MARY BAKER EDDY'S

Lessons of The Seventh Day

MARY BAKER EDDY'S LESSONS OF THE SEVENTH DAY

(Chapters I - IV)

COMPILED BY

RICHARD OAKES

Being a Seventh-Day Call for Individual Recognition and Demonstration of the Complete Six Days of Creation Illustrated in the Founding of Christian Science and The First Church of Christ, Scientist in Boston

~ ~

Chapters V & VI, giving all of Mrs. Eddy's messages and instructions through her periodicals (1895-1910)--in excess of those in Miscellaneous Writings and Miscellany--are now printed separately as "Mary Baker Eddy's Published Writings, Vols.I & II"

~ ~

Prepared for and Using Documentation in

CHRISTIAN SCIENCE RESEARCH LIBRARY
(CHRISTIAN SCIENCE FOUNDATION, Cambridge, Eng.)

ISBN: 0 9507286 4 0

Abbreviations:

COP	Committee on Publication
CSA	Christian Science Association
CSJ	Christian Science Journal
CSPS	Christian Science Publishing Society
CSS	Christian Science Sentinel
S&H	Science & Health with Key to the Scriptures by Mary Baker Eddy
DCC	Divinity Course & General Collectanea
EOF	Essays & Other Footprints
Six Days	Mary Baker Eddy's Six Days of Revelation

M.A.M., m.a.m. Malicious Animal Magnetism

Standard Abbreviations are used for Mrs. Eddy's Other Works, as listed in their Concordance

INTRODUCTION

In the Genesis allegory, the Seventh Day followed the creation of "man in our image" and it was a period of rest-in-action, fulfillment, satisfaction, and eternity. In the forerunner of this book, entitled *Mary Baker Eddy's Six Days of Revelation*, it was found convenient to choose 1894 as the sixth-day climax of a revelation of Christian Science. Yet just as the Genesis "man" was not a material masculine body claiming to be the image of God, so Mrs. Eddy's 1894 unfoldment of "The First Church of Christ, Scientist, in Boston" was not a material structure. It is "*whatever* rests upon and proceeds from divine Principle" just as "man" is *whatever* reflects the perfection of Mind whether called or miscalled animate or inanimate.

In this spiritual sense man and church are synonymous, and individual representations are imperfect unless it becomes clear that these have no value outside the aspect of the one universal Truth they express.

What then is the seventh-day fulfillment of this Church which blesses the race as the one and only institution, wherever and however acknowledged? It is the *unbounded* structure, the City Foursquare, of which Mrs. Eddy speaks in her chapter on The Apocalypse. In this way the Lesson Sermon in her Church does extend from Genesis to Revelation as required in Art.XIV, Sect.2, of the Church Manual.

The city has four sides and consequently is governed by and fulfills the Fourness of God. This fourness governs every set of four concepts that can ever be used to illustrate the activity of Life, Truth, and Love, even in the untranslated human sense of them. It is noteworthy that in pure mathematics if the letter P, for example, is used to denote a set of four persons (properly called "elements" of the set) and the letter Q is used to denote a set of four objects or concepts (again properly called "elements"), then P is said to be "equal to" Q. That is because both sets are governed by the one and the same *fourness of mathematics. In this spiritual sense, all sets of four are "equal", including the set of four developments already noted which Mrs. Eddy introduced into her exegesis pertaining to the Seventh Day: rest-in-action, fulfillment, satisfaction, eternity.

Yet both mathematics and Science recognize individuality and *order* in the myriad examples of FOUR, even while these examples have no inherent creative ability to depart from the unlimited function and attributes of FOUR.

In examining the seventh-day lessons of a period beginning 1895 and closing at the end of 1910, this book finds it helpful to concentrate on four areas in which Mrs. Eddy left instruction, pointers, or advice for those who have glimpsed the idea of the universal Church as exemplified by The First Church of Christ, Scientist, in Boston, and who thus are called on to see beyond all sense of limited personality or material structure.

The chosen areas are healing, preaching, publishing, and teaching, emphasizing four ways in which Mrs. Eddy calls for man to supply the Revelator's legacy of universal Church or the spiritual City Foursquare. Since Mrs. Eddy equates the four sides of the City with the four cardinal points of the compass (and since the latter are "equal to" geometric quadrants which as a rule have a particular mathematical order) the elements will be taken in the order; publishing, teaching, preaching, and healing, to correspond with the Word, Christ, Christianity, and divine Science for the purpose on hand, although any other correlation if scientifically adhered to

---

*The use of a word like fourness is not confined to metaphysicians. For example a book by mathematics professor Georges Ifrah, recently translated from the French by Lowell Bair and entitled "From One to Zero", explains how man first began to notice that sets of three elements (such as three sheep, three stones, three stars) all had a mysterious "something" in common--a something for which the translator simply uses the word "threeness."

would just as absolutely be governed by the Fourness of God's Reality.

Publishing covers the impact of Science and Health up to its 1910 text as the world's scientific textbook; the creation of the Deed of Trust establishing The Christian Science Publishing Society; the founding of *The Christian Science Monitor* as the world's example of correct presentation and assessment of news; the Christianly scientific treatment of the world's problems up to the establishment of peace; and in fact all universal application of Truth. It corresponds with the "casting out of demons" in Jesus' fourfold charge to his followers (Matt. x:8).

It is noteworthy that Mrs. Eddy's final pronouncements to Christian Scientists were made through the world's press (before being copied in most cases into C.S. publications), and that she devoted her afternoon "rest" period to ranging "from the interior of Africa to the uttermost parts of the earth" (My.147:28) in mentally spreading (publishing) the helpful good news.

Teaching covers individualized instruction on how to accomplish the most valuable publishing of the good news. It guides the student to the textbook and quietly reassures the awed learner on the "awful unreality of evil" or malicious mind, and the realization that no teaching is pure unless it includes the understanding that while God may appear as "a teacher," no personal teacher is any nearer God than is any other personal belief. Teaching incorporates Jesus' demand to heal the sick.

Preaching is the identification of the published word with its Source and involves the often slow and labored process by which a churchgoer may learn that there is no personal preacher beside the Person or Preacher who is God; also that there are no "outsiders" to be brought into church, but wonderful partnership to be found already in the society which is church. It corresponds with the command to cleanse the lepers, and our narrative will review *inter alia* the church confrontations associated with Josephine Woodbury and Augusta Stetson.

HEALING in the Seventh Day spreads far beyond the notion of turning sick bodies into well bodies. Rather is it the seeing of all consciousness as whole (healed) and unique. This healing is the recognition of consciousness as the one Soul, governed by the one Mind or Principle. It is the automatic elimination of the belief in another mind, in a mortal (deathly) mind or animal magnetism which finds life where it is not and pretends at other times there is no life where there can be only Life. In reality, consciousness has its Life as All-in-all.

The ultimate healing corresponds with Jesus' command to raise the dead, and celebrates the perpetual resurrection and ascension and descent (second coming) of the God-idea which is the Revelator.

Chapter IV includes the lessons of the "Next Friends Suit", brought against Mrs. Eddy in the name of a natural son, in order to release the mortal, darkened concept of Leader from material birth and personal death into its unborn and unending place in the line of light.

~ ~

While some standardization of spelling and punctuation has been used in the following pages, Mrs. Eddy's text, including her emphasis; has been preserved as actually as possible. Brackets are added to show where context or amplification has been necessary in or surrounding such text. Parentheses are as included in the text itself, whether Mrs. Eddy's or other writers', or they simply indicate words found in such text.

CONTENTS

Page
INTRODUCTION i

I. PUBLISHING 1
"The Lord Gave the Word" 2
Some Statements by Mrs. Eddy 5
The Deed of Trust 7
Correspondence with Trustees 12
Supervision vs. Initiative 14
Lesson for Sacrament Sunday 16
Attention to Copyright 18
Payments, Resignations, Appointments 19
Promotion to Healing 22
Death of Publisher Allison V. Stewart 23
Scope of Trustees' Duties 25
Sifting of Practitioners 28
Lesson-Sermon Committee 29
McLellan Replaces Hanna as Editor 31
Badly-Bound Sentinels 33
Mrs. Eddy's Attention to Form 34
Involvement with Reading Room 37
Involvement with Lesson-Sermon Committee 39
Mrs. Eddy's Watchful Eye on Editorship 42
Changes and True Guidance 48
Historical Facts 49
Directions and Admonitions 51
Watching vs. Watching Out 54
Editor's Rights 55
Advice on Testimonials 57
Introducing the Monitor 58
Publications by Others 61
"The Church in the Wilderness" 64
An "Editorial Too Soon" and the Second Coming 69
Der Herold and Foreign Translations 76
Final Copyright of Textbook 83
The Christian Science Monitor 86
The Line of Light 87

II. TEACHING 94
The Manual Solution 96
Instructional Gems 100
The Class of '98 and Students' Recollections 107
Class Instruction and Col. Sabin 120
Everyday Cares 121
The Kimball Controversy 122
Body and Matter 128
"Line upon Line": Age 134
Death 136
Handling Animal Magnetism 139
Healing 145
Law 146
Miscellaneous 148
Personality 150
Place, Time, Power 152
Poisons 154
Reproduction and Sex 156
Sanity 159
Sleep 160
Supply 161
Treatment and "Patients" 163
The Deathless Dead 166

III. PREACHING 170
Decisions, Problems, Conflicts 171
Vital Role of the Manual 176
Falling "into the Ground" 177
Clubs and Societies 178
Unlocalized Truth 182
No Ecclesiastical Intermediary 186
Persian Rugs and Church Bells 196
Mental Malpractice 203
The "Belief" of a Leg 206
Initiative vs. Compliance 207
The Woodbury Phenomenon 210
Unhandled Beliefs 226
Demands, Reprimands, Recommendations 229

Picture of Mrs. Eddy's Chair 234
Money, Gifts, Property 237
Correspondence on: Church Services 246
Branch Churches 250
Membership and Church Manual 255
Music in Church 260
Readers, Lesson Sermons 263
Reading Rooms, Publication Committees 265
Lecturers, Missionaries 269
Mrs. Eddy's Successor 273
The Fifth Director 282
The Stetson Phenomenon 287
The Carriage Drive 294

IV. HEALING 302
Harmful Personalization 305
Corrective Statements 306
The Manual and Mrs. Eddy's Signature 309
Admonition by Mrs. Eddy 312
Mrs. Eddy's Trustees and The Next Friends Suit 314
The New York World Onslaught 315
The Masters at Pleasant View 325
Peace and Politics 331
Healing and the One Consciousness 337
Preaching and the One Correctness 340
Teaching and the One Man 344
Publishing and the One Government 349

INDEX 355

~ ~

I - PUBLISHING

~ ~

> Thus the heavens and the earth were finished, and all the host of them.
> And on the seventh day God ended the work which he had made, and he rested on the seventh day from all his work which he had made.
> And God blessed the seventh day, and sanctified it; because that in it he had rested from all his work which God created and made. *Gen. ii:1-3.*

In her explanation of this Seventh Day Mrs. Eddy asks "How shall we declare Him?"--that is, how shall we *spread* the Word now that its statement is finished, complete?

This immediately brings up the question: How is it possible or necessary to spread that which is already omnipotent and *omnipresent*? An answer may be found in assessing a similar dilemma at the conclusion of the trial (S&H p.439) when Christian Science eliminates Disease and then sends the roving Word to "whatever locality is reported to be haunted by Disease." The inevitable result is the discovery "that Disease was never there."

In the case of the darkness of Gen.i:4-5 the reader will recollect that as he rose in the line of light he left behind him the darkness which "God called Night." After the light of the Word has *ascended* into the full seventh-day brilliance it may appear that it needs to "spread", or seem to retrace its steps, or *descend* to the place where God reported darkness--only to find inevitably that darkness in the human sense "was never there." This would confirm Mrs. Eddy's statement about the first day, after God had divided (distinguished) the light from the darkness, that "there is no place where God's light is not seen".

Thus darkness becomes simply the "no place" for any belief by which animal magnetism might suggest that there is a mind unable to see the light.

In Mis.172:3-6 Mrs. Eddy explains what is meant by "*declaring* Him" when she writes: "Let us declare the positive and the negative of metaphysical Science; what it is and what it is not." Let us declare the omnipresence of light and the non-existence of the absence of light. The darkness which God called Night merely emphasizes the fact that the opposite of the truth can never be twisted to emit one single ray of truth, except by total reversal, anymore than in the decimal numeration table, 2 x 2 = 5 can occasionally be twisted to be slightly true. The fact that "5" is the wrong answer (i.e. in darkness) does not mean that all "5's" *per se* are wicked, but simply that distinction (division) needs to be made between "4" and "5".

Saying that "the light of ever-present Love illumines the universe" (S&H 503:14) is the same as saying there is no darkness except for a false belief that light is not ever-present to make the needed distinctions; and as the belief is handled we say with the Revelator: "The gates [of our city foursquare] shall not be shut at all by day; for there shall be *no night* there."

"THE LORD GAVE THE WORD"

Our sixth day closed at the beginning of 1895 following the revelation of man in God's image, and coincidentally with the dedication of the synonym, church. Mrs. Eddy's first publication of that year was *Pulpit and Press* designed to record the latter event in words. It was followed two years later by a collage of the full six days, entitled *Miscellaneous Writings* and preserving much of what Mrs. Eddy had elucidated as the days progressed.

In addition to providing a broad view of the ongoing revelation of Christian Science, the publication of *Miscellaneous Writings* gave a specific opportunity to declare what teaching is and what it is not. For after the rising sense of teaching serves to divide knowledge from ignorance (darkness), it is reasonable to ask who will inherit the darkness which the ascending teacher and pupil have left behind. Once again the Word must spread forth and descend into the areas where ignorance was reported to be--and find that ignorance "was never there."

If a person, however letter-perfect he has become, professes to teach another person, he tacitly admits the existence of ignorance on the part of the one being taught--otherwise the operation is futile and unnecessary. Hence the perfect Teacher, too pure to know ignorance, can only be the all-knowing Being who does not have to study or learn to know Himself. His "teaching" is the utilization of His understanding in the infinite expression of His omniscience.

A personal teacher trying to usurp this function would never be able to report that ignorance "was never there," but when the Teacher who is Truth appears as a teacher expressing Truth, there is "no place where God is not seen, evil [ignorance] becomes nothing,--the opposite of the something of Spirit" (S&H 480:3-5).

To emphasize this thought, the publication of *Miscellaneous Writings* coincided with the demand for a cessation of personal teaching, and for Science and Health to be recognized as the sole Teacher together with the lessons of Science and Health as laid out in the workbook called *Miscellaneous Writings*.

Personal teaching as believed in before 1897 was accordingly outlawed for one full year. Then when the year ended and the Board of Education was set up, this seventh-day lesson was in place for those who could profit by it.

Herbert Eustace was one of those certified as "a teacher" by this Board in its early days and by signature of its President (Mary Baker Eddy). As such he was among those who knew better than to encourage the belief of having "pupils" in his classes. He would correct a misstatement along this line by saying: "You mean one who went through class with me?" and by telling the class: "I can teach you nothing that you do not already *know*," that is, I can merely call things to mind with you.

Circumstances and wording used by God to spread the true sense of seventh-day TEACHING are examined in Chap.II.

~ ~ ~ ~ ~ ~ ~

The seventh-day expansion and descension of the Word also required a continuous signpost for the spreading concept of man as church. This appeared in its published form as the *Manual of The Mother Church* in 1895 five months after *Pulpit and Press* had gone on sale. It was necessary to record that Church is governed absolutely by divine Principle and is whatever exemplifies this relationship, and that individual examples called "churches" likewise are "properly *self*-governed only when...guided rightly and governed by...divine Truth and Love" (S&H 106:9).

A few weeks earlier the first *Christian Science Quarterly* was published to show that God's sermons, or preaching, spread from the seventh-day recognition of one complete Church to universal availability. This *Quarterly* carries its message through any church-expression whether called a "group or society or community" or an "individual." Significantly a modern translation of the New Testament (by J.Schonfield) uses the word "community" in places where the Authorized Version uses "church."

The impact and fruition of these developments are examined in the chapter on PREACHING (Chap.III).

~ ~ ~ ~ ~ ~ ~

With the advent of 1895 the *Journal*'s competitive publications had virtually ceased, and the stage was set for the Seventh Day's two major publication events of 1898: the legal establishment of The Christian Science Publishing Society and the inauguration of the *Christian Science Weekly* (*Sentinel*).

The Deed of Trust creating the Publishing Society provided for three independent, self-perpetuating Christian Scientists to take charge of the C.S. periodicals, including *The Christian Science Quarterly*. The three Trustees were chosen for their business capacity (Edward P. Bates), their scholarship (Prof. William P. McKenzie) and their metaphysical or healing ability (James A. Neal).

Although the *Sentinel* finally concentrated on being a parish magazine for the branch churches, it began by trying to cover the field later reserved for *The Christian Science Monitor*. At first its call to "watch" specifically included the need to take into the kingdom of heaven all the world's events of the day. It kept its categories widespread: national, political, religious, scientific, financial, international. Although it may have alerted readers to *declare* the truth about all that was said to be happening, its "sentinel" message was always to *watch*--that is, to *see* God in operation, rather than to take Him to somewhere where He seemed not to be.

PUBLISHING may at first imply that there are places where evil is in charge unless and until we can get the Word into them, yet this "Word" side of our city is not a boundary and is inseparably linked with the side associated with Christian or divine Science. In the study of the Scientific fourth side it will be clear that the first-side call to heal specific diseases and evils by spreading the Word, is inseparable from the universal fourth-side healing which has the Word always in place and showing that "disease was never there." "Our city" is serviced by the ascending Word searching out and correcting (healing), and by the descending Word bringing its universal message of health always in place. Thus Love encircles the squared, yet boundless, city, as examined in the chapter on HEALING (Chap.IV).

SOME STATEMENTS BY MRS. EDDY AT THIS TIME

Strive to work from God, instead of up to God.

No treatment is exact unless it starts from God and starts as God and so continues. Do not look anxiously for results. Cause and effect are one and are already accomplished.

I am learning to take God more and more into every detail of my life. All the Christian Scientist needs in order to remove mountains is the occasion, for God furnishes the power.

Animal magnetism is powerless but you must *declare* against it as though it had all power. And: I have told you that evil has no power, yet I have told you to handle evil as though it had power. This is because of your place in growth spiritual.

Animal magnetism is a strange infatuation to *forget* and not *watch*. The only trouble is we limit God's power. We could even raise the dead from the grave if we did not limit Him. Jesus would not have passed on if the disciples had *watched* with him.

As long as you believe in error at all, you will have to continue with specific claims. And: If you do not master malicious animal magnetism the world will go on another 1900 years sunk into the blackest *night*.

(Recorded by Calvin Frye) A lying argument has just the opposite effect. The wrath of man *shall* praise Him and we rise because of it, i.e. by overcoming it. A lying argument has no power. What we reject cannot be forced into our thought.

Truth reverses every argument of error, and brings out just the opposite results. The belief in fear, sin, and disease is destroyed and cannot return. No mental condition can cause suffering any more than a [so-called] material [condition can].

The only power there is in mesmerism is what we allow it to have. The bigger the error the greater its nothingness.

~ ~ ~ ~ ~ ~ ~

As was noted in *Six Days*, Mrs. Eddy told students that unless malpractice is exposed by Christian Scientists, the world will be little benefited by Christian Science. She also instructed them privately on how to turn the lie of animal magnetism against itself so that it would work to its own destruction and aid the growth spiritual.

To this end she made it clear that so long as it remained necessary for animal magnetism to be handled as having power, the methods of handling should be kept secret from it. Otherwise its assumed power could be diverted into neutralizing the work of destroying it. She even had a code for concealing her own handling strategy by which, for example, a "no" in a telegram could be interpreted by the recipient to mean "yes." Calvin Hill is known to have received a message on one occasion from Calvin Frye which read: "Mother sends you the word 'No.' You will understand it by our key."

Her private instructions for handling evil often emphasized the need to realize that every effort of evil to harm the Scientist could only do him good and increase his strength, that the seeming activity of the lie could only lead to higher spiritual progress, that no weapon formed against him could prosper, that every experience and every day left him better equipped. Thus divine progress and destruction of animal magnetism were linked.

Mrs. Eddy's strictures on the unnecessary PUBLICATION of a lie, or of one's plan to overthrow it, included warnings against the rejoicings that might reasonably be considered appropriate after the lie had been overturned. These warnings are included in instructions Mrs. Eddy gave to her household regarding the "Stetson case" covered in Chap.III and Vol.II of "Mary Baker Eddy's Published Writings." The case troubled the New York field and far beyond throughout 1895-1910. For the correct handling of this and other such problems she is quoted as follows:

> 1) If you take sides...you render yourself incapable of working on the subject metaphysically. [See p.300.]
>
> 2) [In reply to the question: "You mean, Mother, that if we are patient and let God work it out, He will do it in His own wise way at the right time, and in a better way than we would?"] Yes, that is what I mean.
>
> 3) Never notice publicly an error if it can be avoided. Never rejoice in victory over it nor lament. It gives power where it does not belong. Evil is not *something*. Then wherefore give it the honor of noticing it further than to remove it? Then let the dead bury their dead. Have no funeral knell or trumpet blast over nothing, otherwise you will make it something and consistency is especially most desirable in dealing with nothingness. To talk of evil is as inconsistent as to talk of sickness unless it be to untalk it and put it out of mind forever.

THE DEED OF TRUST

Mrs. Eddy's advice to use secrecy to keep the assumed power of animal magnetism from knowing how to upset the plan to thwart it was evident in her establishment of the

Publishing Society. She did not let even the Christian Science Board of Directors know what she was doing, let alone consult them. The rising young scholar from Canada, William P. McKenzie, who was regarded by the treasurer of the Board as being his own special protégé, told other Trustees that this Board member was so upset when he finally learned that the young McKenzie had gained a prominent position without his help and outside the control of the Board, that for a couple of years he avoided speaking to him! Mrs. Eddy's special instructions to the Trustees and the text of her Deed can be found in several publications such as Herbert Eustace's *Christian Science, Its 'Clear, Correct Teaching'*, Hugh Studdert Kennedy's *Christian Science and Organized Religion*, and Alice Orgain's *As It Is*. The special instructions, or rules, include her insistence that animal magnetism be handled as though it had power, and her insistence on secrecy while such handling is being put into effect. The wording she used was as follows:

> "Look over the purposes that the enemy might be trying to accomplish" and
>
> "Have the bird in your hand before disturbing the bush that he hangs upon."

In this way, she wrote, the Trustees would "not mar her success" when "mother foils a demon scheme." Evidently the clandestine creation of the independent Publishing Society was Mrs. Eddy's visible answer to a demon scheme under which the "light that is in thee [could otherwise] be darkness" (Matt.vi:23).

~ ~ ~ ~ ~ ~ ~

The text of the Deed of Trust establishing The Christian Science Publishing Society by signature of Mary Baker G. Eddy on January 25, 1898, stated *inter alia*:

> "Be it known that I, Mary Baker G. Eddy of Concord, New Hampshire, in consideration of one dollar to me paid by Edward P. Bates, James A. Neal, and William P. McKenzie, all of Boston, Massachusetts, and in consideration of their agreement to faithfully observe and perform all the conditions hereinafter specified to be by them observed and performed, and for the purpose of more effectually promoting and extending the religion of Christian Science

as taught by me, do hereby sell and convey to them, the said Bates, Neal, and McKenzie, and their successors in the Trust hereinafter established all and singular the personal property, goods, and chattels which were sold and conveyed to me by the Christian Science Publishing Society by its bill of sale dated January 21, 1898, said property being located in the premises numbered 95 and 97 Falmouth Street in said Boston, including the publication called *The Christian Science Journal* (not including the copyrights thereof), the linotype, all pamphlets, tracts, and other literature conveyed to me by said bill of sale, the Hymnal, the subscription lists of *The Christian Science Journal* and of *The Christian Science Quarterly*, all stationary fixtures, stock on hand manufactured or otherwise, machinery, tools, mailing lists, book accounts, notes, drafts, checks, and bills, whether in process of collection or not, five United State bonds of one thousand dollars each, all cash and bank account and all personal property of whatsoever kind or nature which belonged to said Society and which were conveyed to me as aforesaid, excepting only such of said property as may have been used and disposed of since the date of said sale to me, *upon the following perpetual and irrevocable trust and confidence*, namely:

1. Said Trustees shall hold and manage said property and property rights exclusively for the purposes of carrying on the business...in promoting the interests of Christian Science....

3. Said Trustees shall energetically and judiciously manage the business of the Publishing Society on a strictly Christian basis, and upon their own responsibility, and without consulting me about details, subject only to my supervision, if I shall at any time elect to advise or direct them.

4. ...Once in every six months the Trustees shall account for and pay over to the treasurer of "The First Church of Christ, Scientist, in Boston, Massachusetts," the entire net profits of said business. The "net profits" shall be understood to mean the balance remaining at the end of each six months after paying the usual and legitimate expenses incurred in conducting the business. No authority is intended to be conferred upon the Trustees to expend the money of the Trust for property not necessary for the immediate successful prosecution of the business, or to invest the same for purpose of speculation, or to incur liabilities beyond their ability to liquidate promptly from the current income of the business.

Said treasurer shall hold the money so paid over to him subject to the order of "The First Members" of said Church, who are authorized to order its disposition only in accordance with the rules and by-laws contained in the Manual of said Church....

6. Said Trustees shall employ all the help necessary to the proper conduct of said business, and shall discharge the same in their discretion or according to the needs of the business....

7. The Trustees shall employ such number of persons as they may deem necessary to prepare Bible Lessons or Lesson Sermons to be read in the Christian Science churches...and they may, in their discretion, change the name or style of such *Quarterly* publication as occasion may demand....

8. Said Trustees shall have direction and supervision of the publication of said *Quarterly*, and also of all pamphlets, tracts, and other literature pertaining to said business, using their best judgment as to the means of preparing and issuing the same, so as to promote the best interests of the Cause, reserving the right to make such changes as I may think important.

9. Said Trustees and their successors in Trust shall not be eligible to said trusteeship or to continue in the same, unless they are loyal, faithful, and consistent believers and advocates of the principles of Christian Science as taught by me in my book "Science and Health, with Key to the Scriptures."

10. Whenever a vacancy shall occur in said trusteeship for any cause, I reserve the right to fill the same by appointment, if I shall so desire, so long as I may live; but if I do not elect to exercise this right, the remaining Trustees shall fill said vacancy. The First Members together with the Directors of said Church shall have the power to declare vacancies in said trusteeship for such reasons as to them may seem expedient....

12. Upon my decease, in consideration aforesaid, I sell and convey to said Trustees my copyright of *The Christian Science Journal*....

13. Said Trustees shall each receive annually one thousand dollars for their services in that capacity...or such salary as the said Church may determine from time to time....

The references to "The First Church of Christ, Scientist, in Boston", and to its Directors and "First Members" are interesting in view of the fact that Mrs. Eddy disbanded the First Members in 1908 without changing the Deed. Paragraph 4 presents no problem since there the function of the First Members is shown as negative, not operational. Paragraph 10, however, did figure prominently in litigation that arose in 1919 between the Trustees and the Directors. At that time the Court ruled that since Mrs. Eddy had herself arranged for the "demise" of the First Members, the privileges given to them under the Deed were null and void, and their duties now rested solely in the Directors.

The fact that the Directors' Deed of Trust (1892) stipulated a Board of only four members while the number serving in 1919 was five, also caused some difficulty. But the Court seemed satisfied that since Mrs. Eddy had herself created the fifth director in 1903 she must have intended the requirements of her 1892 Deed thereafter to extend to five persons. As will be seen, however, Mrs. Eddy sought and accepted a legal opinion in 1903 which showed that all requirements under a deed given to four persons remained with those four persons and their legal *replacements* only.

Thus it was that her further legal deeds involving the Board of Directors after 1903 kept carefully to the same original four, emphasizing the distinction she needed to establish between the four and the five.

The litigation of 1919 failed to uncover that the five Directors of that date were a non-legal group that had operated for a while under Mrs. Eddy's direction in the Manual; also that when the original fifth "director" passed on in 1912 he could not be replaced either under the 1892 Deed *or under the Manual*, for the latter specified that such vacancy could be filled only "after the candidate is approved by the Pastor Emeritus."

At that date, 1919, the only Manuals being made available conveniently omitted to name Mrs. Eddy, or anyone else, as Pastor Emeritus in the list of Church Officers, despite the forty or more references in the text to this Pastor's unabrogated functions. The name was restored to the list in 1924 after it became fashionable simply to ignore those references which had been locked, under divine direction, into Mrs. Eddy's own final 88th Manual. The doctored Manual from 1911 on was called the 89th.

Although the First Members and the Board of five "Directors of said Church" were eliminated as legal personages, the legal Board of four Directors was not, any more than "The First Church of Christ, Scientist, in Boston,

Massachusetts" and its treasurer were legally terminated. The 1892 Deed of Trust carefully spelled out the extent and limits of the four-member Board and identified "The First Church of Christ, Scientist" as "the congregation which shall worship in said church."

The symbol of *five* directors is a spiritual concept identified with "this spiritually organized Church of Christ, Scientist, in Boston, [which] still goes on" (Retro.44:30). At the time referred to (1889-92) there *were* five directors (Ira Knapp, Joseph Eastaman, William B. Johnson, of Boston; and Eugene Greene and David Anthony, of Providence, R.I.) arranging services in Boston and promoting Christian Science under Mrs. Eddy's guidance. But they exercised no ecclesiastical authority over the many branches of The Church of Christ, Scientist.

Only when students demanded a reorganization did Mrs. Eddy use four *legal* directors (all necessarily residents of Massachusetts under the Massachusetts law she discovered for creating a non-permanent church organization) to let her students find out for themselves that an ecclesiastical organization is not Science. The fifth director was allowed back as soon as the Manual's estoppel clauses (once obeyed) guaranteed that the concept of five directors should not continue as a personal usurper of God's prerogatives.

CORRESPONDENCE BETWEEN MRS. EDDY AND TRUSTEES

While Mrs. Eddy was contemplating the composition of her trusteeship for the Publishing Society she had an opportunity to assess the value of candidate McKenzie's work. The following correspondence later became part of the Society's files:

-- Letters to Prof. McKenzie [dated Concord, N.H., and signed "Fraternally, C.A. Frye"]:

1) [May 4, '97] Dear Brother: Enclosed I send to you a German translation of part of Science and Health which has been sent to Mother for her approval. She asks if you will kindly find some German person who is well educated and has a good understanding of English

language to have him or her translate the enclosed back into English that we may (see) how it will compare with our textbook.

Of course you know this is a very important work and it is necessary to have a thoroughly reliable person give this decision.

Please attend to this immediately as the party is anxiously awaiting Mrs. Eddy's reply, and send bill for the work. It will be best to consider this matter strictly confidential and not tell the one whom you employ what the matter is taken from.

2) [May 9, '97] Dear Bro. McKenzie: If it is much of an undertaking you had better not have all the copy sent you translated, as Mother does not care to wait long, and the only point now is to find out if the copy which I sent to you is really of any value as a faithful rendering of the text.

3) [May 19, '97] Dear Bro. McKenzie: In regard to the Ger. translation Mother says, what she said in the first place of this German literature, that "She is no more fit to translate my book than a baby."

Mother says she has enough at the first look, where she has substituted "a sacred breath" in the place of "absolute Science."

She says "thank Prof. McKenzie from the depth of my heart for his kind service."

Please return the remainder of the manuscript and bill for translating &c.

Three days before the actual signing of the Deed, Mrs. Eddy put Mr. McKenzie (whom she often referred to as "Prof.") to work on another job which was about to come within the sphere of duties of the new Trustees, namely, assistance with her own publications.

-- Letter to Rev. W.P. McKenzie [dated Concord, Jan.22 '95 and signed "Yours fraternally, C.A. Frye"]:

Dear Brother: Mrs. Eddy requests you to look over the enclosed Church Rules and By-laws and adjust them in a proper way to fit in the proper places in the Church Manual. Then hand them to the clerk of church and have them voted on at the church meeting.

The distance (400 miles) named in Rule is intended to include Buffalo, N.Y. If that place is more than 400 miles from Boston, change the figures accordingly.

-- Handwritten letter to W.P. McKenzie [undated and signed "In haste, With love, M.B. Eddy"]:

My beloved Student: I like your arrangement of Manual. You can use the par. on p.148 of "Mis.Writ." by giving the name of the book and author.

[P.S.] Please transfer as indicated from page 39 to page 38 and erase on page 40.

SUPERVISION vs INITIATIVE

Mrs. Eddy expected the Trustees to work from the standpoint of Life and Truth in all their decision-making, just as she hoped the Directors would constantly "go to God." Yet in both cases the world would always be holding her ultimately responsible for their actions. It must seem a marvel to overburdened man to note how closely she was able to watch over all that these boards did, and in particular how closely she was able to direct, and correct if really necessary, all that went into the periodicals.

An early problem facing the new Trustees was the reaction of the incumbent assistant publisher, who had not been so named in the 1898 Deed. He left town after indicating dissatisfaction, and when a meeting to consider what should be done had to be held over, the Trustees sought Mrs. Eddy's approval for the postponement. She telegraphed back: "Yes if not many days."

-- Further telegram to Rev. W.P. McKenzie [dated Feb.2, '98 and signed "C.A. Frye"]:

Be conciliatory till you get business into your hands ...She says let him be assistant P Now confidential

A telegraphed reply signed "NEAL MCKENZIE" pointed out that the office of Assistant Publisher had been abolished so that the Trustees could "only establish new office and appoint incumbent. Shall we do so?" Mrs. Eddy's response revealed the boundary there must be between her need to be kept au fait and her wish for the Trustees to make their own demonstration:

-- Telegram to W.P. McKenzie [dated Feb.4 '98 and signed "C.A. Frye"]:

She cannot further direct that business Follow deed of trust

"NEAL MCKENZIE's" reply later that day showing that they had gone ahead with their plan to recreate an office of Assistant Publisher, simply stated: "Business completed.... He seems pleased."

~ ~ ~ ~ ~ ~ ~

The management and contents of the new *Quarterly*, with its twenty-six rotational subjects arranged by Mrs. Eddy, was one of the duties put into the hands of the Trustees, subject to her guidance. Hitherto the subjects selected for the series known as the International Bible Lessons had been in use in Christian Science churches. Before the Board's Lesson-Sermon Committee could get fully and correctly into action, the churches had to continue to rely wholly or partially on this international series.

The following letters to W.P. McKenzie, dated Pleasant View, Concord, N.H., and signed "Fraternally, C.A. FRYE", except as shown, record the process of resolution:

1) [dated Feb.13, '97] Your proof of Bible Lessons duly recd. by Mother. She requests me to say she has not time to give this matter her attention, and requests the Committee return to the subjects announced for the International Bible Lessons. She desires to call your attention to your having extracts from "Science and Health" at the head of Lesson on your proof sent, without announcing that it was done with permission of the author. This mistake would have seriously affected her copyrights and would have caused her to prevent your Quarterlies from being distributed, if they had been thus printed. You need to be awake to these subtle errors lest they take you unawares.

2) [dated Feb.15 and signed "Again lovingly, Mother, M.B.E."]: Beloved Student: I see legal points that must

be covered before the new service in church is introduced, so I withdraw the new form till I have time to attend to it.

3) [dated April 15] Mother says that when she last wrote to you she thought you intended to take the golden text for lessons from Science and Health, hence her remark about copyright.

4) [dated April 21] Mother would like to know whether the Bible Lesson Committee are working up lessons from International Series or from topics furnished by her.

5) [To the Committee on Bible Lessons, dated April 26]: Dear Brethren: Mother has prepared the enclosed list of subjects for Sunday services to be used in the forenoon services, and desires that the lessons from the International Series be used for the afternoon or evening services. She requests that you at once prepare lessons from the enclosed subjects so that they may be ready to publish in the Quarterly which is now ready for the press. It is intended that the field will begin to use these lessons on the first Sunday in July 1898.

INTRODUCTION OF LESSON FOR SACRAMENT SUNDAY

The list of "topics" to be covered in the morning services beginning July 3, '98 remained the same as in subsequent Quarterlies except that at first there was no "Sacrament" lesson provided, and the extra subject for the thirteenth week (Sept.25) was "Unreality." The order and wording for the ensuing quarter showed some differences from the practice actually adopted and were as follows:

THE DOCTRINE OF ATONEMENT; SIN, DISEASE, AND DEATH; PROBATION AFTER DEATH; EVERLASTING PUNISHMENT; ADAM OR FALLEN MAN.

MORTALS AND IMMORTALS; SOUL IN BODY; CHRISTIAN SCIENCE; GOD THE ONLY CAUSE AND CREATOR.

CHRISTIAN SCIENCE VERSUS PANTHEISM; DID GOD CREATE MATTER? IS MIND IN MATTER AND THE UNIVERSE INCLUDING MAN EVOLVED BY ATOMIC FORCE? ANCIENT

AND MODERN NECROMANCY OR MESMERISM AND HYPNOTISM.

Since Communion Sunday was observed at the beginning of each quarter, later to be changed to the end of each half-year before finally taking its position early in January and July, the following correspondence from Pleasant View with the Trustees was needed to clarify the situation:

> 1) [C.A. Frye to Bro. McKenzie, dated May 4]: Yes, Mother says that was what she meant, to make your sermon for Communion Sunday adapted for the Communion service and the subjects "God" and "Atonement" can be so done.
>
> 2) [M.B. Eddy's handwritten memorandum, probably May 4]: Communion Service is Morning Service always. Must have *always* a distinct subject, one adapted to it apart from the subjects in the general order.
>
> 3) [Handwritten note to W.P. McKenzie, dated May 14 and signed "With love, in haste, M.B. Eddy"]: My beloved Student: Yours kind, satisfactory. I do want to look up the references in S.& H. before returning reply. Have not had time yet to do this but *once*. The copyright of the Quarterlies henceforth must be mine.
>
> 4) [Typewritten letter to Rev. W.P. McKenzie, dated May 15, '98 and signed "Yours fraternally, C.A. Frye"]: Dear Brother: Mother says that the time for the next Communion Service in both Mother Church and in branch churches is to remain as it now stands; but she recommends that after July the branch churches change, so as to have their Communion service take place on the second Sunday in June and December. The subject for every Communion Service will be "Sacrament." The subject given you for Dec.4 is changed to "Sacrament" and the subject for Dec.25 will be "pantheism, mesmerism, hypnotism." The subjects which she has already sent you cover six months time, and are to be repeated a second six months. So you have with this arrangement subjects to cover a year's lessons for the morning services. But bear in mind that the subject for the Communion Service for June 1899 is to be "Sacrament".

She desires that you request the Editor to give notice of these changes, in this issue of the Journal.

ATTENTION TO COPYRIGHT

Copyright was one of the matters often needing the Trustees' or their editors' attention, as shown in the following letters:

-- Letter to Board of Trustees [dated Mar.21, '98, and signed "Fraternally, C.A. Frye"]:

I would call your attention to the fact that last month's Journal was not copyrighted and would refer you to your deed of Trust regarding copyrighting the Journal.

-- Letter to Rev. W.P. McKenzie [dated April 9, '98, and signed "Fraternally, C.A. Frye"]:

In reply to your letter of recent date, Mother says she desires the copyright of Hymnal to remain the property of the C.S. Board of Directors, and of course the revenue to go to them.

-- Handwritten letter to Archibald McLellan (editor) [dated May 30, '03 and signed "With love, M.B. Eddy"]:

Beloved Student: I have been so occupied with the Manual have not written sooner. I have not had these little verses copyrighted so sent for them. But Mr. Frye says if they are published in the Sentinel that is copyrighted, that will copyright them. If so, please publish without date, or with it, just which is legal. I am not fully informed on this matter. I have another old poem to send sometime but cannot attend to it now....

[*Upward, Written in My Early Years*, by Mary Baker Eddy, was published in the July CSJ.]

-- Handwritten letter to Mr. Editor [dated Dec.23, '04 and signed "In haste, Lovingly, M.B. Eddy"]:

Beloved Student: A student of mine has recently published a book of over 200 pages made up mostly of quotations from my copyrighted books. I have had his books destroyed and his letter of excuse and of repentance also came to me yesterday.

Here I must remind you that our periodicals are infringing my copyright by containing so much quoted from my books, and this furnishes one of the excuses for others committing like infringement.

You must stop this unjust proceedure at once. Please examine the last issue of our Sentinel and note how much it contains of my writings.

Also there must be better literature and more interesting in the Sentinel or it will not stand the test of what I require and the public needs. The last two issues' articles on the first pages are shockingly wanting in quality.

P.S. Thank Mrs. McLellan for her interesting letter. Give much love to her from me.

-- Letter from Board of Trustees of the C.S.P.S. to Rev. Mary Baker Eddy [dated July 16, '07 and signed "Yours faithfully, by A.V. Stewart"]

Beloved Leader: We enclose circular and advertisement from some person or persons who claim to have from you special permission to publish the extract from your writing as there given. ...as it has been customary for you to give public notice through the periodicals regarding any publication which you endorse we find ourselves unable to answer...inquiries with any assurance that the permission...was really granted....

-- Handwritten note added to bottom of above letter [signed "Mary Baker G. Eddy"]:

Beloved: I have no recollection of giving permission to the Thinkright Bureau to publish quotations from my copyrighted books. I have always thought that detached sentences can be made injurious to the real meaning of my writing. I think so now.

PAYMENTS, RESIGNATIONS, APPOINTMENTS

In addition to the half-yearly payments to The First Church of Christ, Scientist which the Trustees were required to make, Mrs. Eddy requested a special payment of $15,000 in April 1898, after the Church had undertaken to purchase Mrs. Eddy's home site in Roslindale, Mass. In a handwritten letter to the Board of Trustees, dated April 13, and signed "With love, Mother, Mary Baker Eddy", she wrote:

> My beloved Students: Please pay to Treasurer of the [sic] First Church of Christ Scientist Boston, the sum of 15000 dollars for my real estate in Roslindale that they have kindly purchased. I would like to have the money this week if convenient. [After receiving this letter Mr. McKenzie wrote on the back of it: "Ck to Treasurer."]

Another early problem demanding a solution by "NEAL McKENZIE" was the resignation in August 1898 of Edward P. Bates whose relationship with official Boston had never been good (see *Six Days*, p.524). Once more Mrs. Eddy wished the two continuing trustees to turn consciously to God when seeking a replacement.

If and when she had to step in, she was not just relieving them of still doing their own work, as events often showed.

Preparations were in full swing for the appearance of the *Christian Science Weekly* (later *Sentinel*) and "NEAL McKENZIE" made the mistake of proposing Judge Hanna as the new third trustee.

The Judge, as editor of the *Journal*, was specially needed to edit the new periodical, rather than be a trustee. The next few messages tell the story:

-- Telegram to Rev. W.P. McKenzie [dated Aug.18, '98 and signed "C.A. Frye"]:

> I wrote you Aug. twelfth that mother declined to nominate a trustee.

-- Handwritten letter to Board of Trustees [dated Aug.23, '98 and signed "With love, Mother, Mary Baker Eddy"]:

> My dear disciples: You failed to see that nobody is yet as ready to be editor of the weekly newspaper as those with whom I have co-operated for years.
>
> Now dear ones nothing but the evil one, could have hindered you from seeing this and so as there is no satan you are not prevented recognizing this important fact.

When Judge Hanna resigns I hereby say that I will appoint the trustee. Please *hurry this matter up*. Call your meeting at once and find enclosed my appointments.

-- Handwritten note [dated Aug.24, '98 and signed "Mary Baker Eddy"]:

I hereby appoint Rev. Irving C. Tomlinson to fill the vacancy on the Board of Trustees.

-- Letter to Rev. W.P. McKenzie [dated Aug.24, '98 and signed "Yours fraternally, C.A. Frye"]:

Dear Brother: Mrs. Eddy requests me to say, Do not elect the person whose name she sent to you, nor any other person, for Trustee till after she hears again from you, and you from her again.

-- Handwritten letter to Trustees [dated Aug.27, '98 and signed "Lovingly Mother, Mary B. Eddy"]:

My dear Board of Trustees: I withdraw my appointment of Trustee. You can forward the name of your candidate for my approval whenever you are ready to do it.

-- Handwritten letter to Trustees [received Aug.30 and signed "With love, Ever Mother"]:

Beloved: I will give you one of my most faithful ones to give him a rest till I may recall him.

-- Handwritten letter to Rev. W.P. McKenzie and James A. Neal [dated Sept.8 and signed "With love, Mary Baker Eddy"]:

My dear Board Trustees: I hereby appoint Thomas W. Hatten to fill the vacancy on your board.

Thomas Hatten was not "recalled" to Mrs. Eddy's home, and like William P. McKenzie he remained a member of the Board of Trustees for the next nineteen years. Irving Tomlinson, whose appointment had been so promptly withdrawn, was destined for the Board of Lectureship as the following letter shows:

-- Handwritten letter to W.P. McKenzie [dated Oct.1, '98 and signed "With love, Mother, M.B. Eddy"]:

My beloved Son: And I have more than *one*, besides many beloved daughters.

I am delighted with the reports of Rev. Mr. Tomlinson's success and only regret that newspapers stinted the Lecture. What I have read of it in the Herald and Globe is just what meets the public need and demand--save in one point which I will name to him. He, the Rev. Speaker was saved from being Trustee for mischief end. I have a big field for him to sow and reap.

PROMOTION FROM PUBLISHING TO HEALING

James Neal was the next casualty on the Trustee Board, but his departure was more in the nature of a promotion. At a time when many energies were going into the building up of church organizations, Mrs. Eddy kept emphasizing the need for healing as the only real way for the Cause to advance. Mr. Neal had shown in his practice a wonderful conviction that God is the Healer and that He alone takes care of every case, with the result that Mrs. Eddy was able to write the following letters to the Board of Trustees:

1) [handwritten, dated Oct.13, '98 and signed "With love, Mother, Mary Baker Eddy"]: Beloved C.S. Trustees: In accordance with Mr. James Neal's willingness and my own desire that he devote his entire time to the great work of Christian Science healing, in which he has been very successful, and which is one of the great needs of the period--

I hereby request that this Board give him an honorable discharge with my thanks for his faithful discharge of his obligations as a member of this Board; and that you elect Mr. Joseph Clark to fill the vacancy.

[P.S., signed "Mary Baker Eddy"]: If requisite--read this letter at a meeting of the First Members of the Mother Church.

2) [dated Oct.21, '98 and signed "With love, Mary Baker Eddy"]: My beloved Board of Trustees: Please accept this as my part of the matter. I hereby appoint or recommend Mr. Joseph Clark to fill the vacancy on your Board occasioned by the resignation of James A. Neal.

For the next eight years the composition of the Board remained set until the decease of Mr. Clark made another appointment necessary. Mrs. Eddy wanted Mr. Neal to remain off the Board; otherwise she left the decision to the remaining members as shown by the following letter:

-- Letter to Board of Trustees [dated Sept.14, '06 and signed "Lovingly yours, Mary Baker Eddy"]:

Beloved Students: I am not so situated as to be informed of the points requisite as you are--hence I leave it to the Trustees to decide who shall fill the vacancy.

Mr. Neal I wish to remain on the Com. on Business and I cannot see that he can fill his position as a healer and have added to his labor aught of what belongs to another office than that he has already.

The remaining trustees proposed A.V. Stewart of Chicago, then committee on publication for Illinois. They pointed out that he had given up a lucrative business career to devote his time to C.S. work, and Mrs. Eddy approved the appointment in the following letter:

-- Typewritten letter to W.P. McKenzie and Thomas W. W. Hatten, Trustees of Christian Science Publishing Society [dated Sept.19, '06 and signed in her handwriting "Lovingly thine, Mary Baker Eddy"]:

Beloved Students: You will please accept my thanks for your long loving *wise* letter.

I am satisfied with your description, and heartily recommend your election of Mr. A.V. Stewart to fill the responsible office now vacant. Our late loved and lamented Mr. Clark has gone to his reward of "well done". May the God of all grace ever guide and bless you and yours.

DEATH OF A DIRECTOR AND PUBLISHER

Mr. Stewart lasted little more than a year as trustee, for he was the one chosen by Mrs. Eddy to become publisher of her works and a director--in both cases in place of Joseph Armstrong who passed on in December 1907. As "Publisher of the C.S. Publishing Society" Mr. Armstrong had been largely independent, but the Society's records do show two references to requests from Mrs. Eddy to the Trustees regarding him. These were:

-- Dictated <u>letter</u> to Rev. W.P. McKenzie [dated Sept.10, '01 and signed in her handwriting "With love to Mrs. McKenzie and her other half, M.B. Eddy"]:

Beloved Student: Your favor of recent date is at hand. Will say in reply: As the Mother Church is oppressed with indebtedness this year I propose that we retain the incumbent Mr. Armstrong one year longer if he is willing to continue as Publisher of the C.S. Publishing Society. I would prefer to have the publisher of my books attend to no other business, but I will yield my preference one year longer to avoid adding expense to the Mother Church.

-- <u>Letter</u> to Trustees of C.S.P.S. [dated Dec.11, '07 and signed "Yours very truly, Calvin A. Frye, Sec.]:

My dear Brothers: In reply to your letter of yesterday received by our beloved Leader, I am requested to say she does not recommend that the Publishing House be closed at the hour of the funeral services tomorrow. She does not approve of recognizing these claims of mortal mind by acknowledging the reality of sin, disease and death, to any unnecessary extent.

She was deeply grieved at the announcement of the decease of our dear Brother Armstrong as all were at Pleasant View. It is a sad loss to our Mother Church.

To fill Mr. Stewart's place, the remaining trustees proposed William D. McCrackan if Mrs. Eddy chose not to exercise her right to make the appointment. In their letter to her they referred to Mr. McCrackan as a reliable metaphysician as well as an experienced author and publisher who "can be well utilized in connection with the increasing scope of our periodicals", while "his training in German and experience of travel, fit him to assist in connection with German and foreign work." He was First Reader in The Mother Church, but with only five months left of office.

-- Handwritten <u>letter</u> to Messrs. Wm.P. McKenzie and Thomas W. Hatten [dated Jan.5, '08 and signed "Lovingly yours, Mary B.G. Eddy"]:

Beloved Students: I highly approve of Mr. W.D. McCrackan to fill the vacancy as a trustee of the Publishing Society.

After only three months, however, Mr. McCrackan resigned on the basis that his work as First Reader involved conditions demanding all his time and strength. In case Mrs. Eddy chose not to make her own appointment, the remaining trustees then sent her a letter nominating Arthur R. Vosburgh, and against the name she wrote: "Please make your own choice. Eddy."

After a few more weeks, they had second thoughts and decided to nominate Judge Clifford Smith instead. In their letter to Mrs. Eddy they cited their association with Judge Smith during his preparation of the pamphlet "Christian Science and Legislation", saying that it "revealed his ability to help the cause." On the back of this letter Mrs. Eddy wrote, on June 18, '08: "I approve. M.B.G. Eddy."

WIDE SCOPE OF THE TRUSTEES' DUTIES

As the financial situation of The Mother Church improved, two letters in April 1905 showed that the funds which the Publishing Society turned over to the Church were being appreciated:

> 1) [handwritten to Rev. McKenzie and signed "With love, Mary Baker Eddy]: Beloved Student: I think it just and a duty for the first provisions of the deed of trust to be carried out for the Trustees. I was glad to know that the income to my Church is what it already is, and I well knew it would be thus when I gave [the proceeds of] my paper to the Church.
>
> 2) [to The Board of Trustees of The Christian Science Publishing Society, signed "Fraternally yours, William B. Johnson, Clerk"]: Dear Brethren: The directors of The Mother Church have instructed me to write you that the following resolution was passed by them this day: "That the salary of each of the members of the Board of Trustees of the Christian Science Publishing Society shall be one thousand dollars annually, payable semiannually, in payments of five hundred dollars, beginning January 25th, 1905." [The amount was raised to $1500 as of Oct.1, '07 "by unanimous vote of the Board and with {Mrs. Eddy's} approval."]

Although Mrs. Eddy usually dealt directly with the editor of the periodicals in regard to wording of individual articles, the Trustees were held generally responsible for appearance, arrangement, overall content, prompt handling, etc., in addition to their special work with the lesson-sermon committee, the reading room and copyrights.

Some of the occasions in which Mrs. Eddy worked through the Trustees in directing or improving the Society's written productions are shown by the following:

-- Handwritten letter [dated Aug.29, '98 and signed "With love, Mother, M.B. Eddy"]:

My dear Board: Alone but not bereft. I name Mr. [Willis] Gross of whom I have heard Mr. Neal speak--to fill your vacancy [as assistant editor to Editor Judge Hanna]. If you please--send for him.

~ ~ ~ ~ ~ ~ ~

-- Other Letters [signed "Yours fraternally, C.A. Frye", except as shown]:

1) [dated Feb.22, '99] Dear Bro. McKenzie: Mother thanks you for the action taken by the Trustees regarding circulation of Sentinel and Journal.

She recommends that you send the Sentinel and Journal to the Concord Public Library in this city regularly if you are not already doing so.

2) [dated March 7, '99] C.S. Board of Trustees: Please send a request to students in all the principal cities in our country to have them get the local newspapers to publish Mother's Address to the "First Church of Christ, Scientist, Concord, N.H." as printed in the last Sentinel (March 2, 1899) on page 4. Please have this attended to at once and caution them to watch that there is no mistake made by the printer, but that it is brought out exactly like the copy. This is Mother's special request.

3) [dated June 25, '99 and signed "Yours truly"]: Trustees of the C.S. Pub. Society: Mother requests that you see that the booklet C.S. History [by Septimus J. Hanna] is largely circulated. Can you inform her how many have already been sent out?

4) [dated Sept.27, '99] Dear Bro. McKenzie: Mother says she would think it much wiser to have Mrs. Williams' article "Homes of Mary Baker Eddy" appear in the N.E. Magazine than in a smaller one....

5) [dated Aug.3, '01] Dear Bro. Hatten: In reply to your inquiry about Mrs. Williams' article, Mother requests me to [tell you to] act at your own discretion. She has no desire about it.

6) [to Rev. Mr. McKenzie, C.S.D., dated Jan.8, '04, and signed "In haste, Lovingly yours, Mary B. Eddy"]: My beloved Student: I gave my C.S. Journal to the Publishing Society on the grounds that it should be well conducted etc. Now I ask you to see that we have more that is understandable and interesting to the general public, more that fulfils this purpose: "I make you fishers of men."--more that is worthy the literary ability that should characterize our periodicals. No matter about the cost of it, but I insist that such writers as <u>Judge Jones</u>, <u>M.G. Kains</u>, <u>Mr. Samuel Greenwood</u>, Mrs. Mims of Atlanta, Edward A. Kimball, Rev. Vosburgh etc. be employed and paid as contributors to our periodicals and <u>constant</u> contributions be had from them.

As it is, only Christian Scientists can find food for the head and heart in our papers. The Rev. Lyman Abbott's last article in the Literary Digest should be reviewed in our papers and quotations from it printed with their authority that would startle the world to see that the great and best men are adopting C.S.

Such articles tend to attract the higher class of thinkers and to dignify our Cause.

7) [dated April 29, '04] Dear Bro. McKenzie: In reply to your letter of recent date [requesting less delay in getting Mrs. Eddy's contributions and corrections back to the editors] will say Yes, I will assist all I can to have less delay in issuing the Sentinel. ...unless special word is sent with matter sent by Mrs. Eddy to be published in the present issue of Sentinel, [you and the Editor] need not delay publication.

...These instructions Mrs. Eddy bids me send. Sometimes proofs arrive here at a time when it is impossible for Mrs. Eddy to give them immediate attention, but she will do the best she can in this matter.

8) [to C.S. Publishing Society, dated Aug.30, '04 and stamp-signed "G.H. Kinter, C.S.B., Pleasant View, Concord, N.H."]: Dear Brethren: Accept our sincere thanks and most cordial congratulations upon the prompt delivery of the September Journal. Everybody from the Leader down was pleased to get it so early.

<u>Sifting of Practitioners</u>

9) [to Rev. William P. McKenzie, dated Oct.7, '04 and signed "In the spirit of true cooperation, I remain, Fraternally yours, Geo. H. Kinter"]: Dear Brother: ...As I understand it, the [Journal] directory [of practitioners] is intended as a book of reference to those seeking help, of reliable Christian Science Practitioners, persons able and ready to heal the sick, and whose first calling is the healing work.

It is a well known fact that there are many names of persons recorded in said register, who not only never do any healing, but who intend not to, and whose time and energy are wholly mortgaged in other matters; furthermore the Journal has become top-heavy, and something must be done, to make room for more reading matter....

10) [dated Oct.13, '04 and stamp-signed by G.H. Kinter]: Dear Brother McKenzie: ...I have in mind to send you the list of "practitioners" in a certain city that I know of, so that you may see how they are employed. It may prove a help in deciding the vexed questions that arise [from the plan to sift through the practitioner list in the Journal, and perhaps drop the advertisements for "Christian Science Institutes".]

11) [handwritten on Nov.19, '04 to W.P. McKenzie and signed "Lovingly thine, M.B. Eddy"]: My beloved Student: Your favor at hand. Please answer your questions as to the By-law "Incompetence and Advertisements" [designed to deal with advertisements by dormant practitioners] by requesting them to *read* that <u>By-law</u> in the Manual.

The present chemical or ferment of mortal mind makes it wise to do thus at present. Thanking you dear one, for your <u>wisdom</u> and fidelity.

[P.S.] Remember me tenderly to your dear wife and the little one.

[P.P.S., sent by telegram signed "M.B. Eddy"] Forgot to say, tell the By-law to all enquirers.

12) [by special messenger from C.S. Board of Trustees, dated Dec.6, '04]: Beloved Leader: After conference with the Editor and Business Manager, we think it would be well to omit further advertisement of Institute Cards in the Journal, and thereby gain about fifteen pages of space. A number of requests have already come from those having Institutes.... The By-law entitled "Healing Better than Teaching" (Art.XXXII, Sect.8) encourages us to devote space to advertisement of healers of the sick, rather than to Institutes; and we notice that the Board of Education is not advertised.... May we learn as soon as possible if [we have your] approval [that] this should be carried out.

13) [dated Dec.6, '04]: Dear Brother Hatten: Your letter by the hands of Mr. Mann was duly received by our beloved Leader this afternoon. The matter is however of such importance she does not feel equal to deciding at once as to the best thing to advise on this subject. I will send you word as soon as she gives her decision as to Institute cards, which may be tomorrow afternoon.

14) [to C.S. Board of Trustees, dated Dec.7, '04 and signed "I remain, Sincerely yours, Geo. H. Kinter"]: Dear Brethren: In reply to your letter of the 6th inst., our dear Leader directs me to write you as follows: "Answer for me that I say do what they, the Trustees, think is best on this subject. I like their decision".... [Their decision was to *omit* the Institute cards.]

~ ~ ~ ~ ~ ~ ~

LESSON-SERMON COMMITTEE NOT UNDER DIRECTORS

There was an early slip-up with the lesson-sermon committee! A letter dated Feb.25, '01 from the clerk of the Church, William B. Johnson, notified the Trustees that "by the recommendation of our Teacher, Mrs. Eddy, and by the unanimous vote of the Christian Science Board of Directors, Mr. John B. Willis, has been appointed a member of the

Bible Lesson Committee." This action trespassed on the preserves granted the Trustees in their deed, and after some letters to Pleasant View, the following was received:

-- Letter to W.P. McKenzie [dated March 12, '01 and signed "Yours fraternally, C.A. Frye"]:

Dear Bro. McKenzie: In reply to your letters of recent date, Mother requests me to say at the time she sent in the name of Mr. Willis for a member of the Bible Lesson Committee, she did not remember that said committee is elected by Trustees. You will please now consider the application for his election as sent to the Trustees and take action accordingly.

Then early in April, and at a time when Judge Hanna's indefinite hold on the editorship of the periodicals was beginning to be doubted, and he and Mrs. Hanna were on vacation, a second letter from the clerk of the Church regarding Mr. Willis threw the Trustees into confusion. A message alleged to be from Mrs. Eddy to the Board of Directors was passed on verbally to the Trustees by Mr. Johnson. It stated: "You must put him (John B. Willis) in first editor now, not wait a day, so as to let him have the run of things. Have the Trustees attend to this business at once." The moment was an awkward one, since the Woodbury suit against Mrs. Eddy (which is dealt with in Chap.III) was in expensive progress.

It was not clear whether Judge Hanna was to remain editor-in-chief with Mr. Willis as first assistant editor, or whether the absent Judge was to be replaced. Besides, as the Trustees pointed out in a letter to Mrs. Eddy, dated April 8 and signed by Wm.P McKenzie: "the Manual forbids us to remove or elect an editor without your consent."

The same day (before the letter arrived) Mrs. Eddy was writing as follows to Mr. McKenzie:

-- Handwritten letter [signed "With love, M.B. Eddy"]:

Beloved Student: Do you not see the danger of letting off Judge and Mrs. Hanna from the editorial chair when they have not found too much help for their present aid? I marvel that anyone cannot see this mistake and the cause *unseen*! I think Mr. Willis and Miss Mary Speakman would substitute for them while they are away. Miss Speakman is a literary woman and the Hannas' vacation will not be long we hope.

I can think of no better way. If the present editors have not too much help, and I think they have not, what would be the effect *just now* to remove two from this office! Let me hear from you on this at once.

A telegram to Rev. W.P. McKenzie, signed "M.B. Eddy", followed later in the afternoon. It read: "I withdraw my proposition just mailed, you and Judge Hanna arrange this important matter." Meanwhile the McKenzie letter reached Pleasant View, resulting in the following:

-- Handwritten letter [dated April 9, '01 and signed "Fraternally, C.A. Frye"]:

Dear Bro. McKenzie: Your letter duly rec'd by Mother. She was not ignorant of the fact that a change of Editors required her sanction. She should have been advised of your intention earlier, and it would have saved her much trouble. As stated in her telegram yesterday she now leaves it for the Trustees and Judge Hanna to arrange the matter.

-- Handwritten letter [dated April 17, '01 and signed "With love, Mary Baker G. Eddy"]:

Dear Mr. McKenzie: It would have been complying with our Church By-laws for you to have informed me of the people you employ in the Publishing Society and a due courtesy for you to have informed Miss Speakman that I requested her to fill the vacancy. It would have been due to me and good manners for the Hannas to have first informed me of their or his intention to leave in this hour of need his post of duty.

-- Handwritten letter to W.P. McKenzie [dated April 18, '01 and signed "With love, M.B. Eddy"]:

Beloved Student: Have learned today that you notified Miss Speakman of my desire. *Pardonez-moi* for a reminder of an omission not omitted.

McLELLAN REPLACES HANNA

In September 1901 Mr. McKenzie began to pursue the possibility of having Archibald McLellan work with the

Publishing Society. Edward Kimball had told him that Mrs. Eddy was interested in getting Mr. McLellan as Business Manager in place of the retiring Joseph Armstrong; but that was before she had prevailed on Mr. Armstrong to continue for one more year, and that matter was duly dropped.

Eventually Mr. McLellan did join the Publishing Society and in June 1902 he took over the editorship from Judge Hanna, who then became a C.S. lecturer, and later, teacher of the 1907 class in the Board of Education.

Mrs. Eddy was unable to meet Mr. McLellan face to face before agreeing to give her approval of his new job, but she sent him a strong reminder of the qualifications needed for an editor.

-- Letter to Mr. Archibald McLellan [dated June 8, '02 and signed "With love, Mother, M.B. Eddy"]:

Dear Student: I am today in receipt of your telegram to Mr. Kimball. I would gladly confer with you on the subject of becoming editor-in-chief of the Christian Science Journal and Christian Science Sentinel, but as I am situated now it seems quite impossible. You are aware that an editor should be reliable in word and deed, adroit, wise, apt in discerning the public need, in rebuking the private evil and unselfish in doing it.

Cowardice, deceit, will without wisdom, have imposed on me tasks incredible. It is wise to protect as far as possible a Leader, instead of putting her to the front in every battle, laying her on the altar and saving themselves. I have now no relatives to defend me and my age requires some consideration after thirty-six years of constant conflict.

I have helped Judge Hanna to the advantageous positions he occupies--but he forgets this. I request the editor of our periodicals to send the proofs to me of special articles they write about me and to head no articles "Defence of Mrs. Eddy"! My history is enough for that. For the sake of our cause I ofttimes change orders and veer like a weather-vane. A direction that is right under existing circumstances may change the next hour for circumstances alter cases, then I countermand my order and it works well.

Mr. Kimball's recommendation of you is very satisfactory. May I name you for Editor-in-Chief of the Christian Science Journal and Christian Science Sentinel. Please wire yes or no.

BADLY-BOUND SENTINELS

Although Mrs. Eddy strove to delegate authority so that students could consciously go to God for His answer, events have shown that she did not hesitate to point out little errors of detail when this turning to Him seemed to be lacking. The following messages cover what can be called the general appearance of the periodicals--particularly the Sentinel:

-- Letters to Board of Trustees (or Publishing Society or individual trustees or editors or both) regarding the look of the periodicals, rather than the literary content:

1) [handwritten to Board of Trustees, dated April 15 {'99} and signed "Mother, with love, M.B. Eddy"]: Beloved Students: Are you awake to the fact that the *Sentinel* cannot be handled long enough to read it till it is out of binding!

Col. Sabin [editor of the Washington *News Letter*, which was at the time still friendly to C.S.] is improving his weekly periodical in binding and beauty. But what of ours! Is it a fact that hypnotism can make black white and nobody know it, or that black can change to color?

N.B. [signed "M.B.E."]: I beg that our Sentinel be immediately bound *properly*.

2) [dated April 22 and signed "Yours fraternally, C.A. Frye"]: Dear Bro. Hatten: Mother has noted that the Sentinels are now bound with staples.

She says she objects to that way, and prefers to have them pasted as before, but to have it well done so there will be no loose leaves.

3) [handwritten to Editors and Trustees, dated April 23, '99 and signed "With love, Mother, M.B. Eddy"]: Beloved Students: I am pained by witnessing the success of malicious minds on the exterior of our Sentinel. Binding and margin of leaves must be changed to the same that the Washington

News Letter now is--or the form must be like other weekly newspapers. There is no comeliness nor precedent for the form of our weekly and I am not willing that the outside of that paper should injure our cause while the inside matter is helping it. There should be pretty compartments for different topics inside, but that can be left better than the other points named. These must be attended to *immediately*.

4) [dated April 26 and signed "With my love and thanks, M.B. Eddy"]: My beloved Students: Your favor at hand. I like the Presbyterian Banner--the size and margins. Please have ours like it--have the front margin same size as the other two.

5) [handwritten to C.S. Publishing Society, dated Jan.27, '01 and signed "With love, Mother, Mary B.G. Eddy"]: Beloved Students: Accept my thanks for your finely bound Vols. of the Sentinel.

6) [dated Oct.24 '01 and signed "Yours fraternally, C.A. Frye"]: Dear Bro. Armstrong [Publisher of the C.S.P.S.]: Mrs. Eddy returns thanks for the beautifully bound Vol.3 C.S.Sentinel which was safely received by her.

7) [handwritten and signed "Eddy" {on letter from Archibald McLellan to C.A.Frye, dated April 15 '01}]: *Thanks*, please print it as I wrote it. I have authority for it.

[The reference here is to the word "thousandfold" as used in My.164:23. Mr. McLellan had written as follows]:

> The word 'thousandfold' is not hyphenated in the Century Dictionary.
>
> There is a rule, but I think it is not now observed by the best writers, that a word of one syllable needs no hyphen between it and the added word, but a word of two or more syllables needs a hyphen before the added word. As examples,--tenfold, hundred-fold. This rule seems inconsistent, and the Century Dictionary does not appear to follow it.

Mrs. Eddy's Attention to Form

8) [to C.S. Board of Trustees, dated Sept.29, '04 and signed "In Mrs. Eddy's behalf, I remain, Fraternally yours, Geo. H. Kinter"]: Dear Brethren: In answer to your letter of

the 27th inst. received by the hand of Brother Clark, our Leader directs that you may make the change at the head of the Editorial page, as proposed, provided you do not make any change in the present form of the cover of the Journal.

9) [handwritten to Mr. McKenzie, dated Dec.9, '04 and signed "In haste, Lovingly yours, M.B. Eddy"]: My beloved Student: Do not have Eds. at the close of a small or large article. If Mr. McLellan writes it Ed. is enough--if the Associate Ed. writes [it, put] full name or Associate Ed.

10) [also dated Dec.9, '04, but signed "Yours fraternally, C.A. Frye, Secretary"]: Dear Bro. McKenzie: Our beloved Leader requests me to say: The enclosed is the form in which she wishes the names of Editor and his assistants to appear in The Christian Science Journal and Christian Science Herold.

[Enclosed]: Archibald McLellan Editor.

John B.Willis Annie M. Knott Associate Editors.

11) [to Rev. William P. McKenzie, C.S.B., dated Pleasant View, Feb.16, '05 and signed "On Mrs. Eddy's behalf, Lovingly yours, William B. Johnson"]: My dear Brother: Our beloved Leader...has sent to the Publishing Society three Journals, has marked the one she prefers, but would like a little lighter shade of green.

12) [to W.P. McKenzie, dated April one, '05 and signed "Lovingly thine, Mary Baker Eddy"]: Beloved Student: I like the color of cover, but the shabby uneven top, bottom and sides I do not like.

The lettering is fine.

13) [to Archibald McLellan, dated July 28, '06 and written by Mrs. Eddy on the front cover of the current Sentinel]: What if you put here the figure of a woman with a lamp in her hand? This would illustrate Longfellow's lines in verse, see page 763.

[This was written on the right-hand side of the cover where at that time there was a torch, while on the left-hand side she wrote]: The same on this side also.

[Further handwritten <u>message</u> to Editor in Chief on same subject, dated July 31, '06 and signed "Lovingly yours, Mary Baker Eddy"]: Beloved Student: You will accept my thanks for your kind acceptance of my proposition for the Sentinel.

14) [to C.S. Trustees, dated Aug.7, '06 and signed "Yours truly, Lewis C. Strang, Associate Secretary"]: Gentlemen: I return the sketch for the cover of the Sentinel. Mrs. Eddy has examined it and endorses it. The only suggestion that she makes is a different style of head-dress for the woman.

15) [to Trustees, dated Aug.10, '06]; Dear Brethren: Mrs. Eddy approves of the new arrangement of the head-dress. The only change that she suggests in the last design submitted is the omission of the C.S. seal--the cross and crown with "Heal the sick, raise the dead," etc. She thinks that the effect without this will be more artistic. In fact, she is very much pleased with it.

[The seal was reintroduced on the cover of the Sentinel after Mrs. Eddy's departure.]

16) [handwritten to Board of Trustees of The C.S. Publg. Society, dated Oct.31, '06 and signed "Lovingly yours, Mary Baker Eddy"]: Beloved Students: Please color the cover of our Sentinel. It looks cheap without this and yet with such fine designs on the cover. I propose a shade of blue. What say you?

17) [handwritten message on letter {dated Dec.21} sent by Trustees to Mrs. Eddy enclosing the first Sentinel with the new blue-colored cover page]: Be sure to extend the color of the cover all over the page and leave no white margin.

18) [to Mr. W.D. McCrackan, dated Feb.14, '08 and signed "Very sincerely yours, Adam H. Dickey, Secretary"]: Dear Brother: In reply to your letter to our Leader under date of February 13th, enclosing new designs to be used on Christian Science books, I have to report that she has selected the enclosed, detached, design, which bears her signature. [The signature "Eddy" was written beside one of the five seal specimens that Mr. McCrackan had sent.]

19) [to Secretary for Trustees of the C.S.P.S., dated March 19, '08 and signed "Sincerely yours, Adam H. Dickey, Secretary"--in response to receipt from the Trustees

of a copy of the new Journal cover showing the new C.S. seal with its celestial crown]: Dear Mr. McCrackan: In reply to your letter of the 18th inst....

Mrs. Eddy was busily engaged on another matter when I presented your [copy] and without making any special comment, she requested me to ask the Trustees to "Keep on the outside of our periodicals, the emblem of the celestial and not the terrestrial."

I take it by this, that the new design was acceptable to our Leader, and that you may proceed with that understanding.

20) [dated March 30, '08 and signed "Sincerely yours, Adam H. Dickey"]: Dear Mr. Stewart: I return herewith the samples you sent to Mrs. Eddy of the new seal to be used on the covers of the different bindings of Science and Health. Our Leader wishes me to thank you for your kindness, and to say that she approves of the samples sent. You may go ahead and use them.

TRUSTEES DROP INVOLVEMENT WITH READING ROOM

-- Handwritten letters to W.P. McKenzie:

1) [dated Aug.14, '00 and signed "With love, Mother, M.B. Eddy"]: My dear Student: Miss Chamberlin or Miss Brown is better adapted to take charge of the Reading Room in Boston than Miss Sargent. She is not adapted to that. Our Reading room is a great feature in our cause. Get the *right one*. And there is no need of but two, the librarian and the janitor to have charge. The scrubbing can be done by an outsider not engaged constantly about the rooms.

There must be more economy used on salaries in order to meet the duties of building and so forth in the near future.

2) [dated Sept.7, '00 and signed "Yours fraternally, C.A. Frye"]: Someone enquired who Mother desired to have pay for the services of the one in charge of Reading Room in Boston--the Directors or the Trustees? Her reply is the Directors should be the ones to attend to that matter. I send this to you because I have an impression that you were the one who enquired.

-- Letters to Mrs. Eddy from Trustees:

1) [dated Nov.12 '02] Beloved Mother: The Trustees have conferred with the Board of Directors in regard to the conduct of the Reading Room in Boston, and all agree that its usefulness would be much enlarged if it were open evenings when those who do day's work have leisure. The hours are now from 9 A.M. to 5 P.M. and the change would be 10 A.M. to 9 P.M. Two persons would be required to have charge, and for the evening hours a man would be preferable. The Trustees (in cordial agreement with the Directors) would therefore nominate for librarian during the major part of the day, Miss Emma H. McLauthlin, C.S.B. and Mr. John W. Reeder, C.S.B. to have charge in the evenings and perhaps for one or two afternoons as may be arranged.

Miss McLauthlin is one of your own students.... Mr. Reeder is First Reader at Roxbury and now is in practice....

The last regular appointment was that of Miss Chamberlin, who left for a vacation by your consent, as we understood....

2) [dated May 23, '05 and signed "Lovingly yours, per Thos. W. Hatten, Sect."]: Beloved Leader: The Directors have advised us that the Reading Room is to be kept open in the evening (except Wednesday and Sunday evening) and have asked the Trustees to appoint someone to take charge. Miss Brown is at present Librarian, with hours from 9 to 5; but...she has to take charge of Mother's Room on Wednesday...; so we have decided to appoint one person for each evening.

It seems very desirable that the Reading Room should be open at hours when working people are free to visit it, and if there is no objection to the plan proposed, we understand that the Directors will make announcement in the Church....

3) [dated Jan.29, '08 and signed "Yours lovingly, The Board of Trustees"]: Beloved Leader: Mrs. Hering who has been assisting Miss Brown in the Reading Room of the Mother Church, has notified us that she will no longer be able to give her services, owing to her moving to Concord, N.H. If you have no objections we will appoint Miss Grace White, a sister of Mrs. Hering, to assist in the Reading Room

when needed. [Handwritten comment signed "Mary Baker Eddy": A good appointment.]

4) [dated June 23, '08 and signed "Lovingly yours, by Clifford P. Smith, Secretary"]: Beloved Leader: An additional Reading Room of The Mother Church having been located on Exchange Street in the business part of Boston, the Trustees have elected J.J. Rome to take charge of it, subject to your approval... [Handwritten comment signed "Mary B.G. Eddy": Approved.]

5) [to Christian Science Board of Directors, dated Feb.4, '09 and signed "Fraternally yours, The Trustees"]: Brothers: Under date of February 2nd we wrote to Mrs. Eddy in part as follows: "The Trustees of the Publishing Society recommend that they be relieved from participating in the management of the Reading Rooms of The Mother Church, and that the Publishing Society be permitted to deal with these Reading Rooms as it deals with the Reading Rooms of branch churches.

"To this end the Trustees recommend that the first sentence of Section 2, Article 21, of the Church Manual be changed [accordingly]...."

Mr. Dickey now informs us by telephone that these recommendations have received our Leader's approval....

INVOLVEMENT WITH LESSON-SERMON COMMITTEE

-- Letters between Mrs. Eddy (or secretaries) and the Trustees regarding the Lesson Sermon:

1) [dated May 3, '01 and signed "Yours fraternally, C.A. Frye"]: Dear Bro. McKenzie: The marked copies of S&H and the Bible which you sent for Mother to examine were sent at an unfortunate time; there are so many other matters occupying her thought at present, she cannot give the matter of new subjects for Bible Lessons the attention which is necessary now. I therefore return the books to you. Perhaps after the J.W[oodbury] suit and Annual Ch. meeting are over she can attend to this need.

2) [to Trustees of C.S.P.S., dated Oct.3, '01 and signed "With love, Mother, M.B. Eddy"]:
It is but just that a part of the travelling expenses of a member of the Bible Lesson Committee who resides out of the state of Massachusetts should be added to his salary. Will you please attend to this matter immediately and report to me? [Notice of compliance sent on Oct.8 to Mrs. Eddy.]
3) [dated March 4, '02 and signed "Yours fraternally, C.A. Frye"]: Dear Bro. McKenzie: Mrs. Eddy requests that Rev. C.D. Reynolds of Manchester, N.H., be elected as substitute for Bro. Tomlinson on the Bible Lesson Committee. She has arranged with Mr. Tomlinson and has his consent to this plan.
If I remember rightly, this is the duty of the Trustees instead of the Directors. If I am not correct, please hand this letter to them to act upon and have Mr. Reynolds notified in time to be at the meeting of Committee next Saturday.

4) [to Trustees of C.S.P.S., dated July 12, '02 and signed "Yours fraternally, C.A. Frye"]: Dear Brothers: About six months ago Mrs. Eddy asked you to allow Rev. C.D. Reynolds to act as a substitute on the Bible Lesson Committee. As Brother Tomlinson has been relieved of the extra tasks he had at that time Mrs. Eddy now requests that you reinstate him to his former position on the Bible Lesson Committee.

5) [to Board of Trustees, dated April 9, '04 and signed "In Mrs. Eddy's behalf, Yours fraternally, Geo. H. Kinter"]: Dear Brethren: Our dear Leader directs me to write you saying, tell them to appoint Mrs. Annie M. Knott upon the Lesson Committee, to fill the vacancy, now existing there. She also wished me to give you her love.
P.S. Both Mr. Frye and I think this appointment is made by the Trustees of the Publishing Society, and if we are correct, you will please refer the letter to the proper person, which will remove the necessity of troubling her about it again.
6) [to C.S.P.S., dated Oct.15 '07 and signed "Yours fraternally, Irving C. Tomlinson"]: Dear Brethren: Because of important duties here, and after consultation with our beloved Leader, she has suggested that I ask you to find a

substitute to act for me, while I am temporarily absent from the meetings of the Bible Lesson Committee.

7) [dated Oct.23, '07 and signed "We remain, Lovingly yours, Board of Trustees, per T.W.H{atten}, Secty"]: Beloved Leader: ...We take pleasure in presenting for your consideration the names mentioned below:...

Rev. Charles D. Reynolds, C.S.B., of Manchester, N.H.
Mr. David McKee, C.S.B., of Boston, Mass....

8) [to Trustees, dated Oct.24, '07 and signed "With kind regards, Charles D. Reynolds"]: Dear Brethren: Your letter saying that I have been selected by our Leader to fill a temporary vacancy on the Bible Lesson Committee, received. I accept with great pleasure....

9) [to Trustees, dated Jan.1, '08 and signed "Yours fraternally, Irving C. Tomlinson"]: Dear Brethren: This is to let you know that I expect to resume my work upon the Bible Lesson Committee on Saturday next.

I return to this labor of love with the approval of our beloved Leader.

~ ~ ~ ~ ~ ~ ~

In October of 1902 the Trustees informed Mrs. Eddy that a Chicago firm was regularly printing the full text of the Lesson Committee's references as given in the Quarterly. They told her they had remonstrated with the offenders (the Malcon Company) on the grounds *inter alia* that the company was guilty of a technical infringement of Mrs. Eddy's copyrights. The response had been that the publication was accepted as a great help to the study of the Lesson and was warmly welcomed by teachers and readers. The Trustees then sent a notice to Mrs. Eddy which she approved for publication in CSS Vol.IV, No.8 (Oct.24). This pointed out that the so-called "Help" which the company was putting out was not recommended by the C.S.P.S., and that if any such presentation became desirable the Publishing Society would initiate it. Support for the "Help" fell off and the publication ceased.

About a year later, the C.S.P.S. offered to the public a leaflet entitled "The Lesson Sermons." This was written by

Irving C. Tomlinson, and regarding it Mr. McKenzie received the following:

-- Letter [dated Dec.5, '03 and signed "In haste and love, M.B. Eddy"]:

Beloved Student: Advertise always on this circular "Science and Health with Key to the Scriptures."

~ ~ ~ ~ ~ ~ ~

Among the long-time members of the Lesson Sermon Committee was Ira O. Knapp, whose passing in November 1910 created a vacancy there as well as on the Board of Directors. After recommending a replacement to Mrs. Eddy the Trustees received the following:

-- Letter dated Nov. 30, '10 and signed "Sincerely yours, Adam H. Dickey, Secretary"]:

Dear Brethren: Your letter of the 23rd instant to Mrs. Eddy recommending the appointment of Mr. Lewis C. Strang as Mr. Knapp's successor on the Bible Lesson Committee has been received by her. Her reply is that she has no special request to make, but that you may elect the one whom you think best fitted for the position.

MRS. EDDY'S WATCHFUL EYE ON THE EDITORSHIP

According to Adelaide Still and other members of the Eddy household the contact between Mrs. Eddy and her editors in chief during 1895-1910 (Judge Septimus Hanna and Archibald McLellan) was almost daily--by visit as well as by mail or messenger. She was known to suggest the line to be taken in the various editorials, and in some cases to give the actual wording for articles to which she required the editor to put his own name or simply "Ed." The following are some of the known examples:

"Rights and Duties" (CSS Vol.V, No.10).
"A Correction" (CSS Vol.VI, No.28).
"Consistency" (CSS Vol.XI, No.14).

It should not be assumed, however, that every article that can be found in the periodicals before 1911 had Mrs. Eddy's scrutiny in advance and her seal of approval. Even though she watched the editorials closely, several of these appeared before she had had the chance to correct them--for example "Watching versus Watching Out" (My. 232:10). She was also known to commend (or criticize) several articles after she had read them in print, and just occasionally she saw the need to secure a correction in a later issue.

The following letters indicate some of the times when she pointed out mistakes and some of the times when she required corrections to be published:

-- Handwritten letters to Archibald McLellan [commencing "Beloved Student" and ending "Yours lovingly, Mother, M.B. Eddy", or some close variant--except where specified]:

1) [typewritten except for P.S., and dated Aug.4, '02, shortly after Mr. McLellan had taken over the editorship]: I never allow hearsay against an individual to influence my judgment so far as to deny that one a chance to be heard on the right side unless that one is openly disloyal....

P.S. I am delighted over what you write about the editorial corps. God bless you. Give my best love to all.

2) [Dictated except for final paragraph and dated Sept.8, '02]: The first mistake that I have seen in the Sentinel since the present editorial corps have conducted it is, the sarcastic allusion to King Edward in "Fashion in Physics", copied from the Chicago Tribune. Your publication of that article may prove very unfortunate for our Cause. Any possible peril to his health, or the loss of his kind attitude towards Christian Science, is not to be risked by newspaper slang however cute,--quoted or original.

A similar circumstance instigated by m.a.m., malicious animal magnetism, and brought to bear on the Court--in my candid opinion--cost our Church at least $40,000. But that money is less in comparison than to lose the friendship of that democratic King. I beg that you will not think I blame you, but only forewarn in order to forearm.

Let our periodicals uniformly maintain a dignified, kind position towards governments not pagan, and churches half civil. The only exception to this rule is when, by returning the enemies' fire you can prevent or check a siege. Never infuriate an enemy and never lose a friend by careless, humorous, or unjust reference.

I dinna ken how you are marshalled as an editorial corps; but I suggest, that one individual have the entire supervision of the literary department of our periodicals. It being thus there can be no deviation from given rules.

Please read this in open meeting of editors.

3) [dated Sept.12, '02] Permit me to indicate what *must be observed* and corrected in our periodicals viz. any error in stating C.S. On page 20, Vol.5, No.2, it reads in *The Education of Man*: "But as love is the principle, the truth, the way and the spirit of all good" etc. This is as incorrect in our writings or statements of C.S. as a grammatical error is in a work on Grammar.

Such an unscientific use of the synonyms or names of God or for God contradicts the rules in your text book and causes the enemy to say justly they use their terms for Deity unintelligently. It should read: As Love is the Principle of all goodness, is Spirit and Truth, humanity fulfils the divine law through love, and the Church does its most effective work by teaching and demonstrating Love.

Strange too it is that a Christian Scientist should write a long article on educational means and never name C.S. as the most efficient of them all. In another instance like this you must either supply the mention of C.S. or request the author to do so or not publish the article.

I hope you will comment on that article in a way that will give your readers to understand our rule on this point in your next issue....

[Six days later Mrs. Eddy dictated a set of rules regarding capitalization which she signed and sent to Archibald McLellan with the instruction: "Please have each editor *copy these rules*." The text follows]:

In abstract Science Good, Truth, Spirit, Love, signify God; and these words should be capitalized when you can substitute the word God and convey the proper meaning. Also spirit, truth, good, love, is used correctly as an adjective or a common noun in Christian Science e.g. It is good. The truth is I love you. The spirit of your saying is cruel. The good you do is evil spoken of. When you can substitute the word God, and retain the true meaning, then Good, Spirit, Love, Life, Truth mean God and should be capitalized.

Always avoid if possible using Principle in any other sense than God. Supply instead the words basis, foundation, etc. It is noticeable that this word Principle is used often in a way that confuses the meaning in Science. To use it only as God, is the rule in Science, and thus its meaning is made clear to the learner and the general reader who knows little, if anything of Divine Science.

I noticed recently a sharp comment in a newspaper on the Christian Scientists' unintelligent use of the word Principle--and it was just, for they often use it unscientifically. I know that this wrong use of the "new tongue" is the effect of m.a.m. and the students should guard themselves against this effect the same as they would against error of any kind.

4) [dated Nov.4, '02] I agree with you that silence on all questions of the court is wise and I deeply regret the absence of this wisdom.

You will pardon my interlines and erasures in your excellent article. "Non-Commit" is our watchword and indirect rebuke of error that fires with one aim and without smoke.

Will you please give your full name to the editorial in Sentinel and I would like to have "Editor" as well. With your permission I will advise Mr. Farlow to give it a wide circulation. Please write to me via express what you think of doing this--i.e. as to its effects on the subject at issue.

5) [dated Nov.6, '02] Since last I wrote things and thoughts have another aspect. I now advise not to circulate your last Editorial that you mailed to me. There are three reasons why but I cannot *write* them. It will do no good in the field.

6) [dated Dec.11, '02] Your kind letter was a "cup of cold water in His name." I *thank* you for it. Few on earth minister to my needs, many--or think that I have any. I enclose a clipping sent by Mr. Farlow [Boston Committee on Publication]. Remember me to your wife.

7) [dated Christmas '02] You will accept my thanks, and present them with overflow to the signers of your "Grace be with you." May the God of our fathers bless you all with His presence and power divine, give you many more Christ-days, and joyful years and time well spent. Then may we all meet --where no partings are--with the spiritual unction and self-conscious approval of "Well done good and faithful."

8) [early 1903, but undated] When a contributor sends a poem for publication in the Sentinel why not give him credit and say either, Written for Sentinel, or merely For Sentinel? It gives more prestige to your paper. Again when copying from other papers why have more than simply Boston Post, at the close of the article? I notice you have it--In Boston Post. Excuse these inquiries.

9) [undated, but probably referring to Harrison letter in CSS Vol.V, No.26]: Please publish enclosed in next Sentinel and return the letter to me. That little newspaper you are making an angel visitant and intellectual guest that blesses and feeds the hungry. God bless you.

10) [dated March 12, '03] I thank you for your letter. Your excuse for its length was kind but a business letter as ample as yours *saves* time often with me.

I agree with you on all its points--they are just what are needed in Journalism. The outlay of about $7000.00 can be over-balanced by the additional subscribers, and I trust an enlargement of the Sentinel. At present it is puny.

11) [dated April 26, '03] Please read the enclosed and if my meaning is not clear as I have now stated it--make it so and publish this article in your *next issue* of our Sentinel.

I have so much to attend to that I may make mistakes in writing. I wish you would correct any that are made; it would be a great help to me. [The reference is to "Significant Question--Who shall be greatest?" in CSS Vol.V, No.34.]

12) [dated May 30, '03] ...Your article in the last Sentinel [Vol.V, No.38] is sound. I have confirmed it with a By-law but either should wait till the subscription to our Church

building is more in the hands of our Treasurer, if we are wise as serpents.

It may discourage pleasure seekers to tell them they need more of C.S. than opportunity to have a good time. I thank you for your last but one letter. It was good to read what you wrote of the Directors. God bless you.

13) [dated June 18] Mr. Frye wrote to you this morning, he tells me, to spare me because I have so much on hand.

But a word from me to the wise is sufficient. I see the need [of] arming and fortifying against the enemy as never before. Publish that article of mine published in the N.Y. Sun that for "dissever" printed "discover" making me confess to the charges against me, and comment *sharply* on such an abuse--if no amends sufficient are made.

Again, the enemy can fire and will through the Press but they cannot *heal* who lie. If we beat in this battle it must be through demonstrating above *their ability*. I started this great work and *woke the people* by demonstration,--not words but works.

Our periodicals must have more testimonials in them. The Sentinel is of late a Shakespeare without a Hamlet. Three pp. of testimonials are the least to have in the Sentinel. Healing is the best sermon, healing is the best lecture, and the entire demonstration of *C.S.* The sinner and the sick healed are our best witnesses.

[See CSS Vol.V, No.42, and My.306:5, where Mrs. Eddy's words to the N.Y. Sun are correctly given.]

14) [dated June 21, '03] The Sentinel must not be issued with the present arrangement of the reply to an *insult* to your Leader, to her students, and our Cause! It is tame, and the Editor assumes as Editor no responsibility of thought on such a matter of importance--even in his editorial!

Please print my article as I wrote it, first--then follow it with the N.Y. Sun's shameful publication of it.

Make the heading a sharp allusion to said word that he supplied--and not as my order! but [as] the proper indignation of the Editor of the Christian Science periodicals; and make it in a way that will not invoke discussion but *stop it*. Get Mr. Willis to prepare it for you if need be and hand this letter to him.

15) [to *Editors* and C.S. Directors, dated July 14, '03 and signed "With love and all the patience God will give me for such *sin* and *folly*, such a waste of time and money, only to obey m.a.m. and make sport for our enemies, M.B.G.Eddy"]: Are you asleep on so important a subject as to make the laying of our Church Corner Stone in Concord a desecration --instead of a quiet, solemn, brief ceremony? You who profess to know there is *no matter* to elevate the usual material ceremony above *all precedent*!

Not over fifty persons shall be present on this occasion with my consent.

P.S. I had not seen your notice in our periodicals till today.

16) [dated July 16, '03] I rejoice to learn that you sent to me a notice of the invitation to Laying Corner Stone. I did not see it. Please pardon it. I cannot remember having made such a sad mistake before. I will correct it to all who know my sorrow over the opposite thought.

P.S. I learned my mistake today for the first time. The sacred hour has just passed of this brief momentous offering to God. O may He grant us our prayer. I was not on the ground.

Needed Changes and True Guidance

17) [to "My dear Editor", dated Aug.24, '03 and signed "In haste your watchman for the Cause, Lovingly yours, M.B. Eddy"]: Drop from the Sentinel articles "For the Children." That article in the last Sentinel is more injurious than physiology, to a child. It makes error more real than physiology could become to a child.

Also give Mrs. Knott her place in the Editor's table, next to your leading article, the same as you did to Miss Speakman occasionally.

The "Testimonials" are not up to date. Please obtain better ones for they do more for the reader than those slim writers on C.S. can do.

18) [dated Aug.29, '03] I deeply sympathize with you in all you wrote. I would quickly, joyfully give you a rule for each need wherewith to supply it, but God alone can do this,

and He will do it. Ask for wisdom of Him, the divine Love, and you will receive it, and as you pray *believe* and it shall be done unto you are the words of our Master.

Our periodicals stand for a system to be established and a Science to be demonstrated. They are not to amuse or to entertain so much as to instruct the public. They should contain only what tends to this result. The dabblers in literature are not the ones to fill this demand.

We need cultured writers to make the abstract interesting; and sound subjects to make the readers satisfied. *Wisdom* and the keen perception of what to write and how and when to write it, are requisite in the Editor, and a fearless stand as to maintaining the rights and rules of periodicals in self defence and the dignity due to our paper and its purpose. Wit and wise repartee are sometimes auxiliaries to this end; and sarcasm blent with love may gain a strong point in human thought. Unlettered novices in C.S. are not the writers that we need.

I recommend that you get *exchanges* with the leading religious or secular magazines and newspapers if possible. This is advantageous in many respects.

Accept my thanks for your labors.

19) [dated Sept.5, '03] Our Master, Jesus of Nazareth, had 82 disciples and these were his "first disciples". My Card should have read, "Call to mind the twelve whom our Master chose to be his disciples." [See My.347:16.] But do not refer to this publicly. I am never quite satisfied (or at least seldom satisfied) with what I write in a constant hurry; hence my habit of revising.

This issue [CSS Vol.VI, No.1] is a good one.

<u>Assemblage of Historical Facts</u>

20) [dated Nov.3, '03 and referring to articles about Major Glover in or destined for CSS Vol.VI, Nos.8-10 and Nov.CSJ '03--and see My. CHAP.XIX]: Your collection is excellent and it does take the pain out of a wounded heart.

I called him, my late husband, *Col.* Glover because he belonged to the militia and I had got mixed on his rank. There were several mistakes in the articles from Mr. Moore's magazine; e.g. my name and the name of the disease that took him from me. They called it billious fever in the magazine to allay the excitement. His was the second case that occurred.

I sent for the distinguished M.D. who attended that terrible disease as an expert. On the third day after the attack he told me he could not conceal the fact that his case was yellow fever of the worst form, and nothing would save the life of my husband.

O, the agony of that hour. I cannot forget it. That being the case the city authorities refused to have his remains taken to Charleston, S.C., his home. He had resided in Charleston many years. The house he built for himself was beautiful. I kept his drawings and specifications of it many years.

P.S. [signed "Again, M.B.E."]: The fever (yellow fever) spread so rapidly I was afraid to have my brother come to me after my husband's death to take me back to the north. My brother George S. Baker wanted to go to me but I declined on that ground.

[P.P.S. signed "Fraternally yours, Calvin A. Frye"]: Mrs. Eddy requests me to add these words: "Mr. Glover had made no will previous to his last illness and the seizure of disease was so sudden and violent he was unable to make a will."

[P.P.P.S. handwritten by Mrs. Eddy]: Another item I recall, viz: Dr. McKee, I think was the name of the expert on yellow fever. Major Glover (my husband) lived but *nine* days after the attack. I prayed day and night for his recovery and the expert M.D. told me that he (my husband) would have died on the seventh day but for my prayers.

21) [to "Dear Editor", dated Nov.13, '03]: I return all that I can find in three Sentinels of what has been published [about] my late husband, Major Glover.

In the beginning of this sacred trust I earnestly requested you to have in one Sentinel all that was collected on the subject. My motive was that I might circulate the paper which contained it, that Pub. Committees could readily find that which they wanted of it--indeed I had sufficient cause for my earnest desire to have it all in *one paper*. But malicious minds caused you to dribble it out and thereby lose as the Scriptures lose their effects by being detached from antecedents.

Now I hereby demand that what I send to you with this letter on the subject above named be properly arranged and placed in next week's Sentinel on the second page after the Contents of this Number.

P.S. [signed "M.B.G. Eddy"]: It is cruel to have this matter so maltreated to furnish a jest for our enemies and a wound to me.

22) [dated Nov.14, '03] I return proof received today for you to use in the next Sentinel, together with all that has been published, and let us have it as I requested at first--all in one Sentinel.

You must be careful not to use aught in this last proof that has been published already in the Sentinel. But be as *careful* to copy from this last proof all that has not been in our issues and make the whole a *connected article* and *including all* that has been printed on this topic. My reasons for requiring this, or a few of them, are named in my last letter that you have received.

[The result can be found in CSS Vol.VI, No.10, and in Dec.CSJ '03 as specifically requested in the following letter]:

23) [dated Nov.16, '03] I hereby request that all which has been published, and whatever may be received in the interval relative to Major George W. Glover, be grouped together and printed on the first pages of our next Christian Science Journal--the December number of 1903.

Further Directives and Admonitions

24) [reply signed "Eddy" to Mr. McLellan's question dated March 5, '04 regarding capitalization in Mrs.Eddy's earlier writings when currently quoted]: When publishing them conform quotations from my works to the capitalization [now] in S. & H.

25) [dated March 10, '04] I have had newly typed the two last paragraphs of *A Correction*. Send no more proof. Please sign your name to the above Article, if agreeable.

[This was Mrs. Eddy's reply to questions about her reference to Sir John Macneill in Ret.3:1. When it appeared in CSS Vol.VI, No.28 the article was duly signed by Archibald McLellan.]

26) [dated March 13, '04] I must confess my astonishment at your arrangement of this March C.S. Journal! Four pages of poetry and *letters* all full of the too much *private* laudation of Mrs. Eddy, at the *commencement* of a literary periodical, are a new thing to me.

Perhaps it is all my fault in sending what I have sent for publication; but I sent it as salt to be sprinkled into food and not to furnish the entire *first* course of a meal, or a book. You will pardon my abruptness--I have not the time to give to detail.

27) [dated May 2, '04] I am indeed sorry to give you so much trouble in issuing my copies. How it happened I cannot tell. Distinctly I recall giving Mr. Frye slips of paper having those By-laws written on them. It must be that my corrections got lost. We have a Babel of *confounded* tongues to encounter at certain times, but the dear God delivers us and teaches us new lessons thereby.

Your copy of notice is just right; be sure and publish the two By-laws. In the first case I requested you not to publish Church Membership, except in our Manual. But since they have gone out together already, it is best not to separate them in republishing.

28) [dated May 16, '04] Correct whatever you see that needs it. I want the questioned By-law understood--then send the enclosed copy to Mr. Farlow to put through the Associated Press or publish it the most conspicuous way he can--he knows better than I know what this way is. Copy it in your next issue of the Sentinel and the Journal.

> [Refers to notice in CSS Vol.VI, No.38 or June CSJ '04 clarifying what is now Art.VIII, Sect.16 of Church Manual.]

29) [dated June 1, '04] In your excellent article The Question of Omnipotence [CSS Vol.VI, No.38] you contradict your assertions. Pardon me, but reread it and you will find you wrote that evil is not "something that enjoys, suffers or is real." Then again you speak of evil "as a mirage that misleads the traveler."

Who is the traveler that is misled and must suffer for it? Who but the evil so-called, and does not evil destroy itself through its own lie, namely, a belief in evil, sin, suffering and death? Yes it does, in belief, and to sever it from this doom would be an evil itself.

30) [referring to "Holiday Gifts" which appeared in CSS Vol.VII, No.10, dated Nov. 5, '04]: Give this a prominent place in Sentinel.

31) [reply to question, dated June 14, '04, whether Mrs. Eddy wished to see proofs of everything destined for Sentinel regarding Communion, Annual Meeting, and visit to Pleasant View, as required in 1903]: Please send only what relates to me or is written by me.

32) [reply to Mr. McLellan's request dated Nov.4, '04 for instructions about widely-wished republication of Mrs. Eddy's article from Oct.CSJ '95, "What We Can Do for the Children"]: Publish the above article as often as is best to do so.

33) [probably early 1905 and signed "Eddy" with final sentence handwritten by her]: Please through our periodicals explain why all the correspondence of my students, that is wise and good is not published in our papers and this "why?" simply lack of room and a genial thought that it will find place in our next issue. The fact however remains that your good articles multiply and our space diminishes.

Make this longer and your own.

34) [dated April 2, '05] Please present my compliments to the Publishing Society for their loving sense of my little poem; and for $100.00 which I certainly do not desire for the service rendered--but greatly prize the courtesy that prompted it. You must not repeat it but [you may] give me the pleasure to know what you think of my old age versification.

P.S. Permit me to say that your Journal of this month is *fine*. The only imperfection is too many pages of Testimonials--24 pages on one subject are too much like patent medicine suggestions to call attention rather than to satisfy inquiry.

35) [dated April 18, '05] Please publish the following with Mrs. Mims' letter commenting on my article on "Divorce".

P.S. (handwritten): Let her letter appear in next Sentinel [Vol.VII, No.34].

[P.P.S., typewritten]: On reading the above letter from our distinguished lecturer and beloved student I was reminded of the following Scripture "For as Jonas was a sign unto the Ninevites, so shall also the Son of man be to this generation."

"The queen of the south shall rise up in the judgment with the men of this generation, and condemn them; for she came from the utmost parts of the earth to hear the wisdom of Solomon; and, behold, a greater than Solomon is here." Luke 10:30,31.

36) [dated June 14, '05] You will accept my thanks for your kind letter. Your growth, editorial, is marked; we do indeed need the best and the wisest in these times. What you may hear of me can give you little idea of what you should know--or what is true of me. May God abundantly bless you and yours and give me time to even receive one call from dear Mrs. McLellan before another year has come and gone. Remember me tenderly to her.

Watching vs. Watching Out

37) [dated Sept.28, '05 and typewritten with only final sentence in handwriting]: I hereby request that the article forthcoming relative to my article ["Watching *vs.* Watching Out" in CSS Vol. VIII, No.3] and to Mr. Willis shall be brief and apologetic, it shall not be explanatory, that is not requisite. Why? Because in the words of Jesus "Why do ye not understand my speech? even because ye cannot hear my word."

A little child does not understand the sayings or doings of his mother, hence my positive position on this point and the good that will result from it, or the evil that would follow the opposite course.

The student is no more capable of explaining my sayings or my life than the student in the two first rules of arithmetic is of explaining or commenting on problems in Euclid. With the student one extreme is apt to follow another--for example I requested you not to pirate my words in our periodicals;

thence followed no quotations from my works, when it should be otherwise, for an occasional quotation therefrom to seal a sentiment is sometimes needed.

The article should have appeared in this issue of the Sentinel. [The McLellan editorial "An Apology" did appear in CSS Vol.VIII, No.4.]

[handwritten P.S.]: Please let these directions be ample and so close all future comment on <u>my writings</u> that is injurious.

38) [also dated Sept.23] *Thanks*; I forgot what I had previously written. My correspondence is so large I can do but little justice to letter writing. This is what I now beg to have done. Tell Mr. Willis for me that I desire him not to refer in writing to "Watching *vs.* Watching Out" again. When I requested him to give us a few words on that subject like those he had written to me in his letter, I did not desire a long article or anything but his kind apology. It is too late now to bring it up. Ask him to please drop the subject--it has done its work all over the field.

P.S. [signed "Again ever yours, Eddy"]: What I have said in this letter for Mr. W. you will please also to accept as to yourself; unless you say in your nice way a brief word for my article as Editor in Chief and have no session upon it.

39) [dated Oct.10, '05] I thank you deeply for our last Journal. I believe it is the best one that has been issued. If you would suggest to Mr. Willis to make his interesting articles more simple or comprehensible to the average reader it might do him good.

I trust your toilsome and most important position now will not weary you but invigorate and cheer which is the nature of goodness.

> [This "last Journal" carried a repeat of Mrs. Eddy's vital article "Watching *vs.* Watching Out", thus making use of Mr. Willis' inexact wording to bring benefit "all over the field."]

<u>Contributions and Editor's Rights</u>

40) [dated Dec.27, '05] You will accept my thanks for your kind letter. Our papers can no more afford to be in-

correct in Christian Science metaphysics than the numeration table in mathematics. Please give the enclosed a good place. I thank you for those points in Heraldry.

41) [dated Oct.7, '05] I did not intend to condemn the article of Mr. Chadwick for it was good--but only that line I pointed out. Had I been the poor Editor in Chief of our paper I should have erased that line and published the article. Mosley and others of your salaried contributors are *talented* and *interesting writers* and you will of course give *precedence* to such. But this is an editor's privilege that whatever contradicts his doctrine and science he can erase or correct and should do.

42) [dated Aug.11, '06] I thank you for your letter. Allow me to say it is right to omit what is wrong in an article contributed to your paper and I advise you to do this and so retain whatever else is useful in said article.

Mrs. Thomson writes some *excellent* thoughts calculated to set the reader to thinking. These I would advise you to publish and if this is not satisfactory to the writer she can stop her contributions and thus spare you this task. I enclose some poetry sent to me that I have taken this liberty with. Personal praise may become fulsome.

43) [further letter, dated Aug.28, '06, about Mrs. Thomson's article "Little Things" which appeared in CSS Vol. VIII, No.51]: The article should not have been published in our periodicals. It contained that which is irritating and unwise relative to priestcraft.

Be very careful not to let appear in our periodicals anything that can offend the Roman Catholics or other religious denominations unnecessarily. And weigh well the results of whatever is published. Let all you send out tend to make friends not foes to our Cause. Let it be a repetition of the angelic announcment at the birth of the Christ idea, Jesus, "Glory to God in the highest, and on earth peace, good will toward men."

44) [undated note {probably early Feb.'09} from Mrs. Eddy, forwarded by "A.H.D."]: Hitherto I have been pleased with the articles contributed by Prof. J.R. Mosley to our periodicals, but I am surprised and disappointed with his

article "The True Orthodoxy" in our C.S. Sentinel of January 30, 1909. Will Prof. Mosley and our readers peruse the scripture according to Jeremiah 6:14,15,19,20,21 on this subject, "They have healed also the hurt of the daughter of my people slightly, saying, Peace, peace; when there is no peace," etc.

45) [dated Nov.29 '05 and signed "Lovingly in Christ, M.B.Eddy"]: Do not publish in our issues the Mayor's kind words on myself again in the *Sentinel*; it would seem too egotistical. Your remarks on the Boston Herald's article should have appeared above it even as you have commented appropriately on other newspaper articles in our Sentinel.

The occasion gave you a grand chance for doing that in a way that would have done much good. Have the Herald article printed in our next Journal just as it is in the Sentinel. But you can now comment on that article in a good heading in the Journal if you please.

46) [dated July 4, '06] It is plainly your duty to speak a word in behalf of "*Personal Contagion*", one of the most important things of thought I ever expressed. Does it cost me no cross to write thus? If you could look into my consciousness you could see it does, even a human rebellion thereto.

If God is not speaking to you your duty to do this now through an awakened sense do not do it because I have written thus.

["Personal Contagion" appeared in CSS Vol.VIII, No.45, and in the August CSJ, with an introductory endorsement by Editor McLellan. For text see My.116-8.]

47) [dated Aug.10, '06] I have now got Mrs. Stetson's article to you for the last time. Pardon the trouble I may have occasioned you. All my part in it has been to shorten it and remove her too much praise of me. Let it appear in both Sentinel and Journal and in our next issues.

P.S. [signed "M.B.E."] Keep this as quiet as possible till it is published. [See CSS Vol.VIII, No.51.]

More Advice on Testimonials

48) [dictated letter to Mr. McLellan, Mr. Willis, Mrs. Knott, Editors, dated Aug.4, '06] One other improvement I

beg to have made in our periodicals, namely: Keep out of them all descriptions of shocking suffering and the symptoms of disease.

Rehearsing error is not scientific. I know that you agree with me in this statement and therefore will adopt what I herewith suggest. Publish as usual the testimonies on healing. Give due authority therefor, and sometimes state the opinions of the M.D.'s on disease, but do this in a way that will not offend them. You can introduce this change to your contributors in a wise way and request them to conform to it strictly.

49) [dated Aug.18, '06] The testimonials are better but are not right yet, not stated so as to prevent an image of disease from getting into thought.

This is the way to keep out a distinct form in thought of disease. If the disease is called "floating kidney", you should write it fatal or dangerous, etc., disease of the kidneys.

Do not give the special name of a disease or of a complaint, but state the disease in general terms. If this is not enough to suit the author of the article, keep it all out.

50) [dated Aug.23, '06] Have no Park nor parks for Christian Scientists. But have more spirituality and power to resist evil. Resist the Devil and he will flee from you: draw nigh unto God and He will be nigh unto thee, St. Paul. I may not have quoted verbatim.

[See CSS Vol.XI, No.1, where Editor McLellan quoted from this letter to quash reports that Christian Scientists were planning a Summer Residence and Assembly Park.]

51) [reply, signed "Eddy", to request for permission to reprint "What Our Leader Says" as first published in March CSJ '99]: You may publish this quarterly if agreeable. [It duly appeared in CSS.Vol.IX, No.6, and Oct.CSJ '06]

Introducing The Monitor

52) [first letter, dated Aug.5, '08 and signed "Sincerely yours, Adam H. Dickey"]: Dear Mr. McLellan: Our Leader wishes you would have some thoroughly responsible outside person, write an article in the Sentinel setting forth Mrs.

Eddy's unexampled leadership in the interests of Christian Science. Let the article be entitled COMPETENCE and have it point out the fact that from the inception of this movement until the present time, not one false step had marred the long line of successful efforts put forth by her in support of her religion.

...Let the article be strong, and carry with it complete conviction as to her ability to lead under divine guidance.

[second letter, similarly introduced]: Since writing the attached letter, our Leader has thought it would be better to have *you* write the article referred to as an *editorial*, for as she stated no one is more competent to do this than you. She further said that the article should make it clear that every move has been made in the line of demonstration....

You will understand that the article is preparatory to making public her intention of starting a daily newspaper....

P.S. Our Leader has not seen either of these letters.

53) [dated Aug.7 and signed "Fraternally, C.A. Frye"]: Dear Bro. McLellan: Mother says Do not publish that article on Competence in this week's Sentinel. [The call to the Trustees to "start a daily newspaper at once" went out the following day.]

54) [dated Sept.29, '08 and signed "Sincerely yours, Adam H. Dickey, Secretary" and endorsed "Eddy"]: Dear Mr. McLellan: ...[Our Leader's] object in saying what she did in the Boston Post [about starting a daily newspaper] was to make it plain that Christian Scientists were not seeking an opportunity for self aggrandizement, but doing this through a purely Christian motive.

In line with your suggestion, Mrs. Eddy does not wish her Boston Post article to appear in our periodicals.

55) [typewritten, dated Nov.18, '08] I hereby forewarn you and demand of you to guard carefully the old landmarks that heretofore have been fought over, and gained their precedence and authority from your Leader and the leading Christian Scientists.

I trust that with you, "forewarned" will result in being "forearmed", to be faithful in history, true to your Leader and her precedents that have been justified by forty years of success.

56) [dated Jan.7, '09 and signed "Sincerely yours, Archibald McLellan"]: Dear Mr. Dickey: I am in receipt of your letter of the 6th inst., instructing me that our Leader wishes her name to appear hereafter, wherever practical and legal, as Mary Baker Eddy, leaving out the initial "G."...

The "G" has been taken out of this week's Sentinel wherever possible, and will be taken out of all of next week's issue with the possible exception of the copyright notice. The validity of the copyright notice with the "G" omitted is under investigation.

57) [dated Feb.5, '09 and signed "Sincerely yours, Adam H. Dickey, Secretary"]: Dear Mr. McLellan: Our Leader directs me to say to you, that she wishes hereafter you would allow nothing to appear in the Christian Science periodicals, either pro or con, that would in any way exploit Christian Psychology or Mental Suggestion. She says that if the Christian Scientists make no mention of them, they will have nothing to make reply to and no reason to force themselves on the notice of Scientists.

58) [dated April 30, '09 and signed "Sincerely yours, Adam H. Dickey, Secretary"]: Dear Mr. McLellan: Yesterday, April 29, our Leader corrected a passage on page 69 of Unity of Good, and after showing it to the members of her household, she requested me to notify you of the change and have it published in the next issue of the Sentinel, together with the date upon which the change was made. The original passage read as follows:

> Job's faith and hope gained him the assurance that by the sufferings of the flesh he should learn how false are pleasures and pains of material sense, and behold the Truth of Being, as expressed in his conviction "Yet in my flesh shall I see God,"--not <u>without my flesh</u>, but <u>in my flesh</u>.

After the change the passage reads as "...'Yet in my flesh shall I see God;' that is, Now and here shall I behold God, divine Love."... [See Un.55:17-22 for full text.]

59) [dated Feb.12, '10] Please publish a strong, clear article on "Quarreling in churches."

PUBLICATIONS NOT CONTROLLED BY C.S.P.S.

Mrs. Eddy watched the rise of Christianly Scientific literature into its peak of seventh-day exactness, eliminating all that is incorrect or "diseased" in the written word. Yet she was also pointing to the spreading descent of the Word into all religious, scientific, political and secular writing--into whatever publication "is reported to be haunted by" evil statements, waiting for the trumpet call that diseased writing "was never there."

She had already seen the leaven of C.S. at work in articles like Dr. Lyman Abbott's in the *Literary Digest* (see p.27, letter to Wm.P. McKenzie, Jan.8, '04). She was already encouraging exchanges with magazines not specifically devoted to C.S. and, before she acted on the need for the *Monitor*, good leading articles in the Sentinel to be taken from other publications. From the other side of the "exchange" came appreciative comments like that in the Salem *Daily Capital Journal* which praised the Sentinel for its choice of extracts from other religious papers and for the fact that it "lets politics alone" (CSS Vol.IX, No.27).

Towards the end of the "Seventh Day" Mrs. Eddy was sending her own articles to the world's media first and even exclusively; and while she gave Scientists the sop of being able to read the authorized C.S.P.S. selection of words in the periodicals, without their being required to do their own analysis with the aid of S&H, she did expect them to be working to bring other writings into the kingdom of heaven. As a step in this direction she advised Scientists to subscribe to secular newspapers "which speak justly of Christian Science" (CSS Vol.IX, No.46).

The process of scientifically translating the writings of "others" could seem at first to involve the need to "expose and denounce" evil writing in all its forms, but later and preeminently it would bring the healing need to "*realize* no reality in" the supposed evil. To Jesus' command "Go ye into all the world" to *bring* Christianity to it, the Revelator was adding: And there *find* the Science of Christianity already in control.

This additive explains the force of her reply to the teacher who asked her to evaluate the public effect of printed articles. She compared published utterances to paper money "which finds its way everywhere and is a wonderful medium of exchange," but which must have the backing of something of real value (gold). To get at the real value the student must therefore first handle animal magnetism through what Mrs. Eddy called "silent declarations of Truth which heal the sick and transform the sinful;" and then they could write or read or translate articles with what St. Paul called "the mind that was in Christ Jesus."

~ ~ ~ ~ ~ ~ ~

Some correspondence follows regarding the writings of others:

-- Letter to Trustee Hatten [dated Feb.22 {'99} and signed "Yours fraternally, C.A. Frye"]:

Dear Bro. Hatten: Mother requests that the Trustees of the Pub.So. order 50 copies of "Spinning Wheel at Rest" from E.A. Jenks of Concord, N.H. (whose article appears on page 12 of last week's Sentinel) and place them on sale at your Publishing Rooms. Send him check in payment for them.

Mr. Jenks is not a C.S. but a very literary man and as you see by his article rather leans towards us at least in his sympathy.

-- Handwritten letters to Archibald McLellan [signed "With love, Mother, M.B. Eddy"]:

1) [dated Sept.18, '02 and signed "Your loving Mother, M.B. Eddy"]: Beloved Student: Under the circumstances it is wise to advertise Mrs. Burnham's "The Right Princess". Then she may write another novel a degree higher and with a clearer sense of C.S. I am *ready* for *it*, you will see what this means hereafter.

I admire the woman, Mrs. B., as a novelist, although I never saw her.

You will excuse the repetition of letters on the same subject. I did not intend to mail the one sent last night. I wrote it in such haste I do not know what it contained so wrote another this morning and sent it via Express. I am half dazed with the amount of care and work on hand.

P.S. [signed "Again, M.B.E."]: Employ Rev. McKenzie if you please. I would like to have a woman on your list of editors if the right one could be obtained. [In due course Mrs. Annie Knott became one of the associate editors.]

2) [dated Sept.25, '02] Please inform Mrs. Burnham there is a church By-law (of recent date) which prohibits our Pub. So. advertising or selling works on fiction. You need not name me in it. Inform her at once.

3) [dated Sept.29] What I have put in pencil will exhonorate us. What I have written of her will not harm her. Please publish my article and tell her at once the novel before being revised is the one I refer to and send her my enclosure.

[in pencil] Also tell her not to add her new chapter to the novel. [See CSS Vol.V, No.5.]

-- Message in CSS Vol.VI, No.52 [dated Aug.18, '04 and signed "Mary Baker Eddy"]:

I recommend to Christian Scientists, and to all lovers of truth, to read the little book--"On The Way There"--by Katherine M. Yates.

~ ~ ~ ~ ~ ~ ~

Mrs. Eddy arranged for the free distribution of hundreds of copies of Judge Hanna's *Christian Science History* and for the sale of a booklet giving a lecture by Rev. Arthur R. Vosburgh, C.S.B., the proceeds from the latter to go to the lecturer.

She requested Scientists to subscribe to the Washington News-Letter when the latter came out with an article favorable to C.S. (see June CSJ '98). Correspondence already cited has shown that she also held up the News-Letter's appearance and arrangement as an example for the Trustees to emulate in their products.

In this case however the story had a provocative ending. When the editor (Col. Oliver Sabin) considered it would be profitable to operate a C.S. magazine outright and to push his own brand of C.S. organization, the decline began. The main points are given in the C.S.P.S. periodicals (beginning August 1899).

On Sept.19, '99 Judge Hanna wrote to Mrs. Eddy to say that "an article intended to meet the Sabin fiasco had been prepared, but upon consultation it was thought best not to publish it." The question confronting them, he explained, was "how to strike the required blows at evil and at the same time avoid giving occasion to the enemy to bring more libel suits [like Mrs. Woodbury's then in progress].... I am told that Sabin threatened to bring libel suits, and he will be on the sharp lookout for anything that he thinks may refer to him."

MRS. EDDY AND "THE CHURCH IN THE WILDERNESS"

Engaging the attention of both Mrs. Eddy and Editor Hanna in 1898 was a book by another cleric entitled "Fragments from the Study of a Pastor." It had been written in 1838 and the author was the Rev. Gardiner Spring.

The book had an account of a vision (later published fully in the Sentinel) which made use of passages from the 53rd and 54th chapters in Isaiah. At the time Judge Hanna was deep into the study of these chapters because of their evident references to the first and second comings of Christ. Seeing a correlation between the vision, the prophecies and the appearance of Mary Baker Eddy in the nineteenth century he sent her a copy of the vision and prepared an editorial for her approval.

-- <u>Reply</u> to S.J. Hanna [dated May '98 and signed "Ever lovingly, Mother, Mary Baker Eddy"]

...Yes, the prophecy was wonderful.

Twenty-one years ago, when the first revolt took place in our church, I had a vision, and uttered it. We then had no funds, I no salary, and C.S. few followers. In this vision [see *Six Days*, p.113] I prophesied great prosperity, plenty of money, blessings numberless, and the utterance was to the Daughter of Zion: "She shall sit under her own vine and fig tree, and all peoples shall hear her gladly."

That was when I had but one or two loyal students. All had deserted me in the darkest hour; the people scorned it, even those I raised instantly from the dream of death would shun me in the street.

In 1898 that dear verse in my hall here was suggested to my thought, that for fifty years had been forgotten. Oh, the goodness and loving-kindness of *our God*! Who can tell it? Oh, the long and still continued nail, and spear, and "My God, hast Thou forsaken me?" Oh, the *Love that never faileth*!"

P.S.: Yes, I would publish in Jour. the prophecy you sent.

~ ~ ~ ~ ~ ~ ~

The "verse in my hall" was as follows:

Daughter of Zion, awake from thy sadness;
Awake! for thy foes shall oppress thee no more;
Bright o'er the hills dawns the daystar of gladness;
Arise! for the night of thy sorrow is o'er.

and the editorial, as finally released for the July CSJ '98, had this to say about the Rev. Gardiner Spring's article:

We herewith publish what seems to us an interesting prophecy.

The article is entitled, "The Church in the Wilderness," and is contained in a little book written in 1838 by the Rev. Gardiner Spring, Pastor of the Brick Presbyterian Church of New York, the work itself being entitled, "Fragments from the Study of a Pastor."

It is interesting to note that the place of Mr. Spring's revelation was on Mont Viso (Mount of Vision) of the Alpine range, at a point whereon the persecuted Vaudois or Waldenses, found an asylum. It will be remembered that this sect arose in the south of France about A.D. 1170. They were the first to protest, as a body, against the corruption of the Roman church, and as a consequence, were of course bitterly persecuted. Persecution, however (as it always does), gave vitality to their doctrines, which passed on to Wycliffe and Huss, and through them produced the Reformation in Germany and England. This sect was distinguished from the Franciscans in that they taught the doctrine of Christ, while the latter taught the person of Christ, or Jesus. They had no official priesthood. They regarded the sacraments as merely symbolical, and with them ceremonies gradually disappeared. They became merged in the general Protestant movement in Germany and England.

As will be readily seen by Christian Scientists, they were among the forerunners of the larger Protestantism which is finding its expression in a general protest against all forms and conditions of erroneous doctrine-- in the churches and out of them.

~ ~ ~ ~ ~ ~ ~

A complete transcription of the prophecy followed the editorial and read in part as follows:

THE CHURCH IN THE WILDERNESS

...I had resolved, if possible, to ascend Mont Viso. Though not so high as Mont Blanc, yet from its solitary and isolated position, it presents a more imposing appearance of grandeur.... Already had I ascended far up the mountain, and all the beautiful plane of Italy was spread out before me.... It was with a feeling of self-reproach that I turned at last, to think...I was standing in the retreat of the ancient Vaudois.

Can this be the place, thought I, where the Woman, described in the Apocalypse, hath a place prepared of God, where she is nourished for a time, and times, and half a time, from the face of the Serpent?... My imagination wandered, I knew not whither. Whether it were that sleep overtook me on the mountain, and what followed was the fancy of a dream, or whether a waking vision occupied my senses, I am unable to tell. I seemed raised in spirit above the world, and yet my hopes and fears were strangely connected with its spiritual welfare and prosperity.

I trembled for the Ark of God. Errors, deeply ruinous in doctrine and practice, were inducing desolation and decay. A smooth theology had taken the place of those wholesome truths which have in every age been the wisdom of God, and the power of God to salvation.... I saw collisions of sentiment distracting the minds and dividing the counsels of those who were once joined together in the same mind and the same judgment....

Such were the thoughts which occupied me in my reverie....

I was by the side of a lofty, weather-beaten mountain. Its top seemed to support the heavens, and its brow frowned over a deep, expansive wilderness, impervious to the eye, and immeasurable in extent.... I beheld a female form of distinguished attractions and beauty, leaning on One like unto the Son of Man. Her countenance was expressive of intelligence and sweetness.... I saw that she was enveloped in a dense and hazy atmosphere, through which a pale light beamed from her countenance and clothed her form and seemed everywhere struggling to dart forth its rays. For the moment it seemed doubtful whether she would not be merged in the obscurity; but the mist was soon dissipated, and she looked forth like the moon walking in her brightness, luminous in her entire form, and like the angel standing in the sun, conspicuous to the world.

I observed that her features were in part covered with a veil. She had an humble, lowly spirit, and though in the full power of youth and beauty, seemed utterly unconscious of her attractions.... One of her loveliest characteristics, as it seemed to me, was this humble, meek and retiring spirit. Her progress was often rapid, yet was it noiseless and silent as the dew of heaven. Wherever she took a false step, she herself was the first to detect it....

And can this be she, thought I, of whom I have so often read, that was cast out into the open field to the loathing of her person in the day that she was born?... Once poor and miserable, and blind, and naked, she now was clothed with embroidered work, girded about with fine linen, covered with silk, and decked with ornaments.... She was the child of God--the adopted daughter of the king of heaven. Her second birth traced her lineage to the skies; born not of blood, nor of the will of the flesh, nor of the will of man, but of God....

Filled with admiration, I could not but again exclaim, Who is this?... The answer was quickly upon my lips. Who but the church of the First Born!--the spiritual Jerusalem from God out of heaven--the Bride, the Lamb's Wife!...

Here she wandered amid the gloom and darkness of the desert. Here she had a place prepared for her by God. With his own hands, he spread a table for her. The rock supplied her, and the manna descended. She fed on angels' food, and ate the bread of life. The pillar and the cloud moved before her. The God of Israel himself was with her,--a friend in need, a refuge in times of trouble....

I stood a while wondering at her zeal and steadfastness, but my wonder ceased when I recollected that she was not alone. She leaned on One who seemed more than mortal.

> In his side he bore,
> And in his hands and feet the cruel scars.

He it was who bore her griefs, carried her sorrow [as in Isa.53: 4], and even made her sins his own. It was her Lord--her Husband [as in Isa.54:5]--her Life--her Sacrifice. It was he who liveth and was dead, and is alive for evermore, to succor and bless his church when all the nations die. I saw the secret of her strength. Her life was hid with Christ in God. Though she was perfect weakness, she had omnipotence to lean upon. Experience had taught her her own insufficiency, and she lived by faith in him who loved her, and gave himself for her. ...Once I saw her so depressed and weary, that she sank to the earth; and then he took her up in his arms and carried her like a lamb in his bosom. Thus she pursued her way--for the most part wakeful, active, persevering--and yet ever leaning upon him....

I observed, that in leaning upon her Beloved, she was often led in a way that she knew not, and in paths that she had not known. She seemed to be under a sort of discipline, designed to subdue her will to an unconditional acquiescence in his; to chastise her self-confidence, and teach her to walk by faith and not by sight....

She was like a city set on an hill. None could help seeing her; none could view her with indifference. Good men beheld her, as identified with the glory of the Redeemer, as identifying their own happiness and glory with hers, as embodying the best interests of mankind in this world and that which is to come....

Bad men beheld her, sometimes to wonder at the peculiarity of her condition--a feeble woman coming up from the wilderness, leaning upon her beloved! Sometimes to admire her beauty, for she was comely as Jerusalem, and the fairest among women; sometimes to acknowledge her influence and power, for she was terrible as an army with banners; sometimes to feel the reproach of her example, for though shining in borrowed splendor, yet was she the light of the world; sometimes to be envious at her allotment, for the smile of heaven played upon her countenance, and the solitary place was glad for her; and sometimes to hate her with perfect hatred, to vex and injure her, to persecute, and if possible destroy her....

I saw also, that God her mighty Maker regarded her. More than all things else, did she illustrate his ineffable glory. He beheld her clothed with his own loveliness. He rejoiced over her with joy; he joyed over her with singing. As a bridegroom rejoiceth over his bride, so did God rejoice over her. God her Redeemer was with her--her shelter and shade, her glory and the lifter up of her head.

He has been her refuge and her strength. To the multiplied mischiefs that have passed through the earth, he has said, Touch not mine anointed and do my people no harm! He has beautified and enlarged her. He has caused her to look forth like the morning....

While this train of thought was passing through my mind, I cast my eyes once more towards the wilderness. No longer was it a desert, but rather an expanse of cultivated fields, and gardens of richest shrubbery, everywhere interspersed with beautiful villages, towering palaces, lofty turrets, and living men. The corn, and the vine, the olive and the palm flourished. Instead of the thorn, was the fir tree, and instead of the brier, the myrtle and the rose. Waters broke out in the desert. The way through this verdant territory seemed a highway. No tedious, intricate pilgrimage was it now. Enemies had disappeared....

No longer did she falter in her course, or turn her eye backward. She was clothed with a divine panoply, and went forth more than conqueror through him that loved her. A banner waved over her of the purest gold, on one side of which was set in rich enamel, The Lord knoweth them that are his; and on the other, Let every one that nameth the name of Christ depart from iniquity. At her approach, every false system of religion was arrested in its progress....

The mountains and the hills broke forth before her into singing and all the trees of the field clapped their hands....

My reverie continued, but the gloom and depression which at first pervaded it passed away.... The bow of promise threw its arch over the eastern sky, and as the sun went down, he cast forth the signals of a still brighter day.

AN EDITORIAL TOO SOON

After Judge Hanna had finished his introductory article and his editorial referring to the vision, he sent them to Mrs. Eddy for her approval, and he received the following letters from her [signed "With deep love, Mother" or similar]:

1) [dated June 10] I have not the time to read your article before Laura [Sargent] returns but have seen it enough to say you may have the Vision and the accompanying circumstances at your control. I would make it a *leader* not editorial.

[P.S.]: I have [now] read your article: 'tis wonderful, *sound*, lawyer-like in argument. Please if you cast this bread on the water add the bit enclosed after fixing it to your liking. God be with us both and He will, *is*.

[The "bit enclosed" read]: We know there is but one God, one Christ Jesus, and one mother of Jesus. But we deem it no infringement to regard the fulfilment of Scripture as indicated at the present period, and named there, a self-evident proof thereof--not confined to personality but the works which declare the Word.

2) [dated June 18] The time has not yet come in which to say the wonderful things you have written in proof [of your editorial] read by me today, unless you qualify it. Now you may hold your ground as therein, but do not say blandly that I represent the *second appearing of Christ.* That assertion will array mortal mind against us, and M.A.M. has been putting it into your mind to say it, and the infinite Love has *inspired you to say it.*

Now be wiser than a serpent. Throw out your truths not as affirmations or protestations, but as suggestions. Then you catch your fish, and make the wrath of man praise Him.

3) [dated June 22] ...Your vision is too grand, *true*, to be tampered with. I ventured to send for it to see if it cannot be held together and be the leader, I want it where all will catch sight of it. I write this before Laura will get here. I am so bothered then to get time. Will add all else I wish to tell you after she brings proofs.

Although Mrs. Eddy was letting Judge Hanna go ahead with publication, he also had her instruction to be "wiser than a serpent." Mrs. Eddy's appearance does of course represent and indicate the second coming of the Christ, but what is the full import of a message which the *human mind* relates to *time* and *space*? For example, suppose some villagers had been waiting for the coming of the Bolshoi Ballet to present "Swan Lake"--and then one day the company came and gave a perfect performance. The villagers could indeed say that "Swan Lake" has come at last.

And yet is it not true that "Swan Lake" in its whole sense has not fully come if it is simply personalized and localized? The villagers would need to make it their own, and everyone else's, before they saw its everlasting glory, and profited from what would be, in Christ's case, but a presentation to them of an always-existing, universal and everpresent concept.

At any rate Judge Hanna wisely pruned his editorial to omit those parts he feared might create opposition. The following reproduction includes in brackets the text as Mrs. Eddy saw it:

"THE SECOND-COMING HAS COMMENCED"

[From Editor's Table, July CSJ '98---
except that sections in brackets were then omitted]

It has ever been a peculiarity of human nature to relegate prophecy and prophets to the past. It is as much a truism that a prophet is not without honor save in his own age and generation, as that he is not without honor save in his own country.

...Jesus' coming had long and repeatedly been foretold, and a Messianic appearing was generally expected among the Jews, the people who, more than any other, refused to receive him.

A second-coming is as clearly prophesied as was the first coming. The Old Testament writers foretold it, Jesus plainly prophesied it, and the apostles reiterated these prophecies. The only question among believers in the Bible has been as to the time and manner of the coming. In respect to this there has been and yet is, much disputation, speculation, and controversy. A personal coming is generally believed in, and the only personality that will at present meet the general expectency of Christendom is the identical personality of Jesus as he appeared nineteen hundred years ago.

Only, as yet, a comparatively small part of mankind are ready to accept the larger coming comprehended in a re-establishment of the religious *régime* which Jesus inaugurated. This small part of mankind are satisfied that the second-coming has commenced and is now manifesting itself in the works which Jesus taught should be the evidence of the fact that the Kingdom of Heaven was at hand. While this coming is, in a sense, general, presaging a universal Kingdom, it is in another sense, individual. As units make millions and trillions, so individuals make an aggregate. Individuality, therefore, leads to universality. Individuality, in the best sense, includes personality. Not the false personality of mortal sense, but the true personality, which, in its individuality, reflects the Divine character. From this point of view Christian Scientists believe in a personal second-coming.

[Who is the personality or individuality manifesting the second-coming? The answer of every true Christian Scientist will be: The person or individual who has done, and is doing, the works, in a sense above and beyond that of the average of those, even, who are addressing themselves to the task of regenerating the race. Is there one such? Christian Scientists unhesitatingly answer: Yes: The Reverend Mary Baker Eddy.]

In the declaration in Genesis that God created man in his own image, male and female, we recognize the divine Fatherhood and Motherhood. That Fatherhood and Motherhood must logically express itself in the male and female.... In other words, there must be a personalized or individualized expression of the male and female of God's creation before there is a full revelation of God to mankind.

[How could such an expression reach human conception unless it were manifested in human form?]

By common belief of all Christians [Christ] Jesus represented the [spiritual type or] malehood of God. Is it not reasonable to assume that a full or completed revelation includes God's [spiritual type of] femalehood?... Christian Scientists believe in a *full* Godhead; and thus believing they believe also in a *full* manifestation of that Godhead to humanity.

[Therefore they see in Genesis a prophecy of the second-coming in female form. In Revelation they see the finality of prophecy.]

To their understanding the Woman of the Apocalypse stands in type for the female of God's creation spoken of in Genesis....

[Must the Woman of the Apocalypse be personalized or individualized to mankind? By every principle of logical sequence in Biblical prophecy, Yes.

[Without undertaking to speak for any but ourself (the writer hereof), we read in the 54th chapter of Isaiah a distinct prophecy of the personalized or individualized woman spoken of in Genesis and revealed in the Apocalypse. All Bible commentators and students agree that the 53rd chapter of Isaiah is directly prophetic of Jesus in his distinctively personal character. We see in the 54th chapter quite as distinct and direct a prophecy of a Woman.]

...Let us look at the 54th chapter of Isaiah. (Then Isa.54: 1-3, then): Mary Baker Eddy had only one son born to her of the flesh, and in his early infancy he was surreptitiously taken from her and for years concealed.... She was, therefore, to all intents and purposes, without a child of the flesh. But what of her other children--her spiritual children? They are now numbered by the thousands, and their numbers are being augmented with amazing rapidity....

In so far as these evidences are being now brought into view through Christian Science, may it not be consistently claimed that the second-coming is here; and in so far as a single Woman has been the instrument of bringing these evidences into view, may it not be consistently claimed that she is the personal representative of that second-coming?...

(Then Isa.54:4-5, then): When we recall the reproaches cast upon Mrs. Eddy because of her widowhood, especially by certain of the clergy, and think upon the irrepressible energy with which the tongue of slander has wagged against her, without any known or apparent reason, it is not strange that we read in the tender words of this prophecy God's purpose to protect his child....

If it be possible for "a widow", still living on this plane of existence, to make her "Maker her husband", surely that widow is Mrs. Eddy....

(Then Isa.54:11, then): Could there be a more explicit fulfillment of this prophecy than the following written by Mrs. Eddy to the writer, but with no reference whatever to the use we are now making of it, and not intended for publication at all, until by special request consent was obtained.

"Twenty-one years ago, when the first revolt took place in our church, I had a vision and uttered it." (Then the rest of this letter of May 1898, quoted above, but without the P.S., then):

Millions are now hearing the "Daughter of Zion" gladly.... Literally enough has this promise been redeemed in the material sense, but with overflowing abundance in the spiritual--present and prospective.

[But what of this material abundance? To no selfish end is it being appropriated. It is fast being converted into the Lord's treasury.

[Such use is being made of it as would be expected of one who in prophetic vision foresaw "prosperity, plenty of money, and blessing unnumbered" for a sacred Cause.]

...In the April, 1898, Journal, Mrs. Eddy, speaking of the financial problem as she experienced it, says: (Then as My.214:19 - 215:6; 215:15-22, then):

The donation of the valuable lot of ground to the Mother Church in Boston, liberal aid to the erection of the church building, countless contributions to indigent students and to charitable purposes outside our ranks...--these are *some* of the evidences of the sense in which the financial fruits of Mrs. Eddy's long years of labor are being used for God's purpose....

[{the last two lines were substituted for}: ...{in which} this Daughter of Zion is sitting under her own vine and fig-tree and dispensing the wine of Life and the figs of Love to hungering and thirsting humanity.

[Has not this Daughter of Zion also witnessed the fulfilment of this promise of God: "No weapon that is formed against thee shall prosper"? Every form of opposition has been made against her and her teaching possible to humanity, saving only attempts to murder her in the ordinary or physical sense. The mental assassin has exhausted his ingenuity and resources in his vain efforts.]

...We shall not stop to enlarge upon the "mighty works." They are becoming well-known and widely recognized. Read of some of them in this *Journal*, and in the newspapers and magazines of the country. Hear of them in the weekly testimonial meetings.... When we observe and think upon all this, may we not justly assert that there is an entirely unselfish disbursement of the trust fund thus committed to Mrs. Eddy's charge? Who can further truthfully charge mercenary motives upon the Leader of Christian Science?

[While, in the foregoing, we plainly see the Woman, as in other Scripture we see the Man, we look beyond all personality and as plainly see the Male and Female--the universal Manhood and Womanhood comprehended in the Divine scheme--and know that the ideal Manhood and Womanhood of God's Word personally typified as we have shown, is--must in the Divine order be--the heritage of every son and daughter of God's creating; and He created *all*.

[Hence we recognize personality in type only that we may thereby understand the unified Individuality of Father and Son, and Mother and Daughter, in the fulness of that Godhead whose second-coming is upon us, wherein we see "a new Heaven and a new earth."]

~ ~ ~ ~ ~ ~ ~

"CHRISTIAN SCIENCE HISTORY"
(Further Remarks on Mrs. Eddy's Place--from Hanna's Booklet Published 1899)

PREPARATORY REMARKS

...Mrs. Eddy, as the greatest religious reformer of modern times, has, in some measure, shared the fate of her predecessors. As in other cases, so in her case, adverse criticism or opposition have come from two classes--those who entirely misapprehend the scope and purpose of the reformation, or those who, having sought a knowledge of Christian Science, as did some of old time, for the loaves and fishes, and having been disappointed in carrying out their selfish ends, have turned with the rage of envy and malice upon her who had been their benefactor, and (vainly) seek to injure her....

HER TENDERNESS TOWARD OTHERS' VIEWS

Mrs. Eddy has recently said in a letter to me: "A new discovery of science always has awakened the world to fierce combat, and Christian Science is no exception to this rule. I have marveled at the press and pulpit's patience with me, when I 'have taken away their Lord' to present the risen Saviour, more spiritual appearing of God's power,--and I thank God, and the vox populi for these signs of the times."...

SPIRITUAL SENSE

In a communication to me dated July 21, 1899, Mrs. Eddy writes:

"In justice to myself, and the readers of your booklet, I send a brief explanation of my writings, that appeared in your first editions [of Christian Science History], and has been quoted by a clergyman and ignorantly or intentionally misconstrued. The spiritual sense referred to therein is, the discerning of the purpose of a mental malpractitioner whose thoughts turn on me with evil intent. This spiritual discernment is neither universal, nor indiscriminate mind reading. It is a consciousness wherewith good is done and no evil can be done. This phenomenon appeared in my childhood, is associated with my earlier memories and has increased with my spiritual increase. It has aided me in healing the sick, and subordinating the human to the Divine. While this metaphysical phenomenon puzzles poor philosophy, and is not in the slightest degree theosophy, hypnotism, clairvoyance, or an element of the human mind, I regard it as a component part of the Science of Mind not yet understood."

[The misunderstood wording in the first edition ran as follows: "I possess a spiritual sense of what the malicious mental malpractitioner is mentally arguing which cannot be deceived. I can discern in the human mind, thoughts, motives, and purpose; and neither mental arguments nor psychic power can affect this spiritual insight. It is as impossible to prevent this native perception as to open the door of a room and then prevent a man who is not blind from looking into the room and seeing all it contains. This mind-reading is first sight; it is the gift of God. And this phenomenon appeared in my childhood; it is associated with my earliest memories, and has increased with years. It has enabled me to heal in a marvelous manner; to be just in judgment, to learn the divine Mind--and it cannot be abused; no evil can be done by reason of it. If the human mind communicates with me in sleep, when I awake, this communication is as palpable as words audibly spoken".]

FOREIGN TRANSLATION OF CORRECT WORDING

Since words in English cannot be fully guaranteed to convey the meaning a speaker or writer believes they will have, the guarantee shrinks still more when even acceptable phrases get translated into foreign tongues. This accounts for Mrs. Eddy's reaction to the first attempts to put Science and Health into German. (See p.8 for her correspondence with Prof. McKenzie on the subject; also Editorial sections of Jan.CSJ '06 and CSS Vol.VI, No.6.)

What then happens when *someone else's* immature understanding of C.S. is conveyed in a tongue which is not English? Will the spirit be enough to govern the letter? The early spread of Christian Science in Germany gave rise to much correspondence about translation between Mrs. Eddy, the Trustees, and the enthusiastic students there. After some local attempts had caused dissatisfaction, eventually *Der Herold der Christian Science* became the official periodical in the German language, as published and supervised by the C.S.P.S. in Boston.

The first publication to be directed at the German market was entitled Deutsches Monatsheft der Christlich-Wissenschaftlichen oder Metaphysischen Heilmethode. An advance circular signed by the editor, Marie Schoen, C.S., said that to cope with the rapid growth of C.S. among Germans who could not manage the English literature available, there would be a German-language periodical beginning October 1, 1900 which would "absolutely rest upon and in every respect represent and comprise the principles and views taught by Mrs. Mary Baker G. Eddy."

The circular created a stir in Boston where officials asked questions about such things as infringement of copyright under translation, including the danger to S&H, in the U.S. as well as Germany, if large amounts were gradually pirated in a foreign equivalent without permission or restraining action. Mrs. Eddy wrote Fraulein Schoen inviting her, unsuccessfully, to come to Boston to edit a German edition of the Journal.

At about the same time other questions were being asked about a special privilege granted by Mrs. Eddy to Frau Gunther-Peterson to teach a class in Germany without earning her degree through a course in the Board of Education. Correspondence dealing with these issues follows:

-- Handwritten letter to Publisher Joseph Armstrong, explaining the special Gunther-Peterson teaching credentials [dated Sept.14, '00 and signed "With love, Mother, M.B. Eddy"]:

My dear Student: ...Frau Gunther-Peterson must have all the privileges of her degree for I granted it to her under circumstances that demanded this exception to our rules which I will name briefly. She came here to enter the Mass. Met. Col. The term was deferred as you remember.

Before she came, some dignitaries in Germany had requested her to teach them. She told them she would after her course at our College. When she was deprived of this course as aforesaid she feared that before she could enter upon it she might lose those important students.

I told her as an exception she might take the normal course with Mrs. Lathrop, and as she [Mrs. L.] was a C.S.D. she, Mrs. P., could take that degree of her as one of the Board of Instruction and so teach her class. This was better than to lose her students.

But Frau Peterson must now pass through the College course and you may credit her tuition to me. Please inform her of this.

-- Letter to Trustee Hatten [dated Sept.23, '00 and signed "Sincerely and lovingly, Joseph {Armstrong}"]:

My dear Brother Thomas: Mother is busy or she would have written Brother McKenzie herself on this matter [of a proposed German translation of S&H].... Fraulein Schoen and Frau Gunther-Peterson are undertaking this...and Mother's word is that you should *faithfully pray* for them. Their purpose is to do good, but M.A.M. has misdirected them, and [you should help] by *kindly* writing to them to deliver them....

-- Dictated letter to W.P. McKenzie [dated Sept.28, '00 and signed "With love, Mother, Mary Baker Eddy"]:

Beloved Student: I have travailed in Soul for the dear students in Germany and have built up a theory for their relief that I want made practical by our Publishing Society in Boston.

It is this: To have the Sentinel and C.S. Journal issued from our House in Boston printed in both the English and German tongue and sent to Germany.

That grand nation should certainly have the means for obtaining a knowledge of Christian Science. And this way of providing it will save breaking the international law on copyright, and dearer far to my heart, it will help Frau Gunther-Peterson and Fraulein Schoen to accomplish a great work which they have nobly and patiently inaugurated for the good of their people and the spread of Christian Science.

Please bring this request of mine to your Board at once and act upon it in the bonds of Christian unity which we all entertain so warmly for our brothers and sisters across the sea.

-- Letter to Joseph Armstrong [dated Oct.15, '00 and signed "Believe me, dear Sir, Yours very sincerely, Frau Dr. Bertha Gunther-Peterson"]:

Dear Sir: ...As to your advice in regard to our German Monthly [the *Deutsches Monatsheft*] I need not answer anymore, since our beloved Leader and Mother herself has acknowledged the necessity of having German Christian Science literature....

Besides you have seen in Fraulein Schoen's letter to you that I am fully in accord with her step and I trust that her letter will have proven to you...that this step was taken with God....

-- Letter from Trustees [dated Oct.16]:

Beloved Mother: Correspondence with Rabbi Wertheimer has at last revealed a willingness on his part to work in connection with a German periodical, in so far as to accept editorial oversight.

In searching for a translator we learned of C.S. work going on among the 300,000 Jews of New York, many of whom know German and would welcome literature in that language....

-- Letters to Marie Schoen in October 1900:

1) [dated Oct.17, '00 and signed "With love thine, Mary Baker G. Eddy"]: My dear Madam: I have the pleasure to invite you through the Publishing Society to come to Boston and edit in that city the German edition of the Christian Science Journal. If this invitation is accepted please inform our Publishing Society thereof immediately.

2) [from the C.S.P.S. and signed "Yours in brotherly kindness, The Christian Science Board of Trustees"]: Dear Sister in Christ: You will be aware that the problem of translating the message of Christian Science into other languages is one which has been long considered here. You also know that Mrs. Eddy could not under copyright laws permit the textbook to be translated and still maintain her rightful control of it. She has been guided of God to a present solution, which is to issue an edition in the German language of the Journal, and perhaps of the Sentinal also....

There are in New York alone 300,000 Jews acquainted with German and in all parts of this land there are thousands who will welcome a German magazine, as well as those who are ready to hear in the Fatherland. To all of these we must minister and it has been proven that literature sent out in the name of Christian Science must be accredited and guarded by those agencies which our Leader has appointed. ...we trust you to accept gladly the opportunity offered to you by our Leader and Mother...by taking charge here in Boston of the translation into German of The Christian Science Journal.

-- Letter [dated Oct.21, '00 and signed "Yours fraternally, Calvin A. Frye"]:

Dear Brother McKenzie: Referring to the German translation of Christian Science literature--the leaders of our Cause, the officers of the Mother Church, and the

Trustees of our Publishing Society in Boston, should adjust this matter, wisely, and in a way that shall retain harmonious relations with the loyal workers in Germany and other foreign countries; and this must be done without placing the burden on Mother or holding her responsible for their decision in this matter. For too many years she has had to carry these burdens alone, but now feels that others should take these cares upon themselves and relieve her.

She emphatically refuses to endorse anything that will tend to make a break between the Christian Scientist Churches in Germany and herself.

-- Next <u>correspondence</u> between Trustees and Frau Gunther-Peterson:

1) [dated March 25, '02 and not signed individually]:

Dear Sister in Christ: You will remember our letter...of September 19th, 1900 [indicating our understanding] that the permission to use the title C.S.B. was to continue only until such time as you could take the course.... We therefore would inquire if you will soon fulfill the requirement set forth by Mrs. Eddy.... The Publishing Society will not have the right to continue advertising your card as now given unless you fulfill the conditions imposed by Mrs. Eddy....

2) [dated May 26, '02 and signed "Believe me, dear Sir, Yours very sincerely, Frau Dr. Bertha Gunther-Peterson"]: Dear Sir: ...When you wrote me that I "eventually" had to complete the course required by Mrs. Eddy, Pres. of the Mass. Met. College, I always have had and have today the intention eventually to complete the course...but am sorry to say it will be simply impossible...this year or in any near future, as we are building here just now our First Church of Christ, Scientist, and I need not tell you what an immense amount of work this means for me in addition to all my other work, which keeps me busy almost day and night literally....

If you think it right, and in accord with Mrs. Eddy's intention, to discontinue advertising my card as now given with the title of C.S.B., you must do so....

~ ~ ~ ~ ~ ~ ~

-- Letter to Mrs. Eddy from Trustees [dated July 23,'02]:

Beloved Mother:...We have at intervals given thought to the German situation, and would present to you our solution.... The claim made by [Marie Schoen and] those who continue to issue [the German Journal in Hanover] is as follows:

1. That their Church is First Church of Christ, Scientist, in Germany....

2. That their Journal is the official organ of both this Church and German Institute....

3. That they have your authorization in publishing this monthly magazine....

4. That they have permission to translate Science and Health and print selections for their lesson-sermons....

We feel that the time has come when a magazine can be published for the service of the German speaking people to be found on this continent as well as in European countries where German is the language of commerce.... We have invited Marie Schoen again to come to Boston, and have also invited Fraulein Bruno, a competent translator, who is working with Mrs. Seal. If they both accept we shall thus have a representative from each set of workers in Germany; and if they come and work together the result will be the unification of effort in Germany....

Although *Der Herold der Christian Science* was duly established a few months later, and it was welcomed by Mrs. Seal, it did not produce a German "unification". The Hanover "faction" remained at odds with the Seal "faction" (Dresden and Berlin) for many years.

-- Letters to Trustees from Mrs. Eddy or her secretaries:

1) [dated Feb.14, '03 and signed "Lovingly, M.B. Eddy"]: Beloved Student [Thos. W. Hatten]: I approve of the German publication but I have not time to examine it. You must have it correct and I leave this with the Trustees to be *sure of.* I am glad that you have changed the day for issuing the Sentinel from Thursday to Sat. I never liked the day it has been sent out. God bless you dear, and prosper you in doing His work, which He surely will do.

2) [dated Oct.19, '04 and signed "G.H. Kinter"]: Dear Brother McKenzie: I have just seen your letter re the cables from and to Germany, too bad I did not know something about this condition.... When I was coming through Boston last fall, en route to Concord, I asked at the Pub. Office about Mrs. Seal, being in need of her address, but was given a most decidedly cool impression of her standing, you know, innuendo, and arched eyebrows....

3) [dated Oct.21, '04 and signed "In Mrs. Eddy's behalf, I remain, Fraternally yours, Geo. H. Kinter"]: Dear Brother McKenzie: Our Leader directs me to write you to settle the matter with the Germans the best you can without bringing her into it at all, as she has more now than she can attend to.

She wishes me to give you her dear love, and many kind thanks for your effective cooperation.

~ ~ ~ ~ ~ ~ ~

Twenty-five years later, when Mrs. Frances Thurber Seal wrote her book "Christian Science in Germany", she wisely refrained from touching on the issue of "Who shall be greatest?" in the pioneer work there. But in Boston there were again arched eyebrows and coolness, and her book was spurned as "unauthorized".

But to return to the first decade of the century, there is some further correspondence about translation worthy of mention.

-- Handwritten <u>reply</u> to Trustees requesting permission on June 27, '06 to translate an article about Mrs. Eddy for *Der Herold* [signed "Lovingly yours, Mary Baker Eddy"]:

You have my permission to do as above requested. Excuse haste.

-- <u>Comment</u> by Mary Baker G. Eddy on letter from Fraulein Bertha S. Reinke dated Sept.20, '06 [for full text of both see CSS Vol.IX, No.6]:

...I will say that the important matter of publishing in the German language my works on Christian Science is not within my jurisdiction, except as I voluntarily assume it.... The Trustees of the Christian Science

Publishing Society are the proper *authorities* to settle this question.

-- Handwritten notes to Trustees 1907-8:

1) [signed "Lovingly yours, Eddy"]: The reprint, Evil Is Not Power, may be printed in French and German if you send me the page proof and it is thought best to publish it thus by Mr. McLellan.

2) [dated Dec.3 '07 and signed "Yours fraternally, Irving C. Tomlinson"]: Beloved Brethren: Our dear Leader requests that in translations of "Evil Is Not Power" into the German and French, you insert her name as the author. [Before the translations arrived from the selected language experts the decision was taken not to issue the translated reprints.]

3) reply [signed "Mary Baker Eddy"] to notification in Aug.'08 that Theodore Stanger was replacing Miss Kollmorgen as editor of *Der Herold*: Beloved Students: I submit this important change to your good judgment trusting a blessing from on high.

~ ~ ~ ~ ~ ~ ~

The translations of S&H into German, and later into French and other languages, did not come until after Mrs. Eddy's direct approval was no longer obtainable.

FINAL COPYRIGHT OF TEXTBOOK

Towards the end of 1906 Mrs. Eddy completed the final major revision of S&H, the one that was destined to bear its final copyright--a copyright which would be due to expire forever on the first day of 1963 (provided of course a renewal was secured correctly in 1934). This was before Congress added 19 years to the renewal allowance, bringing the expiration date to 1982--and before attempts were fruitlessly made during the Nixon administration to allow S&H by special waiver to retain copyright on all editions at least until 2046 A.D.

Much of the routine work of the revision was entrusted to Edward Everett Norwood of Washington, D.C. where copyrights are secured and registered. Mr. Norwood was also asked to redo the whole of the final chapter (Chapter XVIII, Fruitage) by using recent CSS testimonials "revised, primed, mentioning not more than two diseases and given titles."

-- Letter to Mr. Norwood, C.S.D. [dated Dec.1, '06 and signed "Lovingly and gratefully, Your Leader and a Free Mason's widow, Mary Baker G. Eddy"]:

> Beloved: Another word to you. If there are not enough new Testimonials of the new ones to make out the 700 pages of Science and Health you can retain some of the old testimonials that are now in this book. Be sure to have 700 pages in this edition and if it overruns this a little in the make-up, no matter. But the original number may not be lessened.

Twelve days before the above letter was written Mrs. Eddy had completed her elucidations of Chapters I through XVII and she took elaborate precautions to get the revised pages safely to Washington. She demonstrated to members of her household that any belief in their midst of a mind separate from God must be dealt with according to her rule given on p.5:

> "Handle [powerless] evil as though it had power. This is because of your place in spiritual growth."

William Lyman Johnson relates that he had a telephone call from his father on the evening of November 19 requiring him to leave a dinner party as soon as that could be politely done, and go to the clerk's office at the church. Here he learned that a special messenger had arrived from Concord at 7:00 P.M. with a package that needed special conveyance to Washington.

He went home to get ready for the trip which involved taking the midnight train from Boston--except that he was to get out at New London and pass the rest of the night there at a hotel under the name J. Lyman. He could then carry on to Washington the following morning. He writes:

> "I did as directed, and that nothing should happen to the precious package, I placed it in a cloth bag known as a lawyer's bag, which I used every day, and tied its pucker strings to my wrist so that there was no possibil-

ity of its being separated from me in the friction of a crowded street or station."

After his return from Washington the following night he learned that "what I had carried were the last corrected proof sheets of what is now the last edition of Science and Health, and that those sheets with Mrs. Eddy's additions to her text were most precious to her."

Although Mrs. Eddy did make a few more changes and additions to S&H after November 1906, they were still legally protected by this 1906 copyright. Even a major change which it could be argued was extensive enough to be unprotected under copyright law, and therefore in the public domain, would not include a right to appropriate any of the context or remainder of the work.

The letters from Concord which went with the above story were as follows:

1) [dated Nov.19, '06 and signed "Sincerely yours, Lewis C. Strang"]: Dear Brother Johnson: Mrs. Eddy's instructions are as follows: Have your son leave Boston tomorrow and deliver the accompanying letter and parcel to the person addressed. Lyman's business will end with the delivery of the letter.

Lyman is not to take the train direct from Boston to Washington, but is to go from Boston to some station where he is not known, and take the Washington train at that point.

2) [dated Nov.19, '06 and signed "Sincerely, Lewis C. Strang"]: Dear Brother Johnson: Have Lyman meet the Washington train at New London, Conn. To do this he may have to leave Boston tonight and spent the night in New London. Have him travel under the name J. Lyman. Mrs. Eddy's orders.

3) [dated Nov.19, '06 and signed "With love, M.B. Eddy"]: My beloved Student: I want you to send your son Lyman with this priceless, precious charge, in the sacred secrecy needed to save the lives of those who bring to me either the proofs of S. & H. or the electroplates--when finished.

~ ~ ~ ~ ~ ~

In 1908 Mrs. Eddy felt that certain groupings of her works were of sufficient importance to have them in single volumes--with special additional copyrights (to last through 1964 if properly renewed). These were:

Messages to The Mother Church (Pan,'00,'01,'02)
Christian Healing and Other Writings (Hea, Peo, Pul, Pan, '00, '01, '02)
Unity of Good and Other Writings (Un, Ret, Rud, No)

THE MONITOR CLIMAX

Before the close of the Seventh Day (also in 1908) there had to be the final great event of Mrs. Eddy's Founding. Just as in the climax of the Sixth Day she had provided in Boston an example that would "reflect in some degree" *the Church* Universal and Triumphant, so she was now providing in Boston an example of *Communication* Universal and Triumphant. *The Christian Science Monitor* would reflect in some degree the angel message, or evangelic news, from God to man.

The rising journey into the one and only Church had been met with the limited belief that there remain infidels, heretics, sinners outside that church who must be either annihilated or brought into its purifying atmosphere by specified ritualistic examination and observances. Hence the greatest threat that would hinder the downward outreach which discovers no place where His light is not seen is this ecclesiasticism, this holier-than-thou trap which has to face Jesus' dicta: "Judge not that ye be not judged" and "Who made me a judge or *divider* over you?" seeing that those thoughts which start with God must say: "In righteousness *He* doth judge."

To illustrate that a convert cannot sit in isolated redemption in his sense of church or world or universe, God provided the Monitor as another call to go "into all the world" to find Him there. Once again this did not mean that the reader could take refuge from a belief in evil reporting, by hiding exclusively in the columns of the Monitor. While the tangible Monitor would reflect in some degree the News

Universal and Triumphant, the real Monitor as the Advisor, which its name means, will "*spread undivided* the Science that operates *unspent*."

Undivided--it does not judge or divide the world into the holy and unholy, into good guys and baddies, into capitalist exploiters and enslaving commies, but it sends its reporters into every place where dispute is reported to be, only to find that in Science, as opposed to discarded belief, dispute "was never there." This is the glory of the descent of the Holy Ghost after the upward course has divided the light from the darkness (differentiated between the widely varied uses and goals of the Christ message) and is ready to admit that "no night is there."

Unspent--it does not use up part of its energy in battling *midnight* and tempest, for it "sees the face of God in the cloud" and preserves the whole of its goodness while translating the appearance into its original divine language.

THE LINE OF LIGHT

Just as church attendance does not spare the worshiper one single individual experience, so reading the Monitor does not alone turn daily events into pleasant material escapades. But just as C.S. translates Sunday "divine service" into daily deeds, so it expands occasional metaphysical language into minute-by-minute assessment of God's guidance, governance, and activity.

The line of light which moved westward and upward in a materially geographical sense to be found in the "translucent atmosphere" of the far Western students in America (My.197:13-9), fulfills its duty when it "descends" into the uttermost parts of the earth to behold God's light still and always there. A contrary judgment or division is the offspring of a self-righteous ecclesiasticism which the Advisor with its worldwide and universal design naturally removes. It is noteworthy that Mrs. Eddy's warning (My.197:18) that Christian Science could "disappear from among mortals" was not addressed to "students whose words are but the substitutes for works", but to "*the* Christian Scientists" whose duty it is to go into all the world to "illumine the *midnight*" of the supposedly weaker brethren. In this way the "far Western students" could reflect in some degree the *Nation* or *America* Universal and Triumphant.

~ ~ ~ ~ ~ ~ ~

Mrs. Eddy made it clear in several ways that Christian Science, if supposed to be coming into being for the first time, could not really be confined to an historical event in the nineteenth century and one earthly precinct. Otherwise she would not have revealed that "Jesus preached and practised" it in Galilee (S&H 344:23), or that the prophets and apostles "uttered and illustrated it" two thousand years and more ago (S&H 358:16); or that Christian Science existed before 1701 A.D. ('01 24:17).

The "discovery" of C.S. was not a new invention, but it was a second coming, no longer localized, a further revelation that C.S. is ever at hand, an everpresent fact that makes possible such wonderful events in "history" as the Constitution of the U.S. to "reflect in some degree" the Constitution Universal and Triumphant. If, however, a physical amendable document were necessary for C.S. to be, it would be greater than C.S., for "the higher always protects the lower" (S&H 518:14). When Mrs. Eddy asserted that she believed in "our Constitution" (My.282:3) she was careful to add "*and* in the laws of God", allowing the reader to make a differentiation between a material document and the divine, universal, scientific and immutable actuality or <u>Christian Science</u> which <u>is</u> Constitution or Law of God.

Just as a physical expression of church can reflect to some extent the structure of Truth and Love, so a physical document can represent in some degree the government of all the *earth* (in its widest Glossary sense). The realization that the *America* Univeral and Triumphant is not a geographical division of *earth* (in the material Glossary sense) but a divine concept, enabled Mrs. Eddy to see "no place" where it is not.

As early as 1868 she was able to tell a student: "I can introduce Christian Science in England more readily than I can in America" (Aug.CSJ '08 or CSS Vol.X, No.40). Why? Because it may well be easier to illustrate a principle through a special example than to outline the complete principle at one go. The real America is Nation, not a nation in a mortal, territorial sense, "sometimes beautiful, always erroneous". Then its reflection will be found by the metaphysician in "the uttermost parts of the earth" (Ps.ii:8).

If the line of light rose westward to the Golden Shore of Love it did not leave darkness where its light was and originated. Those who understand the significance of Church, Communication, Nation, Universe will spread their understanding north, east and south and find Love already and still there.

Mrs. Eddy recognized that her students were not necessarily ready at the end of the nineteenth century to do this work, but she told them what the work was and that she was doing it (My. 147:26-30). She wrote: "From the interior of Africa to the utmost parts of the earth, the sick and the heavenly homesick or hungry hearts are calling on me for help, and I am helping them" (that is, I AM is helping and healing them).

The periodicals indicate the wide extent of Mrs. Eddy's helping thought, including her interest in the peace movement, as is shown by the many extracts committed to *Miscellany*. In one striking case she made clear to her students the difference between the imposing of peace (such as might accompany the ascending ecclesiastical thought that is still based on division) and the finding of peace by the conviction that God is already there. As elaborated in Chap.IV (beginning p.331), she called for a cessation of the "prayer" which outlines its own comfortable human solution; and demanded the faithful realization that God "will bless all the inhabitants of the earth, and none can stay His hand" for "out of His allness He must bless all with His own truth and love." (See her "Explanation" as found in My.280:28 - 281:14.)

CORRESPONDENCE ESTABLISHING THE MONITOR

1) Typewritten <u>letter</u> to Board of Trustees [dated Aug.8, '08 and signed "Lovingly yours, Mary B.G. Eddy"]: Beloved Students: It is my request that you start a daily newspaper at

once, and call it the Christian Science Monitor. Let there be no delay. The Cause demands that it be issued now.

You may consult with the Board of Directors. I have notified them of my intention.

2) Letter to Mrs. Eddy from Trustees [dated Aug.13, '08]: Beloved Leader and Teacher: ...since receiving your message on Monday [Aug.10] we have been continually at work finding out what must be arranged....

As it is a very large enterprise, careful consideration has been necessary, and we have had to gain advice from men in that work.

To begin with...two presses will be required to print a daily eight-page paper. For the Boston Herald six are used. ...Mr. John J. Flynn tells us that the Chicago Inter-Ocean has over 300 persons employed. We have gone over item by item our smaller needs with Mr. Alexander Dodds of the Pittsburgh Post and Sun... and it seems as if at the beginning our paper could be handled by 90 to 100 employees....

We are agreed to recommend an afternoon paper. The price per year is proposed at $3.50....

New quarters will be required for the daily paper, since practically the whole of the new building is required for our present work. The Directors have consulted the architect and expect that a suitable building could be ready, with night and day work on the contract, in 90 days....

Mr. Dodds...has said that builders of printing presses will expect at least 90 days to fill orders....

Summing up the expenses, apart from the building, we find that for the printing plant an investment of over $125,000 will be necessary, and for the pay-roll, for one year, $125,000. The expense for paper for the editions as printed is usually paid by the money received for subscriptions. The revenue of a paper is from its advertising....

The revenue from the Publishing Society paid to the Church has been about $90,000 a year. If we were to expend as much as that in one year on this enterprise we would have nothing for the Mother Church which now depends somewhat upon this revenue.

...Nevertheless we know the newspaper can be financed, since you see it to be the right time for the enterprise.

3) Letter to C.S.P.S. [dated Aug.14, '08 and signed "Sincerely yours, Adam H. Dickey, Secretary]:

Dear Brethren: Your letter of the 13th instant addressed to Mrs. Eddy comprising the report of your plans for starting a Christian Science daily paper is at hand.

After reading this report our Leader expressed surprise at the amount of capital that would be required. Her original thought on the subject was, that you should proceed to get out a small paper of about eight pages and with a circulation of about fifty or sixty thousand copies, at a much less outlay than the amount stated in your letter. Her intention was not to branch out at once into metropolitan greatness, but rather to begin in a comparatively small way and grow into bigger things with the progress of time.

However she does not wish to hamper your movements by placing restrictions on the amount you shall spend, but wishes you to go ahead with wisdom and economy as your guide.

Our Leader hopes you will not find it necessary to consult with her with regard to details, but proceed with the work in your own way doing the best you can.

4) Letter from C.S.P.S. to Rev. Mary Baker G. Eddy [dated Aug.14, '08]: Beloved Leader: [This letter revised the estimates to $100,000 for the mechanical equipment and to between $120,000 and $130,000 for "salaries, wages, power, and news service".]

5) Reply to editor in chief's request for approval of a managing editor [dated Sept.3, '08 and signed "Sincerely yours, Adam H. Dickey"]: Dear Mr. McLellan: Your letter of the 2nd instant addressed to our Leader recommending Mr. Alexander Dodds for the position of Managing Editor of The Christian Science Monitor, was today handed to me by Mrs. Eddy. After reading the same she requested me to say that she wished you would make this appointment on your own judgment.

6) Letter to Mrs. Eddy [dated Oct.16, '08 and signed "Faithfully yours, The Trustees of The C.S.P.S., by Secretary {Clifford P. Smith}"]: Beloved Leader: We have just engaged Thomas C. Winans of Pittsburgh as Advertising and Circulation Manager for The Monitor.

...We...are about to contract for the Publishers' news service. It will come to us by...leased telephone wire. As this news service will apprise us of hostile news items before publication, it will greatly facilitate the work of our Committees on Publication....

The two printing presses and the eight linotypes for The Monitor are completed and are at their factories ready for shipment. The extension of the Publishing House will be ready to receive the presses on, or before, October twenty-sixth, and to receive the linotypes on or before November ninth....

Assuming that the duties of Mr. McLellan, as Editor of all our publications, and the duties of Mr. Ogden, as Manager of the Publishing Society, will extend to The Monitor, the organization of The Monitor will be as follows:

Managing Editor: Alexander Dodds (Pittsburgh Post and Sun)
Editorial Writer: John J. Flynn (Chicago Inter-Ocean)
City Editor: John L. Wright (Boston Globe)
News Editor: Oscar Stevens (Boston Transcript)
Financial Editor and political writer: Forest Price (Pittsburgh Chronicle-Telegraph)
Foreman of Composing Room: Ames Weston (Boston Herald)

Arrangements are being made with Mr. Frederick Dixon of London; William D. McCrackan (who is now in Switzerland); Edward C. Butler of the City of Mexico; Charles H. Gibbs of Sydney, Australia; and Albert Cope Stone of Melbourne, Australia, to contribute weekly letters to the Monitor. Regular or occasional letters will be engaged from Christian Scientists residing in Australia, Phillipine Islands, Panama, Mexico, Alaska, England, Germany, France and South Africa....

Lewis C. Strang may contribute a daily editorial, and regular contributions may be engaged from ten or twelve well-known Christian Scientists. Sibyl Wilbur will probably be engaged as a special writer to do interviewing and other special work.

All of the persons mentioned in this letter are Christian Scientists, and with one exception, the wife of each of the men is a Christian Scientist.

Monitor Not Copyrighted

As shown by their Deed of Trust, the Trustees are required to manage all the Publishing Society's business "upon their own responsibility" subject only to Mrs. Eddy's "supervision" should she "elect...to advise or direct." Two cases of supervision, one about copyrights, the other about an appointment, are shown below:

-- Letter to Archibald McLellan, Editor-in-Chief, The C.S.P.S. [dated Jan.23, '09 and signed "Sincerely yours, Trustees of C.S.P.S. by Clifford P. Smith, Secretary"]:

Dear Friend: In response to an inquiry as to copyrighting The Christian Science Monitor, or copyrighting articles which our Leader may contribute to the Monitor, her Secretary writes us that she directs him to say that the Monitor need not be copyrighted but that "any articles of hers of great importance" that may be published in the Monitor are to be copyrighted separately in her name. Whenever our Leader contributes an article to the Monitor which should be copyrighted according to this direction, the Managing Editor will inform the Manager, who will attend to obtaining the copyright.

-- Pencilled reply to letter of April 3, '09, from Trustees recommending the division of Mr. Winans' job and the appointment of Albert E. Miller, C.S.B., as Circulation Manager [signed "Mary Baker Eddy"]:

I approve.

~ ~ ~ ~ ~ ~ ~

"The time cometh when ye shall neither in this mountain, nor yet" in Boston worship the Father, for ye shall "worship the Father in spirit and in truth." Just as Church is not a building, but is all that "rests upon and proceeds from divine Principle" (none left out), so "our nation" is the whole World, and "our daily newspaper" everything that comes as consciousness. The examples of the Monitor, The Mother Church, the Constitution, the Leader, are found, and find all, in Spirit and Truth.

II - TEACHING

~ ~

If the Bible and my work Science and Health had their rightful place in schools of learning, they would revolutionize the world by advancing the kingdom of Christ. *No 33:5-7.*

You can well afford to give me up, since you have in my last revised edition of Science and Health your teacher and guide. *Mis.136:18*.

And all my children shall be taught of the Lord. *Isa.liv:13*.

"If Jesus had not taken a student, he would not have been crucified."

"Oh, if only I had not a single student!"

"All the trouble I have is from my students."

"You must teach the Truth so long as error is taught and called Christian Science."

Sayings attributed to Mary Baker Eddy.

Mrs. Eddy writes in Science and Health in her chapter "Teaching Christian Science" (444:31): "The teacher must make clear to students the Science of healing..." and he "must thoroughly fit his students to...guard against the attacks of the would-be *mental assassin*, who attempts to kill morally and physically."

However, she makes it clear that the mission of Christian Science is not primarily one of the "metaphysical healing of physical disease" (150:10), and to the Board of Education class which was destined to approve official teachers of Christian Science, she sent this message in 1902:

> "The only excuse for teaching is in order to teach quietly how error is to be destroyed--and not publish it abroad."

This was consistent with her own instruction to the class of '98 (her "last class") in which one of the members (Rose Kent) records her as saying:

> "The only excuse or justification of teaching is to privately inform the student how to overcome error."

In other words she maintained her advice that until the illusion of the mental assassin is scientifically translated, students must cope quietly with the belief in its power--without broadcasting to it what the elimination tactics are to be.

Six Days (p.366) records a strong hint about the final direction of teaching when it quotes the Norcross article on the Fiftieth Edition of Science and Health (March CSJ, and repeated in April CSJ, 1891). Here it was prophesied that Science and Health "is...intended to be the teacher of the future" and that it would "supersede all teaching, in the technical sense of the word." This would imply that "students" could and would come together to uncover what God's word in the Bible and Science and Health has to say about any and every condition, but personal interpretation or indoctrination would cease.

Until the demand for ecclesiastical interpretation and supervision ceases, it is proper to ask what can and will be done about what will prove to be a fundamentally untenable situation!

-- <u>Account</u> by Clara Shannon of discussions in Mrs. Eddy's home on these points:

> One morning there was some talk about how Christian Science was being taught. There was a teacher who was teaching things that were not in accordance with Christian Science. So Mrs. Eddy said, "How shall I make the teaching uniform and be quite sure that only Christian Science is taught?" She said, "I never thought they would need a Church Manual for the Mother Church until these points came up in teaching"; [so God led her] to make a by-law to prevent the Scientists ruining our Cause.
>
> She told me to write to two of her students [Mary Adams and Elizabeth Webster] who had studied with her from the beginning. They were grand Christian Scientists and such fine teachers. She asked them to come to her and they came. She told them she wanted a Church Manual to govern teaching, and according to their experiences they were to make by-laws which would compel teachers to teach Christian Science as it is in the textbook. As she went on she said, "But we

have other members and this manual must be enlarged so that it will affect everybody."

THE MANUAL SOLUTION

The Manual blueprint for obliterating the sad effects of inferior teaching is well-known, but its progress is worthy of outline here:

First of all, two years after the Manual came into existence, Mrs. Eddy outlawed all official teaching. As noted in Chap.I, this lasted for one year only, but the ban did call into question the assumption that a few designated persons have access to Truth--with a direct line denied to all others except through one of these persons.

For one full year students (in the freer sense of the word) were expected to be taught of the Lord using S&H and their own researching of the newly-published book called Miscellaneous Writings. This step did not prevent "two or three" communing together with Mind (coming together "in Thy name") and enjoying all that was individually meaningful. Yet it did give added incentive and correctives even to those teachers who had faithfully been giving classes with S&H as the textbook, and to those who had looked to such teachers.

In April 1898, shortly after teaching in the earlier sense was resumed, Mrs. Eddy heard one of the faithful teachers (Edward A. Kimball) voice a truth which she had not as yet emphasized in any classes that she had taught. She spun around on him and demanded, "Where did you get that?" According to the reports, he answered, "Why, Mother, it's in Science and Health." She then gave thanks to God, for here at last was proof that the word of God in S&H was sufficient authority and source for the earnest student of the textbook; and now a Board of Education could be set up under the Manual to examine teacher applicants on their awareness of this very point. Mr. Kimball was appointed as the examiner.

Since the charter for the Massachusetts Metaphysical College had never been surrendered or withdrawn (although the college had closed its doors in 1889), the new Board could operate and issue degrees as an adjunct to the old college, and by the end of 1898 the first "examinations" were arranged.

Under the early Manuals loyal students who "have become thus by studying my works or by class instruction" could apply for these examinations. Twenty-one of the applicants (based on geographical considerations rather than on other qualifications) could be certified as ready "for the high responsibilities of teaching Christian Science." [Students who had already been certified by Mrs. Eddy under the original M.M.C. regulations did not have to reapply.]

The method of examination was to hold a series of discussions on Recapitulation and the Platform in S&H. But with 167 applicants in the classroom there was little opportunity for individual examination, or in effect for more than instruction from the teacher's platform.

The results conflicted with the by-law which emphasized that "students of the books of Mary Baker Eddy shall not take lessons from another student" (and this "another student" presumably included the one who was the examiner). Although attempts were made to restrict the tendency to *instruct* as, for example, when the course in Obstetrics was added, and a member of the class was required to prepare a paper for discussion by the rest, the Normal Class did become a course in which instruction quite overtook "examination." After 1902 it was put on hold for five years. The classes which Edward Kimball held in 1903 and Eugene Greene in 1904 under the College auspices, were purely "Primary." They were not called or intended to be "Normal" classes, and no teachers' certificates were granted.

When arrangements were announced in 1904 for teacher training to be reintroduced, Mrs. Eddy decreed that Normal classes be held but once in three years, beginning in three years (i.e. in 1907). Edward Kimball resigned and she was content to wait till 1907 to see if the examination-class method of certifying teachers could be carried on by the vice-president of the Board, namely Judge Septimus Hanna. She herself remained president.

The changeover led to the well-known and detailed letter from Mr. Kimball to Judge Hanna emphasizing the need for uniformity in the Board's classes. The main points in the text will be covered later, but for the moment it is enough to mention the chief rumor about the Kimball teaching. Variants of the letter of this teaching (the letter which "killeth") had gone forth without the spirit (which "quickeneth") and some of the established teachers were decrying the various bits of hearsay. Consequently in outlining the thrust of his statements in class (as a guide for the Judge), Mr. Kimball had to maintain stoutly that he had taught no such nonsense as the "spiritualization of matter."

History does not record the particular passage from Science and Health which Mr. Kimball used to back up his statement to Mrs. Eddy that had so delighted her, but it probably involved either the oneness of good and (nullified) evil (see Un.21:7), or the wholly mental nature of what is called matter or flesh (see Mrs. Eddy's comments on Hon. Clarence Buskirk's lecture in Nov.'07 CSJ, Un.55:17-22 particularly in editions prior to April 1909, Science of Man {EOF 179:24-27}, Mis.154:19-22, etc.).

Mrs. Eddy soon learned that her original classification of matter as a mental expression or "idea of God", possessing no life, substance, or intelligence of its own, did not eliminate the mortal conviction that matter starts out as an evil reality, with simply a hope that it can be *made* unreal. With this false view of matter to face, she had to emphasize (as in the First Edition of Science and Health) that "We are Spirit, Soul, and not body", that "I am...Spirit and not matter" (pp.14,149, etc.). This denial of what was assumed to have independent life as real matter was just as puzzling to the material mind as the explanation of matter as purely an inert *mental* phenomenon--without substance and depending entirely on Mind for life or existence.

Probably Mrs. Eddy realized that the more measured language of later editions, carefully adapting the truths of the "Precious Volume" (the First Edition) to meet current thought, did not obscure the deeper meaning to a reader of Edward Kimball's caliber. But it did not save him from charges of "spiritualizing matter" by the substance-matter enthusiasts who had been unable to accept Mrs. Eddy's original revelation of "matter as shadow."

One of the teachers "authorized" by the Hanna class in 1907 told the compiler of this volume that she thought that one or two of the thirty teacher applicants (the maximum number permitted under the later Manuals) did not get certificates; but even assuming that all thirty did, it remains true that during the eight explosive years of Christian Science growth (1903-10) there was an average of fewer than four new teachers per annum--and this did not allow even for the usual attrition.

Thus if all the new and existing teachers lived to fill their classes each year, the maximum increase in class-taught students from 1903 through 1910 could be little more than 100 a year! This would not nearly keep up with the annual increase in the number of Christian Scientists and C.S. practitioners (some of whose cards appeared in the CSJ without the label "C.S."--and even for a few years after Mrs. Eddy's departure in person).

But instead of being fazed out as the Manual provided, class teaching assumed an aura of exclusivity which was never intended.

The Board of Education had quickly slipped from being an examining body into being little more than a distinguished course for those who had already taken the primary course elsewhere. In 1909 Mrs. Eddy sent two members of the C.S. Board of Directors to New York to meet Mr. Kimball and request him to return to the Board of Education as the "teacher" of the Normal Class (see Edward A. Kimball, published by Horatio H. Wait). He accepted but passed on abruptly as he was returning to his home in Chicago.

Although Mrs Eddy thereupon approved Bicknell Young as the teacher-to-be, the Manual was already in position to bring further official teaching to an end for those with eyes to see. Mrs. Eddy left the scene in person before the 1910 class was held and consequently her signature did not appear on the teachers' certificates as required by the Manual for their validity. She never "resigned over her own signature as President of the Massachusetts Metaphysical College" and if it be thought that the Manual allowed the vice-president of the Board to take her place automatically, it will be seen that Art.XXVIII, Sect.4 still requires her *specific* approval for this transfer of title.

In other words, the Norcross prophecy in his article on the Fiftieth Edition of S&H became valid in 1910, although it was left to existing teachers to continue officially-recognized teaching for as long as they saw fit. The stage had been set for the introduction into schools of learning, as foreseen in No 11:15 and 33:5, to come to pass.

The divine decree that Normal class instruction is not a requirement for the real "healer and teacher" had been given in *Retrospection and Introspection* in 1891, two years after the M.M.C. school had been discontinued. It remains in Mrs. Eddy's final edition (47:16) even though its impact was set aside while the Manual restraints operated. In fact on Aug.31, '01, in order to legalize the Manual's temporary precedence over what is acknowledged as the Revelator's final word, the Directors passed a private by-law, with Mrs. Eddy's full knowledge. This stated: "As in state law, one law supersedes another and virtually annuls it, so our present Church By-Laws have annulled that which was published on p.47 of Retrospection and Introspection on the subject of teaching."

When official teaching was terminated by the Manual itself in 1910, the eternal word in the God-authorized final writings had the effect of annulling in its turn that which was published on page 89 of the Manual (Art.XXIX, Sect.2).

SOME INSTRUCTIONAL GEMS, 1895-8

In the Seventh Day unfoldments leading to the establishment of the Board of Education and the Publishing Deed of Trust, students recorded many gems of elucidation which came to them through Mary Baker Eddy. These statements covered healing the sick as well as the handling of "malicious animal magnetism" (i.e. the "quiet" or "private" understanding of "how error is to be destroyed"). Some examples are given here:

> [From Lydia Hall]: The belief of cancer is induced by arsenical poison mentally introduced. The "enemy" believes he can mentally argue strychnine, mercury, morphine, liquor, ether and other poisons mentally, and that these will be injected into the thought of the patient, so that he will suffer the same effects as if the drugs were

injected physically. These arguments are all harmless because God is All. [See also p.154.]

[From Clara Shannon]: Mrs. Eddy took a medical book and read four pages of diseases etc. coming from arsenical poisoning: extreme thirst, depression, heaviness, etc.

[On another occasion she said]: "I beheld Satan as lightning fall from heaven" etc. means I beheld Satan to be electricity!

In the claim of supply, the so-called power of electricity repels the manifestation of the affluence of good, and this attracts fear of limitation and its seeming manifestation. Know "I cannot be negatively electrified." [For further text, see *Six Days* 302:10-23.]

[From Gilbert Carpenter Sr.]: She kept the whole household working mentally to neutralize the effect of malpractice brought to the home by the students' visits to Pleasant View at the time of the annual meetings in Boston. [And at various times she said]:

When you and all have borne the cross of the Discoverer and Founder of Christian Science, you will be able to tell Mother something she does not know already.

When you enter the presence of any thought to benefit it, find what is already good and abide there until you have lifted them higher. Unfold from that point.

[Quoting James M. Whitton]: "The truly human Jesus has been recovered. The divine Christ from being merely a makeweight in a scheme of divine government fancied to be like that of earthly rulers, has been rediscovered as permanently indwelling in the life of *both God* and *man*." This is a description only of my meaning in the term that I use for the Christ--namely, the *spiritual idea*.

[From Martha Wilcox]: There is no law that can work against me. The only Law does everything for me. The perfection of the divine Mind must be externalized here and now.

[To the Directors, after the death of Flavia Knapp in May 1898]: Oh! what a shock was my information relative to my beloved student, Mrs. Knapp! When others could not help her, why did you not try Mr. Neal and Mrs. Laura E. Sargent? I ought not to murmur and especially to the one most bereaved [Ira Knapp, a director].

[To others]: Mrs. Knapp and her practitioner were treating the case as pneumonia, which was only the decoy; but had they handled mental assassination, they would have healed the case.

[Mrs. Knapp passed on two weeks after testifying in The Mother Church to several wonderful healings she had sustained, and complaining of the persecution she was being submitted to. No doubt she and her practitioner considered pneumonia to be the result of the envy and malice directed against a righteous target, whereas Mrs. Eddy had taught Mr. Neal and Mrs. Sargent to handle animal magnetism as a *lie* or non-existent falsity about the everlasting oneness of divine Mind. It was not a somethingness for the righteous to escape from.]

SOME GEMS FROM LETTERS

In the following letters taken from this period the first eight were written by Mrs. Eddy to Julia Field-King, who had undertaken to trace Mrs. Eddy's genealogy and was thus running into a conflict within, i.e. a conflict between an understanding of divine origin and the untranslated sense of personal history. The letters are included in detail because of what Jesus and Christian Science tell of ancestry. If but "one is your Father which is in heaven", your ancestry is glorious; and since "the perfection of the divine Mind must be externalized" (as Mrs. Wilcox recorded in the truth stated above) the so-called human mind can be conscious of its own acceptance of that statement by Jesus. It could thus say with truth: Your relationship to God means you are related to everything that reflects Truth and Love, and there is no reason why this should not be manifest in a manner that the human mind does recognize.

Mrs. Eddy's perception of the slow weaning of Dr. Field-King from a dependence on the material sense of ancestry is shown in the following series--all written in the year 1895:

1) [March 1] How Mother loves you as she...perceives the experienced woman and the babe in Christ combining. How natural that the babe should be fretted with the friction of material history and the error it includes, and must go to Mother for the milk of the Word and rest on the bosom of God.... Giving milk to babes and meat to men, requires great wisdom, great growth, great love. To lead the world wisely means much; hence Jesus' words: "Be ye therefore wise as serpents."... Search up the history you are upon the verge of discovering fairly and clearly--and write it *wisely*; then send it for publication in the Christian Science Journal and (if it is received favorably there) publish it in pamphlet form.

2) [March 13] I think it not wise to pursue further your chronological research. It is not really in the line of Truth that the thought is forming itself in this investigation, but in the line of material origin and this has an end. Now I would turn away from the subject. My reason for asking you to undertake this historical proof was that the people would sooner be convinced perhaps by it of my legitimate mission; but I fear it costs you too much to direct your thought so materially and the end will not justify the means.

3) [March 19] A feeling of sweet submission has come over me, a sense of "Thy will be done", and I have conquered the reluctance I felt to have what I *knew* was *true proven*--lest it should cherish a sentiment or rather a belief, I so deprecate, namely, a canonization of which I feel so unworthy, and do *dislike*. But, dear one, you deserve the place you have earned, namely the historian of what will thrill the people.... Therefore you may go forward now if it costs you no spiritual loss, as you *assure* me. ...But darling, I charge you *tell no man* till this be accomplished.

4) [April 26] After I told Dr. Foster [Mrs. Eddy's adopted son] what you were doing for our cause, you wrote

me how difficult it was for you to go on. Now handle this question accordingly. "Oh, Absalom" was David's moan [for his unfaithful son].

5) [May 6] I now see clearer than ever the Absalom.... Defend yourself from any Absalom by knowing that evil has no power, and hate and envy cannot rule this event, which love and good will toward men does.

6) [July 17] I forgot to say--The Heraldry and Christian Science will not go together; when the mind is prepared to receive the latter in your beautiful illustrations, it is immediately diverted from receiving your spiritual import by the former. Your present arrangement must be changed before it will do to publish it. As it is, it would do more harm than good to our Cause....

7) [July 23] Now *do not* make a single more research into <u>my genealogy</u>. You have all I want; just type the whole as you named and that is all I shall allow to be historic. I do see it is <u>wrong</u> to pursue the material thought of the dead as having life or of matter kinship, for there is none. Only think of the descent as that of a name. No inherent qualities of race exist. Banish this lie from your mind or it will harm you.... You need Truth; the lie seems more real to you than to me, hence the result above named.

8) [July 24] Send manuscript just as it is to me at once; it will not be published.

<u>Other Subject-Matter</u>

[Jan.2, '95 to Mary Philbrick]: [A rebuke] is not scolding; it is only showing you your duty, and claiming for *once* my own individual rights, even as I would do by others whom I ask not to do my work for me.

[Caroline Foss records that inspite of her attempts to use care and diligence in the way she made Mrs. Eddy's bed, she met with rebukes. So after a while she said to herself: "This bed belongs to God. I am making it up for Him, not for any personality. He sent me here to do it; so I can do it right." She then set about making the bed as before, and found that the rebukes ceased!]

[April 20, '97, to Thomas Hatten]: My precious child: Do not be troubled like Martha of old over anything, do not be disheartened over failure, when at heart you are as faithful as Abraham. We are all to be tried and proved, as by fire.

Now, darling, there is but one Mind. No other mind exists and therefore an evil so-called mind cannot, *does not* affect you or your business.

Keep the first commandment sacredly and know there is but one Mind. Keep the ten commandments, do not let your affections rest for a moment in forbidden directions, but, dear one, have but one God, one affection, one peace.

The senses that lie are nonsense. There is no sensation in wrong directions.

[March 28, '97, to William P. McKenzie]: I have no time of my own, but like the weathervane, change with the elements as perforce of the hand that invisibly is stretched out to point the way with a finger of light.

[July 31, '97] Do not sorrow over your tasks; all things work together for good to them that love God, good. You are now learning how to meet mortal mind in all its false claims; and its evil is less dangerous than its seeming good. You have not nearly as much to meet now as when you cherished (as we all have done) its seeming good that was its greatest evil. [See DCC p.135, line 35, for further text.]

[Aug.9, '98, to Irving C. Tomlinson]: Many times I project and God changes *my* plan and executes His through me which is so much better.

[Oct.28, '98] My moves are not mine but His that moveth me. I waited to have the Bible take precedence of your textbook till the public thought was more enlightened to it....

I have seen that the students of my books when healed by them, if taught by other students, *relapse* and if not invalids relapse morally as all do in said cases. God help you to open the dull eyes and ears to these things and yet to be most wise and gentle in probing these wounds of the people of God.

[Sept.24, '98, to Judge Clarkson]: My dear Friend in Truth: Your letter is opportune. By the way, Church Rules are being made regulating the action of the Board of Education. I have drawn up the Rules. One of these entitles a student of my books to present himself to the Board for examination and if he passes it favorably he is graduated under the auspices of the Mass. Metaphysical *College*. But this student is not a student of a student. He is a student of C.S. as contained in my works. His certificate contains my signature. I have found this order requisite, imperative, owing to certain abuses in teaching C.S. You can excuse yourself [for not entering the class of] dear Mrs. Ewing on the ground aforenamed. I prefer under the circumstances that a student of my works should graduate thus if I have not taught him in a class. Mrs. Ewing is one of my best teachers and she will see the need of the provision for the action of the Board.

[Dec.24, '98, to Edward Everett Norwood and signed "Yours tenderly, truly, M.B. Eddy"]: My beloved Student: Why do you anticipate being removed from your field and the Readership in church?

Do you desire to change your location? I know of no reason why you should change your place. When any strong impression comes to you in such lines "try the spirits" before you submit. Mentally treat yourself that nothing can govern your actions or come to your thought that is not from the divine Mind. Be strong there.

So many sinister suggestions come to mind, watch! And each day commit yourself to the care of our one Parent, trust Him, turn to Him in all your ways for light to direct your footsteps and wisdom to judge well between the human or the evil "suggestion" and the good or divine impulse.

[The follow-up, dated Aug.1, '02)]: I have written to Miss Swazey, of Washington, D.C. to know if her church changes its Readers, and if so I have recommended you for its Reader. I am willing [that] you leave the South if you so desire. You will please remember me kindly to Mrs. Norwood, and accept my warm wish for your prosperity wherever you locate.

THE CLASS OF '98

Two years after Mrs. Eddy had expressed her wish and hope never to teach another class, she invited seventy carefully selected students to meet with her for a special course which was spread over two days and lasted six hours altogether. Sixty-seven of those called were duly in attendance at Christian Science Hall in Concord Nov.20-21, '98. As a preliminary Edward A. Kimball read to them the statement by Mrs. Eddy which appears in My.243:20 - 244:27.

It was already known that she was about to reactivate her college. If under her new Board of Education someone other than herself was going to be directing to Science and Health a batch of new official teachers, she could well take time to assess some students she had taught and some she had not taught and some even who knew little of Christian Science. Moreover the forthcoming Board of Education experiment might not be allowed to sustain itself for very long.

From the many accounts that are extant it seems that Mrs. Eddy was looking beyond the mere "excuse for a class" into an excuse to examine the quality of thought fostered by individual daily study of the Bible and Science and Health. Her recorded remarks laid particular stress on that omnipresent Love which embraces all thought, including any thought wrongly supposed to be "out there" and independent. She stated that she did not intend to go back over the need and means to handle animal magnetism.

The various student recollections here recorded are prefaced by Mrs. Eddy's own statement as published in Septimus J. Hanna's <u>Christian Science History</u>:

> In my last class I did not refer to mental malpractice,--its members generally had taken the primary course, and this instruction properly comes before that class. Without a question the student of Christian Science is not qualified to teach, preach, or to practise divine Metaphysics who knows not thoroughly how wisely and successfully to handle this heinous sin--mental malpractice. Without this understanding he cannot separate the tares from the wheat and destroy the tares--he cannot divide between an impartation from the

immortal or divine Mind, and temptation, or the evil suggestion of human thought and argument, but this must be done in order to obey the former and to resist and destroy the latter, and not till it is done will he be protected and imbued with wisdom and power to rise superior to evil suggestions. This attainment is indispensable whereby to establish a student on the Scientific basis of Christian Science.

Most of the recollections available include some version of the following interchange during the class. The question was asked, How would you heal the sick instantaneously? The general answer was, Realize the presence of Love.

Mrs. Eddy's comment was along these lines:

> You have answered very well--very well indeed. But you don't get quite close enough. Now let me tell you how I'd heal instantaneously. It is not so much to realize the *presence* of Love--but LOVE! Just live love. *Be* it, and love, love, love. Do not know anything but love. Be all love. There is nothing else. That will do the work. It will heal anything. Love enough and you'll raise the dead! I've done it. There is nothing but Love: Love is the secret of all healing.
>
> [A further statement to the class]: The time will come, and I feel it will be soon, when Christian Scientists will not have to make conscious effort in giving treatment, but through the constant desire and endeavor for a Christian life their consciousness will have become so purified that healing will go from them as naturally as the perfume from the flowers to those who are ready for it.

The stated subject for the class in general was *Love*, and the stated purpose was to spiritualize the field, also to elucidate the Scriptures, especially the Decalogue and the Sermon on the Mount. The following prayer and instructions were sent in advance or given to all members of the class:

> 1) O divine Love, give me higher, holier, purer desires, more self-abnegation, more love and spiritual aspirations.

2) *The Trinity*:
FATHER is man's divine Principle, Love.
SON is God's man, His image or spiritual idea.
HOLY GHOST is divine Science, the Messiah, or Comforter.

3) Jesus in the flesh was the prophet, or way-shower to Life, Truth, Love, and out of the flesh Jesus was the Christ, the spiritual idea, or image and likeness of God.

Each member of the class was asked to stand up and identify himself or herself, some of those present being unknown to Mrs. Eddy personally. Each was asked, What is God to you? And most of the answers named one or more of the synonyms* for God as given in Science and Health.

According to one report, Mrs. Eddy then advised them:

> We must be careful that synonyms don't tend to subdivide God when they should always bring out unity, the unity of God, the oneness of Mind, our Mind. If you tell a man that God is the one infinite Mind, he believes that he has a mind of his own and that God gave it to him. How would you go to work to convince him there is but one Mind? Show him that his mind is what he is conscious of, what he knows, and that what he knows, everybody else knows. He can send his children to school and improve their minds, which means, to learn what everybody else knows already.
>
> We need better conditions everywhere, better earth, better bodies, better children. This does not mean that Scientists should go to work and make those children, but they can help others have them. The child is evolved in mesmerism.

~ ~ ~ ~ ~ ~ ~

*Carol Norton recorded the following summary of the synonyms, as given by Mrs. Eddy: Life: infinite, all action; Truth: infinite inclusion of all fact; Love: infinite, all giving; Principle: infinite, all law; Spirit: infinite, all presence; Soul: infinite, all consciousness; Mind: infinite, all intelligence.

STUDENTS' RECOLLECTIONS

At the end of the class the C.S.B.'s became C.S.D.'s, while the remainder were granted the C.S.B. degree. Since the Board of Education was not going to be designed to grant the degree of C.S.D. this title was from now on destined legally to die out.

Some special aspects of the class are given in the following instructional statements as grasped by individual recorders:

1) [From Rose Kent]: All animal magnetism is evil and we must cope with it, not through annihilation, but transformation, which is salvation. Is man male or female? Both, because he reflects Father, Mother, infinity. Man's dominion over the earth, over everything, is the knowing of it. By knowing it you reflect it, because it is simply idea. (Like dominion over 2 x 2 = 4.)

Mrs. Eddy says, There is too much tendency on the part of Scientists to sit still and let God do this or that. They must handle error specifically.... They must first recognize the error, and then it is wise to handle the worst form on the principle that the greater includes the lesser.

We should handle false theology and priestcraft every day.... We should not substitute Science and Health reading in place of our mental action. We need energetic mental activity.... God does not punish evil. Evil punishes itself. Jesus saw perfect God, and the seeing was perfect man....

Affirmation and denial really go together. The mental action must be twofold, because affirmation is denial of all unlike it.

Why did not Jesus heal Judas? Judas had trouble because his sin would not give up until destroyed. This was not Jesus' fault. We can get solace from this, as failure is not always the fault of the practitioner. A student who will not or cannot see evil as something to be corrected is unteachable.

Always treat for fear of death. It may show as a headache, or a sore finger.... Always handle moral questions. The cardinal errors to be handled are envy, jealousy, anger, fear, hatred, malice, revenge, sensuality. Let your treatment be broad enough to handle them all.... A practitioner does not have to translate his patient into a sinner. In other words, do not try to locate and specify sin in human concepts of your patient. Sin is a belief in a cause. Some students search with morbid craving for a cause.

> [Some other statements briefly recalled]: When I can destroy such mental traits as a belief of jealousy, condemnation, etc., when I can emerge from these, I can then afford to talk [about not drinking] coffee.
>
> Succeed by letting it be unknown what your moves are to be.
>
> It is a mistake to give your methods in a Wednesday evening meeting, saying, I realized this and that.
>
> Nothing but the wisdom of God can handle the wisdom of the serpent.

2) [As recorded by Frederica L. Miller]: We are now in Mind speaking the language of Spirit and must strive to express it as accurately and spiritually as possible. To think of God as Alpha and Omega is not the highest conception of God, Who has no beginning and no end. He is the infinite All of understanding that to the spiritual idea is expanding into completeness, self-existent good. Without beginning or end, without time, without place, All is infinite Mind. Christian Science changes the human thought from finity to the Infinite.

[The Sermon on the Mount] is true, absolutely true. It can and will be proved absolutely. It is demonstrable even now by Christian Scientists that no thought need be taken for life or body.

I faithfully followed theology for forty years, but that God is Life did not come to me until apparently on a death-bed. Creeds and doctrines could not teach it, the ordinary teachers of theology understood it no better than the man who advised a thirsty laborer to "hoe" because the Scriptures say, "Ho! everyone that thirsteth."

The philosopher is equally at fault: he theorizes, rises out of sight, returns and is able to impart nothing, no knowledge because he has never risen above the beliefs of matter into the realm of pure Mind where alone true knowledge is found. The healing of the Schools is at best but speculative inquiry--the struggle of the human mind to reach the divine. Mortal man himself is but a struggle for existence whilst Christian Science is a revelation disclosing the world of Spirit, of reality, and proving practically that the ideal is the real.

[Answer to question about need for personal rebukes* when *love* should heal without]: One of the hardest things I have had to do was to deal with this very question. I would rather at any time dwell on love alone and get away from error, but that would not do, it would allow error to increase. Jesus rebuked sharply; I must do so until I arrive at that place in Mind where I cannot see error, where God, Spirit, is All-in-all. The omnipresence of good involves the nothingness of evil, but the mental argument must be used until you can heal instantaneously without it.

[Comments on students' answers to question of what to do when called to help someone said to be passing on]: Is there nothing else you would do? There is one thing that is above all--the healer must have conscious love. Love heals. When called to a death-bed, it is not the time to realize, but to *know* the truth, to know the truth of the infinite Life and Love that heals instantaneously. Being is knowing. Knowing what? Infinity, Love.

---

*The belief in an intelligent, crafty human mind is totally inconsistent with the realization of one Mind, and that one divine; and thus it demands rebuke. Since a person always seems to be involved, the method used requires divine wisdom.

In addition to the examples already cited, the following note to one of Mrs. Eddy's closest workers clearly points to the anguish that might exist, as well as to the right solution. She wrote: "Mother's darling--How can she ever touch him with the rod? Oh, it is so hard to do it. But if I reflect the power that rebukes, then I must use the rod. With deep love."

In his *Precepts* Gilbert Carpenter Sr. refers to the Manual as Mrs. Eddy's God-directed method of exposing the way students did things, rather than criticizing what they did.

The healing love is not a love for a person or for anything--it is Love itself. If you can realize this Love for a moment you will in that moment heal or raise the dying or dead. I have done it three times. It consists in breaking our own dreams of sickness, sin or death.

You all heal, you all have demonstrations. Now with regard to the lingering ones, have patience, keep on and on living the truth and declaring it. Never give up. Be patient and patience will have its perfect work.

Healing is but the result of right thinking and right living. Love is the secret of it all--the love which forgets self and dwells in the secret place, in the true identity, the realm of the real. Sickness is only a dream. Awake yourself from that dream, and your patients will awake. But how do you awaken yourself? By understanding the allness of Spirit and the consequent nothingness of matter; by living, moving, and having your being in the reality, in Love; then, all being Mind, your clear perception of the reality, which is wholeness, harmony, health, will chase away the shadows of sickness from your patient. And how do you attain this understanding? By seeking first the kingdom.

This is the only way to get anything that is real, and nothing but what is real is worth having. The unreal is nothing; it never was and never will be. "Seek first"--that is the only means by which we can reflect God and have "all things." That is the way "all things" came to me, and having got them, I care nothing for them except as a proof of the truth of Jesus' words: "Seek ye first the kingdom."

The attainment of wealth and honor I count as nothing--nothing would I withhold. How gladly would I give up all if by so doing the healing would be accomplished for the cause, for the sake of the world, for those who must find the Christ through the signs following.

When teaching children I am always taught myself through their pure, fresh thought. Science is teaching the children their clear relationship to God, their only parent. The thought of how the belief in other gods came can be illustrated by the relationship of the mortal parent and child. The first few years of the child's existence it follows the father and mother and depends upon them for all; after that the child begins to have a mind of its own, and finally severs its connection with the parent mind. Is that the way the child of God does? No, he always reflects perfectly. Whatever the Father does he does--the communion is perfect. This is how Jesus raised Lazarus: "Father, I know that Thou hearest me always."

[After asking volunteers to read from the Bible while giving the spiritual meaning--not merely the written words]: You must remember it is the language of Spirit we are learning, and we must try to speak in the new tongue. You should translate every day, not only from the Bible but from everything around you. Keep looking towards the things of Spirit and translate every object of sense into an idea of Soul.

However, translating objects of sense does not mean a beginning with the material and dissecting the body to find out what quality of mind the various organs represent or misrepresent, for such analysis would be at least mechanical, savoring of the letter which if used alone killeth the thought that is beginning to be spiritualized.

In Science we can have only as much as we demonstrate. We must work from the inside and patiently go on proving the power of Truth over error. To know that "arm" means strength, and "foot" understanding, makes clear some obscure texts in the Bible but we must not force things [such as treating feet for understanding and gums for hard or soft thoughts]. Step by step from a spiritual standpoint, we will find the present help which will enable us to transform the entire mass of materiality.

Yet it may be necessary to find, or rather to recognize, the specific claim holding the patient in error, in order to touch it with the opposite truth. [By way of illustration Mrs Eddy referred to] a child who had not been instructed in Science. Yet this child's love for his mother did more for her than the efforts at demonstration of the Scientists around her. As she was passing away, he, seven years old, called out, "Mother, mother, you cannot die!" Immediately she revived, but looking around at the Scientists said, "I am surprised...." She was referring to their endeavors to keep her on this plane, when her *belief* was that she was rising to a higher plane through death!

Those Christian Scientists in attendance had not discerned the point of error, that is, the *belief* to handle. Had the child been instructed, he with his love would have broken his mother's dream that death was a friend, and so have saved her the nearly fatal experience.

I want to give you a word of warning: Do not think of me personally nor look to me personally for help. If you do, your thought will become darkened even as it will be if you turn away from me. Think of me only as part of the machine used to carry on the great work. We are all one in divine Principle, Love--one in demonstration. The light has come to me, but you must not look to me as the light. If you do, this will hinder your progress even as turning away from me will darken your thought.

3) [Additional statements recorded by others in the class]: In every case we undertake we must know there is no law which says we cannot heal. There is no wish, rule, or interference that can prevent the healing of the sick. Neither animal magnetism, nor mesmerism, nor the influence of the so-called human mind can prevent or interfere with Christian Science Mind-healing. Expect to heal.

There is no matter, material substance, body or presence that can resist Christian Science healing. There is no law of matter, anatomy, hygiene, materia medica, or anything that can prevent or interfere with instantaneous healing through Christian Science. There is no form of process, development, decay, decomposition or failure, that can obstruct Christian Science healing, or protract the case. There is no matter, nor disease; sickness is nothing but error. Christian Science *does heal* the sick.

There is never a failure. Man cannot be mesmerized or express in thought any doubt or question as to the power of Truth over error, or Christian Science over the belief of disease and sin.

Among other things in healing a case, always declare at the outset, "I can know everything about this case that I need to know, and know it at once; know it now." There are no slow demonstrations. Truth is not slow. Idea is spontaneous with Mind. In every case where the cause seems to be unknown, we must declare that there is no undeveloped, undiscovered, or unknown cause.

In every treatment close with this: This treatment cannot be reversed; its effect cannot be reversed; it cannot be made to produce a result contrary to that which is intended; it cannot be arrested, obstructed, reverted, or controverted; the false claim of malicious animal magnetism has no law of reversal, and cannot act through any belief of law; there is no such law.

When we can consciously [break <u>our own</u> dreams of sickness, sin and death] we will heal instantaneously.

[Answering a question on how to find the discriminant between good and evil]: Ah, now you have asked me what is to me the hardest thing in Christian Science. Yes, you must see and denounce evil. The Bible tells us that Jesus was chosen of God because he loved righteousness and *hated iniquity*. So often I have longed to see and know only love, only the good, but I have not dared. I must uncover and rebuke and *hate* iniquity. When one loves righteousness, one hates iniquity.

[After speaking of the absolute nothingness of error, Mrs. Eddy asked: "What <u>is</u> it?" and the following question-and-answer ensued:

[A {from a student}. False belief.

[Q. What is false belief?

[A {from another student}. Illusion.

[Q. What is illusion?

[A {from a third student}. Nothing.

[Q. What is nothing?

[A {from a fourth student, in a low voice}. Nothing.

[Q {in a still lower voice from Mrs. Eddy}. Nothing? Why so much ado about nothing?]

[Q. What would you do if you found out that someone was malpractising upon you with intent to kill?

[After listening to some elaborate explanations, Mrs. Eddy responded: As for me I would just drop it into the wastepaper basket. {She illustrated this by dropping a piece of paper from her desk.}]

[She also said]: When first establishing this Cause, I needed money, but I have now learned that God is with me, that He gives me everything, and I cannot lack. When you stand before a mirror and look at your reflection it is the same as the original. Now, we are God's reflection and if His hands are full, your hands are full--your hands are full if you image Him. You cannot know lack.

Supply is like a scale. On one side is infinite good--that is the side of Spirit. Everything we put in the scale of Spirit is in the scale of infinity, but materiality means limitation, and everything we put in the side of matter, we put in the scale of limitation. In the human, it is good for us to think of God as our Father and Mother, with us every moment, giving us everything good and beautiful, caring for our human bodies. But in metaphysics man reflects all that God is. God is the trinity, Life, Truth, and Love; man is the idea of Life, Truth, and Love. Man is just as old as God, and he reflects all that God is and all that God has. We must live in the thought of His everpresent infinite Life and Love.

[Giving her concept of "I" as reflection and raising herself in her chair as she did so]: *I* am right here. Where this seems to be, the real child of God is.

[Replying to a young man's response to the opening question of "What is God"]: Now, John, you have said that God is Life, Truth, Love, Spirit, All-in-all, and you have said that He is destruction. Will you tell me how God is destruction. What is there to destroy? [John's ready answer: "Nothing, Mother. God is All, and there is nothing else. He only destroys what seems to be unlike Himself."]

[Giving her concept of God, she said He is] like a father protecting and caring for his child; like a mother taking her little one in her arms and feeding it with the milk of the Word, like a shepherd going out after the lost lamb, calling, calling, listening, listening, parting the bushes, finding it, taking the little one in His arms--and doing this over and over and over again.

[Mrs. Eddy's own example of the spiritual updating of Scripture--using Isa.xl:31]: When we are working to overcome error, or are handling a case that does not seem to yield, we shall not be discouraged or wearied by the work nor can there be any reaction. We shall go on without suffering or being weary, even though the demonstration is slow. [Then]:

My dear ones, I would love it very much--I would feel it a great favor if you would translate for me into the new tongue some passages from the Bible.

I want you to speak distinctly. When you speak distinctly it shows your mental quality. Speak as if you had something that you wanted the world to hear. Speak loud and strong and distinctly.

[She opened to Luke xxiv:2, which Mrs. Sue H. Mims thereupon interpreted as: The stone was the concentrated human belief that life was limited, and they saw that Life had rolled it away and that man was immortal--that he was never both mortal and immortal and that he never dies. They saw what our beloved mother has through Science and Health enabled us to see. Through the book we have all that they saw and more, and we owe it all to her, to this beloved one who is God's messenger today.]

[Mrs. Eddy's comment]: You have given a very beautiful exegesis of the text, but I have one objection--I may say I have one fault to find--it was not necessary to mention me.

[Later, commenting on Judge Hanna's complementary declaration that, in times of darkness and difficulty, he could find a ray of light as soon as he saw Mrs. Eddy as the Revelator for this age]: My dear children, if you had not seen, I would have had to teach you this. I could not have avoided telling you that when my students become blinded to me as the one through whom Truth has come to this age, they go straight down. I would have had to tell you.

[These two comments bring a conclusion similar to the preliminary instruction given to the class about Jesus {p.109}. This instruction could then be paraphrased as: Mrs. Eddy in the flesh was the leader, the assistant towards Life, Truth, and Love, and out of the flesh Mrs. Eddy is the Revelator, the spiritual idea, or image and likeness of God.]

[Some of Mrs. Eddy's references to herself as she was herself being led, were as follows]: The first revelation that came to me was that I could not die. I saw Life, and that it was impossible for me to die.

[Recounting one of the three cases in which she had raised the dead, she was quoted as saying]: When I arrived, the mother of the [sick] child was crying, "Oh, she is dead, she is dead." I put the mother out of the room and went in and took the child in my arms. In an hour I called the mother, and the child was running across the floor to meet her.

[Another early recollection]: We are all learning together, and I must tell you of some of the funny things I used to do when I first saw that I had this wonderful power. My family and the friends around me saw what was done and knew that if they sent for me they would be well, but I could not make them acknowledge it. I could not make them admit what had done the healing work,

One day I said "Oh, I <u>must</u> make them acknowledge it; I must make them see that God does this." Sometimes as soon as they sent for me they would be healed, before I could get there, and then they would not <u>know</u> that it was God who had done it. So one day when I was called to see a child, I was so anxious to have the power of Truth acknowledged that I said to myself, "He <u>must</u> not get well until I get there." Of course that was not right, for I knew I must leave it all to God, but pride had come in and I had lost my humility, and the patient was not healed.

Then I saw my rebuke, and when I reached home I threw myself on the floor, put my head in my hands, and prayed that I might not be for one moment touched with the thought that I was anything or did anything; I realized that this was God's work and I reflected Him. Then the child was healed. [See <u>DCC</u> p.246.]

[Summarizing remarks]: You have told me wonderful things today. Now you must live up to them; you must prove them. That is what Christian Science is--it is practical. God is your Life, and there is no evil.

I cannot tell you the joy this class is to me. I am so pleased and satisfied. I feel the years roll off me!

CLASS INSTRUCTION AND COL. SABIN

The Christian Science periodicals of 1898 and 1899 unfold the illuminating story of Colonel Oliver Sabin, whose Washington News Letter had lost many subscribers after printing a defense of Christian Science. Mrs. Eddy requested Scientists to take out subscriptions to his magazine for one year, and in a letter of gratitude he asked her if he should perhaps take class instruction in Christian Science.

-- Reply to Col. Sabin by Mrs. Eddy [dated Jan.21, '99]:

> By no means [take class instruction]; God is your teacher. Read my books, and this is sufficient. I have known many whose spirituality has been dimmed by taking lessons, imbibing more of the letter than the spirit.
>
> [In a follow-up letter] ...By all means preserve the sanctity of your teaching. As it now stands, God is your Teacher, and I have seen the human teacher turn them from the Spirit to the letter of Christian Science and dim the former. I deeply regret that I did not have you in my last class; but if I never teach another class, keep up your daily study of my books, and that is sufficient.

In this case Col. Sabin did neither--he did not study Mrs. Eddy's works on a daily basis nor did he take class. Absolutely contrary to what he could have found in S&H, he equated his sense of C.S. with ecclesiasticism and sought to organize his readers into a regimented group with himself at the head. Furthermore he was left without the possible "excuse for teaching", since he did not get "quietly instructed" in the handling of animal magnetism.

After Mrs. Eddy had failed to renew her request for subscribers to his *News Letter*, it became the fashion for students of official C.S. teachers to unite in vilifying him, passing it on that he was a Jew, etc. Not understanding that malicious animal magnetism is not a somethingness to be fought, but an impersonal nothingness to be recognized, he struck back and was quickly lost to C.S.

Mrs. Eddy's observations to Col. Sabin were in line with what she wrote to Irving Tomlinson dated Oct.28, '98: "I have seen that students of my books when healed by them, if taught by other students, *relapse*, and if not invalids relapse morally as all do in said cases."

At about the same time (Aug.25, '98) she wrote to a teacher whose students were in danger of relapsing: "My precious student: For God's sake and the sake of the Discoverer of Christian Science cleanse your mortal thought of all that you would not have reflected and seen in the lives of your students. Good healers are the only good teachers. The musician must sing or play well and is judged by his performance, not by his blab. Science is practice, proof, not a profession, neither high-toned wit nor philosophy; these are but apologies for its absence if they possess not the spirit that heals both sickness and sin."

A LESSON ON EVERYDAY CARES

Although Mrs. Eddy eventually found it convenient (1907) to put her estate into the hands of three trustees, there seemed to be no one at the time of her last class who could relieve her of the task of running her home and personal affairs. She supervised the arrangement of her furniture, the care of her grounds, the running of her kitchen, etc., in the same way as she listened for God's voice to direct her in the running of her church. The Board of Directors tried to supply her with a Committee on Help at Pleasant View, but the lesson that seemed to be needed in all such attempts was that without the right mental attitude the help was but a channel for animal magnetism.

-- <u>Letters</u> to C.S. Directors, signed "With love, Mother, M.B. Eddy":

1) [dated Feb.16, '99] My Beloved Students: At last I have found a few moments in which to write my old "body guard" with whom I have fought many a battle. But better late than never, is it not--to thank you for my Com. on Help? At present I am provided for. Dr. Baker has named a florist and sent for him.

The Com. is needed all the same, for the next blow that <u>foils the m.a.m.'s</u> may take him away from me. But they cannot take away my God.

2) [dated March 4, '99] My Beloved Students: I thank you for appointing a Committee on Pleasant View and especially for the one named for Superintendent. At first I felt a touch of memory, and afterwards saw that has nothing to do with the present, and would engage him at once; but we are so unsettled now and have no gardener or florist and no definite state of things, and have all the help we have need of till things are arranged; so I concluded to wait till we get things ready to be superintended. Then I shall apply again to you and if I can get him, be pleased to have you send him here and settle his terms and take charge of my real estate.

A few weeks later Mrs. Eddy extended some advice to members of her entourage regarding their own activities and those of neighbors (like Professor Kent, who lived on the same street in Concord):

> Do not scare nor drive away the fishes you would catch. And too much explanation and not taking the right horn of the dilemma will defeat your good purpose. Animals we please by stroking them the way the hair grows, but stroking it the way we want it to grow will convince *never* a Prof. Kent! I got him once where he loved to hear me talk Science (at least he said so) and I like his frankness; but others have manipulated him out of it--at least his wife has and so has m.a.m. Be *wise* if you would win Concord folk. Go *with them*--as Jesus did--a part of the way and let them talk and then listen to what they are ready to hear.

MORE ON KIMBALL CONTROVERSY

The so-called "Kimball controversy", questioning the authenticity of certain dicta attributed to Edward Kimball, brings many lessons to light on the "what is" and "what is not" of teaching. It is not unlike the "Stetson controversy", dealt with in Chap.III, which challenges one's position on what is and what is not true preaching. It has the same value as the more recent "Bliss Knapp controversy" which questions what is and what is not the personified Woman of the Apocalypse and which faces some answers in Chap.IV.

The modern contender in controversy reflects the same attitude of contention that in the first century proclaimed "I am of Paul; and I of Apollos; and I of Cephas" (I Cor.i:12). It is the old demand for safety in a fortress of orthodoxy, and is synonymous with ancient and modern gang-warfare. It says, My teacher, my priest, my prophet is right--he gets it from God (or else from someone who gets it from God) and therefore I am 100% right, and therefore, if you disagree, you and your teacher, priest, prophet are 100% wrong and should be exposed and obliterated.

What is the divine message about these gangs of educational and ecclesiastical self-righteousness? It is:

1. Follow your Leader only so far as she [or he] follows Christ ('01 34:25, '02 4:3);
2. It is vain to look for perfection in churches or associations (No 4:3).

No assertion that does not stem directly from Principle can be 100% perfect. An opposite assumption would be as fragile as two writers arguing over who had written the correct version, and believing the answer depended on who had used the more expensive pen! Similarly, if two students were translating a passage from Homer, and one was found to be copying out a version slipped to him by his teacher, would that be the one who was 100% right and the only one who was trustworthy?

~ ~ ~ ~ ~ ~ ~

Yet why did Mrs. Eddy switch from Mr. Kimball to Judge Hanna in 1907 when trying to see if teaching could continue to be correctly handled through what were seen as personal intermediaries? Was she dissatisfied with Kimball? or was she wondering whether anyone else could ever be found who would be as reliable? All kinds of guesses are made by that thought that wants to feel it has hopped onto the right bandwagon.

An early Scientist who spent one year in Mrs. Eddy's home was one of those who sincerely questioned Kimball's right to be put on a pedestal. He was and remained a staunch supporter of the Directors, stating openly that any misjudgments they made meant simply that the field was not upholding them properly. He did not feel that a teacher in the Board of Education, or a trustee in the Publishing Society, should take any kind of precedence. When he assisted in the 1930's with the production of a book of Essays attributed to Mrs. Eddy, he sponsored the inclusion in it of a sheet showing Mrs. Eddy's severe corrections to an unsigned typewritten article said to have been written by Mr. Kimball.

His son told the compiler of this volume that the purpose of the inclusion was simply to show the care with which Mrs. Eddy went over articles that crossed her desk. But he and his father were comfortably aware of the effect it would have on contenders in the Kimball controversy.

He later produced the complete article, which was very lengthy. The unincluded portions had no corrections and apparently met with Mrs. Eddy's full approval--so that the places where the language had been considered faulty were actually four isolated sentences, shown in the book as a connected whole. These were no doubt subject to the usual misinterpretations; and the beginner in Science might well wish to know what <u>is</u> this "error" which, in Mrs. Eddy's words, <u>is</u> "walking to and fro in the earth" (Mis.277: 5). Where Mr. Kimball (assuming he was the author) had tried to show the only way error can seem to be or exist, Mrs. Eddy had written also correctly: "it does not exist at all."

The conclusions that can be drawn are very helpful. Primarily the lesson is that no student can take the letter of metaphysical instruction as accurate unless he is at the same time imbibing the Spirit.

When Mrs. Eddy revised Unity of Good in 1909 she told her household it was a <u>correction</u>. This means that either Mrs. Eddy was wrong in what she wrote before 1909, and therefore cannot be called trustworthy, or that the words she was using did not appear to be leading sufficiently to the Spirit back of the letter. Her many revisions of S&H show how she was perfecting her use of the letter way beyond the skill of the average teacher.

If at first she used wording that was misunderstood, that does not mean she must have been a fraud, anymore than it is correct to conclude that the whole of Mr. Kimball's teaching is bad if objections can be made to some of the wording he is said to have used. Actually no personal teaching can be called correct or of any permanent value whatever unless it establishes the paramount principle in the mind of the learner. And sometimes negative encounters can serve to establish that principle more quickly than blind or routine acceptance. It is obvious why Mrs. Eddy was anticipating the day when the thoroughly tested wording of S&H would take the place of courses of personal teaching.

The Scientist works from the Principle and does not decide that the Principle resides wholly in one teacher and not at all in another.

Among the eleven lines reproduced in the Essays book was the statement: "Every organ or function of the body is an idea of God..." and Mrs. Eddy had written beside that: "a lie." Whether Mr. Kimball was the author or not is immaterial, for the statement is worth examining on its merits, and such statements have indeed been laid frequently at his door.

The lesson here is the same as Mrs. Eddy faced in the 1870's: the inability of mortal mind to give a spiritual meaning to words like "body" and "matter"--so that she was later forced to use only the mortal mind meaning, and then deny its existence, rather than persevere with the spiritual identification. She wrote in her original Science of Man (as finally published by her in 1883 but no longer circulated by her then):

> Ques. Is the body of man matter?
>
> Ans. Yes, because man has not a body and because matter as substance is not the idea of God. The soul has a body and this body is immortal, because it is the idea of its principle, and is not a belief of substance, intelligence, and life in matter, but holds these in the Soul, and man the idea of these: this man is the body of the Soul and not the body of man.

Likewise she gave up the attempt to refer to matter as anything but "a belief and error", despite the fact that she had been writing and teaching that matter "held as shadow is the idea of God." This concession was, in Jesus' words, "because of your unbelief."

As Mr. Kimball sought to penetrate the belief that "body" could be used only to designate one of the decillions of human or animal bodies said to be roaming the material world, he encountered the same difficulties Mrs. Eddy had faced with the first edition of S&H. When he wanted to refer to matter as "shadow", a purely mental phenomenon, he found that many Scientists still wanted to use matter only as "substance" to be annihilated or at least shunned. This is why they accused him of "spiritualizing matter" (which after all is what Mrs. Eddy has done with "matter held as shadow" or matter as "the idea of God").

Mrs. Eddy did warn him to watch any belief in more than one mind (i.e. animal magnetism) in the College precincts. She even told him: "Beware of Judge Hanna, for he will always exonerate himself. I say this not to harm him but to protect you."

The letter which Mr. Kimball at length wrote to Judge Hanna to let him know the phraseology he had been using in his Normal classes to illustrate S&H, remained hidden for nearly forty years, but has since had fairly wide circulation. Below are some of its main observations:

"Perfect liver"

-- Letter [dated Nov.29, '07 and signed "Sincerely, E.A. Kimball"]:

My dear Judge: ...I am confident that all of the candidates who have been under my teaching will go to you with a sense of absolute accord and cooperation, and I assure you with unreserved sincerity that there is no flaw in my satisfaction over the fact that you are the one and that they will get nothing but a sound interpretation of Christian Science and the rule of practice....

It seems necessary to see that the...devil will try to make it appear that the College teaching is ununiform and that the teachers work at cross purposes and that they contradict and repudiate each other....

The nearest thing I ever heard [about alleged irregular teaching on the part of Dr. Baker, teacher of obstetrics] was that the Doctor in disposing of error, matter, simply wiped out everything and presented a philosophy which seemed to have annihilation for its ultimate.

Mrs. Eddy spoke to me about this propensity or let me say incompleteness. She said, "I said to Dr. Baker, 'Jesus said stretch forth thy hand', but all you have to say is, 'You haven't got any hand'."...She said to me, "Declare I have a perfect liver, and let the spiritual import of this declaration destroy the false concept about liver." ...Mrs.Eddy said "yes you may declare I have a perfect liver, or there is no liver, provided the thought back of these declarations is right."

...I am under the impression that nearly all the students I taught got a fairly correct appreciation of it, but the ones [in the field] who got it second-hand, or third, or fourth, or fifth-hand [supposed] that Mr. Kimball was teaching that we had spiritual organs; some said each man, a separate spiritual stomach--others that though the material liver was a counterfeit, it was nevertheless a counterfeit of a spiritual organ...and enemies of the College...said that my teaching was defective because I spiritualized matter, or the body. Mrs. Eddy told me she never believed these things about it because she knew where I stood in the matter. I do not need to be elaborate with you in explaining what I taught in order to confirm Mrs. Eddy's instruction but will say briefly by way of outline:...

> Mind's infinite manifestation or infinity of ideas constitute what may be called body or embodiment. Therefore there is one embodiment of Being, one body.... Mind and body are scientifically speaking--One, and constitute the wholeness of unity.

This unity or infinity is inorganic, and includes no organs, spiritual or otherwise. Nevertheless, the manifestation or body does include or show forth all ideas--all things. All the things of body are perfect, complete, immortal, harmonious, and under the rule of divine law. Body is the body of all being, just as Life is "the life of all being divine." There is nothing included in body, but what is perfect. To all intents and purposes it may be said that all men have one Mind and one body.

That which seems to be--the material universe, man and body--is not what it seems to be.... It is not matter at all, but is subjective error--nothing but belief which calls itself matter. ...A lie is always, necessarily a lie about the truth. ...Would it transform or annihilate to have thought limit itself to this concept "there is no body"--"there is no eye", etc.? ...If there were no opposite affirmation to the concept "my liver is imperfect" then the ultimate would be a belief of disaster instead of transformation.

What is the opposite affirmation? It is something like this. Body is spiritual, it consists of spiritual ideas, every idea is perfect--the idea of which liver is a false concept is perfect, in Good....

So then my dear friend no student of mine was ever taught by me that the spiritual man has spiritual organs or that body is organic or that there are bodies many.... To all intents and purposes, the transformation of Mind means also the transformation of body.

I am sorry to bother you about this, nevertheless it may serve to upset an attempt of the enemy to discredit the College. [End of letter extracts.]

Misinterpretation

At this point it is worth making a passing reference to John Willis' article "Watching vs. Watching Out" which Mrs. Eddy found necessary to correct forcefully (periodicals of September and October 1905, and My.232).

According to the recollections of one of Mrs. Eddy's household at the time, Mrs. Eddy told them privately that there was nothing wrong with the Willis article! The problem was simply the misinterpretation she knew readers could be putting into the words.

It was necessary to correct, not what Mr. Willis was hoping to convey, but what might be read into words he was using.

With full faith in the Principle it is possible at all times to learn what Mind knows of the truth that is being presented or even misrepresented, for "God...hath made us able ministers of the new testament; not of the letter, but of the spirit: for the letter killeth, but the spirit giveth life" (II Cor.iii:6). The Christian Scientist reads everything with the eye of God, because the Mind or Principle which is God alone sees.

Since the point at issue in the Kimball controversy revolves around the correct and incorrect use of the word "body" and its functions or organs, and the word "matter", the following pungent and relevant teachings by Mrs. Eddy to close students are copied here. Other subject-matter is listed in the section to follow, headed "LINE UPON LINE."

Body and Matter

There is no error or sin that can mesmerize me into feeling or seeing a body. There is one Body, the body of all being. This body is perfect in form, comeliness, beauty, for it expresses the idea of God. Malicious animal magnetism cannot operate to suggest or produce doubt or fear, or irritation in a Christian Scientist.

Mind is ever imparting perfect modes of expression outlining beauty, form, color, grace, symmetry, refinement, delicacy, beautified being. Know now what God is, and that is what body is. Heaven is here or we would not be here. God is Life and man is the liver. Let Life be seen. Man is the body of God.

Had we the understanding of our God--our being--or the omnipotence of Truth, we should have no fear of matter, and having none, our bodies would become harmonious and immortal. A belief of substance-matter would then give place to substance-Spirit. What if the lungs are thought to be ulcered or decayed? Mind has said this. Action is produced by mind, not by matter.

Change therefore your belief in the case. Contest the error and belief of life in matter with the Truth that life is Soul not sense, and you will form the lungs anew and they will resume their healthy functions. Disease is a belief, its origin mental, not physical, and it matters not what the body indicated. In reality all is Mind. There is no matter, and mortal things are beliefs--not the science of man which is immortal.

There is no substance in: belief. Your matter body is a belief only, hence it is not substance--it is a belief in anatomy. Christ held his person all the same when his body was buried; it could pass through matter and walk over matter (water) with this body; but it could have no pain or inflammation in it because it was not in matter and he never believed his spine was a bone that could be inflamed or that his nerves could pain. In the belief that the body is substance is embraced the whole error of sickness and death.

There are no conditions of matter because there is no such thing as matter. There is no space for a material body to occupy. There never was a thousand years ago.

Jesus said: "Is not the life more than meat, and the body than raiment?" This is a denial of mortal laws and necessities.

All is Mind and Mind's idea. Matter in any form or condition is but the manifestation of a false mentality, mortal mind. If one admits the reality of matter he must likewise admit the reality of all its conditions. If harmonious matter is real, discordant matter is also real. So if one clings to the thought of good in matter he cannot escape the belief of evil in matter. To think of a material body as real while denying the existence of disease in that body is not scientific practice.

The great truth that man is spiritual because he is the image and likeness of God heals sickness and sin. This scientific fact denies the belief of man's materiality, and should be kept before the thought continually. Mortal man must sacrifice the good that seems to be in matter if he would escape the evil that matter produces, for the one is as real as the other, and no more so.

Do not annihilate. Do not say, "There is no strength in arm"; strength and power are omnipotence. The trouble is the wrong sense of body--a wrong sense of Life. First get control of the body, then control of the appetites.

Everything in the material universe is a counterfeit of something real. What is the stomach? A counterfeit of some divine idea. But because it is the counterfeit of something real, do not go any farther and theorize. Just know God is present here.

Rise to the spiritual sense, then your body will respond. This is the resurrection. It is not to be resurrected from matter, dust. There never was any life in matter to be resurrected. The resurrection is seeing the real man that never was in matter. He never was sick to be made well. That was the way I did the healing. I never saw a material man before me, but the real man, perfect, and this healed instantaneously, and no relapse. This is the way Jesus healed.

Jesus read the minds of his students. He saw their sins, but did not believe it was their minds, and this did the healing.

Truth declares itself as our infinite consciousness, which is reflected by right ideas in individual consciousness and individual man. Its manifestations are necessarily universal and infinite. They are constantly declaring themselves according to their divine nature. In every thought, action, organ, function, the infinite Principle, Mind, is showing forth intelligence and law.

Every action, incident, movement, faculty, function, organ, in the divine creation, is an idea of God and is constantly declaring: "I am." Every idea must do this and cannot do otherwise. It does not know how and cannot know how to be unlike infinity. It does not know how to be otherwise than harmonious, lending its tone to the universal infinite harmony of divine, boundless, satisfactory being.

It seems to the material senses that pain etc. is in the lungs or elsewhere in matter, but the fact is that pain or suffering of any sort is no more in the body or matter in our waking state than it is in our night dream, for both states are dreams and not the reality of being.

Error says we are sick or discouraged; we don't say it. It is error talking about itself. If we admit it, we have accepted a lie. Truth says, "I have perfect eyes, perfect heart, perfect limbs, etc.; all there is to me is like God, like perfection." We should discard mortal mind judgment, and pray for the Christ Mind.

Do not deny person and material mechanism without holding the real in thought.

Let love come into his bones like oil--"O Lord, heal me for my bones are vexed" (Ps.vi:2). "O ye dry bones, hear the word of the Lord" (Eze.xxxvii:4), and your bones shall rejoice for God governs them and "make me to hear joy and gladness; that the bones which thou hast broken may rejoice" (Ps.li:8).

"It is not that which goes into the mouth which defileth a man", that is, the belief of physical sensation, "but that which cometh out of a man that defileth a man." That which is taken into the heart (is acknowledged) and a reason given for it, <u>that</u> defileth. If a person is suffering pain, it is merely physical sensation within and cannot defile--but taken into the heart, that is, if one begins to reason with it, it is that which defileth a man. The whole point is if one begins to ruminate about the pain etc. a reason given for it is expressed in defilement.

Don't try to destroy a disease. You have nothing to do with the body. Knowing the omnipotence of God breaks fear. Don't be frightened--know that every seeming effect of mortal mind is a lie. <u>You</u> never were in the dream, and your reality is one with Christ in God. Love made all and governs all and there is naught else and you know it.

"Tell the truth about the lie" does not mean you should say "I have a cold", any more than you should say "I am all right." Better say: "I am tuning in to the truth of being in which there is no cold."

There are two sorts of colds: the cold that is the result of breaking a so-called mortal law, and a cold that is the result of hate. They would want completely different treatment.

The body or matter never yet informed man of disease, but the belief carries this telegram to the body and the body manifests only the suffering of mind.

My health and strength are from the Christ--Mind; therefore no mental arrow can reach me in any part or organ of my body, which is not flesh but is the immortal image of God, my Creator. I bid every claim of evil return and take effect in the sender.

There is but one blood and you reflect that perfect blood. Blood is spiritual idea--there is no material blood. Just as you can neither add to nor subtract from 7 and still have it 7, so you can neither add to blood, take from it or put upon it anything and still have it blood. The scientific fact of blood is the only blood and can never be anything but perfect. Its Life is purity, its substance God. There is but one circulation, but one system (the system of Truth).

There is but one of anything, for instance, one hand. You reflect it right and left, but it is always hand and always perfect. A sore hand would be less than a hand, for it would not be a whole hand, hence it would be a lie. Whatever we see imperfect is a lie about the true <u>one</u>, for the fact of everything is perfect--see every organ as <u>idea</u>, <u>not matter</u>, and that idea always has been and always will be perfect. If sense says it is imperfect, it is a lie about organ.

[If the argument is epilepsy] handle also atavism and laws of ancestry. God is perfect Mind, man is perfect compound idea. No belief of prenatal influence can be reflected in belief. Here is a belief that organs and functions have gone wrong, and affected other organs. Know that all ideas are in Mind, and exist in harmonious relationship.

Matter has no sensation, and no organic construction can give matter hearing. Organic construction cannot give matter sight, nor make matter the medium of Mind.

When you lose your life in sense, for Life is Soul, the disease, pain, suffering will cease. That is why we seem to suffer, for we have not lost our life in matter for life in Soul.

Rebuke and compassion are one. The understanding of this brings out God's Mind and God's Body.

In God is my dominion, my wisdom, my understanding. In God is my dominion over the flesh and evil.

~ ~ ~ ~ ~ ~ ~

The above quotations and examples of Mrs. Eddy's teaching have stressed that idea has no initiative other than the insight it gives into its Principle--and that words have no value outside of the meaning they convey. The care with which Mrs. Eddy watched the impact of her words, and the impact of the words used by her students, have appeared two or three times in these quotations. Two more examples are noteworthy:

1) [From Recollections of Martha Wilcox]: When Mrs. Eddy wrote and added to Science and Health the two lines at the bottom of page 442, she consulted the dictionary, the grammar, studied synonyms and antonyms, and when she had finished she had these lines to add to Science and Health.

I marveled at her perseverance and the time she consumed in writing two lines. [See My.236:24 and My.237:13.]

2) [From Adam Dickey's Memoirs]: While [a letter to the Board of Directors] was being prepared she made several changes in it, each one being an improvement on the former phrasing.

After the letter had been finished, and even signed by her, she called me back again, and said, "Mr. Dickey, I must apologize to you for calling you so frequently, and troubling you so much, but won't you kindly bring that letter back to me?"

...Taking the letter, she glanced over it, drew her pencil through a word and replaced it with another. "There", she said with a triumphant smile, "that is exactly what I want to say."

[Then, reaching for the letter even once more, she wrote on the top for Mr. Dickey's benefit]: Remember that the so-called human mind is expected to increase in wisdom until it disappears and the Divine Mind is seen to be the only Mind.

"LINE UPON LINE"

Instruction such as the above continued at all times in Mrs. Eddy's home in line with the outreach of the Seventh Day. Under general headings some of this teaching is added here, together with related statements made on various occasions:

Age

The added wisdom of age and experience is strength, not weakness, and we should understand this, expect it, and know that it is so--then it would appear.

I ask for you to keep a time for meditation every day. Ponder in thought your infinite harmonious Christ-expressing selfhood, and claim it as you. Drink in its unspeakable safety. All the truth and beauty of God's creation is yours and you.

Enjoy it in sincere prayer and thanksgiving. Preserve your human sense of yourself rightly by dwelling in definite treatment every day, within the sanctity and integrity of your real selfhood.

In that hour of prayer, discard all your false sense of selfhood, all that is involved in the beliefs of birth, heredity, association, time, decay, death. By the grace and authority of God, close your thoughts firmly against the interference of mortal beliefs. Hold yourself open to the plans of God and closed to the plots of satan. Rise into the spiritual forces of your own destiny. Each day will begin and unfold under the authority of divine Mind, and will be well-ordered, rightly balanced, filled with spiritual good.

This magnificent spiritual exercise of treating yourself in devoted prayer, and praying for yourself, will keep you in the secret place which is unknown to the senses and open to all that heaven holds for you.

In proportion as the law of Truth is understood and accepted, it obtains in the personality as well as character.

The deformities and infirmities, said to be inevitable results of age, under the opposite mental impressions, disappear. You change the physical manifestations in proportion to your changed thoughts of the effects of accumulated years; expecting an increase of usefulness and vigor, from advanced years, with as much faith as you look for decrepitude and ugliness, a favorable result would be sure to follow.

Life is eternal and unchangeable, and can never grow old, for time is not, and youth is, immortal--you have always existed, and always will exist a perfect, complete and finished work, a spiritual being created of and by Spirit and subject only to spiritual laws.

You do now and ever must manifest the God-life that is shining in you. It is working always in every part of your being to will and to do.

There can never be any loss of your faculties--for they are of Soul and not of sense. The Life and strength of which you are the constant recipient, are indestructible and infinite, and nothing can prevent their inflow. You are governed and sustained by perfect Love in which there is no fear of helplessness or death. Your faith and trust in the omnipotent power of Truth are perfect, and unclouded, and you know that God is your sufficiency. Never was one of God's children palsied or helpless, for all His works are good and eternal. There is no mortal mind to say you are old or feeble. There is one infinite Mind, which is the understanding of the truth of your being, and holds you in perfect harmony and health.

Malicious animal magnetism haunts you with a personality all distorted by mortal suggestions; makes it hideous and hateful to you and urges you to adopt "this" as being created by God. It suggests a mental picture of age, failing strength, failing memory, dim sight, dim hearing, withered skin, bent form and every other suggestion to bolster up the lie of age.

Mind is God and seeing or vision must be and is an idea of God, never in nor of matter and never impaired nor lost. This vision is your vision by reflection, and as long as you can see the truth of God, your vision is unimpaired and you can prove it. Free yourself from the thought that you have lost your eyesight and that Christian Science can regain it for you. Instead Christian Science is the truth about your eyesight which was never lost and as this idea appears as your consciousness the belief of material or imperfect eyesight will disappear and the idea of spiritual, perfect, indestructible intelligence will appear as the only sight of Mind, therefore as the only sight of man or woman.

Old age is just as much a claim to be overcome as cancer or any other belief. Overcome the belief in it *now*. You have to do it sometime.

God has just told me what age is. Age is God's open door to eternal Truth.

[Said to Mrs Ewing in July 1906]: I am 85 years old today.... I know that you are thinking: "Never record ages", and that is true--never record ages in your appearance.

[Said to Calvin Frye as she looked towards Bow, N.H.]: Over there are the hills of Bow where they say I was born, but I was not. I was born in Mind.

Death

The person is not touched by death. The individual is not touched by death. He is simply throwing off a phase of material consciousness, human consciousness--and that phase has got to meet another phase and another and another till the divine appears. Then comes the immortal and eternal man.

To destroy the belief of death, we must first destroy the belief of birth, for the first enemy is sin and the last enemy is death. The true birth is getting rid of mortal mind and its paraphernalia.

Called to the bed of death, the Truth of being is your only recourse to restore health. On this basis alone can you recognize immortality and dispute personal sense or the apparent fact of death with Soul. Man is not dying, for Truth is mightier than error.

Know that your treatment and its effects cannot be reversed. Patients are dying that would instantly recover if the claim of reversal were handled.

Sin shall not stand face to face with God and live. The soul that sinneth shall surely die. Soul is God and cannot die, only the sinful sense (mortal mind) dies. "Work out your own salvation" and as we lose sight of minds many we grow into the understanding of the one Mind, which is the sense of All, and All in all.

Malicious animal magnetism includes not only the nature of mortal mind but the action. Strike at mortal mind and its claims to law and order. Take up death and relapse in every case. Know there is no law, no lawgiver nor lawmaker to declare that C.S. cannot heal permanently. Your patient and his claims are one belief, illusion--you need only dispel illusion. What would you do if called to a man who had broken his back? Answer: Meet the claim of death by knowing the continuity and unchangeableness of Life.

The destruction of the belief of finite personality, and the recognition and realization of perfection, enabled Jesus to raise the dead. We can enter into immortality here on earth and now, and overcome death. We must do it.

It is easier to raise the dead (which Jesus did instantly) than to cast out devils (seeing it took 40 days to heal Peter of disloyalty). [To keep the pictorial windows of First Church, Concord, in line with the order of these commands by Jesus in Matt.x:8, Mrs. Eddy had the third and fourth windows switched from their original setting.]

This is the point that must be borne in mind, that from every Eden we create in materiality we shall be banished. That condition we call satisfactory from a material standpoint is a delusion of human sense and from it we must be exiled for "to be carnally-minded is death."

Take half an hour each day to declare the Truth about mental malpractice. When you do it know that you are handling error that is trying to prevent C.S. from raising the dead.

[Mrs. Eddy's explanation of her healing of a boy with a carious shinbone]: I knew that if he died he would awake to find he had not that disease, and I wanted to wake him fully to it <u>before he died</u>.

The so-called dead, although liberated from the belief that Life has ended, or even changed to them, are separated from our opinions and recognition of them; and they have no more cognizance of the body we are disposing of than we of their actual existence. These two dreams of life are separated, never to unite again until we pass into their phase of belief, or at length reach the understanding of Life and yield the error of personal sense, or matter man, for Life that is God.

When they leave, they do so voluntarily. Do not try to hold them in this environment, but leave them free to rise, and rise with them at that point of experience.

Work for a patient up to the point of passing but never after. When they are in the vestibule we must loose them and let them go. "Jesus restored Lazarus...not by an admission that his body had died and then lived again."

[Mrs. Eddy's answer to a question as to whether Queen Victoria was still alive {after 1901}]: Yes, and is still a queen in belief.

[Mrs. Eddy's answer to a question as to whether she was demonstrating over death]: I am trying to understand what life is.

[Statement to Adam Dickey]: If I were to pass through the belief of death now, I would still be here.

Infinite Mind provides for the continuity and perpetuity of its own ideas. Mortal mind means dead mind and it provides for its own destruction and also for its own reproduction, not perpetuity. It goes on dying and reproducing, believing that it is reproducing man, and it is only perpetuating its own beliefs, which will continue their evolution until met and demolished by the facts of being.

In Science we find Mind directly and consciously containing all its own ideas. Mind governs and sustains the universe and man. Mortal mind's man is sustained by dead matter, or by the food he eats, all of which must decompose or die for his sustenance. Then we see that mortal mind's man feeds on death in order to sustain life, a contradiction from the beginning to the end--confusion, non-intelligence.

[Published article by Mrs. Eddy, entitled "Heaven" and dated Feb. '05]: Is heaven spiritual? Heaven is spiritual. Heaven is harmony--infinite boundless bliss.

The dying or the departed enter heaven according to their progress, in proportion to their fitness to partake of the quality and the quantity of heaven. One individual may first awaken from his dream of life with a sense of music; another with that of relief from fear or suffering, and still another with a bitter sense of lost opportunities and remorse.

Heaven is the reign of divine Science. Material thought tends to obscure spiritual understanding, to darken the true conception of man's divine Principle, Love, wherein and whereby soul is emancipated and environed with everlasting Life. Our great Teacher hath said: "Behold, the kingdom of God is within you"--within man's spiritual understanding of all the divine modes, means, forms, expression, and manifestation of goodness and happiness.

Handling Animal Magnetism

Animal magnetism is the belief in material man, that Life, substance and intelligence are material instead of spiritual.

1) There is ignorant A.M. which includes all beliefs of colds, damp climate, food, heredity, contagion, producing disease.

2) There is malicious A.M. including belief of anger, envy, jealousy, hate, etc., held against another person.

3) There is malicious mental malpractice (M.M.P.) which is educated thought that has learned the power of thought and uses it for a wrong end.

This is sometimes operated through prayers that Christian Scientists may have relapses, reverses, losses, etc., that they may be discouraged, disillusioned, may have a return of their old beliefs [causing] them to doubt the efficacy of treatment being of God; or through predictions or prophecies of evil to make them consent to aggressive mental suggestions of the power of evil or the peace of dying; or through anathema that all enemies of the Holy Mother Church may suffer. This claim seems to act as a narcotic.

In healing malicious mental malpractice these are the main points to be taken up: Recognition that all mental malpractice is based on the supposition:

1) That there is a mortal mind.

2) That it manifests itself through what are termed avenues--channels or instruments.

3) That it can impart to thought what it suggests through its channels.

4) That it can enforce its beliefs or declarations, its rule, wish, or desire, by means of its law.

5) That it has any object on which to impress itself.

If we are going to forestall animal magnetism's attempt to destroy everything that is good in human experience, we have not a moment to lose. The highest form of evil is malicious mental malpractice, which is educated evil.

Meet animal magnetism without a fight. There is no animal magnetism that can reverse the currents of Truth in consciousness. Arguments are mesmerism. Error is not a person, place, nor thing, and there are no avenues, channels, nor instruments, through which it can act or upon whom it can devolve any power or capacity to act. God is almighty and All-in-all.

Know that God sent it even if it seems the devil brought it.

M.M.P. is not power, mind, or law. It has no sphere of activity, no mind to project its beliefs, no mind to accept its beliefs. It has no dupes, no victims. It is not law--it is not a lawmaker.

Keep the joy of Christian Science and a well-grounded and boundless hope in your success. Remember as Truth progresses, error grows more subtle and aggressive but it does not become something--it always remains an illusion and is always met and destroyed with the understanding that divine Love is the only power.

Know that M.A.M. has no power to touch you with any thought of fear or resentment, envy, hate, jealousy, or malice, for you are with Christ in infinite Good, where error cannot come in in the name of a suggestion to make you believe or listen to mortal mind arguments; for you live in the Infinite Good.

We have a right to expect an immediate uncovering of the claim of cause in any disease--even the laws so-called of physiology if we need a knowledge of such to break the mesmerism of disease.

Analyze every claim of it. If envy, no pleasure in it, no substance in it, nothing to envy or be envious of.

Mental malpractitioners study the C.S. statement that there is only one Mind and argue: Are you Mind? (No.) Are you matter? (No.) Then what are you? NOTHING! for you have not any mind!!

M.A.M. stands ready to argue misunderstanding and the only safe way in hours of trial is to obey the adage "Silence is golden." If anyone has wronged you, you cannot hide it from wisdom. We must all look to Principle and let light dispel the darkness and settle down to peace and prosperity. There is no mortal mind that can influence or darken our consciousness. Love is almighty. Keep declaring for Principle; Life, Truth and Love are omnipotent. It is Love that uncovers and overcomes.

When we are perplexed as to whether we are hearing the voice of Truth or error, we may use this as a guide to the conclusion. If there is any doubt whatever, you may know it is animal magnetism. Truth is peaceful and certain, it leads us with a loving hand. The voice of Truth never pains, or causes any despair or doubt in him whose affections are fixed on God.

Christian Scientists will find the approach and attack of mesmerism to be a sort of paralysis--or inaction of mind, numbness, and fear. When such an attack seems to approach, by immediately reversing the conditions of thought, and mentally inquiring of self: "Am I radiating good or am I absorbing evil?"--and putting that thought into action by addressing the counteracting thoughts of Spirit to whatever seems to be attacking you from mortal mind, you will set yourself free from bondage and render yourself the medium of demonstrations for those blessings you so freely receive from the source of all Good, and not from any person or any belief of mind in matter. S&H 419:8.

Know that God intends you to heal the sick. The divine command to heal the sick comes with the ability to do so. M.M.P. cannot tell you that you cannot heal the sick.

God can never be something external to consciousness for He is never apart from man--"God with me." The claim of hatred never made anyone sick; it is only a belief that did. When you take the fangs from the serpent it is harmless. A Christian Scientist has sufficient understanding to overcome any claim, if he only knows it. "For I will give you a mouth and wisdom, which all your adversaries shall not be able to gainsay or resist" (Luke xxi:15).

Ingratitude, avarice, greed, dishonesty, fretfulness, worry, anxiety, fear must be handled and cast out. We must handle sensitiveness as sin. It is sin that tends to suspicion, doubt, anger, resentment, contrariness, stubbornness, jealousy, and a host of others. We must handle this lie and cast it out. We must know that we are free from sin, God made it not, "The Word begat us", and the Word heals and delivers us.

It is the Word that heals us and saves us from all destruction. Mind has no sad memories. Mind, God, knows only the good, true, beautiful, and pure. Mortal mind never sends forth a positive sound.

In reality there is no animal magnetism, ignorant, malicious or sympathetic. There is no mental malpractice directed against a Christian Scientist or the cause of Christian Science, which has power to make you a channel for error of any nature, mental, physical or financial. It cannot make you its servant, or its slave, its victim or its tool. It has no power to strike through any belief in materia medica, hypnotism, false theology, false science, or any other sense of materiality, fear, hatred, pride, envy, malice, jealousy, ambition, revenge, self-will, self-love, self-righteousness, self-justification, or through lust or sensuality, vice, or through any claim of evil in mortal mind, to pour forth hatred or torment. There is one Mind, and this one is effective and governs the entire universe.

There is no malicious, ignorant or directed malpractice, no mesmerism, no hypnotism, no M.A.M., no fear, no ignorant sympathetic self-mesmerism, no mediumship--no trance condition, no clairvoyance, no demonology, no black art, orientalism, occultism, no witchcraft, no esoteric magic, no Buddhism, no theosophy, no planetary law, no astrology, no materia medica, no scholastic theology, no mental inoculation, no mental contagion, no mental poison.

There is no ignorant latent nor developed transference of mortal thought--no erroneous influence in or out of the flesh --no moral idiocy, no electricity, no electric magnetism, no ecclesiasticism. There is no atmospheric, hygienic nor mortal law, no law of suggestion, no animal attraction, no passion, no lust, sexuality nor sensuality. No sex, no human love, no blind enthusiasm, no prejudice--spite, envy, jealousy, nor hatred, no temper nor violent anger, no revenge, no self-love, no self-justification, no self-will, no condemnation, no self of any kind existing in matter beliefs. Error of any kind is powerless and cannot produce mental laziness or haziness; neither can it blind my intelligence, nor stop my spiritual growth. All there is is God, Good and His Creation, hence I am conscious only of perfection and its manifestation. I cannot be impressed, repressed, nor oppressed for I am the expression of Life, Truth, and Love.

God is all, the only cause and creator, and I am God's child, therefore subject only to the spiritual influence of God and His Christ. Since God, good, is all, there is no carnal or evil mind to influence my action or thoughts.

You (error) cannot produce any new beliefs in me or bring back my old ones. There are no beliefs; belief and believer are one and are mortal mind. Malice cannot produce [new or old beliefs] on myself, friends, family or patients, through malicious animal suggestions, through friend or foe, conscious or unconscious, direct or indirect, willful, malicious or ignorant--cannot reach me through any avenue for every avenue is filled with the Divine Love. I pray that nothing, no evil suggestion or argument may swerve me, frighten me, or deter me from doing the work that is mine to do.

M.A.M. cannot molest me, for there is no danger that can befall; everything is in God's keeping. I deny selfishness by denying all that is unlike Good. I cannot begin with all the world, but I can begin with myself. As the truth of being is wrought out in my life, as God and my true relationship to Him becomes recognized, the evil mortal beliefs will be swept aside, and darkness (ignorance) will give place to light (understanding).

I cannot be enticed by silent unseen arguments. I cannot be impelled into error of thought or tempted into the commission of acts foreign to my natural inclinations. I cannot be made to lose my understanding or lend myself a willing tool to the designs of my worst enemy--even those who would induce my self-destruction. I cannot be made to foster suspicion where honors are due, or fear where courage should be strongest, or reliance where there should be avoidance or a belief of safety where there is most danger. Miserable lies forced into my mind constantly cannot fret or confuse me, undermine my health or seal my doom, for I can find out the mischief and destroy it with Truth. My mind cannot be made dormant, nor can I be put into a state of semi-individuality with a mortal haziness which admits of no intellectual growth or spiritual culture. I cannot be led by secret evil influences into species of intoxication in which to believe or do what I would not otherwise think or do voluntarily, for there is no mortal mind.

There is no malice, no envy, no will-power. All is Love and Truth. God's voice is the only voice that can be heard or speak. M.A.M. is a false claim which Truth destroys. It cannot speak to any of my dear ones for it is a lie. It has no intelligence, no mind, hence no power. It cannot talk, it does not argue, it is no whisperer. Our Father Mother God will not leave us in temptation but will deliver us from evil. God is all, there is none beside Him.

Malpractitioners cannot make laws. The lies they whisper hurt no one but themselves. Lies, hatred, revenge have no power but to destroy themselves every time they try to hurt anybody else. This is God's law, it cannot be broken and it cannot make anybody suffer because we tell you this. You cannot help yourself and nobody can help you till you stop trying to hurt others.

Know that God is your support. His Sword and His Staff support you. His word is quick and powerful and sharper than any two-edged sword piercing even to the dividing asunder of every deadly thing. There is no talking serpent, hence no talking error.

Thinking Good externalizes itself and Christian Scientists should expect good. The reason we seem not to destroy beliefs is because we call belief oneself instead of mesmerism.

The rule to ensure victory for Science is this: Bear faithful testimony to the existence of animal magnetism as an evil belief, which must be met and mastered. A denial of the existence of this error prevents your victory over it.

One needs to protect himself for his own false beliefs alone; therefore the only wrong thinker or mental malpractitioner there is or can be is one's self;--the beam in one's own eye is the whole of evil. All our warfare is located within the confines of our own thought.

Healing

Love is the only and all of attainments in spiritual growth. Without it healing is not done and cannot be, either morally or physically. Every advance step will show you this until the victory is won. You possess no other consciousness but LOVE divine.

We heal by our own perfection. Jesus' perfection healed hundreds. The destruction of the belief of a finite person (personality) and the recognition and realization of perfection enabled Jesus to raise the dead. If you do not heal, you have not much love.

No treatment is exact unless it starts from God and starts as God and so continues. To know there is but one God, one Cause, one effect, one Mind heals instantly. Have one God, and your reflection of Him does the healing.

Do not look to matter to tell you your success, but look up, for your harvest is right at hand. You know the Father's love; trust it. Then when you hear a whisper, "You are a sinner and so and so is your punishment, this suffering is the consequence", put it out; put it out. Animal magnetism says you are a sinner when you know you are not. Then empty your thought of fear and say, "I look to God, my Father, to see what I am. He alone can tell me of myself."

Divine help is ever nigh. O what Love is made manifest in our hours of great need, because we trust then and turn alone to Love for succor and support. We should have faith at all times equal to the demand: then could we remove mountains of obstructions in solution, solved problems. You say, "When shall we learn the way?" I reply, when you have all faith in Truth and no faith in error.

If we take up a reproach against our neighbor, we shall be unable to heal.

Healing is Truth appearing, denying all that is unlike itself. Know that you heal for you are Truth's reflection.

There is no such thing as impersonal healing, for there is always a person in it. There may be indirect healing.

[From Frye Diary April 1, '02]: Mrs. Eddy said "when I began healing" she used no arguments and really did not know how she healed, and only knew that God did the work; but when she began to teach students to heal, she had to work all sorts of ways to start them from their standpoint, for she could not start them from hers, for they could not understand, were not ready to do as she did. But when she dropped down to their methods of arguments she began to fear, and the error began to feel real to her at the time of her husband's death.

Law

MIND is LAW. Mind is the law of perfection, completeness, activity, vigor, vitality to its ideas, to body and to all that is included in body. Mind is the law of elimination or expulsion to the beliefs of abnormality, impurity, discord. This treatment is the enforcement of law. Every Christian Science treatment is the operation and enforcement of spiritual law and it cannot be reversed.

The only laws that govern the reflection or association of the activities of the One Mind are the Laws of God, and they are justice and fairness to each idea.

The "Business" of God's universe is based on unchanging Law, and has no state of inaction or over-action--it is a harmonious and perfect relationship and association of infinite activities, and individual man performs unerringly and surely his part.

Heaven is the consciousness of the law of government. God is Law and man is the manifestation of Law. Mortal mind claims matter is substance, that matter is governed by certain laws such as cohesion, adhesion, and gravitation, planetary attraction and climate, heredity, old age, decay, weakness, loss of memory, loss of power, etc.

Then comes liberated thought such as mesmerism, hypnotism, ignorance of source, M.M.P. laws, so-called association, witchcraft and black art.

Because you are still in matter, in belief, and subject to the laws of matter, in belief--absolute Truth outlines itself to meet the present need.

Realize for yourself that you reflect as your individual consciousness the enduring, consistent substance of Being and nothing can repress, suppress, suspend or make null and void the operation of Truth. Declare: My consciousness and individuality is in God, Love, and can reflect nothing else. Evil (in belief) has no law of malpractice, no activity as law --its whole claim of activity is a lie and the father of it. Love is the only active Principle.

There are no seen or unseen mental arguments that can operate as law, or as any mortal belief, or as a law of mental malpractice through ecclesiastical beliefs to divert or pervert, prevent or interfere with or reverse, the statement of Christian Science, nor can it touch or affect me because I am a Christian Scientist. This treatment is the Word of God and it does not return unto me void, but is final and complete in its effects and the results thereof. This treatment hinders, obstructs, impedes and destroys all supposed power of clairvoyance.

M.M.P. claims it is freqently directed for the purpose of doing evil, but it cannot make a law that I cannot uncover and destroy its intention towards me. I can protect myself against hate, malice, envy, and jealousy. I can handle its supposed law and declare its nothingness.

We must obey the laws of the land until Christian Scientists metaphysically and scientifically understand God sufficiently to cause those laws to be changed.

I am obedient to the will of God and I am governed by the spiritual law of His Christ. No aggressive suggestion from ecclesiastical manipulators can touch my consciousness or enter my thought for all is already filled with Truth and Love.

~ ~ ~ ~ ~ ~ ~

[From Mrs. Eddy's article entitled "The Law of God to this Day"]: There is nothing but complete immunity from all disease. The law of God to this day is the law of exemption from all disease to all Christian Science teachers, practitioners, patients--a law of exemption from the belief of fear, of accident or death. This day is God's day, Mind's day; it is the day of infinite being, the day of infinite Life, the day of infinite substance.

The law of God to this day is a law of infinite perfection, of action, and of perfection in every manifestation.

All things which pertain to this day are already perfected, already arranged and completed; under Christian Science treatment this completeness unfolds. There is no deterioration in this day to mind or body in belief, or at all.

This so-called law of deterioration is broken, annulled, now and forever. There is no growth materially that can result in deterioration and decay. All being is already established and is mature, and perfectly mature. There is no age, no growing old in this day in belief, or at all. There is no law of death or disease in this day; the belief of such a law is annulled now and forever.

This law of God to this day is a law of perfect Mind, perfect consciousness to infinite creation. It is a law of understanding to every Christian Scientist--a law of completeness and harmonious comprehension of Christian Science to all mankind.

It is a law of correct statement, a law of divine understanding, a law of progress, of aspiration and inspiration to every Christian Scientist, and to all mankind.

Miscellaneous

At any time, if we make a mistake and do not detect it as a mistake, and we are shown it is a mistake and are rebuked for it, this is taking sides with error. But if, when error is uncovered to us, we see our mistake, accept the rebuke, and condemn the error in ourselves or to someone else, then we are governed by the Truth, and rise and have overcome error, and become more spiritually-minded. We have gained a step in Christian Science.

You will be condemned until you refuse to see condemnation.

When teaching the Bible and Science and Health, those who talk little if any between the lines of the latter teach it. The effect of my writings is often diluted and sometimes lost by attempting to explain them. It is the seed which once sown springs up, and if seemingly obscure at first, it makes its way in the soil of thought, upward, and though least understood it bears the biggest results of all books--like the seed which when sown is least and the biggest in bearing, that Jesus spoke of.

There is no sin, and consequently no sinner in Science. True, there is not; but of two evils this is the least when working out the problem of suppositional error: to condemn sin as a claim in order to destroy this false claim. To condemn it, you must see its claim, acknowledge and loathe it. This action of mortal mind brings the next step, that you have hated the claims of error and evil, and thus obtained some victory over them.

It is good to be afflicted, to drink in the experience by which we are made meet for the Master's crown. Love is in itself a purifier, and if we reach its glorious behests, we must be purified in the process.

It is good to be afflicted, when the results prove its uses.

May the gentle presence of divine Love so reward your lives that you shall so rise in faith and understanding as never to doubt or dread in a single conflict with evil. God, the divine Love that is your Life will govern it. Take courage and trust in this Love with all your heart, and because of this childlike faith good will deliver you from the sense of evil and the evil of material sense, and establish your way in Truth and rightness.

God blesses and rewards prayer for the divine Principle cooperates with the mind that is divinely inspired--in other words, that thinks aright. "Seek and ye shall find." "Ask and it shall be given you."

People are not our enemies. The arch-enemy is self--self-will, self-pity, self-justification, self-righteousness and all the numerous names for self. Self-pity is the most insidious enemy and disturbing element, caused by seeing injustice. Sensitiveness is the exaggerated sense of selfishness.

We learn in Science food neither helps nor harms man; admitting its power in one direction, we must in another. Man's life is Soul that eats not to live, and immortal man is the idea of Soul instead of sense.

There are no clouds to hide God's face and there is nothing that can come between the light and us--it is divine Love's weather.

Personality

Personal sense is the strong man that the Truth of being binds before destroying error. It being impossible to heal on the Principle of Science, and admit the grounds taken by personal sense--bind the strong man, hold sense in subjection to Soul, and pain as much under control of mind as temptation to sin; then you can despoil his goods, i.e. prevent sin and suffering.

There is no personality. There is no mortal mind to embody itself and call that embodiment by my name, and hold over it the laws of limitations. God is Mind; I have the sense of that Mind and I have no mortal mind to look for pain or pleasure, health or sickness. There is no person or persons that have control over us. God governs. There is no mortal mind, or man, or personality that can think through me to read my thoughts, nor change, influence, beguile, bewilder, or darken my consciousness. It is impossible for darkness to destroy light. Nothing that the divine Mind created can be perverted, reversed, relapsed or changed. The infinite light forever protects its ideas in the substance of Soul. Man was never educated to believe in, or rely on, false theology or materia medica to heal and save him. Man relies entirely on the Principle of being for health, supply and happiness.

The human sense of Love narrows itself down to a human concept of person and shuts out others. That is not love. Really we do not love a person, it is good we love. This true sense of love brings freedom and an enlarged sense of things.

Don't get personal. Don't talk about any person. You may talk about things. Impersonalization of thought is what the cause now demands.

Handle M.M.P. impersonally as impersonal error. One cannot handle M.M.P. as personality--that means resentment. Never connect the name of a person with M.M.P. Mortal mind has no malpractitioner; handle M.A.M. from morning until night.

A treatment against M.M.P. must never have a person in the treatment. The treatment therefore denies the primary claim of mortal mind as existing, and the following claims of law, power, action and objective. Handle the worst form on the principle that the greater includes the lesser. Succeed by letting it be unknown what your moves are to be. Just take long enough to recognize [all these forms of error]. Rise high enough to designate the thought involved.

Mind is the only refuge, the only salvation. The five personal senses do not recognize matter because they are mindless. The fact that the five personal senses have no intelligence denies all the claims of...matter. Matter is a lie about something, i.e. no-thing. The human body is not something, but is a false belief about something. The work of Christian Science is transformation. "Be ye transformed by the renewing of your mind."

~ ~ ~ ~ ~ ~ ~

[From The Seed, said to be inspired by Mrs. Eddy]: Personality is another plant unknown to God, and this must be uprooted. The physical Jesus of Nazareth was but a manifestation of personal sense--a plant which the Father had not planted, and it was destroyed by the Christ. Jesus ever sought by word and works to detract from himself as person, and to point to the Father as the Principle of being. He knew that the physical expression was but an emanation of mortal thought and itself nothing, as was proved by the Ascension, when it disappeared. All personality must recede before the onward march of Truth--this is the law of Spirit.

Jesus rent the veil of matter from the top to the bottom--from the highest conception of the mortal thought even to the lowest. He thus showed that there is no personal God--there is no personal Jesus--there is no personal Founder of Christian Science--there is no personal self; all is Mind. When this spiritual consciousness is reached, we shall indeed be bathed in the light of the Holy of Holies, the supremacy of Spirit.

Man is not somebody or some thing; man is not person; man is a condition of consciousness. Man is a Soul thought. True thoughts constitute the individuality of man. What are these thoughts about? Are they about personality or are they about God?

Don't give life to evil by attaching it to personality or thing. Evil cannot live without body. Error exists only as a belief outside the infinite. We live, move, and have our being in Infinity. Until personal sense is doubted it will never be controlled.

Evil however will always come to you *as* a person, place, or thing. When it is M.M.P. it will always come through its "person." If you cannot take up personality without making it real to yourself, and without harming the individual, leave this out, be sure. This ability belongs alone to spirituality. No human, mortal, or material sense, can enter into it or it prevents the good results, both to the sinner and to the sinned against.

Place, Time, Power

First of all, we must know that Principle and not man does the placing. Paul says that, "For in Him we live and move and have our being." This knowing that man, God's idea, is already in his right place, does the healing work, for that places us in Mind, right now, and therefore his need is already supplied by divine Love. Dwelling in this consciousness we bring into human experience that which we need, whether it be a home or any other good thing, because this state of consciousness excludes every wrong thought, such as mortal verdicts of overcrowded conditions, no good places, fear, indecision, lack, etc., and renders them null and void, and then the facts of being come to light and are manifested in more harmonious experiences. Having cast your net on the right side, you will find your need supplied. Just refuse to accept any man-made verdicts as your own opinion or thinking.

Know that all your thoughts come from divine Mind, and the true thoughts dispel all evil beliefs about place, etc., and their seeming effects go with them. It is right for you to be with your own kind of people, and trusting Him with all your heart will open the right place. There is no place for failure where God is, and He is right with you, every minute. Remember, "Mind has infinite resources", so do not limit yourself in any way.

Know that nothing can hinder or obstruct for an instant the perfect and complete manifestation of God's plan for you here and now.

You cannot enter eternity until you have broken the law or sense of time.

All the past there is to us is own present consciousness of it. According to your steadfastness in excluding evil from thought after you have once unmasked it, do you deal with it scientifically and according to this same steadfastness are you blessed.

No Christian Scientist can be ill this day or die this day, or any day. There is no time in which a Christian Scientist can ever be ill or die.

A Christian Scientist is not in time; he manifests eternity, and his present sense of Life is not involved in time, nor limited, nor circumscribed by any belief of time. His present sense of life is spiritual, indestructible, ever progressive, infinite, immortal, and he cannot be made to believe otherwise, or to manifest any other sense of life.

The Mind that is Truth is silent in its workings; but the power of the living God is with it. Power lies not in noise.

Divine Truth ever appears as our Life. The command to heal the sick comes with that ability and power.

Jesus in his first miracle filled the water pots, thus showing that we must fulfill every manifestation of purity in human consciousness.

I need every moment to know that God, good, is the only Mind, the only intelligence, and the source of wisdom and power--therefore, no other claim to power or mind can rule me, or be manifested in my life or conduct.

The belief in a power opposed to God must be withstood, denounced and denied and must be, shall be, overcome. A suppositional mind to do evil seems to work, but God is true and God works out the purposes of good only and continually. Therefore man, the offspring of God, who is divine Mind, ever active and operative, expresses action also in the grooves of God.

"In Him we live, etc." In Him there is no inaction, overaction, etc. therefore no such supposition can be entertained by man.

The divine Mind supplies all wisdom, all the power, all the opportunity for erring man, and prompts every man to the right action at the right moment, so there is no conflict of interests, no possibility of failure, no discord of any sort. Evil minds have no power to reject, deny, oppose or defy God--no power to stop the work of Christian Science. There is a spiritual reversal for every argument of evil, and to declare it agrees with our adversary quickly.

Be watchful and demonstrate that Truth and Love can and do triumph over every obstacle that confronts us, and vanquish every temptation that assails us. In this critical time we must draw nearer to God and prove Him to be an everpresent help in time of trouble.

Have no fear of [the argument of] mortal mind; it has no power over us. We have full confidence in divine Mind and it is All; there is none other.

Poisons

Vegetable and mineral poisons are the duplicate of animal poisons. Animal poison is a perversion of the love of mortals which is the counterfeit of Love as God.

Inflammation of the lungs is an argument of hydrochloric acid.

Skin eruptions are the expressions of the poison of malice and hate, and they have followed every war, being especially awful after the Spanish-American war against a

Catholic country that was the expression of Roman hatred and curse. These superstitious beliefs in witchcraft use the 28th chapter of Deuteronomy as their guide to work, not the blessings but the curses.

Skin may be likened to a panoply of Love (S&H 571). It is the covering between the inward workings (organs of the body) and the outside influences called material universe, air, universal mortal belief.

As the skin protects the body, so Christ, Truth, the panoply of Love, protects man. "Clad in the panoply of Love human hatred cannot reach you." So skin is especially blessed as the protective agency of Mind governs all its actions and secretions.

Catholicism believes itself to be the blessing of God, and Protestantism the curse. Reverse this and be well.

Begin your treatment with the Allness of God, then handle ordinary material laws, materia medica and theology laws, mental laws, malpractice laws, including relapse, collapse, relaxation and reversal. Handle all poisons, quadruple poison. Surround the claim quickly, then leave the patient to God.

Know: You cannot absorb or secrete any of the poisons: revenge or personal friendship poison, poison of ingratitude, false attraction, disloyalty, cruelty, vanity, misunderstanding, curiosity, treachery, obstinacy, intellect, apathy, procrastination, indecision, sociology, mental stagnation. No thought against you or your patient can do any harm as you are to realize that there is One Mind and that Mind governs and controls. Then stand, for there are not minds many, but One, and you have understanding enough to carry anyone through a belief of mortal mind.

Evil, disease or poison cannot be poured into our thought when we are asleep, to be brought out in action when we are awake.

Man being God's image and nature and expression cannot absorb, secrete, or accumulate any mental poison--mental poison is a mental atmosphere of conflicting human opinions and beliefs. Electricity has no power to send poison through the pneumogastric nerve to cause gas or fermentation. Poison has no active principle, no modus operandi, no chemical effect or consequence.

Poisons: Tin, lead, coppers, mercurial, morphine, opium, morbific residue, electrical, mental (hate), original sin, educated malpractice, vital magnetism, obsession or possession, revery, pride, doubt, fear, apathy, ingratiude, indolence, inertia, instability, lust, egotism, cruelty, vanity, revenge, treachery, obstinacy, indecision, disloyalty, disobedience.

~ ~ ~ ~ ~ ~ ~

[From a letter to Dr. Foster Eddy as quoted in the New York World, Oct.21, '07]: The mental malpractitioners or mesmerists employ arguments of poison to kill people. They cause you or your patients to suffer from arsenical poisons in the blood or stomach, mercurial poison, morphine, or any other form of mineral, vegetable or animal poison which they may name in their arguments. If your patient's symptoms puzzle you and you have tried the ordinary arguments and what is better, the power of Spirit to heal them, but without success, then treat your patient against the effects of this malicious argument, knowing as you ought, that God made all, and that it was good, hence there is no poison and your patient does not suffer from it at all and is not poisoned, also that hatred, envy, and malice, have no power to harm and are not harming your patient, for God has all power and God is Love, etc.

Reproduction and Sex

There are no duplicates in infinity, as this would limit infinity. The one child is born--is created.

The restoration of the lost Israel is the restoring of the spiritual sense of being as perceived by the patriarchs and as exemplified by Jesus. If Jesus had not announced that his mission was to destroy the works of birth and had not said, Blessed are the wombs that never bare and blessed are the paps that never gave suck, he would not have aroused the fear of the high priests. They said: "If we let this man go on teaching this doctrine, soon all men will believe on him; then what will happen to our race? It is better that one man perish than that the whole nation die."

Belief of material creation must fall, never to rise--never did rise! Christ is risen. Lust has no eyes, no ears--no power to hinder sight. Destroy lust in universal thought. Handle fear, regret, remorse, shame, disgust--this is self-abuse. Repentance is the remedy and step.

Know: There is nothing in my thought to respond to evil, or afford it an opening through which to enter my consciousness; for I banish all claims of hatred, malice, revenge, greed, sensuality, lust, pride, personal ambition, limitation, fear, hypnotic human will.

Mental malpractice cannot circulate through pecularities of disposition or through constitutional tendencies so-called, nor can it work as a belief of temperament, nor through impulsiveness or romantic or other feeling, nor through sentiment, nor through longings or yearnings or any other human belief.

If we cling to all the pleasures of earth we surely should fail of Heaven here, heaven within us.

Love reflected in love destroys lust. If you loved person you would have the result of it. To destroy any desire, destroy the belief that man can or ever did create. See the false nothingness of the false presentation of Mind.

"Our Father-Mother" wipes out material birth, sexuality and sexual organs--enabling the obedient son to speak with authority to disease. Birth is the understanding that God is Life, giving strength and action which is perfect and harmonious. There is no material man or woman. There is no sex. Mortal man is a dream. There are no material or female or generative organs--no material conception. Animal magnetism does not think. For claims of suppression overcome the belief that there are any male or female organs, or female desire, or claims called vicarious menstruation.

Unity of Principle and idea is the only marriage. Mortal thought is misconception. Principle only is the omnipresent action. The only Principle is instantaneous in its action and acts without friction and with ease. We can always know when this divine Mind is acting through us because of this law. No discord, no friction, no uneasiness, no fear, no apprehension accompanies this Mind, and there is no other action or actor.

After the Babylonish woman [the "great whore" of Rev. xvii:1] fell, the true sense of Socialism appeared--man's unity with God, therefore at one with fellow man. Human resistance to this divine idea causes the conflict. Government is unity and cooperation in society. The Babylonish woman is the illegitimate sense of power and government, a false sense of human power, just greed and oppression. The Bride (Lamb's wife) is the true, loving, pure, just sense of power and divine government.

[Letter to Helen A. Nixon, in addition to those recorded in Six Days pp.387-93]: The time has come when no woman should have the monthly manifestation of sexuality. I never had it after my discovery of Christian Science in 1866. But to maintain this menstrual error, and then violate the marriage vow will produce the effect of straining out gnats and swallowing camels. Have your mind right and the body in accord with it and then one can reflect the divine Love that will help the husband to accord with pure thought and increase the love and happiness of wedlock. Do not stir this subject until you have done your part as aforenamed.

~ ~ ~ ~ ~ ~ ~

Articles for children are usually written from the point of view that Truth must be simplified to be understood by them--by their limited and undeveloped minds. It should be realized that infancy is a belief of animal magnetism, and when you destroy this belief about the child he will be able to understand Truth in its entirety. So, simplifying the Truth for the child only shows that you accept as a real state of being, the appearance of the lack of maturity. If you handle this error, the child will be elevated to where he will be able to comprehend.

Give children the truth at home, and then let them go. Home is a power. "Going home" is being right. Our one Father-Mother is caring for His children everywhere.

Man calls his body me, and that body is just what his parents first made, and he secondly has made; yet these parents were not matter but mind, as the body proves--the body that is no longer the parent if mind has departed.

Do you love your neighbors' children as your own? If you desire other children to have what you want for your own, your own children will be more apt to have all that is good.

Is man a creator? (No.) Then is he a father of children? (No.) Can he be the father of a lie? (No.) Is the lie a father? (No.) Then is there any lie?

~ ~ ~ ~ ~ ~ ~

[A student's recollection of comments by Mrs. Eddy on "Man and Woman" {EOF p.44}]: The woman (as qualities) includes man, but man does not include woman--the climax (woman) includes all that has gone before, and the feminine qualities come last. The feminine qualities were not clear until Mrs. Eddy brought the motherhood of God. When a man expresses his womanhood he is expressing God, and when a woman expresses her manhood and womanhood she is expressing God. Each individual must be BOTH the male and female for God is FATHER-MOTHER. Mrs. Eddy called it the Mother Church, not the Father Church. The Mother Church was brought forth in great opposition--it was a subjective experience.

["Man and Woman" was written after a lecturer's visit to Mrs. Eddy described by Calvin Frye in his diary as follows: "Judge Clarkson dined with Mrs. Eddy today and after dinner tried to convince her again that she was mistaken and the cause was going to ruin and the men were essential to take the lead of the cause of C.S. and to assert their rights without her dictation. He declared that he and she must come together."]

Sanity

[The argument pretends that if] you say there is no mortal mind, you have no mind for you are not God; also [that if] you say there is no matter, you have no body--and thus you have annihilated yourself!

When you declare "There is only one Mind", you lose your mind if you do not add "and this Mind is my Mind."

Insanity, or moral dementia, is not healed by defending your patient from other people whom you may think are malpractising upon your patient. This state of mind is induced by no one else but the patient's own idiosyncracy, and the patient should not be treated as if it were [induced by some-one else]. It is a constitutional belief, and is liable to be developed by circumstances which bring into action the latent elements or characteristics of the patient. [Refers to a case of insanity said to have been caused by malpractice on the part of students of a certain teacher {see July CSJ '95}].

Nobody but yourself can destroy a belief of yours.

In a case of insanity you argue mentally and verbally against a belief that brains are diseased, the same as in other cases of physical disorders, for all physical inharmonies proceed from mental causes.

Insanity is but another form of mental error.

As you think, you travel; as you love, you attract. You are today where your thoughts have brought you. You will be tomorrow where your thoughts take you. You cannot escape the result of your thoughts, but you can endure and learn, can accept and be glad.

You will realize the vision (not the idle wish) of your heart be it base or beautiful, or a mixture of both, for you will always gravitate towards that which you secretly most love. Into your heart will be placed the exact result of your thoughts; you will receive that which you earn, no more, no less. Whatever your present environment may be, you will fall, remain, or rise with your thoughts, your vision, your ideal. You will become as small as your controlling desire; as great as your dominant aspiration.

Destroy all that error would suggest to prevent your realization of the tranquility of Spirit rather than the turbulence of error. Know: I cannot be mentally confused. God is not the God of confusion. The law of the Spirit of Truth in Christian Science has made me free from the law of mesmerism. I will do as God directs not as man.

<u>Sleep</u>

You do not have to sleep. Mind is always active. Cessation of thought is not what is needed, but the ever-presence of Mind. You rest in God who does not sleep. You need no sleep. Realize this, and the fear that you will not sleep will disappear, and you will sleep.

If you fully believed that Love is all you could have no apathy, for Love is ever-active. It neither slumbers nor sleeps, but is at work all the time and watching.

We must come to see that we do not depend on eating, sleeping, and so forth, for life and health, but we depend on Mind. The spiritual cannot be touched.

There is but one appetite and this is governed by God. Man eats, sleeps, walks and talks harmoniously. There is but one food and one digestion. Truth does the work and there is no delay. Error cannot take away our judgment and make us guilty of the sin of human reason.

I do not depend on the action of the bowels or stomach, eyes to see, ears to hear, and sleep to rest. This knowing will rest me more than sleep.

In order to give up sleep, as in order to give up any other sensual pleasure, a man must be convinced of the unreality of matter, so that he may recognize that that which he is giving up is not a harmless phase of material existence, but rather a phase the harmlessness of which has hitherto been veiled. There is no harmless phase of material existence.

Supply

God is the Principle and Life of all His ideas. Since He is therefore the only source of all that constitutes a "living" man's living is made; God has made it and man is dependent only on God for it.

We are able to recognize that this Principle must be Love because the Principle which sustains and maintains all can include in itself no element of oppositeness. Principle must manifest Love in all its activities. This maintaining power is Infinite Wisdom, and is Omnipotence, and this supply can never fail nor be diminished else God would cease to be God.

Ideas cannot accumulate in one place and be absent from another, for there is no place where the Law of God is inoperative; there can be no such concept as lack in the consciousness of man.

It is sin for us to limit ourselves in any way, for Mind possesses infinite resources with which to bestow on us its infinite abundance, whether it be any what is termed worldly goods, money, understanding to heal, power to heal, intelligence to act and accomplish, or what not.

The very fact that these resources are everpresent shows us that we are with them. They are a part of us and we therefore exist at the standpoint of opportunity to make them manifest; so do not be surprised if you find silver in the fish's mouth--indeed, don't let Love surprise you, but be so open and receptive to it, that you cannot help receiving what it has for you.

We are the creations of our own thoughts. The altitude of our thought is the magnitude of our God. God is infinite. Therefore there need be no limits to any supply that we can widen our souls to receive.

We demonstrate Life, Truth, and Love and <u>they</u> give us our supplies; we do not demonstrate material things.

God is law; you are obedience. God is answer; you are prayer. God is supply; you are demand.

God is abundance. God supplies only abundance. Malicious mental malpractice cannot rob me of this abundance. It cannot impoverish me spiritually, mentally or financially. A demonstration of this is an abundance of light, Truth, intelligence and all material needs. All is God--Good--All is Mind.

Mortal mind cannot embrace me in the claim of poverty, in the claim of matter or fear--all this is mesmerism and cannot embrace me in it. What a glorious inheritance is ours through the understanding of omnipotent Love. We cannot want to have a more sweet assurance than this: "Peace, be still." (See Mis.307:5.)

~ ~ ~ ~ ~ ~ ~

Sad, sad thought that money regulates the actions of so many students. Had your Leader been governed thus, Christian Science would have been minus today, instead of overcoming all opposition, ruling and reigning.... I have worked for all without money or price till God paid me in His own way. It is safe to go and do likewise. I left house, home and friends, and I gave up a large salary, as a writer, in order to serve the Cause of Christian Science. I have endured all shame and blame in its behalf, and I have lived these down. This is the experience of your Leader.

Are her followers willing to take up their crosses, as she has taken up hers, in order to follow Christ, or do they demand all that they humanly want?

My income is the incoming of right ideas. It comes instantly, constantly, continually day and night. It is my God being. We do not work for money to come through personality.

Divine Love increases and blesses our supply. Whatever is mine, is mine now; nothing can come between me and my perfect supply--neither time nor space. Supply is therefore here and now. There is nothing that can take it away from me, for there is but one power, all harmonious, beautiful. It is possible for us to do everything that it is right to do.

God cannot be impoverished; man cannot be impoverished. I know poverty is an error that Truth destroys.

There is no illusion of poverty. God made all, owns all there is, and it is good. I am joint-heir with Christ, in God, and have my share of everything. I am exempt from want, loss, lack or limitation of any kind. There is no material resistance that can limit me. "The Lord is my Shepherd, I shall not want."

Abundance cannot lapse into lack, since God is my fountain source of infinite riches and plenty. I can and do demonstrate the wealth which comes from God with no interruption in its flow. I am prosperous and successful, kept so by an inexhaustible supply. Animal magnetism cannot touch me with a claim of poverty in any way in myself, nor in anyone, for Spirit is my unlimited source of supply.

<u>Treatments and "Patients"</u>

How many Christian Scientists give treatments as though they knew that Mind really heals the sick?

The real thing is the presence of Mind and the realization that there is no other presence.

Know there is one Mind and that this one Mind governs you and your patients. Know that no ignorant or malicious malpractice can interfere with you or your patients. Know that your treatment, the word of Truth, is with power.

Treat yourself before you treat your patients.

The world is mentally and morally paralyzed to the Truth of being and this must be handled in every case. Our treatment must be universal as well as individual.

Sometimes when you do not get any results from your treatment, declare: This treatment is God with us, this treatment is the very essence, presence and power and activity of infinite and perfect God; it does its work because it is God with us, and it does wipe out, blot out, obliterate and reduce to its native nothingness any mortal belief in a power apart from God. God is the only power, God is the only Life. There is no law of reversal. M.M.P. cannot make a law to reverse this treatment, or cause it to do anything that it is not intended to do. There is no such law. The great safety is to treat the impersonality of error (in Science) and keep the claim out of thought.

Remember that a treatment is "Peace, be still." We must not fight--otherwise there will be something to fight back.

Treat impersonally from the standpoint of man's perfection and always destroy sin if it is the case. Good is man's nature--kind, gentle, etc., qualities of good, attraction to the good. All claims must be handled separately.

Deny also the power of malpractice claiming to act as hatred, envy, jealousy, malice, revenge, anger, fear, etc., the claim of old discordant beliefs, the claim of reversal. Treatment cannot be reversed. The belief in a law of reversal is canceled by C.S. because Christian Science is a treatment which proceeds from the divine Mind.

Put physical ailments in the mental. Know they are the results of fear, anger, envy, hate or some wrong thought; and we do not fear the physical. Just ask for more light and goodness. That the action of Truth can produce fear, painful chemicalization, confusion or aggregation of symptoms is a lie, and is only an evil belief, for God is all and the only action of Truth is in the production of harmony.

We should anticipate error, otherwise error will get the advantage of us. How shall the Christian Scientist guard himself in advance?

Ask yourself what mortal mind would do to prevent Truth's appearing in the project about to be undertaken, and then destroy the belief in its power to do anything. Know scientifically, not in a general way, that there is no M.M.P. to affect your patient or yourself.

You must do this because there is a claim of law that says these things can affect you and your patients. Declare and know that M.M.P. cannot reach the patient through you--through your belief, etc.--and that fear cannot touch you.

Know that animal magnetism cannot use malice as a channel to affect man, for there is nothing in man to see any such condition. Man is the reflection of God and never was touched by evil. Know that ecclesiastical thought can do nothing but destroy itself; it is a self-destroying error and can see nothing in me but its own belief of a lie--it never saw man.

There is in reality no patient, no transference of thought. There is only the reflection of God. Your treatment is the Word of God. It cannot return void. It is all power, for God is omnipotent. The omnipotence of God means the omnipotence of Good. Whose Good? YOUR GOOD. It is your good and has all power. The treatment of the Christian Scientist must know enough to know it is all-power. How much power has the treatment? All the power there is.

M.A.M. cannot make a law that will close the avenues of Love to me. It cannot make a law that I cannot heal; that I will have no patients, and no success in God's work.

Realize for yourself that there is nothing but God and harmony. We must go to the "patient" strong in that understanding and if they do not respond, we must seek for the error that holds, find where the lie is, and expose and destroy it. Since rebuke and compassion are one, know that compassion antidotes.

Thank God that we have all that is to be desired. Only accept and demand the best for everyone. Say to your patient and make him say, "God is Life." Acknowledge God in all thy ways.

Don't give patients into other hands for that is acknowledging your neighbor as better than yourself--while God said to hold him as yourself. Purify yourself. Your patient gets more benefit from your purification than you yourself get.

Treat against drugs and applications, against animal magnetism. Treat as long as the Spirit saith. Garrison your own household, don't leave it unprotected, for when error is in your own thoughts you cannot drive it from your patients' thoughts. Clear out and watch your own thoughts. Matter cannot destroy Spirit. When you go to a patient feel that God is there. There is no mind to create a fear or hold a fear, for there is but one Mind. If we do not heal morally, we are the worst kind of sinners.

You do not have to wait for your patient to tell you what to meet. You should see it and meet it.

You must get rid of the "old man", the old woman; you cannot make them better and keep them. You are not getting rid of the old man if you try to make him better.... The resurrective sense is positive; it....does not listen compromisingly to error. It is *always* about its "Father's business"--reflecting Principle.

HISTORY AND THE DEATHLESS DEAD

-- Letter to First Church of Christ, Scientist, Charleston, S.C. [dated July 16, '02 and signed "With love, Mother, Mary Baker G. Eddy"]:

Beloved Brethren: It is impossible for pen to portray the depth of tears, love and joy this dear church gave me, when I read the narration in our Journal [Vol.XX, No.4] of that grand, successful search for the records of St. Andrew's Lodge, of which my late husband, Col. George W. Glover, was a master in Charleston, South Carolina. Not all the utterances of love and reverence from those who knew him, nor the reticence of storied pile, could say as much for the dear departed as your persistent, faithful search for those few sacred words. They stir the soul of a Free Mason, and fill this heart of mine with memories saintlier for their years.

The effacing mold, the noiseless steps of time, touch not our deathless dead whose works survive to tell of the past. My love for the South and its noble sons and daughters is ever allied to the memory of my early loved and lost. May the presence and power of Truth and Love rest in holy benediction on this dear Church, and peace, prosperity and unity hallow its inner sanctuary.

-- Letter to Edward Everett Norwood [dated Aug.1, '02 and signed "With love, Mother, Mary Baker G. Eddy"]:

Beloved Student: Pen cannot express my thanks for your fidelity and defence of our Cause in the dark South. My late husband, George W. Glover, was born in Boston, Mass., if living, his sister, Charlotte Glover, now Mrs. Shute, resides in Quincy, Mass.

I understand that he went to the South when quite young. He was an architect of the rarest kind and a builder. At the time of his attack of yellow fever he had a contract for a cathedral in Haiti for a large sum of money. His title might have come either from the Governor of the State of South Carolina, given because of his being a member of his staff, or he may have belonged to the State militia. I cannot say as to that, but I know it was military. Before I left the South I gave some of his military equipment, an elegantly decorated coat and a fine sword to one of his many friends. I cannot now recollect who it was.

He was in Wilmington, North Carolina, on business (where he had taken me with him) when attacked with the 'yellow jack' as 'twas called. I never attempted to remove his remains to the North. I was not allowed to take them to his home in Charleston, South Carolina, on account of the fear of the contagion. The dear Masons did all that could be done for him. They conducted the funeral with music and a large procession. I never knew where his body was allowed to be laid.

Let this tragic history of my dear departed drop now. His character and reputation stood high--it is above the enemy's aim and above all need of further research. I kept for many years his diploma as Royal Arch, etc., but cannot find it now. I shall keep the sacred evidence of his standing in Masonry that you have forwarded to me in grateful memory of your noble, persistent search after them. I have in my Scrap Book a leaf taken from the Masonic Magazine in 1844 containing the date of his death and a tender obituary. (See also pp.49-51.)

-- Letter to E.E. Norwood [dated Dec.21, '03 and signed "Sincerely yours, Mary B.G. Eddy"]:

You will accept from me a small sum [$500] in payment for your expensive search for the items regarding my loved and lost husband. I can never pay you but in gratitude what I feel in the remembrance thereof, and for your noble grand discharge of the divine duties of a Free Mason.

-- Earlier letter to Frances J. King and Edward E. Norwood [dated Aug.21, '96 and signed "With love, Mother, Mary Baker Eddy"]:

My dear Children: You will pardon this delay when I tell you I had on hand what God called me to do before giving me a moment to pleasure. Accept my thanks for the pretty cotton branches. You cannot know how they touch my heart with tender tones. I have seen them for the first time since I looked on them with my loved one who has gone to the realm of the departed.

Oh, may the Father of all bless you, heal you, mind and body, make you white as the cotton blossoms, bud, blossom, and fruit all on one branch of being; even that vine of which our Father is the husbandman.

-- Letter of thanks to E.E. Norwood for other services rendered [dated Dec.1, '06 and signed "Lovingly, gratefully yours, Mary Baker Eddy"]:

Words are weak to express my gratitude for your strict demonstration and success in conveyance; also, your fidelity in all I entrusted to you. I was not mistaken in my man if I were in some men. My prayer is for all that learn through suffering, and for all who learn by enjoying, to enter into the rest of rightness; for every experience human is met, compensated or punished by divine Love. Dear one, learn with me to have but one God, and know of no other Mind, for this will bring peace and spare us the sorrow and agony that so-called mortal mind has in store. One Mind, and loving others as we would be loved is the panacea for all our wrongs, trouble and strife. I hope sometime to reward you for your dear heart and your helping hand in my behalf.

Give my love to Mrs Norwood.

~ ~ ~ ~ ~ ~ ~

-- Recollections of instruction by Mrs. Eddy Oct.25, '09:

...when we can waken ourselves out of the belief that all must die we will then be able to bring back all that death claimed to have taken away from us. In other words we will be able to reproduce the presence of those who thought they had died, whether it was ten minutes ago or ten years ago. However, when that time comes death will not appear to us what it now seems to be, and it is hard to predict even in the light of Science just how things will appear to us under changed conditions.

In S&H p.72 the author is trying to explain the impossibility of evil being communicated from the departed to mortals, and incidentally remarks that good may come to us in this way. Thought on the other side of the grave is not different from thought on this side. Edward Kimball is not dead and has not stopped his Christian Science work. In fact he knows that he has not died, and he still teaches and holds association meetings. Good therefore may flow from him to his students through the efficacy of enlightened thought. That evil can flow from the departed to mortals is the false belief. That good may thus flow is the spiritual fact.

[On Aug.21, '09 Mrs. Eddy sealed the package that became Miscellany, but reopened it once, a few days later, to include her latest, glorious, crowning message: "There is No Death" (p.297). Here she immortalized the above sentiments by stating that "Edward A. Kimball...is here now" and that his "clear, correct teaching {still} is an inspiration to the whole field."]

III - PREACHING

~ ~

> There is only one [method of treating disease] which should be presented to the whole world, and that is the Christian Science which Jesus preached and practised. S&H 344:21.
>
> Jesus established his church...on a spiritual foundation of Christ healing. S&H 136:1.
>
> The Jews had agreed already, that if any man did confess that [Jesus] was Christ, he should be put out of the synagogue. John ix:22.

By 1895 Mrs. Eddy had left to the world and the Boston Christian Scientists the complete, spiritual definition of Church and also its visible example on Falmouth Street. The building she called "a prayer in stone"; and just as words of a prayer have no validity without the spirit back of those words, so the edifice of The First Church of Christ, Scientist, in Boston, Mass. has no validity outside of its spiritual thrust. The message is individual and absolute, and is not regulated for persons by persons, except so far as Principle may appear as person, it being understood then that it is Principle speaking through what is called person, and not a person initiating something.

Dr. Alfred Baker has recorded that in response to a question in class about organization Mrs. Eddy said: "The church in Boston should be the center--The Church of Christ, Scientist--all others tributary to it, not separate organizations."

Church as exemplified in Mrs. Eddy's writings is indeed the governing and ruling authority for all churches, in the widest possible sense of the word, just as God's Seven determines the total functioning of all sevens.

In the Church universal and triumphant there is one member, one Christian Scientist, expressed in countless ways. Mrs. Eddy had already shown that this true sense of church or group organization could be advanced by a "dissolution" of the material compact into a "voluntary association of Christians" (Six Days p.321 etc.). Yet she realized that her disorganizational example might be understood and followed only by a reorganization allowing the students themselves to "complete its history", as forecast in *Retrospection and Introspection*, 1st edn.

WHO SHALL DECIDE ON MEMBERSHIP?

A belief that Church is a material organization, lodged precariously among thousands of differing material organizations, immediately invites the problem of determining qualifications for membership. Which external human minds are acceptable within the church confines, and which internal human minds are capable of discerning that acceptability?

When Mrs. Eddy saw that persons were expected and expecting to assume authority over the quality and thinking of church members, and over outlying churches of Christ, Scientist, she was compelled to write the "laws of limitation" known as the Church Manual. These laws, or guidelines for behavior, began to appear early in 1895, and in book form gained on September 11 their first of ten copyrights.

Among the first essential rules or by-laws was Mrs. Eddy's demand that "This Church shall have no leader but its Pastor--The Bible and Science and Health", i.e. no leader but individual interpretation of the divinely inspired Word. Another essential requirement was: "One member of this Church shall not be guided by another. One good member is no more than another good member to this Church."

She also encouraged the democratic concept of rotation in office, by immediately limiting the term for the church president to "one consecutive year, and once in three years."

Yet it is interesting to note that until 1902 a reader's term was not confined to the present three years; and even in 1906, after branch churches had adopted the new practice of The Mother Church, Mrs. Eddy agreed to let John Lathrop read beyond three years in Second Church, New York City (see letters in CSS Vol.VIII, No.24). This shows that the developing purpose of the Manual is to draw attention to its Principle or Spirit, exemplified by "Rotation in Office", rather than to make arbitrary decisions for blind slaves to the letter.

At first the office of first reader in branch churches was virtually reserved in perpetuum for the local teacher, until they chose to follow the 1902 by-law. It is evident that a three-year limit saves endless argument on how best to apply the democracy and rotation principles, even if it encourages the false security of obedience without understanding.

According to Mrs. Eddy's original rule in 1895, Judge Hanna was to remain Reader "as long as he is acceptable" (Six Days, p.523). Later (August 1896) she proposed a limit of five years for the readers (almost immediately reduced to three years). A limit on reappointments followed in 1902 with a by-law stipulating that the Directors elect the readers and president annually, with eligibility limited to but once in three years. An exception was then made for the readers, extending their term of office to an absolute total of three consecutive years, and no more. Thus, after many years in office, with but a single break in 1895 to allow Dr. Foster Eddy to read, as explained later, Judge Hanna was finally replaced by Prof. Hermann Hering, the First Reader for the three years from 1902 to 1905--his election having by now become subject to approval by the Pastor Emeritus.

IMMEDIATE PROBLEMS AND CONFLICTS

Elsewhere in the closing pages of Six Days (pp.522-5) are many references to the problems that quickly arose after the students were ushered into the fulfillment of Mrs. Eddy's church illustration--at least as it became viewed through the eyes of personal sense.

Even though Mrs. Eddy's Church is ruled wholly by divine Principle, the individual's response to this spiritual ideal may bring apparent conflict. His response to the Principle could be mistaken, or there could be a need, or an attempt, of another individual to claim to be the Principle.

If Principle appears as person unfolding its divine plan all individual thought can be blessed. If however the person thinks he can usurp the role of Principle to his own ends the individual has the lie of ecclesiastical control to handle according to his best understanding of what the Principle really is.

The Manual at first gave widespread right to individuals (the "First Members") to make their own decisions as to what Principle is. They could even have outvoted the Pastor Emeritus on the fundamental identification of the Pastor. The more that personal opinions rather than subservience to Principle threatened to determine their acts, the more it became necessary to emphasize the absolute authority of Principle, of the Word or Pastor of all that Church is.

To this end the Manual became both less and more democratic. That is to say, those in charge became less free to act out beliefs in an unchecked personal authority; and branch churches and individuals seeking a personalized authority were required wholly to turn to Principle (Art.XXIII, Sect.1). As far as the Directors of The Mother Church were concerned, they were able less and less to make personal determinations, being required more and more to accept the absolute authority of Principle voiced through the Pastor Emeritus. When the Pastor Emeritus was withdrawn as a materially visible guide, their control (direct as well as indirect) ceased under the 29 "estoppel" clauses in the Manual, for they returned to their limited legal status under their 1892 deed of trust (and as reaffirmed in 1903).

~ ~ ~ ~ ~ ~ ~

Evidence follows of how Mrs. Eddy in the early days required the First Members to do their own work about acceptance of members.

-- Letter to The First Church of Christ, Scientist, Boston [dated Feb.12, '95 and signed "Affectionately yours, Mary Baker Eddy"]:

> My Beloved Students: I cannot conscientiously lend my counsel to direct your action on receiving or dismissing candidates [see Mis.146 for full text].

-- Letter to the First Members and Clerk of the Mother Church [dated March 13, '95 and signed "M.B. Eddy"]:

> If you have not a rule or a By-law already that defines your position as to receiving or rejecting those who left this Church, draw one up. Call a meeting and adopt it, then publish this rule or By-law through the

> C.S. Journal. I have myriads to answer on these subjects and cannot do it because it is not my duty but it is yours.

The First Members thereupon drew up a by-law which was passed at their quarterly meeting April 6 as follows:

> Individuals who have heretofore been members of this Church, or were members of the Church of Christ, Scientist, organized in 1879 by Reverend Mary Baker Eddy, but have either voluntarily withdrawn, or were expelled therefrom,--may be received into this Church on one year's probation, provided they are willing and anxious to live according to its requirements, and make application for membership according to its By-laws and Rules. If at the expiration of said one year, they are found worthy, they shall be received into full membership, but if not worthy their applications shall be void.

On the question of worthiness, the First Members naturally had great difficulty in deciding, either unanimously or by majority vote in a quorum fixed at seven, who was or was not worthy, or who could be passed as loyal to Mrs. Eddy's teachings. More and more Mrs. Eddy began to word the by-laws herself and to reserve the right to make decisions from her own observations.

Over the next few months the following by-laws dealing with membership were passed on Mrs. Eddy's recommendation or instruction:

1) Applicants for membership with the Mother Church who have studied Christian Science with Rev. Mary Baker Eddy, and who are loyal to its teachings, need no invitation or indorsement, and will use the first form of application.

2) If an individual on probation or a member of this Church is found to be unworthy of this Church's membership and another member in good standing shall, from Christian motives, make this evident, and the offence shall include what is prohibited and specified in [the] Church Rules, a meeting of this Church shall be called and the name of that probationary member or member of this Church shall be dropped forever from the list of membership. [This became Art.VI, Sect.3, which was amended as shown below.]

3) A complaint...if said member belongs to no branch church, and if the complaint is not for mental malpractice, shall be laid before the Board.

4) A member of the Mother Church who is professionally teaching or healing, but is disobeying the Church rule, or the C.S.A. By-law relating thereto, as published in the Christian Science Journal of April 1895, shall be dropped from Church membership.

The major offence that the by-laws aimed to eliminate was of course mental malpractice, first by identifying and uncovering it, second by handling it as having no mind to give it credence--thus annihilating it.

Also, in line with a wish for emphasis on reformation rather than on penalizing, Mrs. Eddy sent the following letter [dated Dec.3, 1895 and signed "With love, Mother, Mary Baker Eddy"]:

> My beloved Brethren: You have already reaped the good result of executing the stern By-law in Article VI, Sec.III. It has relieved you of a large portion of the plottings and machinations to destroy the <u>unity</u> of your church. But I foresee the danger of a future possible misuse and abuse of the uncompromising By-law, which I would have you avoid. Therefore I have asked the clerk to call a special meeting at which you will reconsider your vote on the By-law, and vote to amend it by striking out...the word "forever."
>
> I am led to request this, that we may never knowingly deprive a single mortal of a single hope that may be an incentive to his reformation; or involve at present a precedent for settling the question of mental malpractice.

The same problems were confronting the Christian Scientist Association, whose membership was confined to those taught by Mrs. Eddy but where iniquities were occurring. To the C.S.A. Mrs. Eddy sent a proposed by-law with the following covering letter:

> As a Mother in Israel seeking the good of all, tenderly as lovingly, I recommend the following Rule and By-law for the purpose of advancing my students,

and encouraging and justly dealing with theirs. Thus practically maintaining the doctrines of our denomination and Christ's golden rule, "As ye would that others do to you, do ye."

[The by-law, which was duly adopted, read]: If a member of the C.S.A. claims to be teaching Christian Science, but is found either disobeying the rule of the Mother Church, or the Christian Science By-law published in the Christian Science Journal of April, 1895, it shall be the duty of the Christian Scientist Association at a meeting of this Association to demand of this member compliance with these rules. And if this member refuses or neglects to comply with either of them, his or her name shall be dropped from this Association.

THE VITAL ROLE OF THE MANUAL

The Mother Church Manual is the masterpiece of this Seventh Day, and Mrs. Eddy could say of it: "I never had a Church until I had the Manual. I wrote the Manual as I did Science and Health. I study Science and Health [and therefore the Manual] constantly."

To John Lathrop and others she said: "Every By-law in the Manual is inspired. I did not write them any more than I wrote Science and Health. Teach your students, patients, and everyone, to be loyal to the By-laws, and they will be blessed."

Just as Science and Health is the written exponent of the Science of Christianity, so the Manual is the written example of the spiritual Law of all Reflection or Relationship. A written Manual has the same kind of connection with Universal Law as a physical Jesus does with Christ, or a personal sense of Mrs. Eddy with the immortal Woman of the Apocalypse, or the paper and ink of Science and Health with the Little Book that is written in heaven.

The Principle that produces the Manual is the same Principle that covers all activity whether it be associated with what is called church and religion or not.

In Mrs. Eddy's own words: "This Church Manual is the law of God, and it is as much God's law as the Ten Commandments and the Sermon on the Mount, and I mean to keep it so, and the time is coming when it will be acknowledged as Law by law, I mean the laws of our State."

FALLING "INTO THE GROUND"

Individual church, just like individual man, is strikingly covered by Jesus' statement recorded in John xii:24-5:

> "Except a corn of wheat fall into the ground and die, it abideth alone: but if it die, it bringeth forth much fruit. He that loveth his life shall lose it."

Translated into terms that cover church, he could have said: "Unless a church is grounded in the one and only Church, it will struggle along on its own, falsely believing it can generate life for itself. Yet the one and only Life is identified exclusively with the one Church. A well-grounded example of Church will alone bring forth unlimited fruit of activity. A material example on its own without resting in its Principle, is dead, powerless, futile. To love and cherish the effect without recognizing cause loses both cause and effect".

Jesus' statement is of course as true of human knowledge as it is of church ritual, as Mrs. Eddy makes known in Ret.10:11, where she says: "After my discovery of Christian Science, most of the knowledge I had gleaned from schoolbooks vanished like a dream." That is, as the Principle of Science or Knowing is gained, the separate illustrations fall into the ground and die (i.e. surrender their belief in an independent life) in order to honor the Principle which is Love, and extend it to everything seen and known.

In S&H 66:13 the lesson is given in these words: "Spiritual development germinates not from seed sown in the soil of material hopes, but <u>when these decay</u>, Love propagates anew the higher joys of Spirit, which have no taint of earth." Jesus also said (John xvi:7): "It is expedient for you that I <u>go away</u>." (Emphasis added in both cases.)

The message is that if a branch church should seem to fold, it is either because it was not grounded in The Church of Christ, Scientist (which is universal and unlocalized) or because it already is seeing all its surroundings as Church.

CLUBS AND SOCIETIES

The development of thought about peace societies and the regulating function of the Church Manual is shown by the excerpts given in "Mary Baker Eddy's Published Writings" for July 1907. Here CSS Vol.IX, No.48 quotes a letter from Mrs. Eddy to the Second Editor of the periodicals requesting that he "obtain a large number of Christian Scientists to become members of the American Peace Society." Nine months later she formulated a by-law which withdrew permission to "form [or join] outside organizations...except those specified in the Church Manual" where the American Peace Society is not mentioned as such! This same by-law remains in her final Manual with little word change, and another current by-law stipulates that the "wide channels of The Mother Church [furnish] dutiful and sufficient occupation for all its members" (see Art.VIII, Sects.15,16). Why the apparent shift?

When it is clear that "church" is any and every "institution which affords proof of its utility and is found elevating the race" and that the Principle governing the Manual is the same one and only Principle of all idea, members of that "church" do not divide His work into religious zeal on the one hand and secular worthiness on the other. All work is the conscious reflection of the One Principle, and the Manual's examples are of temporary value unless they take the individual to the Principle which provides them.

In this Seventh Day Mrs. Eddy is telling her followers to "take God...into every detail" even as she told members of her household that she herself had been learning more and more to do. In effect she is saying that the only way students have any right to appear to be "joining" something is with the understanding that they already belong, since there is no activity outside the activity that is their God's and which they reflect.

To the student who complained about all the material work she had (when she thought she deserved more time to "get down to her books"), Mrs. Eddy said, "I did not know there was any material work." In Christian Science there is no activity which is not governed by Principle.

If "eternity awaits our Church Manual", is Art.VIII, Sect.26 defying eternity when it forbids a member of The Mother Church to "haunt Mrs. Eddy's drive", no such drive having taken place since December 1, 1910? Or does the member have to wait until Mrs. Eddy returns in eternity, so that he can show his loyalty and worthiness by avoiding certain streets in Chestnut Hill during the early afternoon?

Eternity comes to the Manual as the everlasting Principle which dictated its rules is seen as the All-in-all. Then the member of Mrs. Eddy's Church needs no reminder that he must not "haunt her drive"; for he never looks for transference of good from one person to another person, but derives his good continually from the one Good which alone is the cause of every effect. This is knowing no Leader but the Pastor which is S&H and the Bible, and no guidance of "one member of this Church... by another."

~ ~ ~ ~ ~ ~ ~

Despite its insistence that a member's attachment to human organizations, however praiseworthy, come under the Spirit of the Manual, it should be remembered that the Manual does not put any ecclesiastical restriction on the formation of C.S. Societies, which have to be simply in consonance with the Manual to be what their name implies. C.S. social "clubs", which in fact begin with a localized distinction between "me" and "thee", are however barred as the following letters show:

-- Extract from Letter from C.A. Frye to William B. Johnson [dated July 13, '99]:

> Mother requests that Article I, Section 5 [of the By-law sent yesterday] be amended by inserting after the word, trustees, the words, "nor syndicates." She says the students had better mingle with other people than form syndicates, but better still would it be for them if they would keep apart from all worldly schemes and work with God.

-- Extract from Letter from Mrs. Eddy to Edward A. Kimball [dated Nov.7, '03]:

> One should not plan outside of what is in his church Manual.

-- Letters from Mrs. Eddy to Laura and John Lathrop [with reference to their C.S. Club in New York City]:

1) [dated April 21, '04]: You know not what you do, were the merciful words of our great Master. If I were not thus tender, I should not write to you, who have taken this perilous step without consulting your teacher and Leader! Did you read in the Sentinel what Russell Conwell D.D. of Philadelphia said of organizations separate from the church? If you go into clubs you go out of the church in spirit, and God will show you this. It will be a severe lesson this time if you do not heed my warning and M.A.M. has lured you into this membership of a club, just as it drew you into that act.

God save you both. You can teach and heal and form churches; is not this enough? Yes it is, and waken in time to see it.

2) [dated April 22, '04]: All true Christian Scientists adopt two textbooks, the Bible and Science and Health--and one code, the Manual of *the Mother Church. Therefore they are aware that not one of these books furnish a precedent or rule for a Christian Science club!

You address me as your beloved Leader, but you have not consulted me as to forming such a club! Also the spirit of our Church rules is based on our textbooks, the Bible and Science and Health, but nowhere in either are you bidden to form such an organization. But, per contra, you are forbidden to do thus. For example, Paul says, "Be ye not unequally yoked together with unbelievers."

On page 451 you read in Science and Health [1904 edition]: "Christian learners must live under the constant pressure of the apostolic command to come out from the material world and be separate. They must renounce the pride of power", etc. I do not assert the unfitness of each member of this organization to be a member of *the Mother Church, and hope in his worthiness; but I do declare that this church consents to no organizations being formed that are not specified in its Manual. Such has ever been the spirit of its By-laws, and has now become one of them.

---

*As noted elsewhere, "the" Mother Church was in general use until about 1904.

My heart holds nothing but loving thoughts and a high hope for each member of your club--while I admonish each and all to dissolve this organization, that is opposite to the rule of the Mother Church, inasmuch as I know that by so doing they will advance more rapidly in the paths of His testimony and the footsteps of His flock. Christian Scientists already have on hand weekly and semi-weekly meetings, Students' Associations, Teachers' General Associations, churches, public reading, lecturing, teaching and practising Christian Science. Are they individually and severally doing their duty in these departments? If so, then they have no time to spend in other directions.

~ ~ ~ ~ ~ ~ ~

Just as the Manual represents the Principle governing all church, all "institution", so Pastor Emeritus represents the Pastor or Word governing The Church of Christ, Scientist, as a universal whole. A book outlining "laws of limitation" that must fall into the ground and die could glorify a Pastor Emeritus which must likewise fall into the ground, i.e. which must re-emphasize its identification with the ordained Word, or impersonal Pastor, of The Church of Christ, Scientist. Hence the wonder and inevitability of what are now known as the "estoppel" clauses of the Manual (i.e. those that cannot function without approval or consent of the Pastor Emeritus and must therefore "fall into the ground and die" in order to "bring forth much fruit").

The re-identification of Pastor Emeritus with the universal Pastor removes the "laws of limitation" that had to be written into a printed Manual (i.e. into a physical example of the everlasting Manual or Law of God) so long as it was believed that "idea" may usurp the initiative of "principle". The "death" of the Pastor Emeritus (i.e. this proper grounding in Principle) was the "death" or elimination of control by persons belonging to an ecclesiastical hierarchy, and the correct appearance of the one divine control everywhere.

The inference here is not that churches lose their own "truly democratic and liberal government" in some kind of general anarchy but that priestcraft gives way to individual acceptance of what the majority finds "nearest right under the circumstances" and to "rotation in office" (see My. 361:21 and Mis.288:13).

By 1911, "The First Church of Christ, Scientist, in Boston" under its original deed of incorporation was left with no right to divide Church into a ruling church--and wayward churches needing ecclesiastical control. The date which thought may affix to this grand event is immaterial.

UNLOCALIZED TRUTH

Some of Mrs. Eddy's observations or instructions about Church, the Manual and the correct definition of preaching, follow:

Truth, Life, and Love are formidable wherever thought, felt or spoken or written: in the pulpit, in the courtroom, by the wayside, or in our houses. They are victors, never the vanquished.

Our cause is immortal. It rests on nothing temporal. It is the cause and effect of all that really exists.

There are many members of my church who should not be, and some time there will be a sifting in my church.

[1901] There is need of a revival of religion in our ranks. O for more Christliness, more meekness, more truth among us. O for the Golden Rule to actuate our everyday life.

[An 1896 By-law by Mrs. Eddy]: Any member who cannot nor will not live in Christian fellowship with another member who is in good and regular standing with this Church,--shall either withdraw from Church membership, or he shall be excommunicated.

It is the duty of any member to complain to the Church of another member who does not live up to the above named requirement; and it shall be the duty of the Church to enforce this By-law. [This By-law made it possible to uncover the subversive activities of Mrs. Woodbury and her students, as unfolded later in this chapter.]

[In answer to Joseph Mann who asked Mrs. Eddy why he felt error more in Boston than elsewhere]: What is it that personalizes or localizes--Truth or error? Error, because error locates Truth [explained as meaning "confines Truth to a location"].

[The conclusion Mr. Mann came to was: "It is a very human headquarters. Headquarters is in Boston, and yet it is not there. If we are really Christian Scientists and want to be merciful to the Bostonians, we won't locate Truth, that is, we shall not be guilty of the error which locates Truth."]

[1900] There is no darkness, no mental depression, no failure in God's Cause. You are to take up for the [Mother Church] Directors daily, Mind is All: Do not name them by name [leading to the worker's conclusion: "i.e. do not localize them!"]

[1901] Keep apart from the Sunday students in our midst who trample His divine word under foot all week [i.e. localize Church] and expect forgiveness on the Sabbath.

[1902] Take for your one unworthy patient the Mother Church of Christian Science which needs healing from its sins this day.

[Undated] Often I sent out an angel (a new By-law) and it would come back bruised and bleeding, and I would have to take it in and cherish it until the field was ready for it. [Many of the constant modifications of by-laws were aired in the periodicals, and can therefore be found, as they arose, in the text of "Mary Baker Eddy's Published Writings." Also, the step-by-step development is carefully outlined in Alice Orgain's "Story of The Mother Church Manual."]

[1904] The Mother Church is founded on [i.e. grounded in!] Truth and cannot be removed nor taken down. Weary in days of trial but freshened in His service [Mrs. Eddy] waits till all unworthy ones come neath the shadow of His wing.

The reluctance of mortal mind to "fall into the ground and die", that is to admit that matter has no life or intelligence of its own, and that All is Mind, appeared to this mortal mind as immense resistance to the by-laws grounded in Principle. When some action in Boston or elsewhere involved a specific disregard of Principle, and a rule became necessary to demand attention to the particular principle involved, mortal mind saw the rectification process as turmoil. This mortal mind then saw God's representative, or Pastor Emeritus, in painful battle with its wishes for its own glorification.

-- Letter to Christian Science Board of Directors [dated Feb.27, '03 and signed "With love as ever, Mary Baker G. Eddy"]:

Beloved Students: I am not a lawyer, and do not sufficiently comprehend the legal trend of the copy you enclosed to me to suggest any changes therein. Upon one point however I feel competent to advise namely: Never abandon the By-laws nor the denominational government of The Mother Church. If I am not personally with you, the Word of God, and my instructions in the By-laws have led you hitherto and will remain to guide you safely on, and the teachings of St. Paul are as useful today as when they were first written. The present and future prosperity of the cause of Christian Science is largely due to the By-laws and government of "The First Church of Christ, Scientist" in Boston. None but myself can know, as I know, the importance of the combined sentiment of this Church remaining steadfast in supporting the present By-laws. Each of these many By-laws has met and mastered or forestalled some contingency, some imminent peril, and will continue to do so. Its By-laws have preserved the sweet unity of this large church, that has perhaps the most members and combined influence of any other church in our country. Many times a single By-law has cost me long nights of prayer and struggle, but it has won the victory over some sin and saved the walls of Zion from being torn down by disloyal students. We have proven that "in unity there is strength."

N.B. [signed "M.B.E."]: I request that you put this letter upon our church records.

Adam Dickey, who served in Mrs. Eddy's household 1908-10, deals with this struggle phenomenon in his "Memoirs of Mary Baker Eddy" pp.45-8. In effect he wrote that inattention to the Principle would appear as pain and grief to the Pastor Emeritus, and that as soon as the by-law was formulated which redefined the Principle, mortal mind was outmaneuvered and harmony immediately re-established.

Other workers have recorded that there were some nights when the whole Eddy household was in turmoil, and their efforts to handle the appearance of a sorely suffering Pastor Emeritus were utterly ineffective. When the truth of the situation was seen and the remedy put into words as a by-law, morning would break with the household exhausted. But Mrs. Eddy was up and at her desk as though nothing had happened to give her a grievous and sleepless night! To the Pastor of The Church of Christ, Scientist, there was no change, and the Pastor Emeritus had simply been acknowledged as voicing this Pastor, yet as able "of mine own self to do nothing."

Calvin Frye recorded many such nights in his diary, and one entry for 1909, probably Aug.3, reads: "Intense pain last night--she requested an M.D. to administer an hyperdermic [sic]", followed by "Mother heard an audible voice from God saying: 'Leave alone successor contention before it is meddled with'."

Parts of the Frye Diary were in shorthand, and the word "successor" is unclear. But it is generally accepted as a correct rendition, and this seems likely. The biggest threat to mortal mind's claim to have a right to usurp the church authority of divine Mind lay in those by-laws giving ultimate jurisdiction to the Pastor Emeritus. In its need, therefore, for suitable changes in the Manual, this mortal mind used fear in the field and among the Mother Church Directors--fear that, at Mrs. Eddy's death, both Church and branches would become untended. The Directors no doubt felt they would be looked to as the obvious successors in authority. Yet mortal mind's attempts to kill the Pastor Emeritus without understanding that in reality the Pastor Emeritus can only merge into the unborn and undying Pastor or Word of God were the great threat to the personal representative, as evidenced by the suffering they seemed, in the unillumined human mind, to cause.

NO ECCLESIASTICAL INTERMEDIARY

None of the above suggests that in reality there is a misguided Board of Directors to be destroyed anymore than there is an unsound Pastor Emeritus to be lost.

According to the instructions in S&H we must begin "by reckoning God as the divine Principle of all that really is." Then who do we reckon are our Pastor and our Directors? They are the one and only Authority, called God, expressed in countless forms, forms which "can of [their] own self do nothing." And what is our Church that God alone is directing? It is everything that Principle unfolds to us as His compound idea "including all right ideas."

The Church of Christ, Scientist, established by the deed of trust in 1892 gave no supervisory position to someone called Mrs. Eddy or to any personal successor; hence the apparent overlapping of a Board designed to be guided by God alone and a board operating between 1892 and 1911 and needing guidance by Mrs. Eddy towards the goal of being divinely guided!

There were many early instances where Mrs. Eddy insisted that the church board make up its own mind, i.e. demonstrate the one Mind or Pastor for itself; and others where she had to operate for the time being as this one Mind or Pastor, and force or even override the board. On the other hand, when she saw a move by the board which was in line with Principle, she was ready to applaud it.

The following letters from Mrs. Eddy to the Board of Directors give instances where she implied that the final decision remained with the Board:

1) [dated April 9, '95 and signed "Mother": Beloved Board of Directors: "Is it lawful to do good on the Sabbath day?" Yes. Selling doves--is to slander or gossip in God's house. Selling Quarterlies and S. & H. is to give or sell and take money for the Word of God--and the workman is worthy of his hire. You have my hearty thanks for doing the latter.

N.B. [signed "Mary Baker Eddy"]: I suppose the C.B. Directors [sic] are aware that they own legally the Mother Church in Boston, where the church owns it beneficially.

2) [dated July 2, '95 and signed "With love, Mother, Mary Baker Eddy"]: Dear Brethren: I have received a letter from one of your number in reference to collecting pew rents. I think your honorable body abundantly able to adjust this matter on business principles without any advice from me. [Pew rents were soon discontinued.]

3) [dated Sept.4, '95 and signed "With love, Mother, M.B. Eddy"]: My beloved Students: I want to say this morning that the suit you have at law you alone had better decide as to its continuance and the result. I am not willing to decide those matters. I can only say in the words of Jesus, "If they sue you at law &c."

To avoid those necessities would be my mode of procedure, but as matters now stand, I beg that you four Directors will act your own judgment in carrying out your lawsuit, or compromising.

What I said to Mr. Bates I really did not mean, if it meant a lawsuit. I meant to settle it but not unjustly. I beg that you will not consult me on such matters again. You as well as I have a God to direct you. Perhaps my more spiritual thought cannot be carried out in such matters at present, wisely.

4) [to Mr. I.O. Knapp, dated Sept.29, '95 and signed "With love, Mother, M.B.E."]: My dear Student: Under the circumstances perhaps you had better take the key of the Mother's Room into your care, but you must decide this matter. Mrs. Laura E. Sargent will be in Boston soon. Nothing would please her more than to care for my Room, but you must pay enough for this to remunerate her for the time spent.

I would let the local children contribute for flower fund for one day per week, but drop fund for keeping the lamp aflame. I had no idea you were running into debt for flowers.

5) [dated Oct.8, '95 and signed "With love, Mother, Mary Baker Eddy"]: My dear Board of Directors: Mr. Chase [treasurer and member of the Board] is a precious Christian Scientist, he is my student, and I see no cause for auditing his accounts. But if a fight is waged because of my confidence in him, you have the By-laws of our church, and the church not I, must settle this question.

6) [dated Oct.29, '95 and signed "With love, Mother, Mary Baker Eddy"]: Beloved Students: I have sent Mrs. Sargent to Boston and given her directions to obtain the key that I sent to Mrs. Munroe of Mother's Room and remain subject to your orders. I ask that the salary of the one who has charge of this room be not less than $500 annually and it be paid monthly.

Also I have selected Mrs. Sargent to take charge of this room if such be the mind of this honorable body.

~ ~ ~ ~ ~ ~ ~

In an attempt to shift responsibility for church decisions from herself to some select body, Mrs. Eddy set up an Executive Committee which did not last long, as the following letters show.

-- Letter to First Members [dated July 1, '95 and signed "With love, Mother, Mary Baker Eddy"]:

My dear Students and First Members of the Church: The reports from the field show that the purpose for which I designed to have the Executive Com. elected, is not carried out; and is not understood by those applying to this Committee to investigate their charges against any member of this Church; thus opening a gap through which misled minds can rush in their blind opinions and perhaps uncharitable conceptions of any member, and the Church be kept constantly judging one another, which is contrary to Scripture.

I therefore request that this Committee be dissolved at this quarterly meeting of the Church.

-- Dictated Letter to W.B. Johnson [dated July 4, '95 and signed "Yours truly, M.B. Eddy, C.A.F{rye}"]:

My dear Student: Please put the following into my request to dissolve Committee which I sent, namely, that what the Committee has done is admirable, but the purpose for which the Committee has been used was not what I designed as its legitimate function.

In our meeting at Concord I said distinctly "Form a committee called an Executive Committee whose duty it shall be to see that the Church Rules are carried out."

Please add the above, to my letter under N.B.

-- Letter to Wm.B. Johnson [dated July 5, '95, signed "With love, Mother" and enclosing the following]:

BY-LAW--The Reader in the church who conducts the other parts of the Sunday services, and the Friday evening meetings, shall examine the candidates for admission to the church.

The above By-law is the one that is not understood.

[The letter itself read]: My dear Student: The above means you shall have no Examining Committee on Candidates, but you must dissolve your Committee. And adopt the above By-law.

~ ~ ~ ~ ~ ~ ~

Whenever Mrs. Eddy saw the need to step in, she did not use half-measures. The requirement that the Church accept no leader but S&H and the Bible, and that all good members be accepted as resting on an equal footing, was written into a by-law designed to be free of any human majority vote. After summoning the 21 First Members to Concord to secure their compliance in this instance she wrote [on May 3, '95 in a letter signed "With love, Your Mother in Israel, Mary Baker Eddy"]:

Beloved Brethren: I ask you to act on this By-law for two reasons viz. (1st.) I cannot be your Leader [into the understanding of what Leader means] unless I have the power to guide you when you need this guidance.

(2nd.) Because I will pray earnestly and watch for God to guide me in knowing that I am right in my decision before entering a complaint against a member of this church. And from long tests I know that He will show me the way that is just and then I will follow it.

Despite her early expectation for autonomy in the Board over the question of admission of members, she took over direction of operations in at least three cases of members whose practices brought them into conflict with the church authorities: Josephine Woodbury; Benjamin Foster Eddy, her adopted son; Augusta Stetson.

At the time of this meeting of First Members in Concord Mrs. Eddy was already in effect "entering a complaint against a member of this church", namely Dr. Foster Eddy! She sent the clerk a statement which he was to read to the First Members back in Boston, also a private letter with more exact details. The open letter read as follows:

> Beloved Students: When a student tells you that I am influenced in my conclusions or work in this field by anyone but God, or when he says I am mistaken in my knowledge of who is attacking me mentally and thus malpractising--know then that this student is disloyal to the core and is not be be trusted.
>
> This I have proven true 30 years.

The cover letter to Wm.B. Johnson [signed "With love, Mother"] stated:

> My dear Clerk: Do not read the following in meeting: Write me at once as soon as the meeting is over the action and what the Dr. said, if anything. He and Mrs. C. are attacking me mentally with apparent intent to kill. This is proven beyond a doubt.

If the malpractice could not be recognized and destroyed, Mrs. Eddy was prepared to see if her adopted son could function better in some different but useful position, even away from Boston, so that the pressure of beliefs in many minds might abate. Similarly she hoped (in vain, as it turned out) to provide reformation for Josephine Woodbury by twice ordering that she be accepted into the healing atmosphere of the church.

As for Mrs. Stetson, Mrs. Eddy was always conscious of and appreciated the wonderful aspects of this pioneer's character. But when Mrs. Stetson failed to let her fine qualities fall into the ground and die, that is, failed to lose her pioneering and mothering sense in a realization that God, not person, is the only Mother and Leader, Mrs. Eddy had to let her start learning her new lesson away from an organized, mothering, or ecclesiastical sense; and had to let the ecclesiastical sense in Boston likewise fall into the ground and die--albeit involuntarily.

The basic attitude of the Pastor Emeritus to church membership for straying students is shown in "Overflowing Thoughts" (Mis.310) and in letters like the following:

1) [To First Members, Jan.21, '96 and signed "With love, Mother"]: ...Call Anna [Osgood]'s case up, notify a meeting as soon as legal, and settle her case. A rebuke should be sufficient. Anna is not an old sinner. Forgiveness and advice; then try her and let her teach her students to avoid her errors.

This will work better than to drop her name now. But I am not the one to influence in this case; the Church must decide it. But do not adjourn the meeting that tries her case until it is decided by vote. Finish up this awful stir; if you do not you will regret it.

[P.S.] Don't wait for Anna to attend the Church meeting. Simply decide her case as I would, if you want to follow my example. There is no rule for having [offending] members present and fighting in my church.

The rule is if you, the First Members, wish to drop her name, do it, and if not, vote to let her go on and see how she does hereafter.

2) [To Julia Field-King, Nov. 11, '96]: You cannot include in your thought personality without a risk. So take none. You injure yourself if you injure another. This is my golden rule: I would no sooner harm Richard Kennedy [an early student whose practice became malpractice] and J.C. Woodbury than you or myself. I would never have consented to have her [finally] dismissed forever or a day from our church had I not known that it was better for her as well as for the church. I did all in my power to help her even when I knew she was trying to injure me.

3) [To the Christian Science Board of Directors, Nov.21, '02]: Relative to the discipline and excommunication of offending members, I have only this to say: Confine yourselves strictly to the By-laws of the Mother Church and be merciful and just according to the Golden Rule. I hope said members can be reformed and retained in our Church.

I close with this emphatic declaration: No members of this Board can consult me on the discipline of members, or the excommunication thereof.

~ ~ ~ ~ ~ ~ ~

The next batch of letters serves to illustrate occasions when Mrs. Eddy's requests to the Board of Directors amounted to demands (including her first "order" that Mrs. Woodbury's application for membership be accepted):

1) [to Wm. B. Johnson, C.S.B., dated April 17, '95 and signed "Lovingly yours, M.B. Eddy"]: My dear Student: I request that you pass out notices at once for a special church meeting and convene as soon as possible. Read this letter to the church and thus give, as Jesus did, a chance for sinners to reform. You take no risks when doing right.

> ["This letter" {dated April 17 and addressed to The First Church of Christ Scientist} read as follows]: My dear Students: Adopt at this meeting a By-law that all members who withdrew from your church or who have been put out of it and thereafter apply to be taken back into it, and are anxious to live according to its requirements, be received on probation for two years. Then if found unworthy, you can deal with them as you think best for our Cause. But I also require you to remember Jesus' words, "Go ye and learn what that meaneth, I will have mercy, and not sacrifice."
>
> You will bring my white hairs into remembrance in years to come, when you remember the unchristian acts that keep me in perpetual broils. I order that after this By-law is passed, you vote to accept the application of Mrs. J.C. Woodbury to join this church.

2) [to Wm.B. Johnson, C.S.B., Clerk of The First Church of Christ, Scientist, Boston, Mass., dated May 3 and signed "Mary Baker Eddy, Per Clara M.S. Shannon"]: The services for the children shall be held once in four months on the second Sunday in the month, as once monthly is too often in order to perpetuate harmony in the general services of the Church.

3) [to the First Members, dated May 14, '95 and headed "Read this in open meeting" and signed "With love as ever, Your afflicted Mother"]: My beloved only in the Lord: How doth my heart wrestle with the angel of the Lord for you all! You are weighed in the balance and who of you are found with doors guarded when the thief cometh?

A man is said to be no stronger than is his very weakest point. What then shall be said if there is in one of you a vulnerable spot to malicious mesmerism so exposed as to admit its influence and rob you of free moral agency? Or one of you in the bonds of iniquity, yet having on the mask that hides your face and the Father's face from you?

I know there are some among you that are not by reason of their sins and lack of truth and love cast out of this vineyard of our God. Oh! let not the senses drown your hearts in the depths of apathy; or sear your consciences with the heat of pride, envy and revenge. God grant that a word to the wise be sufficient. [For a similar and more gently-worded reprimand of church members, see Letters To The Mother Church (Mis.129-32), which appeared first in Nov.CSJ '96.]

4) [to Board of Directors, dated Nov.6, '95 and signed "With love, Mother, M.B. Eddy"]: My dear Directors: Will you have a fire kept in the church day and night to save the moisture affecting the church? It is necessary--for you must look sharply after the iron rust.

5) [to Mr. Clerk, dated Dec.3, '95 and signed "With love, M.B. Eddy"]: My dear Student: Please call even another special church meeting...at once. Read my letter to the church. Then see that my directions are carried out. Hand copy of the By-law to the Editor of our Journal, and request him to publish this By-law in the Jan. number of the Journal....

~ ~ ~ ~ ~ ~ ~

As explained in Six Days, Edward P. Bates was found a place on the Board of Directors in March 1895 after William B. Johnson had volunteered to resign; but there remained resentment against Mr. Bates among other members, probably on account of his display of greater worldly knowledge and general savoir faire. At the same time Dr. Foster Eddy was angling for the position of First Reader and trying to get his mother to arrange it for him.

The opportunity to let false pride run its course came when Mr. Bates tired of the position he found himself in, and wished to leave the board. It was then possible to appoint Judge Hanna to the board and to give his position as First Reader to Dr. Foster Eddy. However, when the latter decided after one Sunday that the task of First Reader was not for him, Judge Hanna was duly reinstated as First Reader and William B. Johnson as a member of the board, as the following letters confirm. Also the expiry of Dr. Foster Eddy's term as president of the church left a slot open for rewarding or reappointing some prominent member like Mr. Bates who would otherwise be out in the cold.

-- Letter to Wm.B. Johnson after he had made it possible for Mr. Bates to be elected to the Board [dated April 8, '95 and signed "I am your loving teacher, Mary Baker Eddy"]:

My dear Student: I thank you deeply for your precious letter. Your action has been grand, well worthy of crowning the office you have so well performed as a Director, and gracefully laying it down. I could not have permitted it had I not seen that you had more on your hands than was best for you. You are faithful in business and now can attend to the details of the Clerk of a large church with more ease and give it more time.

-- Letter to Christian Science Board of Directors following the Bates resignation [dated Sept.9,'95 and signed "With love, Mother, Mary Baker Eddy"]:

My dear Students: I have accepted, after serious consideration, the resignation of Mr. E.P. Bates as a member of your Board, dated Aug.30, 1895. I also recommend that you elect Judge S.J. Hanna to fill the vacancy. Also I recommend that you elect Dr. Foster Eddy for the First Reader of our church.

God bids me fulfill the command in the Sermon of our Master, to all Christians. I ask dear Mr. Bates to give this example to the church and then God will take care of the rest, and the wrath of man will praise Him and the remaining wrath He will restrain.

The vote on the time for offices to expire must first be taken at a special church meeting. I have notified Johnson. Then you can elect as above, and show yourselves followers of Christ's command.

Please say to Mr. Bates that I especially request him to nominate Dr. Foster Eddy for First Reader, and have it voted on, before his resignation is accepted by the Board.

Please let me hear immediately from your Board. "What I do ye know not now but shall know hereafter."

-- Telegrams [dated Sept.30 and Oct.1, '95 and signed "M.B. Eddy"]:

1) To Joseph Armstrong, care Board of Directors: Re-elect the same president.

2) To E.P. Bates: I telegraphed yesterday re-elect Bates. Tell Armstrong to get express letter sent yesterday this noon sure.

-- Letter to clerk [dated Oct.10, '95 and signed "With love, Mary Baker Eddy"]:

My dear Student: First business of your Church meeting is to adopt the enclosed By-laws. Then close the meeting by adjourning to meet in Concord at my house the same day, Oct.13, and afterwards in Boston. Bring all the [First] members but Dr. Foster-Eddy with you; he cannot come.

N.B. I charge you to say nothing of this last till your meeting convenes. If the circumstances admit of any change in this program I will let you know in time.

~ ~ ~ ~ ~ ~ ~

The lesson on the Rest-in-action of the Seventh Day, where "the absolute ideal, man, is no more seen nor comprehended by mortals, than is his infinite Principle, Love" (S&H 520:7) was appearing by reversal as the turmoil resulting from this lack of comprehension by so-called mortal mind. The Manual, which is designed to remind the student that what is not in line with Principle is unprincipled or chaotic, permitted in 1895 the idea of missionaries to go into the outlying parts to set a standard among the churches. The incumbent in Philadelphia had abandoned her job and here was another outreach by which Dr. Foster Eddy might look to Principle and learn to be grounded in Love. Mrs. Eddy was prepared to make use of it, emphasizing the nature of its importance as a stimulant to thought.

-- Letter to C.S. Directors [dated Oct.23, '95 and signed "With love, Mother, Mary Baker Eddy"]:

Beloved Board and Students: I want you to meet to-morrow A.M. and appoint Dr. Foster Eddy the mission-

[ary] to fill immediately the vacancy in Phila. Miss Anna Osgood has left, and it is a most important post to hold and have strongly guarded.

-- Instruction [signed "With love, Mother, M.B. Eddy"]:

Send missionaries to only destitute places, and recall all others sent into other fields, and change the By-law at your next meeting to read thus, so you will not again break an important By-law. Oh when? and how long, Oh Lord!, How long? I cannot carry this church, or in other words, I will not unless the members do better.

N.B. Do not do such an outrage as to appoint a missionary that you do not know well.

PERSIAN RUGS AND CHURCH BELLS

In Pulpit and Press, pp.77-8 and 86-7 there are accounts of the attempts, first by Mr. and Mrs. Bates and later by the Board of Directors, to get Mrs. Eddy to accept the newly-built church edifice in Boston.

The Bates invitation to accept this "testimonial to Truth" was conveyed on a scroll of solid gold. The Directors' invitation came with a facsimile of the cornerstone in granite, plus an inscription in a box of solid gold.

Mr. and Mrs. Bates had little right to issue such an invitation, and Mrs. Eddy did not respond to the call to be present at the church edifice at the time stipulated for formal acceptance. The Directors' legitimate gesture was respectfully declined by letter as given in full in Pul.87:11-28.

Two months later, after Mr. Bates had been put onto the Board, he and the other three directors thought of a different and costly gift for Mrs. Eddy. They used church funds to procure several valuable Persian rugs to adorn Mrs. Eddy's home in Concord. The following letters unfold the saga:

1) [to the {sic} First Church of Christ, Scientist, Boston, dated June 7, '95 and signed "Lovingly yours in Christ, Mary Baker Eddy"]: My beloved Brethren: Your royal gifts to me are such refreshing types of your loyalty to God, your love of Love, and "good will to men",--that I thank you from the depths of a grateful heart.

2) [to My Beloved Church, dated June 8, '95 and signed "And the God of all grace be with you, Mother, M.B. Eddy"]: My beloved Students: Your exquisite addition to the finest manufactures of Persia is safely put in its place in my home, Pleasant View.

I did not dream of the value of these royal rugs until Mrs. Kimball told my household. I estimated the one that hangs in the library at $1000, but was afterwards told it was $300, and next by Mrs. Kimball, $3000! What a price, what a gift, what a type of your estimate of Christian Science, God's gift to you, and my lifelong purchase for you!

Beloved, I can only say I thank you deeply, and may the God who gave all, and most of all his dear Son, also give you the daughter of His appointing by covenant and adoption--to help the sons and daughters of Adam (of which she is one) out of sense into the liberty of Soul. Please sent me nothing more of this earth, but send a token of Heaven as often as you please, viz., love one for another.

3) [to the C.S. Board of Directors, dated Aug.19, '95 and signed "With love, Mother, Mary Baker Eddy"]: My dear Students: To relieve me of some worldly care I ship to you in care of Mr. Moore four of my Persian rugs with this request: Will each of the Directors take one of these rugs to his home, use it, and care for it, and keep it until Mother calls for it? Do not remove the labels.

I shall keep in Concord six of these rugs and send to Commonwealth Ave. four to be taken good care of till I call for them.

~ ~ ~ ~ ~ ~ ~

There were many occasions when Mrs. Eddy did express deep appreciation for gifts, and at one time she used to send lists of Christmas gifts to her for publication in the Journal. Then in 1891 she had a notice inserted in the December CSJ which read: "Do not send me another material Holiday present.... But give me this gift, the knowledge that you have risen above personality, and are giving your good gifts to God."

The gifts continued, however, and in April 1908 she sent the following for publication in the Boston Herald: "Will the dear Christian Scientists accept my thanks for their magnificent gifts, and allow me to say that I am not fond of an abundance of material presents; but I am cheered and blessed when beholding Christian healing, unity among brethren, and love to God and man" (for full text, see My.274:20-8).

The Executive Members (that is, the newly-renamed "First Members" including the four directors who had sent the Persian rugs) presented a loving-cup to Mrs. Eddy on her 82nd birthday. Her "heartfelt acknowledgment" was printed in CSS Vol.VI, No.1 and in the Oct.CSJ '03, but when included in My.347 the final paragraph was changed from the original which said: "While I treasure my LOVING CUP, with all its sweet associations, who shall say that Mrs. Eddy is fond of her cups!"

With the attitude "Maybe I can find something Mrs. Eddy wants and doesn't have", the gift might well be superfluous, but with the attitude "I am making sure my sense of Mrs. Eddy is complete" the gift already has the blessing of Truth and Love.

The following letters give examples of her unlabored thanks:

1) [to Emily Hulin from Mrs. Eddy, dated Sept.24, '95 and signed "Thanks, dear one, <u>thanks</u>."]: Your rug is a complete success. It just suits Mother and I had almost thought that you had done for me a kindness never to be <u>undone</u>. Also you have demonstrated what must be and can be accomplished, even what opens the way to victory over all else. To master sin is much more than to heal the sick in other directions. May Love crown you with "well done, good and faithful." Oh! I thank God that there is some wakening and stir among "the dry bones" all over the field. You set others a good example.

2) [to Augusta Stetson, dated Nov.24, '95 and signed "I am thine, tenderly, truly, Mother"]: Beloved Student: Much thanks and gratitude for your gift of the first Old Testament translation by woman, unless it was Mother Eve's!

I am glad to get the original Hebrew text. I always liked it and now I know why. May such a treat of inspiration, and such a feast of fat things flow into your consciousness today, as has come forth from mine and fed all around me....

3) [to C.S. Directors, dated Dec.15, '95 and signed "With much love, Mother, Mary Baker Eddy"]: ...Accept my deep-felt thanks for your gift of curtains. They are beautiful and I prize them for your kindness and being like the covering at our church.

4) [to Augusta Stetson, dated Feb.8, '01 and signed "With love, Mother, M.B. Eddy"]: My precious Student: ...I never wear my bonnets without gratitude to you for breaking the law that I shall have nothing fit to wear....

5) [to Mr. W. Nicholas Miller, K.C., and Mrs. F.L. Miller {see '01 16:7}]: For your precious gift, Wyclif's translation of the New Testament, I thank you beyond expression. I often decline to receive presents. Last summer I returned shares of mining stock valued at $1,000 each, and other gifts magnificent from afar and near because I had no need of them; and were as grateful for the offer as I could have been for the presents. No so for your dear gift, sacred to the memory of the past, and to you tender thought of the Christian Science textbook with its hallowed meaning, 'knowledge of Salvation.'

~ ~ ~ ~ ~ ~ ~

The purchase of the Persian rugs coincided with arrangements the Directors made to purchase a clock from England which would ring out from the church tower, each quarter of an hour, the famous "Westminster chimes." The local folk were tolerating the church bells used to summon the faithful to church services and meetings by means of hymns, particularly after the bells were properly tuned. But the frequent clanging of the time-telling chimes was considered to be disturbing. Mrs. Eddy decided to have them curtailed or stopped, and sent the following:

-- Telegram to Board of Directors [dated July 26, '95]:
Better stop chimes than cause disturbance by them.

-- Letter to C.S. Board [dated Aug.11, '95 and signed "With love, Mother"]:

My dear Students: I say give up the chimes Westminster, even as all else that does not talk of Heaven on all occasions, and chime for proper occasions, meetings, etc., such as you were calling through chimes before the clock came--hymns suggesting what C.S. is, namely spiritual, and not material in a single suggestion.

~ ~ ~ ~ ~ ~ ~

She also treated the local press to the following accounts in lighter vein of her thoughts on the subject:

-- Letter from Mrs. Eddy to Editor, Boston Herald [dated Aug.15, '95]:

With your permission, and through your columns, to confess my part in the tragi-comedy of the Londonshire, Westminster chimes, would ease my conscience. The Board of Directors [printed without initial capitals in the Herald version], sent this inquiry to me, "Shall we have the Westminster chimes, in our church?" I answered in substance, "If you want them, yes." Now our presidential administration makes it wise and popular to act like unto the London folk. So the Directors [directors], purposing to show their generosity to the public, fell into the ignorant atrocity of calling the costly clock from across the waters to disturb the peace of Boston.

The faint-hearted, and the sensitive auditories, could not stand that sort of Salvation Army heraldry, and the one who keenly sympathizes with such distress was wholly ignorant that she had lent her hand to give unto others "too much of a good thing", but in extenuation of this crime will now say she advised that the soft chimes be let loose but thrice per day.

The question now is "To be, or not to be", that is, would not three lesser doses of sweet sounds sent forth at morning, noon and eventide, instead of disturbing it, serve to rest the tired thought and to soothe the sufferings of the sick and suggest to the heavenly homesick the call to a better land, the welcome of saints and angels, the final bliss of our harvest home?

-- Further letter to Editor, Boston Herald, following his publication of the above:

"O the bells, bells, bells"--Poe. Accept my thanks for giving my suggestions on the Westminster chimes a good outing and airing in your popular daily. There is another side of this question, "To be, or not to be"--namely, Shall our church clock ring on betimes, or shall it be rung entirely out of the question? If its less frequent voice is a relief to the sick, perhaps the latter may find more rest by suppressing it altogether. The sick, sooner than all others, should decide as to the quantum sufficit for their pillow.

St. Paul wrote: "If meat make my brother to offend, I will eat no flesh while the world standeth." Now the good Directors [directors] of our church will certainly concur with the writer in wishing to do likewise in this, as in all Christian endeavors, except, peradventure, the "eating of the flesh."

When the danger ebbs and flows and the less of the bells is the better, it is well to be willing to drop the Westminster chimes and accept the Westminster catechism so far, at least, as its first question extends: "What is the chief end of man?" "To glorify God." This must mean, or include, to return good for evil; "and all things whatsoever ye would that men shall do to you, do ye even so to them."

To this end, be it understood, that the Westminster chimes will be heard no more in the old Bay State. May it rest pacific on the shores of the Atlantic.

~ ~ ~ ~ ~ ~ ~

The climax to the saga of the Rugs and Bells was a letter to the Board of Directors congratulating them on complying with the need to acknowledge a mistake, and continuing with the following metaphysical lesson covering both episodes:

-- Letter to C.S. Board of Directors [dated Aug.18, '95 and signed "With love, Mother, M.B. Eddy"]:

My beloved Students: Your obedience is proving that you will conquer the world, the flesh and evil. "In the world ye shall have tribulation, but be of good cheer; I have overcome the world", said our Master.

Each article of mine to the press had the word, "Directors" with a capital, but each time it appeared with a small letter. Now, I had gotten the press on our side and the M.A.M.'s were waiting and watching to get them back on their side. Your expensive purchase of the clock and its too frequent voice gave them this chance; and it was malicious animal magnetism that caused you to buy it. Now, why did I consent: It was Mary that answered without waiting for God. Oh, the pity! I will watch,--that she does this not again. She did not even know what Westminster chimes were. Had she known, she would have seen at once that it was just what the enemy wanted for the purpose of breaking the thought that she left in the minds of the pressmen as to the [hymn-ringing] chimes from our church. Do you remember it?

Again I must tell you that your royal gift of rugs that are so beautiful, and all of which I so appreciate from my beloved church--was started by the thought, and for the purpose of, Theosophy. Hence, my first feeling when the first ones came to my house was from the right side,--(it was a feeling I do not want them around my home). But I have conquered this feeling and also their motives so far as to have no thought or care about matter or its pros and cons. Still I intend to send them sooner or later to 385 Commonwealth Avenue, Boston.

The moral of my letter is to help you, dear ones. Before you act again, watch and pray that you enter not into their temptation. I am much wiser from what God has taught me, and you certainly will be.

...Note this--and let it save you. The mesmerists carry their points more or less every time, and with all the students, and Mother has to go over the ground and patch up the fissures as best she can. "These things ought not so to be." Their purpose is to disgrace us and squander the Church funds. Note this every time you take one dollar out of this fund.

-- N.B. to letter [dated Oct.8, '95 and signed "M.B.E."]:

...Let the clock be silent till God speaks and tells you when to restore its speech. Let the chemical produced by it subside. Say nothing of what I write. But when the time comes let the clock strike the hour at 7 in the morning, at 12 M, at 6 P.M. NO MORE. When this shall be done I cannot say, but God will tell me when it is right to have it strike again.

[Further N.B., signed "M.B.E."]: I open again this letter to say, Do your mental duty towards the Editor of the Herald and counteract the effect on the press. "These things ought ye to have done and not have left the other undone", are the words of our Master.

-- Letter to C.S. Board of Directors [dated Jan.22, '96 and signed "Lovingly, Mother, M.B. Eddy"]:

My dear Students: I want you to give me your promise in writing signed by the entire Board: That the clock in the church shall not be chimed but three times daily, striking the hour. This is important. It will save future trouble.

-- Further letter [dated Jan.29, '96]:

...if you are willing, I am, to let the clock chime 3 times per day when the clock strikes the hours of seven A.M., 12 M, and 6 P.M.... [They] would sound sweetly and could not disturb anyone.

-- Telegram to Mr. Joseph Armstrong [dated Feb.18, '96]:

Ring the chimes [that is, not the clock] for all good occasions. All hail!

MENTAL MALPRACTICE

The final story of Mrs. Woodbury's brief acceptance into the church is told in CSJ Vol.XIV, No.3, and of Mrs. Eddy's efforts on her behalf in CSJ Vol.XV, No.2. These extracts show that there was a 17-week break in her probationary membership between November 1895 and March 1896. The occasion for this break was a long justification of her behavior which she voiced at a Friday meeting in October 1895, and which was more than the First Members could accept.

In addition to Mrs. Woodbury herself there remained the question of the students who had gone over to Mrs. Woodbury's camp and had even been retaught by her. Technically many of them were and remained members of Mrs. Eddy's C.S.A., and in her article "Overflowing Thoughts" (Mis.310) she had "cordially" invited such to "unite with The Mother Church in Boston." After a couple of years or so, many were weaned from the Woodbury brand of mental science and did join the church.

Yet even if Church might prove to be the salvation of disloyal students, Mrs. Eddy did not want them in her Association in 1895 if they had chosen to follow other paths. She had coached them in the method of handling thought, and now false teaching was inviting them to mass with others to misuse it. Some of her warnings were:

-- Letters to Wm.B. Johnson:

1) [dated March 9, '95]: Handle malpractice but never at the suggestion of any one unite on handling it--unless it comes with my name written by me.

2) [dated May 14, '95 and signed "With love, Mother"]: Yours having important inquiries just read. Yes notify for next meeting of the C.S.A...Mr. Bangs and wife [whom] I put into the C.S.A.--hence until these are expelled they must be notified. But the disloyal students must be expelled.

Those who can show certificates in my handwriting recommending them to become members of the College Association, the C.S.A., are entitled to be notified if loyal and if not vote on their expulsion and allow no person to belong to this Society that cannot show certificates as above named.

N.B. [signed "M.B.E."]: Say not a word of the contents of this letter. Notify the members by mail.

The C.S.A. had dissolved itself Sept.23, '89 as an organized group, and after that date met simply as a "voluntary association of Christians." Its disorganized status had curbed any mass impact it might have had on the running of the reorganized church, and Mrs. Eddy had even canceled its scheduled 1894 reunion.

Nevertheless, in June 1895 she did send an invitation to the members to meet at Pleasant View.

-- Invitation to 180 C.S.A. students [dated June 3, '95]:

> Mrs. Eddy's compliments to the members of her College Association, and will be pleased to receive a call from them at Pleasant View, Concord, N.H., June 6th, 1895 at one o'clock, P.M.

Mrs. Eddy greeted them all by name, although some she had not seen for several years. When it came time for her remarks to them she concentrated on unity, love, healing, and she made no direct mention of mental malpractice.

It was of course imperative that students be aware of malpractice and be ready to handle it scientifically (not simply ignore or condemn it). Yet Mrs. Eddy knew that personal accusations, even when complaints seemed justified, would be extremely difficult to establish if someone chose to challenge them in court. The days had gone when credence was given to anything resembling alleged spells or curses of the evil eye.

At the time not all rules or by-laws governing teaching and associations were given through the openly-published Manual, and the following requirements for the C.S.A. were worded differently when they did finally reach the Manual in some form or other:

1) If it is made known at a meeting of the Christian Scientist Association that a member is mentally malpractising, and thereby knowingly is injuring another member, upon a complaint being entered, it shall be the duty of the members of this Association to immediately expel this guilty member.

2) Careful observation has shown Mrs. Eddy that a student who had been taught by her and afterwards takes lessons of a student, is not benefited, but darkened and deteriorates thereby.

Therefore be it known that for the sake of our Cause, no student of hers can be a member of the Christian Scientist Association, or considered loyal, who from this date, June 5, 1895, shall take lessons with or sit in the class of a student after having been taught in a class by the author of our textbook and the Discoverer and Founder of Christian Science.

3) [As referred to in a letter to Wm.B. Johnson, dated Sept.29, '95 and signed "Yours fraternally, C.A. Frye"]: Mother says she saw and corrected in galley proof a By-law relative to students' students calling anyone Mother except the Founder of Christian Science, unless they were so related by family relation. She does not find it in the Manual. She requested that it be looked up immediately and be placed in the first edition of the Manual, whatever the delay may be.

A further letter gave her unequivocal reason for requiring the Manual by-laws to refer to The Mother Church alone:

-- Letter to Wm.B. Johnson [dated Oct.2, '95 and signed "With love, M.B. Eddy"]:

My dear Student: The By-laws are not for other churches, they are adapted only by the Mother Church and made for that.

You can see for yourself they would not apply to a Church that I was not leading.

THE "BELIEF" OF A LEG

It is not clear what effect, if any, the Woodbury students--and the church's attitude to them--had on the quality of the experience meetings they attended. Nevertheless the terminology in use among testifiers quickly proved to be a stumbling-block for strangers. The clerk and his assistant (Wm.B. and Wm.L. Johnson) undertook to let Mrs. Eddy hear some samples, which she found amusing, apart from the serious implications.

The problem was not new. Words have no meaning outside of the thought conveyed by them, as has been covered in Chap.II where the "Kimball controversy" is examined.

Students in her household recall that she told them to "tell the truth about the lie", and this was thought to mean the need for an accurate rehearsal of all that mortal mind was claiming. Yet there would remain the demand (S&H 447: 20-2) to "realize no reality in it."

In CSS Vol.XII, Nos.43 & 44 can be found an excellent article by its Second Editor (John B. Willis) showing the corrections, or rather elucidations, which Mrs. Eddy insisted that he include in a reprinting. She required "the claims of evil" to be replaced by "the false claims of evil" and "nervousness" by "a belief of nervousness", etc.

Some church members, convinced that it was "error" to mention error, would lower their voices if they had to use the word, and determined to know that there was no material leg, would testify to the healing of damage to a "belief of leg."

Mrs. Eddy therefore commissioned the Johnsons to request some good students to set the pace at these experience meetings by testifying rightly, that is, by reflecting the right spirit back of such words as would be intelligible to the newcomer. Their students then followed the example and improvement was soon obvious.

Yet the individual need to resolve the difficulty of language and meaning remained, as is shown by the answer Mrs. Eddy had to give in CSS Vol.II, No.7 (Oct.'99) to a question about the existence of the material body and the existence of disease in that body. (For her answer see My.217.) It was evident that there could be misunderstanding even among good Scientists over the right use of words when dealing with the body and its functions.

Among the cogent statements they did record about testifying was this advice by Mrs. Eddy: It is a mistake to give your methods in a Wednesday evening meeting, saying "I realized this and that."

INITIATIVE vs. COMPLIANCE

The First Church of Christ, Scientist had been legally identified in 1892 as those worshipers who would serve to promote "the doctrines and practice of Christian Science as taught and explained by Mary Baker G. Eddy...in 'SCIENCE AND HEALTH'." The holding of church services in its building was specifically mentioned as not expected as a permanent requirement [Man.131]. In fact the consequence of premature termination of services had to be legally circumvented when the congregation moved to the Extension. At that time there came the following:

-- Letter to Mrs. Eddy [signed "Lovingly your students, The Christian Science Board of Directors, by William B. Johnson, Secretary"]:

Beloved Leader and Teacher: The enclosed draft of deed is submitted by [Lawyer] Elder for the purpose of releasing the Directors from the necessity of maintaining services, each Sabbath, in the original Mother Church edifice. If this deed is satisfactory will you kindly execute it, then return it so that they can accept it and record it as required.

-- Reply to Mr. Johnson [signed "As ever yours in Christ, Mary B.G. Eddy"]:

Beloved Student: The aforesaid draft of a deed I have read and find it satisfactory.

I will execute it and return it to the Christian Science Board of Directors as soon as I can.

The Deed of Trust had verified that Mrs. Eddy had found a way for worshipers to "have and hold church property without going back to outgrown forms of church organization", even while recognizing the church's possible need "to organize a second time for the completion of its history" (Six Days, p.440 & p.380). Was there evidence of spiritual progress after a couple of years of this terminable "second" organization? And how far was the field benefiting from Mrs. Eddy's presentation of the Seventh Day rest, including full acceptance of what Church is and what it is not and how it must be grounded in Spirit? Let us examine.

She had already warned that "for students to work together is not always to cooperate" (Mis.138:9) and she advised each student to "seek alone the guidance of our common Father". How then was this church activity operating, with its teachers' groups (associations), with four Directors and growing numbers of First Members called to make majority, and even unanimous, decisions?

The "good member" might well demand the right to follow his own initiative and "go to God", quite sure he was therefore doing right. Or he could be guided by someone who he thought was closer to God, including someone called Mrs. Eddy or a director. Or he could unselfishly give way to the views of others, perhaps others of more assertive or dictatorial trend, feeling this was loyalty to the One Mind.

Thus in 1895-6, as at other times in the historical picture, there were:

invaluable people like the early Directors who would set aside initiative in order to seek and follow Mrs. Eddy's guidance--with the paradox that she might truly be wishing them to be in their "closet" listening individually to the One Mind;

those who would follow Mrs. Eddy's instructions, but with the reservation that they must still get satisfied themselves as to the why and wherefore;

those who would follow Mrs. Eddy's instructions only if they had not avoided getting them;

those who would follow some other exalted person while belittling those following a different exalted person, thus continuing the "I am of Paul" complex;

those who thought they could get to God without having to believe God could single out Mrs. Eddy as His voice to this age; and

those who thought they could get to God quite as well as Mrs. Eddy, if not better--particularly on her "off days."

There thus remained plenty of scope for "coelbowing."

~ ~ ~ ~ ~ ~ ~

There were likewise varying views on the purpose of the church organization, and a common view was that the one and only true Church (of Christ, Scientist) must reach out through personal envoys into the places where the Church was not. This meant that pliable persons could then be saved and coaxed into church, while others would have to wait until they were either destroyed or found worthy of the chance of salvation.

The physical smallness of the C.S. organization after seventy years and more has led many earnest thinkers to wonder where are the "millions of unprejudiced minds" spoken of in S&H p.570. Often the bewilderment is accompanied by an identification process of the "foe in ambush" seen at work in other people. Yet Mrs. Eddy's advice and instructions are not directed at "you" the "informer", but at "you" the "listener"; and advisedly so, for "a man's foes are those of his own household" and "what thou seest, that thou beest" (see Hea.8:16). She says: "Listen and be wise."

S&H does not refer to millions of unprejudiced people, but of "minds"--mental illustrations that come flooding in to "you" ready to tell of God's goodness and omnipresence; and "shall we plead for more at the open fount, which is pouring forth more than we accept?" If they are people, they still must be unprejudiced, that is, un-pre-judged. If they are prejudged as being (at least initially) spiritually inferior, politically misinformed, morally deluded, etc. the cold water is being poured on them, rather than being shared with them at the "open fount." With one Church and "you" the one

Church member, Church unfolds itself in its millions of ways daily and hourly.

The illustrations of the previous pages could be summarized as saying:

1) Welcome into Church the "millions of unprejudiced" Mind-illustrations which come flooding in from God, the only Source;

2) Entertain only those thoughts which uphold the true sense of universal Church and its Pastor;

3) When the Pastor issues a call to work for the church, do not assume "you" are right and people in the church are wrong, for the call is to recognize what is wrong in a false sense of Church and thus correct it.

4) A call to work against some designated ecclesiasticism or heresy in any church group is to eliminate the thought of any church other than God's.

THE WOODBURY PHENOMENON CONTINUED

Prejudiced or prejudged thinking by church members in regard to Mrs. Woodbury and Dr. Foster Eddy might well conclude that these persons did not and could not really belong in "my" Church. When Mrs. Eddy tried to make the point that Mrs. Woodbury must be rightly seen as everlastingly under God's Church-law, and they twice went through the motions of letting her in, this does not mean their thinking about her changed. Nor did it when they obediently appointed Foster Eddy to the First Readership, or sent him as missionary to Philadelphia. Unaware of the opportunity its Pastor was giving for demonstrating Church with one universal member, the cloistered thought merely wanted to duck an unpleasant situation rather than heal it. The result was the lack of solution and the appearance of damage to the visible Pastor or Pastor Emeritus.

Dr. Foster Eddy lasted only a few months as missionary, and then retired to Vermont, shorn of his position as a First Member as well as his position in Philadelphia.

Two entries in the Frye Diary illustrate the arguments of animal magnetism that still needed to be handled:

[April 11, '96] Mrs.Eddy told me this morning that Dr. Foster Eddy has gone to Vermont to take her up mentally and she can live through it only by fighting against his mental influence.

She was attacked with suffering on reading Dr. Eddy's letter to her on the 8th last and could get no permanent relief until she wrote the C.S.P[ublishing].So[ciety]. today to reinstate Dr. Eddy on the Bible Lesson Committee.

[Feb.25, '98] Ever since Jan.22 when Mrs. Bates told her about the threat of theosophy...Mrs. Eddy has from that time until now had more dangerous beliefs to contend with which threatened her life in belief.

Today she told Miss Shannon and me that it was not caused by the theosophists but by a concerted effort of Dr. F.E....and Woodbury, and that the story about the theosophists' threat was only a scare sent out to cover [them] from recognition.

The fundamental issue was not met, however, for there ensued the apparent mental liaison between Dr. Foster Eddy and Mrs. Woodbury, and later between him and the "Next Friends" who brought suit against Mrs. Eddy in 1907, hoping to have her declared "non compos mentis", and thus hoping to control her funds.

As for Mrs. Woodbury, besides insisting twice on probationary membership for her, Mrs. Eddy identified the precise ways in which animal magnetism was claiming to use her. She gave careful instructions on how this wrong thinking could be corrected; but Mrs. Woodbury was unable to benefit from the advice and the church members were never able to view her as "one good member."

Her story, including her claim to an immaculate conception, probably to avoid embarrassing explanations, and her uninspired withdrawal from the 1879 organization, are touched on in Six Days (pp.300-1, etc.). Although she acknowledged Mrs. Eddy as her teacher, she felt that her presence in the Normal class of February 1886 had forever established her as a teacher in her own right, and she had even coaxed into her orbit some of Mrs. Eddy's students. By 1894 she found herself watching an imposing church come into being in Boston, comprising a far greater number of students loyal to Mrs. Eddy than she could ever claim for herself.

On the basis that "if you can't defeat them, join them" she tried during 1894 to convince Mrs. Eddy that she wanted to assist in the promotion of the church in every way possible, and that she was sincerely sorry for any misdeeds she may have committed and for any embarrassment she may have brought to the cause of Christian Science.

Once the services in the new church were open to the public she encouraged her students to attend, and they used to arrive in time to take the front seats, apparently with instructions that they use their mental powers to disrupt the services, particularly the Friday experience meetings. The plan of malicious animal magnetism was to wreak confusion rather than earn a reconciliation, the apparent aim being to dominate or aggravate the First Members sufficiently to make them see no way out but to succumb to the extension of membership. Mrs. Woodbury had advertised that until she was granted membership, Mrs. Eddy would be unable to visit the new Mother Church. Mrs. Eddy thereupon decided to satisfy mortal mind that the malpractitioner could make no such law. As already recorded (Six Days, p.525) she paid an extensive visit to the Boston "prayer in stone" on April 1, '95 and spent the night there in Mother's Room.

Yet the "good members" seemed unable to handle the mesmerism, and the Directors hoped that by renting out pews (only to desirable worshipers) they might keep Mrs. Woodbury from trespassing upon the services; but one of her students promptly applied for a pew in her behalf and the Directors then tried to stall by ruling that Mrs. Woodbury would have to apply in person.

Mrs. Eddy showed (letter of July 2, '95) that she was not to be involved with pew rents, but she did see the Woodbury affair as an opportunity for the First Members to stand by what Church is, quite as much as it was a problem for Mrs. Woodbury. Her correspondence with Mrs. Woodbury is given below, also her permission for it to be used in effect to wave in the face of the First Members. As shown by the letter of April 17, '95 to Wm.B. Johnson she did finally demand that the church rise to the occasion and admit Mrs. Woodbury, and she did so again in the following March.

The lesson however was missed which would "agree with thine adversary quickly, whiles thou art in the way with him", and Mrs. Eddy accepted the failure to resolve the Woodbury phenomenon as evidently showing a need to "go thy way for this time" and await "a convenient season."

Mrs. Eddy's letters to Mrs. Woodbury follow:

1) [dated Feb.27, '95 and signed "With love, Mary Baker G. Eddy"]: Dear Student: I have your letter asking my assistance in getting admission to the Church. I have made a rule, which has been published in our Journal that I shall not be consulted on the applications for membership to this church or dismissals from it. The responsibility must rest on the First Members according to the rules of the Church. Hence I return your letter to you and the church.

May the love that must govern you and the church influence you and your motives, is my fervent wish. But remember, dear student, that malicious hypnotism is no excuse for sin. [Mrs. Woodbury had conveniently blamed the external forces of m.a.m. for any "misdeeds" she may have committed.] But God's grace is sufficient to govern our lives and lead us to moral ends.

2) [dated April 8, '95]: Now, dear student, try one year not to tell a single falsehood, or to practise one cheat, or to break the decalogue, and if you do this to the best of your ability at the end of that year God will give you a place in our church as sure as you are fit for it. This I know. Don't return evil for evil, and you will have your reward.

3) [Answering Mrs. Woodbury's request that the correspondence be shown to First Members]: My dear Student: I am willing you should let them read my letter. I forgot to mention this, hence my second line to you. Now mark what I say. This is your last chance, and you will succeed in getting back, and should. But this I warn you, to stop falsifying, and living impurely in thought, in vile schemes, in fraudulent money-getting, etc. I speak plainly even as the need is.

I am not ignorant of your sins, and I am trying to have you in the church for protection from temptations, and to effect your full reformation. Remember that M.A.M., which you say in your letter causes you to sin, is not idle, and will cause you to repeat them, and so turn you again from the church, unless you pray God to keep you from falling into the foul snare. In the consciousness that you and your students are mentally speaking to me, I warn you this is forbidden by a strict rule of the by-laws as well as by conscience.

-- Letters to First Members:

1) [dated Jan.21, '96 and signed "With love, Mother"]: Settle your questions with W[oodbury]'s students at once. It must be done for reasons most important.

2) [dated March 18, '96 and signed "With love, Yours in Christ, Mary Baker Eddy"]: My beloved Brethren: I hereby request that you reconsider your vote on excommunication of Mrs. Josephine C. Woodbury and receive her again into your church.

This Christian forgiveness can do you no harm, and it will help her spiritually, this effort will be worthy of your Christian endeavors and of my sincere hope and inexhaustible charity.

3) [dated April 1, '96 and signed "With love, Mother, Mary Baker Eddy"]: My beloved Students and Brethren: I wish to thank you for indulging my request to give Mrs. Woodbury one more trial on probation. This you have nobly done.

Now, it behooves you as Christians to consider her case at this meeting, and the evidences of her character and present conduct, fairly and finally, and act as it becomes this church, justly.

Since your last acceptance of her on probation, instead of genuine gratitude therefor, she has been circulating letters, wherein the specific charges are against me and our church. But I make no complaint. Now it is requisite for the members to speak out and testify of what they have heard her say and give due evidence that their action today is just and proper.

-- Letter to Wm.B. Johnson, after receiving one from him giving reasons why First Members had finally turned Mrs. Woodbury out of church forever [dated April 29, '96 and signed "With love, Mother"]:

My dear Student: I have no chance to return this record of crimes except via express. God will settle her account and I have nothing to do with it. How prosperous our cause is, truly we have great cause for rejoicing. Oh, that God will save her in His own way.

~ ~ ~ ~ ~ ~ ~

Failing to get any further mediation from Mrs. Eddy after her second excommunication in April 1896 (just 11 days after reinstatement) Mrs. Woodbury started to hold Sunday services called "Christian Science worship" at a hall on Huntington Avenue, a few hundred yards from The Mother Church.

Her activities had gone beyond the alienation of some of Mrs. Eddy's students. For example, among those she was cultivating were Col. Sabin of the Washington News-Letter and Rev. J.H. Wiggin who had been employed by Mrs. Eddy to help with the editing and precise wording of the original editions of S&H. Mr. Wiggin had composed the extensive index to S&H 16th edition and acted as editor of the CSJ in its early days. (See My.317-24.)

He now agreed to conduct a Bible study meeting for Mrs. Woodbury in her Huntington Avenue hall; and when Mrs. Woodbury published a volume of poems in 1897, he wrote a long and flowery critique emphasizing his respect for the authoress particularly in view of the persecution to which she had been subjected. He obviously was referring to her skirmish with The Mother Church. As a result Mrs. Eddy felt unable to ask him to be "proofreader for my book 'Miscellaneous Writings'" (My.318:4) that year, but she did write a tactful note to him warning him of too much association with the discredited Josephine Woodbury, as shown by the batch of letters given lower down.

Two years later (May 1899) Mrs. Woodbury went vigorously into print herself in "The Arena." After airing the old story that Mrs. Eddy had stolen her ideas from Phineas Quimby, she devoted a section entitled "The Book and the Woman" to a violent attack on Mrs. Eddy and her views, citing poor scholarship, phony college degrees, ridiculous claims, and greed!

During the next two weeks Mrs. Woodbury's husband died and shortly thereafter the public was given the text of Mrs. Eddy's communion address to her church on June 4, '99. With some justification, Mrs. Woodbury felt identified therein with "the Babylonish woman" who "would enter even the church...and...pour wormwood into the waters--the disturbed human mind--to drown the strong swimmer struggling for the shore..." (My.125:29).

Mrs. Eddy was referring to a type, a mental concept in consciousness, but Mrs. Woodbury seized the opportunity to bring a suit against her and her church, seeking $150,000 damages for alleged defamation of character. For some two years it caused a good deal of commotion in the ranks of Scientists and in Pleasant View itself, but the judge and jury in the case were finally able to see that Christian teaching is by trope and metaphor, and that its ideals and illustrations are types, not persons. The account of the favorable judgment is given in CSJ Vol.XIX, No.3.

The lawsuit was however evidence that if church officials in 1896 thought that excommunication simply got rid of the Woodbury problem, they had a needed lesson coming. For by 1901 the church found itself confronted with legal bills amounting to $40,000 and a possible need for salary cuts.

~ ~ ~ ~ ~ ~ ~

The following correspondence, with its many references to Mrs. Woodbury, fills in the story leading to the lawsuit with its consequences:

-- Letter to W.B. Johnson referring in earlier days to Mrs. Woodbury's husband [dated Feb.12, '96 and signed "With love, Mother, Mary Baker Eddy"]:

My dear Student: ...I have...remailed those applications for church membership from Mr. and Mrs. Buswell. I am thankful for the By-law that gives me exemption from knowing what you do in Boston with applicants and with members under discipline. If there is aught to abhor it is quarreling. Love is our God. Let us obey Him as I said to you when here. Take no defensive steps. I shall not notice Mr. Woodbury's false statements in his letter. I taught him Christian Science and if I did him good that satisfies me.

P.S. [signed "Again, Mother"]: The hardest thing I had to bear was his declaration that I tortured his wife! When I never knowingly gave her the least trouble. But have as my church knows and she knows tried to restore her to the church and save her character. But I am done touching her case.

-- Letter to Mr. Lamb who was circulating a story about Mrs. Woodbury's mental prowess [dated March 21, '96 and signed "Respectfully, Mary Baker Eddy"]:

Dear Sir: In reply to your letter of February 27, 1896 in which you relate a story about a pear tree blossoming in January which you say Mr. R. Cushman heard Mrs. Woodbury tell is absolutely untrue.

While Mrs. Eddy was in a suburban town of Boston she brought out one apple blossom on an apple tree in January when the ground was covered with snow. And in Lynn demonstrated in the floral line some such small things. But Mrs. Woodbury was never with her in a single instance of these demonstrations. [See DCC pp.259-60.]

-- Letter to Rev. I.C. Tomlinson referring to Mrs. Woodbury's misuse of the press [dated March 30, '99 and signed "With love always, Mother, M.B. Eddy"]:

My beloved Student: I had not time to write you. I am trying to attend to my book, but do not get over one hour in the day to read proof. I should have said, have Mr. Farlow read the letter to you.

This was in substance its contents to Board of Directors and Pub. Com. Do your duty mentally for the press. Break the spell of W[oodbury] on it; defend the constitutional rights of ours. See if you cannot do as much good as others evil. The first plan included to work mentally; if this has been carried out, are the best and leading Scientists showing by their works they are unequal to so small a task mentally? And if it has been neglected, why is it? More mental work for the field must be done.

N.B. [signed "Again, Mother"]: The letter I sent to Mr. F[arlow] was not addressed to you and did not include you. He is a gem of character, as is the Judge [S.J. Hanna]; but they are not watching with me in this crucial hour. I am as usual alone.

-- Letter to Mrs. Eddy from Clerk, The First Church of Christ, Scientist, in Boston [dated June 23, '99 and signed "Your loving student as ever, William B. Johnson"]:

Our Beloved Mother: Your letter to the Directors received, and the work [of making a private and secret investigation into Mrs. Woodbury's morals for possible use in the upcoming lawsuit] is being attended to.

Shall we report progress from time to time or wait for you to ask for information?

I ask this because we do not know how mortal mind is working as well as you do, and we do not want to lose the fruition of our labors by any unnecessary act on our part.

-- Reply to above letter [undated and signed "Mother"]:

Beloved Student: You alone as students must do this. God demands of me other duties than these. And you must seek wisdom for those occasions--and with faith you will find it. You may report occasionally.

Never report through mail and do not report often. Work out your own salvation.

-- Further letters from Mrs. Eddy to C.S. Directors referring to Mrs. Woodbury:

1) [dated June 24, '99 and signed "With love, Mary Baker Eddy"]: My beloved Students: At last I am driven to protect myself with a by-law ["Alertness to Duty", now Art.VIII, Sect.6] in order to save our Cause from a new means of destroying it by disgracing Christian Scientists.

Once when I referred to a mistake made by a student he would see it--and kindly apologize. Now he or she does not see it even after again and again being reminded of it,--hence he does not excuse it. This sad fact indicates a certain downfall for this church. In a quarter of a century I have never seen one failure in this sign.

Three years almost I have had no rest from defending our Church and Cause from the blows of two students [Woodbury and Foster Eddy]. But now instead of exposing them and W. specially, I am the one you refer to before the public in a manner that foreigners deem disrespect to Leaders, and such it will appear, although I know it is not intended for that.

[P.S. to Wm.B. Johnson, signed "Mother"]: My dear Student: Read this letter in public meeting and please say to Mr. Nunn that I thank him for his kind article in reference to me published in the Boston paper. It is best to have this by-law, but do not publish it in our periodicals. Put it in the Manual. So many students yield to the tempter and forget my warning voice, this by-law is all that can save them on this important point. When another comes up then we must have another by-law! Alas for the Sleepers and for me!

2) [to Wm.B. Johnson, dated April 22, '00 and signed "With love, Mother, M.B. Eddy"]: My beloved Student: Your letter and the good old man's testimony [about Mrs. Woodbury's behavior] are just read and such a laugh as I had is a rarity in these times. I could almost hear him talk, so characteristic was the written vernacular. Will you say to Judge Hanna and yourself, I thank you for the penning of it.

Do not trouble yourself to copy testimony for me to read. I thank you, but have not time to indulge in it.

N.B. [signed "With the hope of Heaven sometime, M.B.E."]: Have got the clinch over the Pub. Com. settled by dint of wisdom. Carol had chosen to remain on Board of Lectureship rather than the Pub. Com. Both, none can be, for the stuff she [Mrs. Woodbury] publishes would go into the newspapers always when the lecturer would be off on his lecture tour and no Com. there to attend to it.

3) [dated Aug.9, '00 and signed "As ever, Mother"]: My dear Students: Do not you know that Mr. Armstrong's dear son is put in just the wrong place for his own good, and the good of our Cause? This move of subjecting him to the full fire of m.a.m. is all done by W[oodbury] showing you how you are controlled by her and so would do such an imprudent, unwise act. This has caused another by-law to be

enacted and put in the Manual. Oh, how long will even the Board of Directors be led by sin and Satan? If another act like this is consummated by you, I will change the entire Board. You give me little cause to have any faith in you.

N.B. Call a meeting at once and act on this as the By-law demands.

4)[dated Nov.8, '00 and signed "With love, Mother, M.B. Eddy"]: Beloved Students: Enclosed find copy of my letter to Dr. Foster [text given below]. I knew it was needed. W[oodbury] does not mentally neglect him for witness against us.

You will remember that when the charge of the Dr. having been a "counterfeiter" [i.e. criminally at fault], was sent to the Mother Church, or brought there by Mrs. Chanfrau--I objected to having it laid before the church and you kindly complied and it was dropped. This is what I refer to in my letter.

[P.S., signed "Mother"]: O for the peace of a dog in my old age.

> [The letter to Dr. Foster Eddy referred to above, dated Oct.28, '00 and signed "Affectionately, M.B. Eddy", read as follows: Dear Doctor: A few moments I give to you this calm, sweet Sunday. How good God is to us who know so little how to be good to Him. But Love is divine --is always Love, and in its objects, whether it be the rod or staff, it comforteth us and points the path. I have longed for time enough to say to you that I acted not, in your dismissal from the Mother Church. I only assented in order to choose the least of two evils viz.--your case coming before this church from a branch church, and the charge being criminal according to law--or simply to drop your name and reject the other charge. May God bless you in all your paths in life--make them straight and leading onward and upward. May you realize that mother has done the best for you that she knows, even if she is not understood; yet she is faithful. You are better to be removed from m.a.m. in Boston.]

> -- Telephone message from Calvin Frye to W.B. Johnson [dated Nov.8, '00]:

> Mother charges you and the other Directors not to name outside your meeting together what she has writ-

ten in a letter now on the way to you; nor the contents of enclosed letter to Dr. Eddy. Also show these letters to Judge Hanna with same charge: not to speak of it to anyone. This she says under authority of our Church By-law.

-- Letter to W.B. Johnson [dated Dec.26, '00 and signed "Fraternally, C.A. Frye"]:

Dear Brother: Mother requests that the Directors get from Mrs. Wiggin the letter Mrs. Eddy wrote to Mr. Wiggin [who deceased the previous month] about Woodbury--demand it from her, of course pay for it if need be--and ask her if she has ever shown it to Mrs. Woodbury. [This letter did not become an issue.]

~ ~ ~ ~ ~ ~ ~

The strong wording of the letter Mrs. Eddy sent to the entire Board on Aug.9, '00 indicates the need she saw for each member to keep on handling the animal magnetism that had been initially neglected in the Josephine Woodbury case. For here was a dominant member of the Board (Joseph Armstrong) suggesting that the job of librarian (in the local Boston reading room) be given to his son--and the other members thinking they were being "nice guys" by acquiescing without seeking alone (individually) "the guidance of our common Father."

The need to have someone tried and true in such a position forced Mrs. Eddy to demand enactment of her by-law which stipulated that the librarian "shall have no bad habits, shall have had experience in the Field, shall be well educated, and a devout Christian Scientist." Mr. Armstrong's young son did not have the safe or requisite experience in dealing with the "malpractitioner", that is, with the belief of many minds.

As part of the Pastor's call to the church to deal with these beliefs voiced through someone called Mrs. Woodbury she included the First Reader (Judge Hanna) in the need to contribute. The following correspondence shows she was prepared to take stringent measures like imposing salary cuts for top officials.

The existing salaries followed the pattern laid down by Mrs. Eddy on Oct.24, '96 when she wrote the Directors to say "God has spoken to me on fat salaries." Although she claimed no "legal right" to fix the amounts, she did send "a poor sketch of the discount on some and a slight increase on the bell ringers." This gave Judge Hanna an annual salary of $6000, with $1500 each to Publisher Joseph Armstrong, Treasurer Stephen Chase, and Clerk William Johnson. Soloist Elsie Lincoln received $1200, Organist Lewis $900, and William L. Johnson, assistant clerk, $208. The Lesson Sermon Committee (Mary Armstrong, Septimus Hanna, Wm B. Johnson, Ira Knapp, Mary Munroe) each had $700 p.a.

<u>Letters</u> from Mrs. Eddy to the Christian Science Board of Directors or individual members:

1) [dated May 19, '01 and signed "With love, Mother, M.B. Eddy"]: Beloved Students: On account of the increased expenses of the Mother Church this year, the Reader and not the Church, must pay for the rent [set at $2000 p.a. in 1896] of my house, 385 Commonwealth Avenue, Boston.

If anything in the Manual conflicts with this, you must change it to read that way.

2) [dated May 22, '01 and signed "With love, Mother, M.B. Eddy"]: Beloved Students: I see nothing...to prevent my doing whatever I wish with my house except to sell it. I know that was the intent of [lawyer] Mr. Walker and my own when the document was drawn up. But there is so little that I can do or say now that is not either misunderstood, or purposely belied, you had better do nothing about this at present. When, O when, will this law case be settled in Boston? <u>Perhaps</u> on the 29th inst. and <u>perhaps not</u>, it will come to trial.

3) [to Mr. Stephen A. Chase, Treasurer of The First Church of Christ, Scientist, dated July 31, '01 and signed "Accept my thanks, With love, Mother, M.B. Eddy"]: Beloved Student: On the 27th inst. I received from the clerk of The First Church of Christ, Scientist, in Boston, Mass., a letter which reads as follows:

> Beloved Mother: At the semi-annual meeting of the First Members held Nov.7th, 1899 it was unanimously voted "That the expenses connected with the lawsuit

now pending against our beloved Mother and Teacher, including all lawyer's fees and incidental expenses be entirely defrayed by the Church. That it is a privilege and joy to relieve our Mother of this annoyance and burden. That the clerk be instructed to notify her at once to this effect and that the treasurer be authorized and empowered to defray such expense."

A copy of the above was sent to you at the time.

The Board of Directors wish on their own account, that the above vote be carried out. Therefore they hereby ask you to kindly send to them any bills that may come to your hands on this account, and they will cheerfully attend to their being paid.

Lovingly yours for the Directors
Benjamin Johnson

At the time the above offer was made there had been seven libel suits entered by Josephine Woodbury, in the Superior Court in Boston, Mass., all based on practically the same complaint. If I remember rightly, I did not accept this kind offer of my Church, feeling that the party to each of these suits should meet the responsibilities themselves individually. But I find now that the termination of the suit against me, (which was decided June 1901, with a verdict in my favor by the jury,) has also disposed of the other six suits.

In view of this fact I do not feel it would be just for me to pay the total cost of the defence which virtually covers all these suits. I will therefore withdraw my previous objections and accept the kind offer of my Church to assume and to settle the cost of defence in this suit of Woodbury vs. Eddy.

Some of the bills seem enormously large, and I suggest that you use your best endeavors to have them reduced. I have paid to Mr. Morse $2,000 and to Bartlett $2,000.

4) [dated Aug.19, '01 and signed "As ever, M.B. Eddy"]: Dear Students: You kept from me the awful charges made public [by prosecution lawyer Peabody, despite the verdict in the case] until it was too late for me to defend myself! And this after the cruelty of the conduct towards me in the onset of the suit, when, if I had been obeyed, the suit would have been settled at the first opening of the court, the case thrown

out in Concord. Now I demand that you act as the church by-laws require, or take the just reward of stopping the advancement of Christian Science. Those awful newspaper libels of your Leader who is not guilty of a single one of all those charges but the lies are allowed by your lawyers before the case is put out of court. Our lawyers can contradict Peabody, and they must be made to. Do not pay them till they do this.

You will bring God's curse on our cause unless you change your sinful measures of doing nothing yourself, and giving the one He has appointed to do His work no opportunity to meet such lies with Truth. I cannot trust you in anything. The sale of His word is going down. You have the word of Farlow for saying that the Editor of the Herald said Peabody is insane. The Editors that published are liable for libel. Now do nothing without letting me know what it is beforehand.

5) [dated Aug.23, '01 and signed "As ever, Your leader, M.B. Eddy"]: Dear Board: I have so much to attend to now in consequence of your not coming to see me in the awful hour of sacrifice--that I cannot see you now.

Pass this by-law at once. ["This by-law" was in effect reducing the salaries of top church officials!]

P.S. [signed "M.B.E."]: Cannot Hanna help you now? You did as he said before. God is your help if you do your duty.

6) [to Clerk, dated Aug.23, '01 and signed "With love, M.B. Eddy"]: Dear Student: The Bible Lesson Com. is not included in the last by-law. This Com. belongs to the Publishing Society.

7) [to Clerk of the Mother Church, dated Sept.4, '01 and signed "With love, mother, M.B.G.Eddy"]: Beloved Student: Call a meeting of the Board of Directors today at the earliest moment and vote to annul the last Church By-law relative to the salaries of Church officers for one year. Telephone at once today to all who have been informed of the By-law to meet and have it adjusted today. The By-law was not intended to include musicians or janitors.

Have the Board of Directors do as they think best on the purchase of real estate. If I have written in favor of the Church getting in debt, it was because I did not understand the situation. Do not consult me again on purchasing Church property. I decline to give any further attention to it. You know the Church By-laws. Act in accordance with them.

Stop at once the stir in Boston.

8) [to W.B. Johnson, dated Sept.5, '01 and signed "With love, M.B. Eddy"]: Beloved Student: Your map and letter explain what is to be purchased. I do not believe in getting in debt, especially on church property. Why I asked to have the Church By-law repealed was that compulsory giving is not my idea of church charity. Let the church consider all that I have done for it, and give without being asked. Cancel their account with God is my advice to the church officers--not including its musicians and janitors. I consider it a silly expenditure to build a church that costs what ours does to run it. I said "let the defence in that lawsuit pay the cost" but what I said was overruled and this lawsuit that could have been settled the first year was prolonged and the cost three times as much as it might have been, because I was again unheeded. I think now you had better look after m.a.m. before acting.

-- Letter to Wm.D. McCracken from Mrs. Eddy [dated Dec.3, '01]:

I cannot quite forgive my students for depriving me of that golden opportunity to have answered the libel of Peabody's. Only a page of reply would have shown him a liar. All he said could be met by dates and proof of its falsehood. I could have written it not in reply but simply stated the facts and not called him a liar, but left the reader of them to know that he was. But it was over a week after his lecture before I was told of it, and then it was too late.

If Farlow had written nothing on that subject and let his silence speak, it would have been decent. As it was, the whine he sent out was all the enemy wanted. Dear Mr. Farlow, that was once smart, seems dwarfed into something besides himself. His last public reference to me was, He knew that "Mrs. Eddy had had one tooth extracted without pain." Think of this! I cannot and will not bear it much longer.

I approve of your having a [C.S.] Institute of your own [in New York]. But have I not some rights, some claims that should be respected at headquarters? His case is one of hypnotic mental malicious malpractice. O take warning; watch continually that thy house be not broken open. So far I have noticed no signs of this. God grant you exemption.

[William D. McCracken, scholar, historian, C.S. lecturer, served for a while as Publishing Committee in New York. More on publishing committees under COP's section, p.265.]

CONTINUANCE OF UNHANDLED BELIEFS

The final sentence in the above series of letters to the Board of Directors gives the key to the lesson they were bringing home. The thought that Church is a localized concept which kicks sinners out into the cold, rather than being the home of all, needs to be handled sooner or later.

The belief that human law alone could take care of the Woodbury phenomenon was no more scientific than the belief that excommunication could. The proposed salary cuts simply served notice that more positive mental work had been needed, also a better realization of the truth about Church and Pastor for the future.

At the height of the Woodbury suit--in an unrelated incident--Mrs. Eddy sent instructions to Clerk Johnson which were aimed at showing the Directors how really to dispose of an error. She wrote (May 6, '00):

> "Do not record one word of the slander on the accused members. Bury it among the offal of lies."

Later (May 29, '00) she added:

> "Dismiss all complaints. Pass the addition to By-law and deliver yourselves from M.A.M."

As a warning against any feeling of triumph over the ejection of wrongdoers, she once said: "To rejoice in the fall of an enemy is murderous and malicious" (see DCC pp.220-1).

"Mrs. Woodbury" was just a name given to mistaken views asking for acceptance, just as the Pastor had shown that thinking of "Mrs. Eddy" as a personal "Mary" did not necessarily bring the right guidance.

As long as materialistic views could remain even after a dismissal of the libel charges, Mrs. Woodbury's lawyer Frederick W. Peabody was able to hurl forth all the misconceptions he had been gathering about the Discoverer of Christian Science. After giving lectures on the subject, he published his words in a pamphlet entitled "Complete Exposure of Eddyism or Christian Science", and even sent copies to the Directors and Trustees. These officials, who may have thought it would not be very kind, or very self-serving, to worry Mrs. Eddy, kept quiet.

Henry Nunn records that Mrs. Eddy called Judge Hanna, Alfred Farlow and himself to Pleasant View after the Peabody attack and berated them for the way they had failed to tackle events. Seeing that Mr. Nunn was taken aback, she turned to him and very gently explained that the force of her words was simply showing that he was ready to understand he could demand to reflect the one omnipotent Mind, see the real Pastor, and witness the good results.

~ ~ ~ ~ ~ ~ ~

Among those who could profit from rebukes was Wm.B. Johnson who took to heart the September 5 lesson about <u>compulsory</u> giving, as the next four letters show:

-- <u>Letter</u> to Christian Science Board of Directors [dated Sept.10, '01 and signed "With love, M.B. Eddy"]:

> Beloved Students: God is numbering you this year and he has set down our clerk, William B. Johnson, as number one, who donates his salary for one year to the Mother Church.

-- <u>Letters</u> to William B. Johnson:

1) [dated Oct.3, '01 and signed "With love, mother, M.B. Eddy"]: Beloved Student: I have found you very faithful in your office. If I recollect rightly I <u>personally</u> requested you to dissolve the committee in question. However, we all are liable to mistakes, but allow me to ask that all letters of yours hereafter containing accounts of the Church business shall be addressed to me personally....

Here let me thank you for Christian love and fidelity in your office. Enclosed find a letter of mine to substitute the one you have received--please [act on] this letter and destroy my prior letter on this subject.

N.B. Leave out the amendment of By-law on Publication Com. and destroy it. Let this Com. work under the Manual By-law as it is, at present.

2) [dated Oct.4, '01 and signed "With deep love, Mother"]: Dear Student: Not until today did I know your experience yesterday and tomorrow will be better than today.

Thank God and know that it is because He loves you that He gives you higher lessons than he gives your classmates. Be of good cheer. The By-laws I sent yesterday will not prevent your re-election but secure it. Also I shall see that you have your annual salary. You have given it this year to the church. You set the example. "It will return to you after many days as bread cast upon the water."

3) [dated Oct.10, '02 and signed "With love, Mother, M.B. Eddy"]: Beloved Student: Continue your salary [which this time he had donated to the Building Fund for the Church Extension]. If you do not earn it, no person in Boston does.

4) [dated Feb.3, '06 and signed "Lovingly, M.B. Eddy"]: My beloved Student: I desired especially to have you return to me the papers I gave you to ask for dismission from the C.S. Board, that you might help your Leader.... I hope you have not shown them to the other Directors. I do not wish to lose you on that Board if it can be helped. On reading your communication, which says that [my assistant secretary] Kinter demands what the by-laws of our Church makes no provision for, I can perceive no way that is better than to have you present at once your request, arrange your business immediately to come to me. Will you do it? Wire me "yes" if you can come. I must have help. Mr. Frye and I cannot do the work alone.... [Mr. Johnson wired "yes" and the next day received the following letter]:

5) [signed "Lovingly yours in Christ, M.B. Eddy"]: My beloved Student: Don't resign from the Board of Directors. Let me wait on God, but you be ready when I appeal for help and come to Concord when I send, or when God sends you to aid me as He did at this time.

Remain on the Board and make no mention of what we have said on this matter. Dismiss for the present the thought of any change.

DEMANDS, REPRIMANDS, RECOMMENDATIONS

The Woodbury phenomenon brought to church members Mrs. Eddy's dose of demands and reprimands, but always the recommendation that problems be grasped as something more than just events to be lived through; furthermore, that when animal magnetism hinders the loving lesson the One Mind is bringing, accompanying events simply get repeated in one form or another. Woodbury and Peabody were still on hand to figure in the Next Friends Suit, with its repeated press attacks, as covered in Chap.IV.

In other fields--readers, lectures, music in church, gifts, adornments, handling of funds, etc.--there was the continual balance of demands and recommendations, as the following correspondence shows. Also there was the everpresent instruction, as given in Six Days p.332, which could be paraphrased here as follows:

> If your church is empty, if your lectures are unattended, if your Pastor seems unreasonable, if the "wrong" people (call them morally inferior, call them theosophists, women, Jews, blacks, Catholics, communists, terrorists, what you will) are in control in your world, your nation, your church, your home, your newspaper, etc. you can know this is all part of one erroneous mental picture being suggested to you--and first you "handle animal magnetism" or the belief that there are hoards of minds to delude or poison or drug you. Then you hear God, the only Mind, talking peace and dominion to you. Remember Jesus said to self-righteousness: "The publicans and harlots go into the kingdom of God before you."

"Animal magnetism" was the coverall term Mrs. Eddy used, in her specific instructions to students and officials, to signify the belief that one effect can affect (magnetize) another effect. At times she used poisons, drugs, various forms of ecclesiasticism, etc., to show the different aspects.

But always she meant mental arguments which would induce the apathy or destruction often thought to be reserved for some physical intake.

Students have preserved the following instructions from Mrs. Eddy for handling animal magnetism in some of its various forms:

> [As mental poison]: Find out the leading fear in the patient's mind and if that be mental malpractice or poisoning, judge from the symptoms what the poison is; then declare against this. Name it! Say: "There is no such poison, no fear of it; no belief that you are poisoned. Awake from this dream. Know that God is your only Mind and divine Love is caring for you. You have no arsenical symptoms, no symptoms of narcotics, cyanide of potassium, or any other poison."
>
> [As other mental arguments]: Know that: A.M. cannot think--do--feel. It has no existence or creation. It cannot gain or assert power or action through any mortal or mortals. It never has been--nor will be and cannot manifest itself in grades of error, electricity or mediumship, spiritualism, theosophy, agnosticism, psychology, astrology, sooth-saying and hypnotism, or any other form of sin, sickness or death, for God is All-in-all and the only Creator of the only universe and man, and we are His children and realize the only completion, the only fullness--the omnipotence of God.
>
> [For further instruction on the handling of mental malpractice and poisons, see the lists beginning on pp.139,154.]

Another student (Mary Freshman) has recorded that while John Linscott was reading in Denver before he moved to Washington, D.C., he found himself having a great deal of physical discomfort to meet from malicious animal magnetism (operating as a person so-called). During a visit to Mrs. Eddy he was completely healed of his illness.

In relating this to Mrs. Freshman he said: "She came into the room, and said to me, 'You are drunk with animal magnetism', and she shook me. She stood very erect and turned to me. Then uplifting her hand she said with great force, 'I see you, begone!' speaking audibly the name of a man in the West! She further said that if I had understood and done that, I would not have had to come so far to be healed." [As clarified in the later quotes, this treatment simply demanded recognition of a wrong thought asking to be accepted as "your own thought"--and calling for elimination right there. It was not a waiver of the rule: "Take up nobody personally."]

-- Some general letters to church officials:

1) [To Irving C. Tomlinson and dated July 8, '99]: I wish mother could be excused by divine Love from speaking as I did to my fresh happy callers! I thought I was done when I went to my room but the Scripture I opened to and the leadings spiritual sent me back. What I said I no more expected to say than when I wrote S&H. Afterwards I recalled your kind care of me getting everything ready, etc., when I went to Boston and said--O what have I said?

I also knew that these Sinai detonations make the student grow most rapidly into the holy fitness for every demonstration; or they (under the fire of the enemy) cause him by degrees to dislike mother and keep aloof from her counsel.

2) [To William B. Johnson, dated Jan.5, '00 and signed "With love, Mother, M.B. Eddy"]: My beloved Student: I can almost say "Lettest thou thy servant depart in peace" I am so joyed over your waking up. Now do not be caught even napping again. Mother has prayed for you....

N.B. [signed "Mother"]: You are above temptation; now do not go down into the house to find anything to take out of it. You are God's image. God is the only Mind.

3) [To W.B. Johnson, dated Aug.9, '00 and signed "M.B.E."]: Beloved Student: The one devil, evil, takes thought by drugs as well as siege. The drugs are morphine, opium, hashish, arsenic, rhus radicans, strychnine. There is need of awakening before it is too late. [The emphasis on "thought" and "awakening" shows that Mrs. Eddy was referring to accepted promoters of mental drowsiness, not to material objects or persons.]

4) [To Wm.B. Johnson, undated, but probably late 1902, and signed "With love, Mother, M.B. Eddy"]: Beloved Student: You say, "When shall we learn the way?" I reply, When you have all faith in Truth, hence no faith in error.

Gain this point, overcome evil with the good by knowing that good is supreme--is the master of so-called evil. Work mentally with this consciousness and you will overcome evil just as I have done so many years, and carried on a cause in the midst of all opposition, to such heights of success.

True, I am battle-stained; but I still love and give orders that are blessed and foil the enemy.

Read this letter to the C.S. Board of Directors and let your noble son [William L.] study it.

N.B. Naming persons in prayer, is the fight between beasts. Overcoming their evil and lies with good, and Truth in your prayers, is C.S.

5) [to the Watchers at headquarters who are mistaken, dated Dec.21, '01 and signed "With love, Mother, M.B. Eddy"]: Beloved Students: Disband your meeting today and never meet again to do what is not carried out scientifically. Each one to do the work of daily duty. Each one realize the allness of God, Good, and that there is no opposite evil. Do not meet together to discuss or to direct the prayers of Scientists unless I call you together.

Each one pray daily and not ask amiss. I have known of the discord before of prayer that is amiss. You all can know that newspapermen will not publish aught against Christian Science. Please know this--and also know that you can do this separately as well as together.

[P.S. addressed to Wm.B. Johnson and signed "With love, Mother"]: I forgot to say this: Take up nobody personally but let your prayer be impersonal and God will bless the right.

[P.P.S.] Do not think of me or my affairs. Let God do this and you invoke a general blessing.

6) [to Wm.B. Johnson, dated March 19, '02 and signed "With love, Mother, M.B. Eddy"]: Beloved Student: ...I shall not decide the question about giving letters of recommendation to other churches outside our denomination. I should hope you would see the folly of beginning such a system of letters. Now do not say "Mrs. Eddy has decided this question", for I have not. But you should at once and forever, if persons wish to leave our church, let them go, and without a letter.

7) [to C.S. Directors, dated Nov.8, '02 and signed "M.B. Eddy"]: Beloved Students: Call a church meeting on receipt of this letter and vote on the enclosed By-law [removing the First Reader from acting with the Directors in matters of discipline]. It is just that my old church shall not become the victim of m.a.m. without my interference in its behalf. I see what you do not in these cases of discipline. If I were to have the students that break faith all excommunicated without sufficient effort on my part and on yours to save them, how many members think you would be left in it?

Also vote on my recommendation to make Annie Dodge a First Member of the Mother Church. God give you the wisdom to obey the Golden Rule and bless you, is the prayer of mother.

N.B. [signed "M.B. Eddy"]: Remember your church By-laws and that my communications to you are not to be named to anyone outside of your meetings.

8) [to the Christian Science Board of Directors, dated Nov.21, '02 and signed "With love, Mother, M.B.G. Eddy"]: Beloved Students: ...Relative to the discipline and ex-communication of offending members, I have only this to say: Confine yourselves strictly to the By-laws of the Mother Church and be merciful and just according to the Golden Rule. I hope said members can be reformed and retained in our Church.

I close with this emphatic declaration: No members of this Board can consult me on the discipline of members, or the excommunication thereof. Please read the enclosed amendment of By-law, Article XXII on page 52 of Church Manual, and after voting upon it, inform me as usual of your vote. The information I received yesterday about the offending members has shown me the wisdom of restoring the By-law as it read on discipline and excommunication.

9) [N.B. in letter to Rev. I.C. Tomlinson, dated April 11, '99]: When I speak of men or women afraid to meet the defence, I mean afraid to come out in open noble, loving, rebuke to certain secret crimes or immoralities--uncover them and <u>show the remedy</u>.

By this I do not mean mental or audible attacks, but kind strong rebuke that will <u>heal</u> and not <u>wound</u> the good folks.

PICTURE OF MRS. EDDY'S CHAIR

One area of church activity which called for frequent correspondence could be named the secular side: gifts, displays, and financial deals.

Shortly after services began in The Mother Church controversy arose about "the picture of Mrs. Eddy's chair" and how it should be displayed. This picture had a slight similarity to "Seeking and Finding" in *Christ & Christmas*, but the table showed a vase of roses and (as related in the Boston Herald of June 9, '95) "copies of the Bible, Science and Health, the Christian Science Quarterly, and the Christian Science Journal; and in the background an open copy of the Boston Herald of January 2 [1895], containing an account of the dedication of The First Church and the full text of Mrs. Eddy's sermon on that occasion."

No one was seated at the table, but shown beside it was the black walnut chair in which Mrs. Eddy did much of her writing.

Towards the end of 1895 the picture was moved from the Publishing House to the church vestry, where the lighting was found to be inadequate. Finally it was hung over the center door leading into the auditorium and secured by pulleys and ropes so that it could be raised enough to allow the door to be used at gatherings and services.

This brought unfavorable comment as well as the following two letters from Pleasant View:

> [To Wm.B. Johnson, dated Dec.10, '95 and signed "Yours fraternally, C.A. Frye"]: Dear Bro. Johnson: Mother directs me to say that she does not like the idea of having the painting of the chair arranged as it is; it suggests too much of the theatrical exhibition, being raised and lowered. She says if there is not room enough for it to be permanently placed in the auditorium it must go into the Mother's Room.
>
> [To the C.S. Board of Directors, dated Dec.11, '95 and signed "With love, Mother"]: My beloved Students: I said in the first place that the painting of the chair should not be itinerant, nor placed in the vestibule, but placed permanently in the auditorium or in Mother's Room. The present arrangement is M.A.M. giving an-

other occasion for saying "personal worship of Mrs. Eddy!" Pulling it up and down for exhibition is enough to make people say you are gone wild over Mother and the church is turned into a theatre, while the fact is that if you loved Mother you would keep her commandments. It destroyed the dignity of the history associated with the chair to twaddle it up and down on the walls.

Mrs. Eddy objected to displays of materiality, even to many of the pictures of herself; and yet, as though to test the waters, she had her portrait sometimes in and sometimes out of S&H. If a picture or design speaks of character, God-qualities, the One Spirit in action, it enhances the reign of Spirit. If it conjures up a belief of special powers in material things or persons it achieves nothing in the right direction. The interpretation is said to be always in the eye of the beholder--hence is problematic unless the real Beholder is known to be God Himself, and one looks with the eyes of God. (See Six Days, pp.465-9.)

Mrs. Eddy was evidently testing Adam Dickey's beholding when (Memoirs, p.71) she asked him if she should not perhaps throw away some of her trinkets as "too childish." He replied that each item spoke of the love and appreciation of the donor "and there is no reason why you should not have it." When taken back properly to Mind, nothing is ever lost; otherwise, even if thrown away, the thought of it remains to be handled, and if handled properly, appreciated.

-- Letter from Mrs. Eddy to Emma McLaughlin [dated June 27, '95]:

...I have no pictures of myself that please me. I mean [one] that looks as I feel sometimes. This is what I want to get, this is the expression that artists have not yet caught.

-- Letter from Mrs. Eddy to Julia Field-King [dated Aug.7, '97]:

...My life is a perpetual slavery to the world and it is a hard matter. So much the students demand of me and yet I need help above all persons on earth in everything but Christian Science. But the law is not yet broken by them--that they "can do nothing for me." So I have the care of my house, my grounds, my clothes, my entire mass of what I despise, and want to lose sight of.

-- Contrasting letter by Mrs. Eddy [dated April 17, '02 regarding her portrait as painted by Emilie Hergenroeder for First Church, Baltimore]:

...I can never express my full appreciation of the loving care which prompted the dear church in Baltimore to give a portrait of me to the world. I have often wondered, when thinking of the indifference that other churches have shown on this point, it does concern the history of Christian Science at present, and will in the future, more than today.

Mere memorials, in churches or in graveyards, can be equally inappropriate, as indicated in the letters which follow. The first letter came eight months after the "twaddle" of the chair picture. It showed that another by-law had to be written decreeing that "no pictures coming from outsiders shall be exhibited in the room where the Christian Science textbook is published."

-- Letter to C.S. Board [dated Aug.7, '96 and signed "With love, Mother, M.B. Eddy"]:

My beloved Students: ...Next follows another picture hung up in the pub. office for examination! which is shocking after what has already been said on this subject. This forces me to turn from my paths of duty on hand, and make another By-law for the rebellious Israelites....

N.B. [signed "M.B. Eddy"]: Have this By-law added to Article 14, Sec.1 [similar to present Art.XXV, Sect.7].

-- Letter to Mrs. Eddy [dated Memorial Day, '07 and signed by Rev. Irving C. Tomlinson]:

Beloved Leader: ...This Memorial Day, when dear hands lay fragrant blossoms on the resting places of forms beloved, I am reminded that I should be glad if I might have the oversight of those sacred spots where rest those of your family near and dear.

I have visited your pretty plot in the well-kept Tilton cemetery. I have also gone with General Baker to the spot in Bow where sleep your grandmother, Mary Ann Baker, and other members of the family.

I have also visited with the General the Pembroke resting place of your father's uncle, Thomas Baker, and others of his family.

May I be allowed to see that these dear places are properly cared for and that upon Memorial Day they also have their symbols of beauty and eternity?

-- Reply from Mrs. Eddy [signed "Ever and forever Thine in Christ"]:

I love you and thank you, but they sleep not there. "Let the dead bury their dead" (Jesus).

-- Recorded statement to Mrs. Stack: Flowers are an idea; you get it by knowing it, and not by cutting it. If you know it, you will always have plenty of cut flowers.

-- Letter from Mrs. Eddy to Directors [dated Dec.14, '09]:

No picture of a female in attitude of prayer or in any other attitude shall be made or put into our Church, or any of our buildings, with my consent.

This is now my request and demand: Do nothing in statuary, in writing, or in action, to perpetuate or immortalize the thought of personal being; but do and illustrate, teach and practise, all that will impersonalize God and His idea man and woman. Whatever I have said in the past relative to impersonation I have fully recalled, and my Church cannot contradict me in this statement.

MONEY, GIFTS, PROPERTY

The subject-matter in the following letter was the "Lynn Property Trust" formed by Christian Scientists to preserve what seemed to them to be significant, historic real estate in Lynn; and the by-laws Mrs. Eddy was referring to were to regulate thought about trusts, syndicates, and the like.

Letter to Clerk of the "Mother Church" [dated March 15, '96 and signed "With love, Mother, Mary Baker Eddy"]:

Dear Students: I request you to call a church meeting as soon as legal. Also to read the first page of the enclosed letter at the opening of the meeting. Then adopt the By-laws. Next read the 2nd and 3rd pages and vote to act as therein requested.

[The "first page" signed "Mary Baker Eddy", stated]: Children of the Mother Church: I ask that at this meeting you adopt the...By-laws which God has given you to save you from much sin.

[The "2nd and 3rd pages" signed "With love, Mother Mary Baker Eddy", read as follows]: I also at God's command (as I discern it) order you to dissolve the Board of Trustees of the Lynn property, and to refund to each contributor every dollar in their hands contributed for the purchase of this property; and to pay from the income of your church to Mr. Eastaman, the money that Mr. Eastaman has paid already for said property. And if an individual member of this church desires to possess said property, let him or her purchase it, but not the church.

[P.S., signed "Mother"]: The last of this letter is to be read in open meeting after the By-laws are adopted.

-- Telegram to William B. Johnson, c/o J. Armstrong, 95 Falmouth St. [dated March 16, '96 and signed "M.B. Eddy"]:

Don't read number one in meeting. Return it by Laura [Sargent]. Ask members through Lynn estate, are you worshipping matter or Spirit? You cannot serve two masters.

The occasion for this next letter was the presentation to Mrs. Eddy by the First Members of a clock valued at $1000:

-- Letter to First Members of The First Church of Christ, Scientist [dated Dec.31, '98 and signed "Gratefully and lovingly, Mother, Mary Baker Eddy"]:

My beloved Students: For your last Christmas gift I feel quite bankrupt in thanks. You have made me a timely present, one that gives a new tongue to time, that calls my attention to the loss of moments, and to the gain of what is timeless, even eternity. It speaks to me in cathedral tones of the Mother Church, the temple of our God, and of the dear worshippers therein.

Although I am not with you as of old, the music of mind is not missing, and the chiming of our thoughts calls us together in one general assembly where hearts keep time in love one for another.

The blessings vouchsafed to us as a denomination are superabundant. The uplifted cry of the people seems poured forth with this one utterance, "Give us to know Christian Science, to know more of Soul, man's origin and being."

We cannot sufficiently thank God for all His great goodness to us. But we can acknowledge this by conforming our lives more to the divine image, and thereby feebly expressing His praise.

I feel a great sense of gratitude to you for what you are trying to do, and have already done. From the depths of a loving, lonely heart, I thank you for your rare Christmas gift to me and for your labors in the vineyard of our Lord.

N.B. [signed "M.B. Eddy"]: I herewith recommend the following four candidates for First Members of the Mother Church: First, for their faithfulness in the field. Second, for the advantage to them individually. Third, from a desire to have them grow up with the First Members of the Mother Church who receive more directly my counsel and assistance:

James A. Neal, Carol Norton, John Carrol Lathrop, Daphne S. Knapp

The remaining items selected under this section's heading are taken from correspondence by Mrs. Eddy with her Board of Directors (or the Clerk):

1) [dated July 31, '96 and signed "With love, Mother, Mary Baker Eddy"]: My beloved Board of Directors: Please read this in meeting. When you voted to adjourn all the meetings one month, you should also have voted to close the church building to all visitors during that month! Our Master asked, "Which is greater, the temple or the gift that sanctifieth the temple?"

2) [dated Sept.1, '96 and signed "With love, Mother, Mary Baker Eddy"]: My beloved Students: Will you take my estate 385 Commonwealth Ave., Boston, into your hands and thus help me in carnal things, while I minister unto you in spiritual, even as St. Paul said? If you do, I shall refuse to take any remuneration from you when I may speak in our Church, and not take a car to myself.

This is my request, that you rent for me my estate on Commonwealth Ave., and at $2000 per annum. The rent there of the adjacent house was $3000 annually when I left Boston. Also I give you the right to sub-rent to parties that I would not object to--I having the privilege of occupying it for one week if desired, at the cold season perhaps. The rentor paying nothing for rent, but paying the city and water taxes. One room is never to be rented, that is, my chamber; and your rentee is not to rent any part of my house, or to let a family but his own occupy the house and to take no boarder, to take no class, and have no practice with patients in my house. He is to keep it in good order and repair any damage done to it.

P.S. and N.B. [signed "With deep love, Mother"]: Please make two writings as rentor that include the conditions named in my letter, sign and send them to me by express. I will return one of them to you by Laura. Name the length of lease 5 years.

[P.P.S., signed "M.B.E."]: I desire to have Judge Hanna and family occupy it as long as they want to, or rather as we want them to.

3) [dated Sept.5, '96 and signed "With tender thanks for your kind help in relieving me of the care and burden of real estate, Ever lovingly, Mother, Mary Baker Eddy"]: My beloved Students: No words can express my thanks for your relieving me of the rent of my house 385 Commonwealth Ave.

The present occupant [Judge Hanna] remains in it at my request on the terms I wrote you. No other lessee has the house on such terms. I do this, or rather, make this exception because of the purpose to support the First Reader and leader in Boston for the welfare of our cause. When Rev. Mr. Norcross went out of the city proper to make his home, it worked ill for him and the church. Keep the Judge in Boston near the Church as long as he acts wisely and does as much good as at present, be sure.

P.S. [signed "M.B.E."]: I will rent my estate at 385 Commonwealth Ave., to the C.S. Board of Directors at $2000 per annum for five years subject to my occupancy, at which time this rent ceases. When I occupy it they pay no rent for my house.

4) [to Clerk, dated June 23, '02 and signed "With love, M.B. Eddy"]: Beloved Student: Call a meeting immediately, vote on this By-law [establishing 385 Commonwealth Avenue as the First Reader's official residence]; then inform Prof. Hering [the new First Reader] of the By-law and publish it in our next periodicals.

The Hannas had my house all furnished and the furniture was used and spoiled by them as well as the former occupants, then sold for second hand. So he should consider this and sell his furniture at a discount to the Directors. I still own a writing desk and some other things in my house at Commonwealth Avenue. Have them all left in it.

5) [to Mr. Ira O. Knapp C.S.D., Joseph Armstrong C.S.D., Wm.B. Johnson C.S.B., Stephen A. Chase C.S.B., dated A.D. 1897 and signed "With love mother, Mary Baker Eddy"]: My beloved Students: Accept from your teacher and former pastor a trifling momento of her affection that derives its sole value from the associations connected therewith. This silent picture [of The Mother Church] can speak from your walls of one conquest. But may the better trophy of victories, be each one of our lives gathered into one signal, for future history to float over this church.

6) [to Wm.B. Johnson, dated May 1, '97 and signed "Yours truly, M.B. Eddy, per F{rye}"]: Dear Bro. Johnson: In reply to your request to frame my letter [reproduced in item #5 above], I am willing provided you will first have Prof. McKenzie examine it and if he sees any errors in it, he may note them and return it to me, and I will rewrite it for you to frame. Tell him please that I wrote it in 10 minutes and did not take the pains I should.

7) [dated May 31, '98 and signed "With love, Mother, Mary Baker Eddy"]: My beloved Students: Your generous

check for $1000 is received. I thank you! but most of all do I give thanks that you still go on in this office and our old tender church relations are not severed. God grant that they may remain worthy to be perpetuated.

8) [dated July 7, '98]: Your triplicate mirror that you present to me, arrived safely. Its "three in one" is noticeable. My heart thanks you. May this mirror reflect the unity of spirit that shall characterize our friendship; and oft remind me, not of age and personality, but of what we have won on the field of battle--and of God's great goodness.

9) [Telegram dated April 15, '00 and signed "With love, Mother"]: God bless my old Board of Directors and their plants [sent in old-fashioned commemoration of Easter. See also Man. Art. XXII, Sect.10].

10) [to Mr. Ira O. Knapp, C.S.D., Mr. William B. Johnson, C.S.B., Mr. Joseph Armstrong, C.S.D., Mr. Stephen A. Chase, C.S.B., dated March 30, '02 and signed "With love, Teacher and Mother, M.B.G. Eddy"]: My beloved Students: Your loving Easter greeting was a ray of sunshine. I love to remember the many years we have journeyed on together in storm and shine. Also to recall the great growth of our Cause and organizations since its birth. May this Easter morn bring from the sepulchre of sense sweet chimes of spiritual tones--awakened during all these years to sound their loudest notes today. And so give the waymarks of our walk together a clear impress of our labor and its fruits for the whole world.

11) [dated December 29, '01 and signed "With love, Mother, M.B. Eddy"]: Beloved Students: I thank you for your recent affectionate [Christmas] letters, caring and kind. They are a balm to one who is so alone, so bereft of earthly ties. Accept my tender loving wishes for you and yours; for your growth in spirit-divine Science--your health and your happiness.

12) [dated May 5, '00 and signed "With love, Mother and teacher, M.B.E."]: One more thing to be said: Raise Mrs. Sargent's salary [for taking care of Mother's Room] this next annual meeting to $800 per annum. She needs it and is striving to help our cause.

13) [to Clerk, dated March 7, '02 and signed "With deep love, Mother, M.B. Eddy"]: Beloved Student: Mr. Chase wants $500 of Church funds left at his disposal for ch. purposes. This sum he accounts for annually. Please call a meeting of the Board and vote on this yes or nay. I suggest that you give him $300 for one year and then increase the sum if need be and it works well....

14) [Telegram to Mr. Wm.B. Johnson, dated Sept.3, '02 and signed "M.B. Eddy"]: I do not think it advisable to take that land it would be too heavy a burden.

Explanatory Letter [of same date and signed "With love, Mother, M.B.G. Eddy"]: Beloved Students: I saw your sketch of the lot of land, or site for the Publishing House, and admired it--but when I learned of the price, I took not two minutes to decide as to purchasing it.

We cannot prosper on a wrong premise. We take the Bible for our guide, and find in it this Scripture: "Owe no man." A slight sum of indebtedness with a speedy prospect of payment would not break the spirit of that Scripture, but so large a one does. Why? Because it involves a material thinking and acting and taking thought that is not advantageous to spiritual growth. The Scripture saith, "Take no thought for the morrow."

Now, dear ones, you have my reasons for deciding not to purchase that site, and I know you will agree with Mother's view when you think thereon and remember the demands of Christian Science.

15) [dated Nov.21, '02 and signed "With love, Mother, M.B.G. Eddy"]: Beloved Students: Since my interview with Mr. A.P. DeCamp [the treasurer who briefly replaced Stephen Chase] yesterday, almost the reverse of what was then deemed right relative to the Church Building has come to my thought, and I must accept it as God given, and report it in this letter as follows:

Do not commence to build the addition to the Mother Church until after the Annual Meeting next June. Allow Mr. S.A. Chase to perform his part as not according to the Church By-laws. Have the Directors and Finance Committee cooperate according to the Church By-laws. By all means let the Church Building Fund remain with Mr. Chase and continue him as the custodian of this fund.

I ask the Directors to report to Mr. DeCamp the manner in which the funds for our first church were lost and let that be a warning. [See Six Days, p.224.]

16) [dated Dec.17, '97 and signed "Always thine, Mary Baker Eddy"]: My beloved Church: For your love I have no words to express my thanks. But I can say of your money, it was munificent, and it more than pays for my beautiful little organ [being installed in Concord's "Christian Science Hall"]; therefore, will you please receive from me the balance through Mr. Neal who has my check for it, and take with it Mother's gratitude to God and man for such a dear church, that ere long will form forever with her in a body triumphant.

17) [to The Mother Church, dated June 25, '04 and signed "Lovingly yours, Mary B.G. Eddy"]: My beloved brethren: Your munificent gift of ten thousand dollars wherewith to furnish First Church of Christ, Scientist, of Concord, N.H. with an organ is sweet proof of your remembrance and love. Days of shade and shine may come and go but we will live on and never drift apart. Life's ills are its chief recompense, they develop hidden strength. Had I never suffered for the Mother Church neither she nor I would be practising the virtues that lie concealed in the smooth seasons and calms of human existence. When we are willing to help and to be helped divine aid is near and if all our years were holidays sports would be more irksome than work. So my dear ones let us together sing the old new song of salvation and our measure of time and joy be spiritual not material.

18) [dated July 28, '04 and signed "Lovingly yours, Mary B.G. Eddy"]: My beloved Students: I thank you for remembering me and for the beautiful trowel with which you performed the custom of the times [at the start of building the Extension]. May our God who is Spirit be worshipped by you in spirit, and the house you are about to erect be built on the Rock of ages; while you, my dearest ones, are rearing in your own consciousness a temple not "built with hands"--and consecrated to the One-and-All apart from all material considerations. Be careful not to drop into the usages of other churches in thought or act--only so far as you can unite on the one spiritual basis and not the material.

19) [dated April 23, '06 and signed "Sincerely yours, Mary Baker Eddy"]: My beloved Students: Your generous cheque of $5000 April 23, 1906 is duly received. You will recognize my gratitude and emotions also the touch of memory. The above sum was unexpected at this juncture but not the less appreciated.

I have Message to my Church all ready for you: It is not sufficient to publish in book form for I thought it wise to be brief on this occasion of Communion and Dedication which include much time and talk and work.

My By-law I submit to your action upon it, and trust you will see as I foresee the need of it.

Now is the time to kill the lie that students worship me, or that I claim a divine homage from them to me. This historical dedication of our Church should date some special reform, and the aforesaid is one that is greatly needed to do justice to the history of our denomination.

20) [dated June 23, '06 and signed "Lovingly yours, Mary Baker Eddy"]: My beloved Students: You will accept my thanks for the pew you have selected for me in the center of the auditorium of our magnificent Temple [i.e. the "Extension"]. I hope you let all have it to use who need it when I am not there. Allow me to remain central in your hearts like the pew.

21) [dated Aug.1, '06 and signed "Lovingly yours, Mary Baker Eddy"]: My beloved Students: I thank you for giving me this great help on perpetuating the history of The Mother Church. I have amended the Church By-law Our Church Edifices, page 78, to read consistently with this movement. But it should not be published in the Sentinel until the History is engrafted into Pulpit and Press. [See Manual Art.XXIV, Sect.1,2, and Pul. p.22.]

Keep all this matter out of the knowledge of anyone but parties concerned so long as possible.

N.B. [signed "M.B.E."]: Will you defer making a public move on this matter until you hear again from me: You can have this history written and ready whenever you have time to do it.

22) [from Mary Baker Eddy, dated April 5, '09]: My beloved Board: You know that God, divine Love, reigns, and

the Catholic prayers this [holy] week or any week, to harm your Leader, are powerless. Will you as my Church realize this Truth that destroys error?

Do not take me up personally but know mentally and prayerfully that the Catholic prayers to harm anyone are utterly powerless. Evil and sin are nothing. Good and divine Love are infinite, and there is no other power. They are all and govern all.

FURTHER CORRESPONDENCE
on
Church Services

-- Letters from Mrs. Eddy to C.S. Board of Directors (or the Clerk):

1) [initiating a Sunday afternoon service, dated April 10, '96 and signed "With love, Mother, M.B. Eddy"]: Beloved Students: God bids me say to you: Tell Judge Hanna to appoint next Sunday from the pulpit, that [two] services, one in the A.M., the other in the P.M., will be held thenceforth in the Mother Church in Boston. Confer with the Judge as to the hour of the afternoon service and appoint the hour when you give out the notice.

N.B. [signed "M.B.E."]: Let me hear from this as soon as attended to.

2) [follow-up dated April 11, '96 and signed "With love, M.B. Eddy"]: My beloved Students: I discern the need of having two services, one in the forenoon, the other in the afternoon in order to feed the multitude on Sunday. To do this there must be a change in the salaries of your Readers in Church. Mrs. Hanna has lost her income from the Committee service; and I consider it but just that the Judge have $5000 annually for his service for the Church. He does for us unpaid much, beside his labors that are remunerated; and other Churches pay larger salaries for their pastor than you for both Readers. As your Pastor preaches to you without money and without price--save the salvation of sense--you can afford to raise his salary and Mrs. Gragg's also. Also dear Laura's wages should be raised to $1000, the sum you first named. She proves herself worthy of it--and her car

tickets supplied her for going on errands for our Church and for her weekly trips to Mother's Room....

3) [Telegram to William B. Johnson, dated June 28, '02 and signed "M.B. Eddy"]: You may announce tomorrow there will be but one service in July and August.

4) [to Board of Directors and Judge Hanna, dated April 30, '00 and signed "With love, Mother, M.B. Eddy"]: Beloved Students: As an exception to the positive rule that our Annual Meeting shall not be over-run, I herein say, Let them come at our Annual Meeting this year, as many as want to come. Leave it to their option.

5) [dated Sept.10, '01]: I propose that because of the many recent gatherings together of the several Churches, we omit a universal gathering, and have the business of the church transacted...at the forthcoming semi-annual meeting in November.

6) [to Clerk, dated April 23, '02 and signed "M.B. Eddy"]: You may hold Annual Meeting in Mechanics Hall on Wednesday and announce it in our Sentinel and dailies. [See CSS Vol.IV, Nos.42 & 43.]

7) [Telegram to Mr. Wm.B. Johnson, dated April 24, '02 and signed "M.B. Eddy"]: Yes invite all to come to annual meeting this year. Hold communion in our church.

8) [to Clerk, dated March 15, '05 and signed "Lovingly, M.B. Eddy"]: Beloved Student: I see the feeling is against postponing the dedication of our Church [Extension] till it is finished throughout and paid for. So I withdraw my suggestion on this subject and will here say have your dedication thereof at your June annual meeting.

May God guide in all, and better loyalty be manifest among some of the local members....

N.B. [signed "M.B.E."]: Please inform at once those students that already knew what I have said before on the dedication of our Church--that I have changed my order or request as within named. ["Local members" did later accept a delay in celebrating the dedication, as indicated in the next letters.]

9) [to Mr. William B. Johnson, C.S.D., dated March 14, '06 and signed "Lovingly yours, M.B.G. Eddy"]: Beloved

Student: In my prayer it has come to me: Do not have the Mother Church dedicated until it is completely finished outside and inside. I can see the wisdom of this, and the directors will see it if they follow this direction.

10) [follow-up, signed "Lovingly yours, Mary Baker Eddy"]: Beloved Students: Under the present circumstances I deem it wise to have the Annual Convention and the Church dedication in Boston observed on June 10, 1906.

You can finish that which requires another year to complete as you named, hereafter. I do not believe in Christian Scientists making conspicuous anything that includes materialism.

Let the dedication serve only as a form of usage. [Others may choose to] spread their grandeur to its extinction. We give ours to God, Spirit, and avoid all unnecessary forms in or for our worship.

God cares for us.

~ ~ ~ ~ ~ ~ ~

As noted on p.207, the trustees under the 1892 deed (i.e. the Directors) needed a further deed when the Extension to The Mother Church foreshadowed a lapse of more than one year in the holding of services in the original building.

The Manual for its part lays down that Mother Church services be continued twelve months each year--in line with the accompanying aphorism that "A Christian Scientist is not fatigued by prayer, by reading the Scriptures or the Christian Science textbook. Amusement, or idleness, is weariness."

A year or two after the two services were introduced, it is reported that Mrs. Eddy slipped into a Sunday service in the Concord C.S. Church to determine the quality of the reading being offered the public. Her comment: I never would have known that they were reading from the Bible or my book, because they put no healing thought back of it!

Other views on the type or quality of church services are contained in the following:

-- Letter from Mrs. Eddy to First Church of Christ, Scientist, Troy, N.Y. [dated Dec.3, '97]:

...I hope the church shows [connected with dedication] are now over....

I recommend to all Churches to give no publicity and particularly no public pictures of their churches. It is...too like a surprise that one can have a church edifice. I feel so even in regard to the Mother Church although that is an exception to all others.

Gilbert Carpenter Sr. records that the Annual Convention in Boston could be just another of the "church shows" which Mrs. Eddy deplored in her letter of 1897 to the Troy church. He said it left the local fields unattended, and when it included a pilgrimage to Concord, the ensuing personalization of the Leader proved to be a problem of animal magnetism which the workers at Pleasant View were required to handle.

At least the Leader elected to keep clear of personal appearances in Boston as shown in the following letters to the C.S. Board of Directors:

1) [dated June 2, '00 and signed "With love, Mother, M.B. Eddy"]: My beloved Students: Your kind request for me to be with you at your Communion season is gratefully acknowledged. I am with you in my Message. In propria persona I shall be at Pleasant View, be in durance, watching for the dear descent of divine Love--at the feast of Soul. I cannot find time to meet you otherwise, and I am sure it will be a Pentacost for you all tomorrow.

2) [Telegram dated June 21, '01 and signed "Mary Baker G. Eddy"]: Your request for me to be present at our communion received. It will not be convenient. God is with you.

3) [to Church Committee, dated June 14, '02 and signed "With love, Mother, M.B. Eddy"]: Beloved Students: I cannot, much as I love and desire to see my church--I cannot immediately after our sacred sacrament meet them on the Fair Grounds in Concord; and think it wise to leave this subject this year as I have left it in my Message.

[Thousands of Scientists had gone to the Concord State Fair in 1900 and 1901, following the Annual Meeting, to enjoy Mrs. Eddy's appearance there.]

Branch Churches

Some letters to the C.S. Board of Directors about branch churches follow:

1) [dated Dec.19, '96 and signed "With love, Mother, Mary Baker Eddy"]: My beloved Brethren: For several reasons I see it would be advantageous in the branch churches, for the Mother Church to amend her By-laws relating to the quarterly and annual meetings so as to hold the quarterly meetings semi-annually and the annual meetings bi-annually. This will enable the leader of the several churches to meet with you and also to attend to their own duties in the intervals.

2) [to William B. Johnson, replying to a question {shall Branch Churches have First Members?} and signed "With love, M.B. Eddy"]: My beloved Student: I have answered all letters to me on this question: No! and explained the reason why. The best way is for you to form a church By-law, call a meeting and vote on this By-law prohibiting Branch Churches having that form of our church government....

3) [dated Dec.19, '98 and signed "With love, Mother, Mary Baker Eddy"]: Beloved Students: The question of churches opening up around Boston is one to be deeply considered, and you should look to God for guidance in its sacred interest.

If the Mother Church is full in the A.M. on Sundays and the dear little churches would relieve her of this surplus so she need have but one service--would it not be a good thing, provided, the churches in the suburbs of Boston only take from our church those that come from the suburbs to attend it?

Be careful and not monopolize the reading of our textbooks, the Bible and Science & Health. I want to encourage the building of all the church edifices that can be built; and the organization of as many churches as do not interfere with each others' interest, but rather promote it. Read this letter in your church meeting called for discussing this subject.

4) [dated Jan.1, '99 and signed "With love, Yours in Christ, M.B. Eddy"]: My beloved Students: Have Mr. John-

son call a church meeting and read this to the brethren, as my special desire. Make no refusals to reasonably advertise C.S. Churches for local Christian Scientists. Explain to them the reason for not having too many societies and but one church in small towns, and the churches not too near the Mother Church. Ask the applicants for advertising to consider this. Then at your church meeting decide the distance to be maintained between the Mother Church of Boston and the churches outside of Boston proper. Have all done in love, unity and fellowship with each church. This is Mother's request.

5) [dated Feb.25, '02 and signed "With love, Mother, M.B. Eddy"]: Beloved Students: Whenever you pass the By-law, or after you have passed the By-law that we proposed today as to defraying the expenses of the lawsuits, which By-law you shall print in our publications, then vote on the following:

> No member of the Mother Church shall form a church organization or erect a church edifice in Brookline, Mass., until a By-law shall be passed, permitting such organization or edifice.

Now remember that the Directors formulate and vote upon these two By-laws and not Mother. Word them as you please and act upon them voluntarily, and a majority vote of the Board shall decide concerning them. Do not publish the By-law relative to the church in Brookline, but should you ever hear of any movement looking toward a church organization or edifice there, then notify the parties of the By-law.

6) [dated May 16, '02 and signed "With love, Mother, M.B. Eddy"]: Beloved Students: I will try to make an appointment to see you as soon as I can before the annual meeting. O how I wish you could see what I see before us in the history of the churches, unless a change takes place. I will appoint next Monday for you to see me at my house at about 3 P.M. If anything prevents will telephone you "not now" and try again <u>Deo volente</u>.

7) [dated Jan.17, '06 and signed "Lovingly yours, Mary Baker Eddy"]: Beloved disciples: The six churches of our denomination in Chicago are in need of help out of con-

fusion in acting on church matters without conferring together on said matters.

For this purpose I propose the enclosed amendment.

To prevent a difficulty caused by a conference, I sent this article to you years ago, and it did prevent all troubles at that time; but now a change comes over the spirit of their dream and they write me that they must meet and confer or tumble one on to another in acting. I struggled too hard to plant C.S. on a Rock in Chicago to let the worms, or the gates of hell prevail against it, hence this amendment for you to act upon [see present Man. Art.XXIII, Sect.1].

I am sorry to trouble you, Mr. Armstrong, with these changes in your new addition of our Manual, but so fate has it whenever you issue one,--I have noted this. I am used to all sorts of shocks when getting on well, but can pity others who are in my predicament.

8) [dated March 19, '07 and signed "With love, M.B. Eddy"]: Please act at once on the by-law as to "mercy and justice" in the tenets of the Mother Church, then inform the branch church of which Mary B. Glover is a member to act on her case according to the By-Law which drops her name from that Church. For she with her father, my son by birth, has brought complaint against her grandmother for what is not true [i.e. joined in the Next Friends Suit] and this when I was supporting her with a home--and after the death of my husband, Gilbert Eddy, I offered to her father all my real estate, house and money, but one small government bond that I reserved for myself, if he would come with his family and live with me, but he refused to do it. That was unmerciful and unjust.

-- Letter to Rev. Irving C. Tomlinson from Mrs. Eddy [dated April '99]:

...I have a problem to work out that you will not have for many years. If you and others give me not sufficient chance to do it, the Science is not demonstrated.

I did not want a church so near me as Concord. I have all I should do for mine in Boston. But Mr. Buswell started the Sunday service without my proposing it and then ran out. Could get no place or hall fit to use.

Then to save dishonor to our Cause, I got the Hall. My next step to organize was influenced by others that I do not name.

Now I see the care is increased that I need diminished and if there were no Sunday services and [only] healers here, I sincerely believe it would be better for me and the world. I seem to be beyond this organized work. I have had my experience and it worries me more than all else. If only I had what time I could work to give to writing, it would do more good than I can tell. God governs me.

When I sent for Mr. B. I told him I did not want a church or Sunday services which lead to it, but healing done where I was. This was God's first order, and in 33 years I have not yielded to depart from His first order without being driven back to take it up. I see His hand is resting in this hour and that my need, not the church's, is what should be regarded, till I have overcome mental malpractice and age, but which I am not given time sufficient to attend to as I need.

[Two months before she wrote this letter, Mrs. Eddy was shown the by-laws proposed for the new Concord church. They were modeled on those of The Mother Church and she accordingly disallowed them.]

-- Telegram to First Church of Christ, Scientist, London celebrating dedication of first church across the Atlantic [dated Dec.'97 and signed "Affectionately yours, Mary Baker Eddy"]:

Beloved Brethren across the Sea: Today a nation is born.... With you be there no more sea, no ebbing faith, no night....

[The true sense of nation thus comes with the true sense of church, and vice versa. Neither one precedes the other, for the one church is the one nation. For remainder of text of telegram, see My.183 12-5.]

-- Letter to the [sic] First Church of Christ, Scientist, Edinburgh [dated June 27, '02 and signed "With love, Mother, Mary Baker G. Eddy"]:

Beloved Brethren: Your united excerpt with its wealth of love, and valuable comments on my revise of your textbook, gave me great gratitude and joy. Accept my humble thanks and affection.

A Church in Scotland is dear to my heart,--it brings to memory the golden days of childhood, when Scotch tales were told at the fireside of my home. May the bounty and beauty of holiness gladden this church, hallow its meetings, rest in the hearts of each member,--and birds of the upper air sing their sweetest songs and build their nests in this dear branch of His planting. Though you wait long for the ripe harvest, you wait in hope, for the arm that upholds you is strong; and you are bringing your ripening sheaves into the storehouse of Love that has opened the window of Heaven and is pouring you out blessings infinite.

Be joyful in His reign of righteousness, though its coming may seem slow to sense, swift are His chariots of Love. Look up--and you will see, they that are for us are more than they that are against us.

-- Letter to Second Church, Montreal from Mrs. Eddy [dated July 18, '02]:

...Your deep desire for more grace and spiritual understanding is akin to all Christian endeavor and encourages my hope in the present and future growth of our cause. May you see of the travail of your hope and faith and be satisfied. This consummation awaits one and all who awake in His likeness; who are constantly looking and walking midst thorns and flowers, through deserts and green pastures, to rest at length beside the still waters, in thoughts that have dissolved themselves in a solution of divine Love. Thus laboring and waiting patiently you reach the rest of the righteous, sit down at the right hand of God, receive the reward of these words, "well done, good and faithful" and partake of the "fruits of thy labors."

-- Letter to Washington churches [dated July 15, '05 and signed "Lovingly yours, Mary Baker Eddy"]:

...Your request for my permission to unite the two churches in Washington, D.C. I hereby give you; but this does not settle the question, because I have no right to do so. I hope that you all will see your duty in the case and do it in the interest of Christian Science.

Membership and Church Manual

-- P.S. to Letter to Judge Hanna [dated Jan.17, '98 and signed "With love, Mother, M.B. Eddy"]:

Please find the amendment to by-law for next edition of Manual. I read and showed my woman document to lawyer of Concord who is considered smart. And he said, "There is nothing incorrect in it."

Well, had I been its author, I scarcely could have believed it. But I was not more the author of that than of S. & H. as I regard it.

-- Further letter clarifying the above [dated Jan.18, '98 and signed "With love, M.B. Eddy"]:

Beloved Student: For special reasons and to prevent unhappy results this transaction had to be rattled off that night in time for the meeting was called. I employed a lawyer called smart. His father was our Senator at Congress. I had scribbled it for a schedule but there was not time for the Lawyer to read and rewrite it and mail it in time, so I read it to him and he said it was "right" and I signed and Mr. Ladd, my 2nd cousin, treasurer of The Loan and Trust Savings Bank, Concord, put down his signature.

The lawyer is of the firm of Stevens and Leach, city. Names, Fred. N. Ladd, Henry W. Stevens. Do you think best about adding the signatures.

-- Letter to Clerk Wm.B Johnson dealing with the above [dated Jan.21, '98 and signed "With love, M.B. Eddy"]:

My beloved Student: After adopting this Church Rule and you have looked over the list of First Members, then drop the names of those that reside not within the distance specified for First Members. I am constrained to have a limit named because of the calls of distant applicants to be made First Members....

-- N.B. added to letter to C.S. Directors [dated March 11, '98 and signed "Again M.B.E."]:

It is of utmost importance that the Mother Church retain no members that are not strict adherents of its Tenets.

-- Other messages to C.S. Board of Directors or Clerk:

1) [Telegram dated April 10, '98 and signed "Mary Baker Eddy"]: Correct By-law just sent to read: and her testimony or the testimony of a member of the Christian Science Board of Directors shall be found sufficient evidence in the case.

[The By-law in question, before the correction was made, read as follows]: The Christian Science Board of Directors of this Church shall not fill a vacancy occurring on that Board except by a unanimous vote of all the First Members of this Church.

The Board of Trustees of this Church shall not fill a vacancy occurring on their board except by a unanimous vote of all the First Members of this Church.

The Readers of this Church shall not be elected except by a unanimous vote of all the First Members of this Church. And no person shall be a member of this Church or be eligible to the said offices who has made attempts to greatly injure Mrs. Eddy and hers or any member thereof, and their testimony thereto shall be received as sufficient evidence in the case.

This Church By-law can neither be amended or annulled except by the consent of Mrs. Eddy, The Pastor Emeritus, of this Church over her own handwriting.

[The above By-law, in both old and new versions, gave remarkable evidence of the trend of the Manual. Not only did it make a distinction between the Board of Directors of a church in Boston and the Church Trustees under the Deed establishing The First Church of Christ, Scientist; but it also was evidence of the growing role of estoppel clauses {in the Manual, but not the Deed of Trust} requiring Mrs. Eddy's signature.]

2) [to Wm.B. Johnson, dated Aug.27, '98 and signed "With love, Mother, M.B. Eddy"]: My beloved Student: ...I

send you the enclosed to print in the Manual on page 9, Art.2, Sec.4 in place of that section. You must vote at your next meeting to adopt it.

[Enclosure]: Sec.4. Seven First Members shall constitute a quorum for transacting the church business. A majority of all the First Members elects a First Member.

3) [to Wm.B. Johnson, dated Aug.29, '98 and signed "Fraternally, C.A. Frye"]: Mother requests that you have this adopted immediately:

Church By-Law

If a weekly newspaper shall at any time be published by the Christian Science Publishing Society, it shall be owned by The First Church of Christ, Scientist, in Boston, and shall be copyrighted and conducted according to the By-law relating to the Christian Science Journal.

["The First Church of Christ, Scientist" is defined legally in its 1892 Deed of Trust--not in the Manual text.]

4) [to Clerk, dated March 14, '99 and signed "With love, M.B. Eddy"]: The Church Manual in Article No.II, Sec. III, must be restored to its original form at the close of this Sec. Circumstances require this vote to amend so as to read as it was in the revised edition of 1897.

I hope not to trouble you again in this wise. Have it corrected as above in the last edition, if this has not already gone to press.

[The correction enforced the forbidding of membership to someone like Mrs. Woodbury who had been "twice excommunicated." It showed that if the church failed twice to see a "good member" in some individual, it was better for the church and that individual to "await a convenient season" for the healing thought.]

5) [to C.S. Directors, dated Feb.6, '99 and signed "With love, Mother and teacher, M. Baker Eddy"]: My beloved Students: The call from Littleton, N.H. for a lecturer is not a breach of church By-laws, when you carefully study all of them. This call must be met, and in this manner. Have our brother fill one of Mr. Tomlinson's appointments in Mass. and send Rev. Tomlinson to Littleton. As he has gone to the

capitol of our state to work for C.S., he should do the lecturing in N.H. This will be best for our cause.

6) [dated Nov.23, '02 and signed "With love, Mother, M.B. Eddy"]: Beloved Students: Do not delay publishing the new edition of the Manual on my account. This is the cyclone hour with our cause when my weather vane must veer with the wind in order to indicate the right course. What seems best today, tomorrow may make not best. Be strong and clear in your conviction that God, not m.a.m. is influencing your actions. In order to be this, you must surely pray daily that God, good, divine Love--your only Mind--be followed, be loved, be lived by you.

7) [dated April 18, '04 and signed "Lovingly yours, M.B. Eddy"]: Beloved Students: ...I am in receipt of a letter from Mr. Farlow containing almost absolutely what I saw in that By-law which caused me to hesitate to send it to you. Read his letter and do not, if you have not already, adopt or print that By-law. If it has been adopted and printed expunge it--remove it from the Manual and destroy it.

8) [to The First Church of Christ, Scientist, dated Dec.19, '96 and signed "With love, Mother, Mary Baker Eddy"]: My beloved Brethren: ...It is important that a By-law be made and passed...concerning the student's students, empowering them to sign applications for membership with this church to be countersigned by their teacher, who must also be a member of this church. Mrs. Rose E. Kent's son, Morgan B. Kent, must be admitted to this church at this quarterly meeting. He rises each morning at the St. Paul's School in this city, earlier than the others, for the purpose of reading <u>Science and Health</u>, one hour. The St. Paul's Church had requested him to unite with them, hoping thereby to prevent his becoming a Scientist.

9) [dated May 30, '99 and signed "With love, Mother, Mary Baker Eddy"]: Beloved Students: I request that under the present circumstances you suspend the church by-law and without the preliminaries permit Lord and Lady Dunmore's son Viscount Fincastle, to become a member of the Mother Church--The First Church of Christ, Scientist, in

Boston, Mass. [Lord Fincastle was in America briefly on his way to an appointment overseas.]

~ ~ ~ ~ ~ ~ ~

Mrs. Eddy's requests and demands in the letters above were often calls to view the Manual as a whole (i.e. to imbibe the overruling spirit even while studying the letter).

According to members of her household some by-laws were thought to be too specific (too devoted to the letter) to be included publicly in the Manual. They were sent to and passed by the First Members or Directors in case a specific need arose or in case Mrs. Eddy needed to make an instant change. Three of the "in case" by-laws read as follows:

> 1) If in the course of observation our Pastor Emeritus has seen the need of exterminating a By-law, or a Rule of this church, it shall be the duty of the First Members to vote to expunge it.
>
> 2) If at any time editors should refuse to publish the Publication Committee's reply to some abusive article unless they are paid for it,--if it be of sufficient importance to warrant this--the manager of the Committee, on furnishing himself with an indorsement by the Board of Directors, can apply to the Treasurer of this Church and receive from him a reasonable sum to pay for the publication of said article.
>
> 3) No Church funds [may be used to assist in] a lawsuit against any member of The Mother Church.

By 1907 Mrs. Eddy was contemplating a change in "Alertness to Duty" in the Manual to require members to "purge" themselves rather than "defend" themselves. The distinction balanced the question whether evil was a suggestion coming from without to be handled, or whether evil was a suggestion harbored within and needing to be kicked out. The current version (Art.VIII, Sect.6) was however chosen in preference to:

> It shall be the duty of every member of this Church to daily purge himself of all aggressive mental suggestion and not be made to forget, nor to neglect his duty to God, to his Leader, and to mankind.

-- <u>Letter</u> to William B. Johnson, C.S.D. [dated Aug.4, '06 and signed "Lovingly yours, Mary Baker Eddy"]:

I am sending you the printer's copy of an important revision of the Church Manual [in its ninth copyright].

It is important that our Church By-laws shall be letter-perfect when they appear in book form, and I desire that the Christian Science Board of Directors see that the printers follow this revised copy exactly.

I have retained a duplicate copy of this revision so that it will be possible to detect any discrepancies.

<u>Music in the Church</u>

-- <u>Letter</u> to C.S. Board [dated Aug.7, '96 and signed "With love, Mother, M.B. Eddy"]:

My beloved Students: Call a church meeting at once and put this By-law [regulating the music permissible for Mrs. Eddy's hymns] in the Manual.

I sent the Mother's Evening Prayer on sheet music composed by Mr. Case, by the Dr. to Miss Lincoln, telling him to have her sing it and return word to me what she thought of the music. I had not accepted the music, but was having it examined, and never dreamed of having it sung in church till I did conclude to have it published in that music. The mistake was made by m.a.m. causing my directions to be mistaken or knowingly disobeyed. I have not yet heard Miss Lincoln's opinion of the music, although that was what I expressly sent it to her for, and my only purpose. Now it has furnished a bone of contention as the demons direct. But I declare this subject shall be dropped and no more be thought or said of it.

Look up any By-law that has been made relative to the matter of music to be sung in church and send it to me.

When, if ever, will all the members of this church, even while under the rod, behave themselves as Christian Scientists, and not have to be put into straight jackets to keep them from quarreling in the sackcloth of this solemn hour!

The "quarreling" Mrs. Eddy referred to arose inter alia from Composer Henry Lincoln Case's association in New York wih Augusta Stetson (see Six Days, pp.519-20). Such was the opposition in Boston to Mrs. Stetson that Mrs. Eddy had already found it necessary to suppress dispute by enacting the by-law (Art.VIII, Sect.11) to which she drew Mr. Johnson's attention in the above letter. This stated:

> "No hymns nor words composed by students of Christian Science that are not at this date, January 22, 1896, in the Christian Science Hymnal shall be sung in the Mother Church, The First Church of Christ, Scientist, in Boston. As a necessary barrier to inharmony in the Church this By-law has become requisite" [emphasis added].

An attempt was then made by the Stetson group to circumvent the by-law by telling the soloist that Mr. Case's rendition was an "ode" rather than a hymn, and therefore that she could sing it. This did not get by Mrs. Eddy, as the correspondence below will show.

The Directors, for their part, were wanting to have Mrs. Eddy's hymns, as currently accepted for congregational singing, available for the soloist, but found no by-law to permit this.

Without the Spirit, words and music can be just noise--"sometimes beautiful, always erroneous"--and Mrs. Eddy was insisting that her hymns follow the tones of Spirit, in the music just as much as in the words.

She accordingly kept objecting to tunes which simply danced to the rhythm of words, and she made a distinction between music for congregational singing and music suitable as accompaniment for a solo.

Her aspiration was well worded in this letter to a friend: "I long for music spiritual with healing in its wings--only thus can my hymns reach hearts ready for them."

-- Letter to Mr. Wm.B. Johnson [dated Aug.18, '96 and signed "Eddy"]:

> My beloved Student: A Hymn is a song or ode composed for the church. An ode includes the music as well as words, hence the By-law has been broken for neither words nor music were in our Hymnal at the time Mother's Prayer was sung. See Webster's dictionary.

-- Further <u>By-law</u> by Mrs. Eddy [forerunner of present Art.XIX, Sect.1]:

If a solo singer in The First Church of Christ, Scientist, Boston, shall either neglect or refuse to sing alone a hymn composed by our Leader and Pastor Emeritus as often as once a month, and oftener if the Board of Directors so direct, a meeting shall be called and the salary of this singer shall be stopped.

-- <u>Letter</u> to Christian Science Board of Directors [dated May 10, '99 and signed "With love, Mother"]:

My beloved Students: One thing I have delayed for months owing to so much else I have on hand. It is this: to have my hymn "Shepherd, Show me How to Go" either taken out of the Hymnal, or set to better music. It must not be sung again with that tune. When Miss White sang it to me in Concord a few months ago to the music, or rather, no music, published in your Hymnal, I was shocked. The spirit of the words was gone.

This is another special order. Remove it from your Hymnal or give music that I will approve. It may be sung as arranged on the sheet music if you desire to have it.

N.B. [signed "Mother"]: Have this matter attended to in time for your next edition of the Hymnal. I have not heard my other hymns sung according to the music given them in the Hymnal, but if it is not better than the one I have referred to, they shall all be served in the same manner--left out of your Hymnal Book--which certainly would be a disaster to the Mother Church.

-- <u>Letter</u> to C.S. Board of Directors [dated Sept.30, '98 and signed "With love, Mother, M.B. Eddy"]:

My beloved Students: I call your attention to an important point. Mr. Metcalf gave us the church organ; he is dissatisfied with the organist's playing. Now it is but just and right that we satisfy him if we can. To this end and to show him our appreciation of what he has done for us, I direct you to call a meeting of your Board and appoint a Com. of one (and that one Albert Metcalf) to engage for our church the organist. Then at the expiration of this present one's term of service, he can suit himself to the man that shall play our church organ. After your appointment of him as Com. write a kind respectful letter to him informing him of your appointment, and that it was my request.

The clerk's son, Wm. Lyman Johnson, was also in the picture. He had studied music before and during his Harvard days, and had sent to Mrs. Eddy his own verbal analysis of her Communion Hymn along with the music he had written to match. Despite her approval and authorization for it to be sung in the church as a solo, some of the audience sent in anonymous comments which more than matched Mrs. Eddy's uncomplimentary views on some of the hymn tunes they did like! Later Wm. Lyman tried "Mother's Evening Prayer", but found it too much of a challenge, particularly after learning from Mrs. Eddy that "my child" in the poem is "none other than Christian Science." His settings for "Feed my Sheep" and "Christ my Refuge" were however included in the 1903 edition of the Hymnal and remained in the 1932 revision (Nos. 253, 306).

In the unpublished supplements to his "History" he records his estimate that the main opposition to his musical offerings came from Archibald McLellan, who seemed to be handled by a dislike of the younger Mr. Johnson somewhat equal to his dislike of Augusta Stetson (as dealt with later on in this chapter).

Mr. Johnson felt that Mrs. Eddy could have overruled the McLellan objections or let the other directors outvote him, but she once again was prepared to wait on God for a more "convenient season", thus giving the truth about God and man a chance to manifest itself in its own way.

More on Readers, Lesson Sermons

The following correspondence took place between Mrs. Eddy and the Board of Directors (or the Clerk):

1) [to William B. Johnson, dated Aug.1, '98 and signed "Mary Baker Eddy"]: My beloved Student: ...I recommend that now you take two thirds more matter from S&H than from the Bible for your C.S. Quarterly.

2) [dated April 2, '96 and signed "With love, Mother, M.B. Eddy"]: My beloved Students: I have taken your kind advice, at least Mr. Armstrong's and as I really need Laura--with your permission will keep her here all but the Friday on which she will be in Boston to tend Mother's Room.

She will go there on Thursday and return to Concord on Sat., and pay Mrs. Weller for opening the Room on Sunday, tending guests and closing it. Also will leave the key with Mr. Irving, where Mrs. Weller can find it and leave it. Now if you think best thus to accommodate me, please return this reply. Again I will remind you that Mrs. Sargent [Laura] must go on the Com. for preparing the C.S. Lessons. She is important there and will send or leave with you her MSS.

3) [dated Feb.23, '01 and signed "With love, Mother, M.B. Eddy"]: Beloved Students: Please meet and appoint Mr. John B. Willis a member of the Com. on Bible Lessons. He is a good Biblical scholar and such a one is needed. Attend to this immediately.

4) [dated April 8, '04 and signed "With love, M.B. Eddy"]: Beloved Students: I recommend that you fill the vacancy on Lesson Com. with Mrs. Knott. She will have time apart from her office as Assistant Editor to fill this office....

5) [to William B. Johnson, dated July 13, '99 and signed "Yours fraternally, C.A. Frye"]: Dear Brother: Mother requests that you change the last part of the By-law sent yesterday on qualifications of readers to read, [to] "read and spell well", instead of "correctly."

6) [dated April 30, '99 and signed "With love, M.B. Eddy"]: Beloved Students: Appoint at once Judge J.R. Clarkson of my last class and residing in Omaha, Neb. a member of the Board of Lectureship. He is not a First Reader but a first and grand man.

The lectures are doing much for our Cause but the Readers must not be called so much away from their churches; hence my putting the new candidate in to fill the appointments that the dear Readers give up of lectures on file.

7) [dated June 11, '02 and signed "With love, Mother, M.B. Eddy"]: Beloved Students: I have just received a letter most kind from Judge Hanna signifying his willingness and pleasure to leave the Readership and editorial chair for a rest [after the three-year limit for readerhip was established]. This now gives you opportunity to secure Mr. Cameron of Chicago and Mrs. Ewing if you can, to take the readership; and Mr. McLellan of Chicago the place of editor-in-chief of our periodicals.

Mr. Cone reads my Message [for 1902]. Mr. Bingham is to be our President, and then all is provided for in case the Readers named will serve--is it not? [Prof. Hering was appointed First Reader instead of Mr. Cameron.]

With lone and dreary foresight of my tasks I look on this hour--unless you help me more to help new officers know what is best to do and how to do it. But you must help in this, or give up your office on our Board, for I cannot and I shall not do it alone.

[P.S. {signed "With love, M.B. Eddy"}]: Elect Judge Hanna a member of the Board of Lectureship.

8) [dated June 23, '02 and signed "With love, Mother, Mary Baker Eddy"]: Beloved Students: It is my desire and established usage, that a person having a well-earned title--when he becomes a Christian Scientist--shall retain that title or appellation. The members of our denomination will please comply with this usage in every instance.

Our [newly-appointed] first Reader in the Church is Professor Hermann S. Hering.

> -- Message from Mrs. Eddy to all First Readers [undated]: I request that you pray once every day for the principal editors of the principal periodicals in your city and for the clergymen in your pulpits. The lying influences sent forth to deceive our clergymen and our pressmen would, if possible, "deceive the very elect."

Reading Rooms & Publication Committees (COP's)

9) [dated May 16, '00 and signed "With love, Mother, Mary Baker Eddy"]: Beloved Students: Once more God thunders in your ears--"Get a reading Room in Boston and

locate it in that part of the city where people will be most apt to go into it."

Again I say unless you do this at once and have it ready, furnished, and ready, before our Communion season, it will be ill with thee. I see this; I know it. You have not prospered since you disobeyed God in not getting the right location and at the time He bade you do it, for another church building, and publishing house for His Word to be heard therefrom. I beg for God's dear sake, for your own, and for mine, that you obey this call.

Announce at once and not stop till you have accomplished my request in this letter. Write to me.

[Following the aborted appointment of Mr. Armstrong's son as the librarian, Mrs. Eddy on Aug.18, '00 sent in two other names that she could agree to.]

Other correspondence on these subjects follows:

1) [to Irving C. Tomlinson from Mrs. Eddy, dated early Jan. '00]: Yours just read. Before I received it I had typed my By-law relating to Publishing Com. I thank you for your dear interest in our cause. I thank God that I can call on you for help. But dear one, never attempt to steady the altar. God had told me what to do before the subject was named to you. And you will be delighted to hear that I had requested the clerk to read my letter requesting the Church to elect Mr. Farlow.

2) [to William B. Johnson on the same subject, dated Jan.8, '00 and signed "With love, M.B. Eddy"]: Beloved Student: I only asked Mr. Tomlinson to write that By-law for me but he sent it to the church before I had examined it. Herein find the proper By-law as written by myself. Wipe out the other one. Do not vote on a By-law except when I have sent it.

N.B. [signed "Again, M.B. Eddy"]: ...Say in open meeting to my church that Mother recommends that this church elect Mr. Alfred Farlow, C.S.D., to constitute the Publishing Committee.

3) [to Mrs. A.E. Stetson, dated Oct.25, '03 and signed "With love, M.B.G. Eddy"]: My beloved Student: I did not

get your letter in time to reply before you left N.Y.--to your question on selling my books downtown in your city. That movement would be unwise in many ways and would not prosper, abandon such a thought. You have fulfilled the By-law in our Church relation to a Reading Room; and it only remains for you to carry on your Reading Room and for the downtowners to unite and have a Reading Room that is centrally located. This is what must be done.

4) [to Alfred Farlow, dated Jan.8, '06 and signed "With love, yours, Mary Baker Eddy"]: My dear Student: Your report on Libraries in N.Y.City received. Thank you deeply for having instituted this important work on reform; it is much needed. I have not the time to inform myself on this subject sufficiently to suggest other than what you are already attempting. May God prosper and speed your undertaking. Have no <u>lawsuits</u> about this.

[P.S. {signed M.B.E.}]: I called a halt to inquire as to results before writing you. Litigation must not attend this work.

N.B. In Church Manual see page 34, Art.6, Sec.1, on your duty as a member of my Church and show your plans to the Directors for their approval before you execute them.

[P.P.S. {signed "Eddy"}]: W[oodbury] sends those papers that report me done as Leader all over the country. You wrong me and your correction is not read by thousands and injures our Cause in the eyes of thousands, every time you allow such lies about me to be published and if you cannot or will not stop doing this, you are unfit for the General Pub. Com. and will be removed.

~ ~ ~ ~ ~ ~ ~

This sharply-worded letter shows that the COP's duty (i.e. the one Scientist's, the one COP's duty) is not simply to look for and correct errors. The call is: not to "<u>allow</u> such lies...to be published." The COP must be able to send his "best detectives to whatever locality is reported to be" misinformed, and learn that the lie "was never there" (S&H 439:31).

In words which Mrs. Eddy wrote to a student Feb.16, '07, the starting point is:

"There are no lies. All is Mind and governs. What is matter? it cannot talk. Then hold to Mind and the rest will take care of itself--the rest is nothing.... Life is divine, immortal, and there is no other life. That is all the Life there is and it is ours."

Yet despite the sharp criticism of Alfred Farlow's handling of some of his duties (notably regarding the Peabody attack, and the Wiggin "mistake" mentioned in My.317:9), Mrs. Eddy was nonetheless appreciative. To the Board she wrote: "His salary does not pay his rent and clerks! Please vote to amend the By-law to read instead of three thousand dollars annually for the Pub. Com. not less than three thousand dollars. Then vote to increase his salary to five thousand dollars annually." At another time she sent this:

-- Letter to C.S. Board Directors, Mr. W.B. Johnson, C.S.D. [dated March 27, '04 and signed "Lovingly yours, M.B.G. Eddy"]:

Beloved Student: ...The By-law that I forwarded relative to members of our church and to publishing house I want you to read to Mr. Farlow and ask him for me, if it in any way will hinder his official duties, and if it will not please act on this By-law and the one on S[unday] S[chool] immediately and inform me. [See May CSJ '04.]

Individual Scientists who rightly respond to the call for COP activity may need to know Who is the one and only COP. In April 1901 Dr. "Fighting" Buckley, Methodist minister in New York City, challenged any Christian Scientist to meet him in debate. Rev. Arthur S. Vosburgh, C.S.B., accepted the challenge--valiantly ready to go into "whatever locality is reported to be haunted by" error and lick it right there. Such an attitude led to what is now Article X in the Manual, and the following:

-- Letter to W.B. Johnson [dated April 18, '01 and signed "With love, M.B. Eddy"]:

My beloved Student: ...It has become imperative for me to make some more By-laws to prevent the sheep of my fold from going over the wall and scattering into by and forbidden paths. Please call a meeting and vote on them and publish them in our periodicals.

Lectures, Missionaries

Further correspondence with the Board of Directors (or the Clerk) on the above subjects follows:

1) [to Clerk, dated Jan.21, '98 and signed "With love, M.B. Eddy"]: My beloved Student: ...an answer must be given those asking to be added to list of lecturers.

Please look up William B. Dickson; he has applied to me for a place on the Board of Lectureship. I am willing he should have one if he is the right candidate. The far distant West ought by right to have one lecturer in its precincts. Call a church meeting as soon as convenient and vote on these matters.

2) [dated March 11, '98 and signed "With love, Mother, Mary Baker Eddy"]: My dear Students: Some ones, and you seem to be the ones, must look after the "Lecturers", who are liable to make mistakes because not familiar with the circumstances that surround them. I cannot take the Board of Lectureship on my hands, and our cause demands that the teachers of the students (if the students have confidence in them) should look after their students; and that you should inform them, the teachers, of any impending danger that surrounds their students, and they should at once inform them thereof.

3) [dated Sept.12, '98 and signed "With love, Mother, M.B. Eddy"]: My dear Students: I am informed that the experience meeting flags. You are directed to advertise through the C.S. weekly and monthly that the Wed. eve meeting will be changed to a meeting of interest on other subjects as well as personal experience, and will hereafter be called the Wed. Evening Meeting. Also a member of the Board of Lectureship will lecture at these meetings as often as once in three months annually and the Directors will select the lecturer and request him where and when to deliver his lecture within the boundary of his section or precinct.

4) [dated Sept.28, '98 and signed "With love, Mother, M.B. Eddy"]: My beloved Students: ...I send a list of names for you to consider in your choice of missionaries according

to the By-law last sent. Please do not let people know that I selected them....

Missionaries

Prof. McKenzie John F. Linscott
Mr. Ira O. Knapp Mrs. Ellen B. Linscott

5) [dated Oct.30, '98 and signed "With love, Mother, M.B. Eddy"]: My beloved Students: The Missionary Board is to be dissolved and the By-law annulled at your next meeting and left out of your Manual. Why? I saw at a glance on receipt of proceedings how it would be prolific of discord.

Missionaries are needed in the field but Mother had better recommend the ones adapted to it--the work--to go where they are needed, and then leave it to them to decide whether or not they are willing....

[The missionaries went out into the field to assist outlying groups of Scientists on the spot--in a way that a centralized hierarchy could not manage from Boston. Even though Mrs. Eddy insisted on supervising the appointments, she wanted the Directors to do the "paper work" as shown in the following]:

6) [note to Ira O. Knapp, President, dated April 8, '99 and signed "With love, M.B. Eddy"]: My beloved Student: You, the C.S. Directors, must attend to this matter of missionaries according to your own best judgment.

N.B. [signed "Again, Mother"]: ...Please call a meeting of your Board and elect Judge Ewing of Chicago as one of [the Missionary Committee] members and inform him at once of this election.

7) [answer signed "With love, M.B. Eddy" to a letter from the Clerk dated Sept.26, '00]: Beloved Student: This is the first time I have heard of your selection [of Judge Joseph Clarkson as next] lecturer [in the Mother Church]. Yes, I highly approve of it.

8) [to Clerk, dated Jan.25, '02 and signed "With love, Mother, M.B. Eddy"]: Beloved Student: ...Nothing could injure our Cause more than the general silence that prevails on the topic of your Leader's Character. This silence is causing

the press to publish...lies, for it looks as if the Board of Lectureship was ashamed to speak in defence of your Leader, or has nothing to say in her behalf!

...I will write to the members of the Board to do their duty, and Mr. Tomlinson will also write to the Board on this subject.

9) [dated July 22, '02 and signed "With love, Mother, Mary B. Eddy"]: Beloved Students: I have learned that our able lecturer, Dr. Sulcer is suspended [for immoral behavior] till further orders. I hereby request you to reinstate him or retain him in office, whichever applies to the situation. I request that you call a meeting for this purpose immediately and that you also elect Edward H. Hammond a member of the Board of Lectureship and name his circuit the Southern and Middle States. Then send a notice of this to our Editor in chief for publication.

10) [dated April 16, '04 and signed "Lovingly, M.B. Eddy"]: Beloved Students: I have received Lawyer Clarence Buskirk's reply consenting to my request that he become a candidate for election as member of the Board of Lectureship. I think he will honor our Cause if elected.

11) [dated Feb.4, '06 and signed "Lovingly yours, M.B. Eddy"]: Beloved Directors: Do you understand this is what I mean viz. To qualify four Students not as surgeons, but only to give epidermic injections <u>safely</u> as to puncturing a vein or injecting too large a dose of morphine. Bone surgery requires too long time and too much material thought and practice, to make a safe surgeon, for Christian Scientists to undertake. It is their privilege to handle bones mentally as I did in practising, but if they cannot, to employ an M.D. Three more Students who are <u>unmarried</u> and free from family obligations should be selected and instructed by Dr. Strang (who taught Mr. Lewis Strang, his brother, how to inject morphine. He is an M.D. and qualified therefor as I am told).

The By-law on "<u>Missionaries</u>" is ambiguous necessarily. It means that the Church shall pay them except when I send for one to remain with me one year. Then that one comes under the terms of the By-law--"Opportunity to Serve our Leader" [see Man.67:24] and I pay him.

N.B. Be wise in selecting Missionaries--their office is very important.

12) [note dated Feb.3, '06, signed "Mary Baker Eddy" and written below the by-law referred to above]: By the above word and classification in the Church Manual is meant: The members of The Mother Church who act in administering hypodermics and those who are chosen for Watchers, and those who are selected for maids to attend upon its Pastor Emeritus.

-- Letter to Irving Tomlinson from Mrs. Eddy [dated Jan.7, '98]:

My dear Brother: You can lecture occasionally as you see the need thereof, if not called upon to do this by the churches. Be careful and not berate any religion: be charitable towards all men. Make a strong point showing the practical excellence of Christian Science. Arm yourself with divine Love; then when you "are lifted up you will draw all men unto you."

-- Letter to Mrs. Sue Mims, C.S.D. [dated Nov.26, '05 and signed "Ever lovingly thine, M.B.G. Eddy"]:

My beloved Student: Your letter and lecture are treasures. Can I half thank you for them, pen can never do it but my heart can and does. God will fill you with the fatness of his house and the rivers of his pleasure flood your being with beauty and bounty. That which you impart either impoverishes or enriches being. And the fruit of your labor has already declared it from the garden of God, the tree of Life....

Darling one, how I long to have time to see you and say something that I think, and yet I know that you hear it whether absent or present.

-- Watch Prayers given to Henrictta Chanfrau:

1) [Feb.10 '02]: Take up at once the so-called C.S. lecturers that they do their duty to their God,...and the life of their Leader must be shown as it is. The scandalous attacks on the Discoverer and Founder of Christian Science will stop if the truth about her be shown to the world.

2) [Feb.2 '06]: Take up...strong, clear voice for Christian Science lecturers. Error tries to hinder Truth being heard in public....

CHURCH EXPANSION AND MRS. EDDY'S SUCCESSOR

By 1906 the pattern for CHURCH UNIVERSAL (alias one Consciousness, one Nation, one World, one Universe) was set and clear. The guidelines put in place by Mrs. Eddy were there for the individual to follow--whether obediently and blindly, or understandingly and God-prompted.

Yet into her revelation of one God, one church, one man, one Scientist, lurked the "belief in a mysterious, supernatural God, and in a natural, all-powerful devil" (S&H 450:1-4). This belief of more than one mind kept shouting "Who shall be the greatest?" and "Who will join me in fighting off my devil in ambush?" Students have preserved these two pungent sayings by Mrs. Eddy:

1) When the Christian Scientists stop shooting at each other, the Cause will make some progress.

2) The method of error, to divide and conquer, prevails like an epidemic in the Field, and no office is high enough to be beyond its reach. That is why I have taken a hand in church affairs and intervened. I have been called a pope, but authority has been forced upon me by necessity. Why, the Board had five dear churches under discipline at one time, and to what end? Good people do not change at once from good to evil anymore than bad from evil to good. And who of us can cast the first stone? Our organization is made up of members, and if we do not understand this, must it not disappear from the face of the earth?

Is it not simple? When one says that Christian Science is the Way and the only way, he is ready for church membership, and there is no other requirement. Then one's ability to heal the sick through Christian Science, and this alone, shows his position as a Christian Scientist. Not the cries of "Lord! Lord!" and not the bowing to ecclesiastical despotism; but by their fruits ye shall know them.

~ ~ ~ ~ ~ ~ ~

This chapter is however to record the Seventh Day's lessons, not to judge them on how well they are heeded.

With Mrs. Woodbury the church officials had been united in their ability to detect the error and in their inability to correct it.

As the "hour has struck for Christian Scientists to do their own work" (Mis. 317:5), it became inevitable that the prop of a visible Pastor Emeritus would "fall into the ground and die", and that each individual would need to become consciously grounded in Principle. The belief in many minds would then be vying for the top honor of sitting "on the right hand" of the Lord in His kingdom. These many minds were thus contemplating their chances of being the successor to a personalized Mrs. Eddy in the inevitable but hardly mentionable event of her death.

Mrs. Eddy had defined her successor in the most far-reaching way she could--by getting mortal mind to speculate widely on the subject and then using the largest news agency (the Associated Press) to tell the world on May 16, '01 that her successor is no "man today on earth" but is "man the generic term for mankind." Although this statement was included in 1909 in the sealed package which was to become *Miscellany*, publication was delayed until 1913, when men today on earth were already established in many minds as her "successor."

No Christian Scientist will point to a delay in publication as an excuse for misunderstanding Mrs. Eddy. Gilbert Carpenter Sr. records that during his year in Pleasant View (1905-6) she startled him by telling him he was her successor. Later he confided this remark to Laura Sargent who said "Oh yes, she says that to all of us!" "You", as the one Christian Scientist, succeeds to the one goodness the Revelator has established.

Mrs. Eddy was known sometimes to add C.S.B. to names she wrote to, even when they had no such official qualification, and although she was never at fault with names on College or Board of Education certificates she had signed. Also, at a time when no change was required, and no change was made, on the Board of Directors, she wrote to Edward Kimball (July 26, '01): "I want to make you one of our Church Directors in Boston."

It is evident that director, successor, graduate are automatic qualifications of the Christian Scientist, who is responsible at all times for correct thinking on all these functions. They involve the understanding of what and who Pastor, Revelator, Teacher, is; and are independent of material certification. In fact, "state honors perish, and their gain is loss to the Christian Scientist" (Mis.358:7).

What then are the lessons that accompany a belief in personal direction and submission, in personal revelation and acceptance, in personal instruction and obedience? They involve the handling of jealousy, hero-worship, suspicion, dependence, mad ambition, subservience, etc.--by corrective realization of the truth of one God, one man.

For the Bostonians who wanted to climb the worldly ladder there seemed to be the threat of the "Chicago invasion": Kimball, Ewing, McLellan, Dittemore and others. There was always the New York threat--centered around Augusta Stetson. There was the local threat of gossip, and of their own failings (unless m.a.m. could operate to offset these by counter gossip).

Mortal mind's game is to find some criticism (preferably by Mrs. Eddy) of a rival and thus label that one 100% wrong, even as one brand of thinking tried and tries to do with Edward A. Kimball. Praise by Mrs. Eddy likewise gives an opportunity to label others, or others' favorites, 100% right. Mrs. Eddy's remedy is always to detect the error--and recommend it be healed with Truth and Love, rather than cherished it as a "sweet morsel" to be used for personal advancement.

She said moreover (No.41:12) that "it is vain to look for perfection [100% rightness] in churches or associations." The whole of Truth is not in some single object or person, but the object can point to the subjective truth governing all objective appearance.

There were plenty of words of praise, and of caution, for Mrs. Stetson, for the Directors (including McLellan), for Judge Hanna, for Judge Clarkson, etc., just as there had been words of encouragement and concern for Mrs. Woodbury.

On one occasion (July 1898) Judge Hanna and William McKenzie slipped out of Boston to find some moments of relaxation from the heat and pressure. Mrs. Eddy located them and wrote sternly as follows:

Return at once to Boston and find your retreat for an outing within a short distance of human help, if indeed there is the least occasion for it. Had I known sooner the place where you were sent by M.A.M., I would sooner have delivered my message to you no doubt.

Could this now be interpreted to mean that in everything the Judge wrote and did he was liable or even certain to be propelled by M.A.M.? The belief of many inimical minds would love to say so, but such a thought needs to be reversed not magnified; and Mrs. Eddy did just that in other parts of her letter:

You can take my method, bar your doors, and then hold your solitude with moral dignity by meeting the merciless selfishness of callers with a fixed rule and the divine imperative Principle to be alone with God, and never break this rule till you have your interval of study and prayer.... The mail and the male and female claim undisputed powers to break my peace and rob me of all individual exemption from labor. But you have no need of thus surrendering your rights for others'.

Similarly, can the following letter be interpreted to mean that Archibald McLellan was always right--at least on all matters of importance? To substantiate this it could be pointed out that Mrs. Eddy publicly proclaimed him as the trustee "I knew I could trust" (CSS Vol.IX, No.51).

-- Letter to Board of Directors [dated Feb.5, '03 and signed "With love, Your teacher, M.B. Eddy"]:

Beloved Students: I send the enclosed By-laws. Please convene immediately and vote on them. They are of equal importance to our cause. After adopting the By-law on the number of C.S. Directors--then consider and act on my candidate for Director, viz., Archibald McLellan, our Editor-in-Chief. I have watched him and so far he has been right on all important subjects. You will have three in unity that leaves a majority when they are right.

Also you can now remove a member of your Board. "Mother" lives and learns by the things she suffers. [Here was further evidence that one "member of your

Board" could be removed in God's good time in order to re-establish the concept of a unique four-member Board under the 1892 legal deed of trust.]

No personal sense is the complete Truth--or the complete error. Mathematics, as often, furnishes its parallel: A personally wrought example of a quadratic equation on the blackboard may be figure-perfect--or may have a slip. If there is a slip, the healer works from the Principle, points out the mistake, and corrects it; he does not destroy the board and the chalk, and the operator! If there is no mistake, the Scientist does not then enshrine the board and the chalk, and tell the world the board is incapable of working out quadratics incorrectly!

Moreover, just saying "Oh, that's an terrible error" does not correct the mistake, as the following statement shows:

-- Written Instruction by Mrs. Eddy [dated Sept.20, '09 and entitled "Dreams"]:

Admitting that mortal life is a dream is admitting that it is something, when the fact remains that it is nothing, since there is no mortal life. God, Truth, is the only Life and a dream is not Truth. Eschew that statement of life unscientific--state it scientifically, and commence your solution of the problem called life with fact and not fable. Then you begin with Truth, not error; with God, not man; with Principle, not idea; and solve Life as having no beginning and no ending, the eternal now and forever.

In 1905, when the Directors conferred together to make a list of candidates for the position of First Reader, Mrs. Eddy rejected every single name as "entirely unsuitable." The Directors had been like mathematicians assessing boards and chalk, rather than recognizing examples of the Principle. When they went individually to the Principle the right name was approved.

Examples already given of Bostonian rivalry named these two:

1) Flavia Knapp, wife of a director, who believed that the locals were after her because they were jealous of her

outstanding healing work. She passed on two weeks after revealing this fear in a testimonial given in The Mother Church. Mrs. Eddy attributed the failure of Scientists to help her to the fact that they thought they were handling a physical disease, rather than malicious mental malpractice and the latent fear of it.

2) William P. McKenzie, who was one of the original Publishing Society Trustees--and so named by Mrs. Eddy without prior consultation with the 1892 Trustees (i.e. the Board of Directors). He told a colleague that a director who had assumed the position of his mentor would not speak to him for two years after that!

Letters too are quoted in this book and in Six Days showing that the Directors felt obliged to settle charges of immorality by casting out the Nickersons, Joseph Eastaman, Dr. Sulcer, and others from their positions in the organization.

In these cases Mrs. Eddy ordered reinstatement as though to emphasize that the Christian Science Church is an outreach of true healing and purification, not a fortress for self-righteousness and condemnation.

In 1902 questions were raised about the integrity of Treasurer Stephen Chase, leading to his temporary replacement by Mr. DeCamp as noted earlier. Mrs. Eddy insisted that Mr. Chase continue to be responsible at least for the Building Fund, even if "not according to the Church By-laws", while the lesson of Who is the one and only Treasurer was being sought and reinforced.

-- Letter to Messrs. Johnson and Armstrong [dated Dec.4, '02 and signed "With love always, Mother, M.B. Eddy"]:

Be of good cheer.... Meantime restore Capt. Eastaman to the First Membership when I write you to do this.

I will inform you what to do before that is done as soon as the time seems long enough after your call on me, not to be seen as the mover of it. I feel that God alone has shown me just what to tell you. "Knowest thou not the way to come unto me?"

-- Letter to C.S. Board Directors [dated Dec.8, '02 and signed "With love, Mother, M.B. Eddy"]:

Beloved Students: ...as soon as you read this letter, call a meeting and [re]elect Mr. Stephen Chase a member of your Board. Then read in meeting this letter of Captain Eastaman's and vote to put his card in our Journal; also to restore him to the First Membership of our church, and wire me that this has been done. I am meeting too much to bear this delay another day. You know what I refer to.

This lying about my student and causing him and his innocent wife so much suffering, is one of the deepest plots laid since my prosecution for repeating the Revelation of St. John. What has happened since Mr. DeCamp was here shows me that I am right in what I say on this subject. God is guiding me as I act.

Read Manual 25th Edition, page 54.2, and page 60.3, and see if we are straining out gnats and swallowing camels. Eastaman has not directly broken a By-law, but somebody else has. Please return to me Capt. Eastaman's letter. Jesus Christ forgave repentent sinners. Capt. Eastaman is repentent for his sins. I have spoken in my letter to him plainly, and now I require you to do your duty as aforenamed.

-- Letter to Clerk [dated Dec.11, '02 and signed "With love, Mother, M.B. Eddy"]:

Beloved Student: What do you say to putting [Thos. W.] Hatten on the Finance Com...? [Hatten, a Trustee and later a member of the Building Com., had just been voted down by the Board as DeCamp's replacement on the Board, for reasons of their own.] We must have members of our Boards and Committees who are loyal, obedient to God and to the author of S.& H.

You know him and his adaptability to such a position better than I do and I leave the decision to you. If you think he is ready for it, put him there.

There may questions arise for the Board to decide in which we shall need the majority to vote for what I indicate to be done. And our cause needs now that this Board uphold their Leader publicly when the occasion demands it.

The dawn of the Twentieth Century enabled Mrs. Eddy to hail Love's expression on earth of "one race, one realm, one power" (Po.22)--that is, one man, one nation or church, one Pastor. She also saw it as both "God-crowned" and "patient."

It is God-crowned because God has foreordained every event of its unfolding; and it is patient, because it remains true no matter how long the human mind takes to acknowledge its perfection, or how many negative illustrations intervene "through understanding, dearly sought, with fierce heart-beats."

The years 1901-3 saw the

1) final chapter-arrangement of S&H (226th edn.)

2) ultimate resolution of personal teaching (Board of Education class of '02)

3) visible representation of independent branch church (Mrs. Eddy's own branch in Concord)

4) end of motherhood (Man.Art. XXII, Sect.1)

5) start of the Extension, or visible communion-place of the independent branches (as noted in Man.72nd and previous edns) and as taken right out of material sense by Man.73rd edition (the "authority") and as explained in My.140-1.

6) necessary appointment of a fifth director to emphasize the distinction between the "God-directed" four and the "patient" five.

It could be said that the lessons of the Seventh Day were complete by the middle of 1903 as reckoned in calendars of time. But the completion of any lesson does not mean that all students comprehend or are proficient. It is obvious that the "Bethlehem star looks down upon the long night of materialism...'and the darkness comprehendeth it not'." Students still had to absorb for themselves the principle behind their lessons--and perhaps wearily.

In 1903 Mrs. Eddy had responded to the abuse, in practice, of her 1892 Deed of Trust by making the distinction between the four Directors under that Deed, and five directors thinking they were running a growing but unharnessed group of lesser individuals. She selected Archibald

McLellan as the fifth director (i.e. one not sanctioned or governed by the irrevocable 1892 Deed) to hasten the movement's chance to cope with examples that could uncover the principle Mrs. Eddy had illustrated and insisted upon.

The cause would need directors who could actively and individually turn to Principle, quite as much as those who would passively not question the Principle as presented to them by Mrs. Eddy.

In 1909 there were still on the Board two members (Ira O. Knapp and William B. Johnson) who were outstanding and useful C.S. patriots, in the sense that they would be ready to say "My leader, right or wrong." These two would accept the 29 estoppel clauses in the Manual as inspired and demanding obedience, even if they expected or hoped Mrs. Eddy would do away with them before her departure.

Some of the others in authority could accept that "my Leader is right" but would want to examine what it was that made her instructions right, and to be sure for themselves. Hence they were ready to "try the spirits."

On the Board, Messrs. Knapp and Johnson (with the help of Stephen Chase) could outbalance the other two directors if these ever felt they had graduated to the point where they could be just as right as the elderly Mrs. Eddy--and maybe more so.

The 3:2 ratio had to be adjusted if a rift was to be averted--a rift which might give no chance for a clearly-defined course to be tried out. If a lesson has to be learned negatively, it has to be clear exactly what it is that has deviated from principle.

~ ~ ~ ~ ~ ~ ~

Similarly in 1904, after permitting Primary Classes, but no "annual" teachers' course (Normal Class) for two years, Mrs. Eddy publicly announced that from then on Normal Classes would be held but once in three years. She thus allowed five years to go by without a single increase in the number of official teachers.

When it became obvious that the goal of Ret.47:16 would not be reached without the negative lessons that accompany "official" teaching, a normal class was held in 1907, with Judge Hanna as teacher. And that was the last and only such class ever held under the Manual after 1902; for before the next triennial normal class could be held, the personal Pastor Emeritus (who was also President of the College and whose signature was necessary on the official certificates) passed on. "Authorized" personal teaching was left to phase itself out in favor of divine teaching which knows no priestly intermediaries.

More on the Fifth Director

According to Wm. Lyman Johnson and other writers, Archibald McLellan (who had never thought highly of Wm.B. or of son Wm.L.) felt the church needed a clerk who was not blandly dependent on guidance from Mrs. Eddy--i.e. a clerk who might be counted on to support McLellan's own ambitions!

He began suggesting to Mrs. Eddy that a change was necessary, and the replacement he recommended was naturally one of his former Chicago buddies: John V. Dittemore, an efficient and experienced businessman. At the third attempt, Mrs. Eddy acquiesced--quite aware of the lesson God was preparing for those who would learn in no other way. She even agreed to Dittemore as the replacement, but added, prophetically: "If you want him, take him--and all that goes with him!"

There is a parallel here with Jesus' remark to Judas: "What thou doest, do quickly." In Judas' case it was like saying, "If you have to learn, by a visible proof on the cross, and your own attempt at death, that I am not in a mortal, material body, I can only say, Get on with it!" In the case of the ecclesiasticism associated with names like Dittemore etc., Mrs. Eddy's remark was saying, "If you have to learn, by the certainty of error's self-destruction, that Church is not a material organization, at least be ready to profit by the negative result that must follow!"

Dittemore was a name used by God to highlight many developments in the Divinity Course on church. His first official duty outside of Chicago was COP in New York City where he became aware of animosities and irregularities concerning Augusta E. Stetson. These he nurtured and denounced, without realizing "no reality in them." Later he and his friend McLellan turned on her with vigor, just as they would turn one day on their fellow-citizen from Chicago, Edward Kimball, the man who had virtually sponsored them.

He could have profited by the letter given below which Mrs. Eddy sent to a COP predecessor of his, although the lesson of "What thou doest, do quickly" was probably now the only way God's plan would shine through.

-- Letter from Mrs. Eddy to Wm.D. McCrackan, newly-appointed COP in New York [dated Jan.12, '05]:

Beloved Student: I hasten to ask: Have you been elected for the Publication Committee of New York State? If so, then I am prompted by our God to write to you solemnly, earnestly and lovingly on this special subject, namely that you act lovingly and wisely towards Mrs. Stetson and her church.

The enemy will tempt you to do otherwise, but if you have the desire to do rightly, and watch and pray daily for guidance, then no one can misguide you in this or in any other respect, and no one can harm you and you cannot be made to hurt anyone and will "do thyself no harm"; and God will bless you abundantly.

[Mrs. Eddy was here insisting that Mr. McCrackan move in to heal, not condemn. She needed him in New York for, as she further wrote him: "If Mrs. Stetson and her students would do their duty to the Press these malicious articles against their Leader would not appear."]

-- Simultaneous letter to Mrs. A.E. Stetson [dated Jan.12, '05 and signed "Ever yours lovingly, M.B. Eddy"]:

My precious Student: Who is your Publication Committee? If it is as I am told Mr. McCrackan, then let me comfort you with the lessons of my own experience and the proof of their value. The great Teacher of you and me has said most emphatically, "It is not enough that ye love them that love you, but I say unto you, love your enemies."

I have learned from experience that we can never escape from the cruelty of our enemies in any other way than by loving them, as Jesus taught, and that this way gives us not only escape but victory over them.

Now, darling, just try this toward Mr. McCrackan and I am sure you will overcome yourself and him. I know you can do this, dear one, and triumph in this way. His office only lasts one year and this year can be the happiest year of your life, if only you will have faith enough in me to do as I ask; and have faith enough in our great Teacher to believe that this demand must be met by us all before we can be real Christian Scientists.

Write me on receipt of this. You know in part now how much I love you and others know it, but you never will know this wholly till you overcome your enemies with love, if you have not already done so. I had to do as I do to others--have Mr. Frye typewrite this. I am so oppressed with work for and the care for all. God bless my dear precious student who helps me to clothes, while I am helping to clothe her with righteousness, the robes of heaven here and now.

Eventually Dittemore found himself more and more in disagreement with his fellow-directors, who voted to replace him in 1919 with Mrs. Annie Knott. After aligning himself with the breakaway "Parent Church" of Annie Bill for some years, he then co-authored a book which attacked Mrs. Eddy herself.

Nevertheless he did recant somewhat shortly before his death in 1935; and he was the one who, as clerk, started the full-fledged Archives of The Mother Church. Since he kept his own copies of what went into the archives, and since he was ready and even anxious to make them available, some of Mrs. Eddy's legacy to the world can first be associated with the name Dittemore (used in this way in quite a different and better light)!

To go back however to 1909--he was the one allowed to replace Wm.B. Johnson as clerk on the Board of Directors. And with the decease one year later of Ira Knapp, the board ratio was reversed in favor of the active "independents" rather than the more passive "listeners." The lesson of the estoppel clauses--faithfully included in the Manual by Mrs. Eddy--was thus deferred until the negative impact of disobedient independence could reverse the human-mind thinking about these clauses. Mrs. Eddy's dictum about the value of "negative" lessons remains valid however, for "the reverse of error is true."

As soon as Mr. Wm.B Johnson learned of Mrs. Eddy's agreement to a change of clerk, he dutifully and characteristically sent in his letter of resignation and received the following:

-- Reply to Mr. Johnson [dated June 1, '09 and signed "As ever, lovingly yours, Mary Baker Eddy"]:

> Beloved Student: I thank you deeply for your loving letter. I think it is for your own good that you take the step you name. Having no office work to meet in a business way will give you a better chance to attend to yourself and we must all do this sometime or the weeds will choke the growing grain.
>
> One of the gladdest moments of my life would be to have more time in which to help myself, and for others to give time to help themselves. You have named to me in confidence certain needs of your own. Now dear one attend persistently to them and you will conquer and be blessed in all ways.

After the departure, eighteen months later, of the visible Pastor Emeritus, Albert Allen, publisher of the Columbus [Ohio] News, asked Mr. McLellan how the board was going to get around the estoppel clauses in the Manual. The reply was now inevitable and simple: "How can we get the consent of a dead woman?"

McLellan and other directors had sought the haven of human law after failing to get Mrs. Eddy to change the sections requiring her written or verbal consent. Consequently he was ready with his response--based on the law's assurance that "the law does not require the impossible"!

Appropriately enough McLellan was the only member of the Mother Church board of directors who was not a legal member of the 1892 Deed of Trust setting up the Board of Directors of The First Church of Christ, Scientist--and Mrs.

Eddy was fully aware of the fact, and he knew she was. She made this known in a:

-- Letter to Archibald C. McLellan [dated March 19, '03 and signed "With love, M.B. Eddy"]:

Beloved Student: ...I was delighted to meet you and intended to invite you and Mrs. McLellan to P[leasant] V[iew] when we get over the present purchase of land in Boston. I reminded the Directors of this intent and my inability to meet you that day, and told them to tell you.

N.B. [signed "Again, M.B.E."]: I regret that your name cannot appear as a member of the C.S. Board of Directors in their deeds. I have twice urged this question but Mr. Elder [lawyer] finds it cannot be legally so.

~ ~ ~ ~ ~ ~ ~

There now remain three points in this church "divinity course" which need mention: the forestalling of a mother church in New York City; the Massachusetts Commonwealth's refusal to permit large legacies to a materially-organized church; and the proof of Mrs. Eddy's total competency in the years following 1903, along with her awareness of all that was being done in her name.

The last item was taken care of by God in the conclusions of the so-called Next Friends Suit, dealt with in Chap.IV as part of the ultimate wholeness (or healing virtue) of the discovery and founding of Christian Science.

The question of Mrs. Eddy's financial legacy to her Church was taken care of by the 1892 Deed of Trust itself. But first, in 1907-8, suitable steps were taken to prevent her relatives acquiring under human law the growing proceeds of the sale of S&H etc., and the copyrights by which they could have stopped further publication. CSS Vol.X, No.16 and Jan.CSJ, '08, gave details of the "Christian Science institution" by which Mrs. Eddy planned to donate her funds to "the special benefit of the poor and the general good of all mankind." This proved to be an unnecessary legal device.

The trust establishing The First Church of Christ, Scientist, provided for the end of "preaching, reading or speaking in" the church and showed that its Church activity was fundamentally the worldwide promulgation of "the doctrines and practice of Christian Science as taught and explained by Mary Baker G. Eddy in...'SCIENCE AND HEALTH'." The millions of dollars which Mrs. Eddy left to it were therefore not for the purpose of maintaining a localized, material church organization, but were for the benefit of "her heirs and assigns" which are the whole world, i.e. all that is meant by generic man. Although it was necessary to name a body corporate to handle the funds, these were not limited to the $1000 or so then permitted by Massachusetts as legacy to "a church."

The will which names "the Mother Church--The First Church of Christ, Scientist, in Boston, Massachusetts" (emphasis added) as Mrs. Eddy's residual legatee was dated September 13, 1901. It thus preceded the necessary distinction made between "The First Church of Christ, Scientist" legally identified in 1892, and "The Mother Church, The First Church of Christ, Scientist" with its five directors reestablished in 1903. These five directors are not identified legally in the human sense, but represent in reality the divine direction of The Church Universal and Triumphant.

The money left under the will was to be held "in trust ...for the purpose of more effectually promoting and extending the religion of Christian Science as taught by me." The Boston "church building" had to be kept "in repair", but there is no permanent demand for church services in the localized or old-fashioned sense.

THE STETSON PHENOMENON

Finally there is the illuminating saga of Augusta Stetson and First Church, New York City.

The story goes back to 1884 when Mrs. Eddy became aware of the great qualities Mrs. Stetson possessed, and when after much persuasion she got her to attend the November Primary Class, convincing her of the truth of Christian Science. This was during the "Demonology" era when S&H carried a chapter with that title (in its 3rd through 15th editions) using actual examples and personal accounts of malpractice.

Much as a physical scientist becomes aware of a great principle by observing the behavior of ingredients which of themselves have no importance and which can easily be replaced, so Mrs. Eddy had been observing the results which followed treatments given by Richard Kennedy, her young first partner in the healing business.

In "Demonology" she outlined in detail the results which had followed treatments by use of a "mind" Kennedy believed to be his personal property. Instead of knowing he reflected the divine Mind, he had experimented with a belief in a personal mind to be used for his own ends.

Her students did not always understand that Mrs. Eddy was explaining the need to handle and correct any use, in themselves or in what appears to them as <u>others</u>, of this separate-mind belief. She showed them how to work against the <u>error</u> which "Dr. K--" and "D. S--" (abbreviations for Kennedy and Spofford in the Demonology chapter) had kindly revealed. In the 16th and subsequent editions of S&H Mrs. Eddy removed the personal illustrations and changed the chapter title to "Animal Magnetism", words which her students found easier to divorce from the personal channel.

It was the old story: an incorrect calculation on the blackboard must first be recognized as incorrect and even deplored, and it must be rectified, lest it become an example for others; but the correct use of the principle is all that can really correct the powerless chalk and board.

Mrs. Stetson may have realized that a mistake can appear to be "corrected" temporarily by erasing the entire bad example, and she and other early students may have quoted instructions from Mrs. Eddy which seemed to sanction such an action as the first step. But this provides no <u>healing</u>; and Mrs. Stetson did do wonderful healing work after coming into Science.

Some of the Stetson healings were sought by Mrs. Eddy for the early Journals. As late as 1906 Mrs. Eddy told her to write an account for the Sentinel of an impressive healing of cancer in New York. And although she later modified her request, a shortened account did appear in CSS Vol.VIII, No.51. The following letters tell the story:

-- Letter to Mrs. A.E. Stetson, C.S.D. [dated July 14, '06 and signed "Lovingly ever yours, Mary Baker Eddy"]:

I want you to write me a letter containing your statement of the case of cancer that you cured,--and also copy some other portions of your last most excellent letter to me. Make the letter short enough to be published in our periodicals. I thought your comparison of value was very apt. You can make a most valuable contribution to our papers by extracts from your letter that I refer to. Shall I mail this letter to you, or can you do as I desire without it?

-- Letter [dated Aug.3, '06 and signed "Tenderly, Lovingly yours, M.B. Eddy"]:

My darling Student: Since writing to you on the subject of giving testimony on disease, God has shown me that error of any sort is no help to Truth.

Therefore I shall publish your dear letter to me, but not the testimony on disease which I requested of you.

Some hundreds of letters passed between Mrs. Eddy and Mrs. Stetson over 25 years, and facsimiles can be found in Mrs. Stetson's books ("Sermons and Other Writings" etc), also in the Huntington Library, California, and the CSF library in Cambridge, Eng. Nearly all of the Eddy letters are entirely in her own handwriting. A few random samples are given below:

1) [dated Dec.17, '98 and signed "With oceans of love from your teacher and Mother in Israel, M.B.G. Eddy"]: My precious Student: ...I am overwhelmed with work and need your help. I cannot remember anything but what serves to save our Cause from the jaws of the devourers. Another plot is to organize churches within the vicinity of the Mother Church and no one in Boston lifts a finger against whatever is abusive to our Cause in such ways, but turns to me to meet it all. Will you not help put this down?

2) [dated Dec.17, '00 and signed "Your loving Mother and Teacher and Leader, M.B. Eddy"]: Darling Augusta, my precious Student: I always explain Christ as the invisible and

never corporeal. Jesus was a man corporeal. Christ was, is, and forever will be the Holy Ghost, or in scientific phrase, the spiritual idea of God. I am corporeal to the senses, even as Paul was. But God has anointed me to do His work, to reveal His Word, to lead His people. And your faithful adherence to my directions and love for me has caused you to prosper in the field even as you have....

Jesus was the man that was a prophet and the best and greatest man that ever has appeared on earth, but Jesus was not Christ, for Christ is the spiritual individual that the eye cannot see. Jesus was called Christ only in the sense that you say, a Godlike man. I am only a Godlike woman, God-anointed, and I have done a work that none others could do. As Paul was not understood and Jesus was not understood at the time they taught and demonstrated, so I am not. As following them and obeying them blessed all who did thus--so obeying me and following faithfully blesses all who do this....

3) [dated Aug. '02 and signed "With thanks and love, always thine, M.B. Eddy"]: My precious Student: I want you to give most of your time to healing. This department of C.S. is the one in which no student has equalled me. It is the one to which every student should aspire more than to any other. It is the one most vacant at present.... How I wish my best students would strive most to attain the standard of Scientific healing!

I pray daily for all the members of my church and hope and pray they will lead in healing the sick, more than in teaching or church making. Why? Because, my darling student, healing is the foundation of Christian Science. A poor healer can never be a good teacher....

4) [dated Oct.4, '05 and signed "Lovingly ever, Thine own, M.B.G. Eddy"]: My darling Student: Your letter was a feast for my hungry heart. You, dear one, little know what an effort I have to make in order to keep the students awake to the subtlety of M.A.M. O! I am so happy that <u>you</u> are <u>saved</u>.

...Give my <u>thanks</u> and <u>love</u> to your dear students for what they did to <u>honor</u> you.... God bless my precious Augusta--my faithful helper.

5) [dated July 7, '06 and signed "Ever lovingly yours, Mary Baker Eddy"]: My precious Student: Your dear letter of the 7th inst. is just received. It comforts me. Now let me say--that mental malpractice must be met daily by all the Students; met by your mental protest that breaks the so-called law of a lie, or you are liable to be affected by this lie all unconsciously. Dear one, remember this. Our Master said, "had the good man of the house watched, his house would not have been broken open."...

N.B. [signed "Again tenderly, truly, M.B.E."]: Your kindness to me has been an example for others and I shall not forget it nor cease to speak of it as the great cause of your prosperity.

6) [dated Jan.8, '02 and signed "Be happy in well doing, be happy this and every year, Mary Baker Eddy"]: My dear Student: ...Now dear one, remember you cannot be swamped or harmed by M.A.M. God, good, is your life, health, hope, salvation. Then what is there left to harm you? God knows all about our every need and will build your church-edifice, if you do not make it a "skyscraper." But the divine Mind makes the human meek, and lowly in spirit, binds up all wounds and heals the sick and weary ones. You are healed, and every trial of your faith in good makes you stronger and better, if you improve this lesson from Love.

You are able to judge of the interest of your church. Let not a single element of discord outside or inside trouble you. Do right and Love will bless you. There is no harm in doing rightly before a stated time, meeting, or assembly.

7) [dated March 22, '03]: Beloved Student: ...One thing in my haste was forgotten, namely, the designation of The First Church of Christ, Scientist, as my church. The question will be, is, asked, whose church is it? We cannot say it is Mr. Hering's or the Board of Directors' church, for it surely is not. It was my church in the beginning as much as Mrs. Stetson's church is hers.

We must be orderly in these things or it will lead into difficulties that you do not see, but I do see them.

[Mrs. Eddy surely explains here that each individual accepting One Mind is solely responsible for what he sees as "my church."]

8) [dated April 11, '03 and signed "Ever tenderly, lovingly thine, M.B. Eddy"]: My precious Student: ...I invited you and your dear church to come here at our next Communion season, but I meant that if my church came generally, to be sure that you, dear one, and your church shall come also. I want my church to act in unity and each one to prefer another, and to love one another, even as I have loved them....

9) [dated Nov.30, '99, signed "Mary Baker G. Eddy" and sent for inclusion in the cornerstone of "Mrs. Stetson's church"]:

> To Mrs. A.E. Stetson: Beneath this corner-stone in this silent, sacred sanctuary of earth's sweet songs, paeans of praise and records of Omnipotence, I leave my name with thine in unity and love. [See "History of the New York Organization", CSS Vol.IX, No.36.]

10) [dated Aug.30, '09, typed, and signed "As ever yours in Christ, Mary Baker Eddy", the signature being handwritten]: My dear Student: ...You know that I love you and you know that God has made, and is making His ways and works manifest through Divine Science. I trust He will direct your path in the footsteps of His flock.

The Holy Bible, Science & Health and The Mother Church Manual are your safe guides, follow them.

I have not the time to think of the Students in all their varied duties of life, but I have the faith to leave them in the hands of God who giveth to all men liberally and upbraideth none.

~ ~ ~ ~ ~ ~ ~

Mrs. Eddy was clearly able to identify Mrs. Stetson by the qualities God used her to express, just as she was able to point out the remedy for the wrong beliefs associated with Mrs. Stetson. Someone who can be called a dominant personality has several problems to handle, for the tendency to tell others what to do includes false motherhood, rigid political standpoints, assumptions about the perceptions of others, and so on. Where the priest-thought directs and condemns, the Science-thought works out from the Principle that heals.

<u>Six Days</u> (pp.373-4) gives an example of the motherhood tendency which tricked Mrs. Stetson into wanting to regulate the reading behavior of students. Other such incidents brought remedial exposures by Mrs. Eddy in various ways, as shown below:

1) [dated Dec.17, '04 and signed "M.B. Eddy"]: My darling Student: ...Do not doubt my <u>love</u> for you, my faith in you, and my faithful rebuke if need be. Above all, dear one, know that God knows your good works and will reward them, that He loves you, and she whom He has called loves you, just as tenderly in giving you His rod as His staff, and by them both--the rod and support--you cannot doubt His care and love for you, my precious one. Now, be of good cheer, be not afraid, for such are God's proofs to all His own that they are His and <u>none can</u> pluck them out of His hand.

2) [dated May 1, '07 and signed "Lovingly ever thine, Mary Baker Eddy"]: My darling Student: ...Remember this that I charge you, viz., avoid being identified pro or con in politics. If you do otherwise it will hinder our cause, remember this. Keep out of the <u>reach</u> of such subjects.

Give all your attention to the moral and spiritual status of the race. God alone is capable of government; you are not, I am not, but God has governed through His anointed and appointed one in the way of divine Science;--not politics, nor the making or breaking of national laws or institutions. He, God alone is capable of this.

3) [dated March 7, '07 and signed "In haste, Your loving teacher"]: Beloved: By the "evil one" I by no means refer to personality but the <u>one evil</u>, viz. Hypnotism or m.a.m. [There were charges that Mrs. Stetson and her students were giving Mrs. Eddy as authority for attacking evildoers personally.]

4) [dated July 23, '09, typed, and signed "Lovingly your teacher, Mary Baker Eddy", the signature being handwritten]: My dear Student: [For text see My.359:27.]

5) [dated Dec.9, '08 and signed "M.B.E."]: Darling: I charge you not to have your students think that it is I personally that changes your action and thoughts for it is not I. It is God and He has moved the world in that way. If you plant this change on a person it will not prosper....

6) [dated April 15, '08 and signed "Lovingly ever yours, Mary B.G. Eddy"]: Mrs. Stetson and her Students, Darlings: Do not send me another thought or thing material. My treasures are spiritual and laid up in Heaven.

7) [dated April 15 {'09} and signed "Again thine, M.B.E."]: Darling: A temptation is upon you, viz. to have a quarrel with Anne Dodge. I shall not take your side nor her side in this quarrel but only God's side namely to love.... [See also CSS Vol.XII, No.13, "Letters to Our Leader".]

~ ~ ~ ~ ~ ~ ~

My.361:9 makes reference to a meeting "over a year" ago between Mrs. Eddy and Mrs. Stetson, as well as to the letter of Aug.30, '09 already included above.

The meeting was an important one and included an hour-long carriage ride which the two had together just one year and two days before the date of the letter referring to it. The arrangements were made as follows:

-- Dictated letter to Mrs. A.E. Stetson, C.S.D. [dated Dec.7, '08 and signed "Lovingly yours, M.B.G. Eddy"]:

My beloved Student: I have tried and hoped all through the past season to have you come to me and take a drive with me around the Chestnut Hill Reservoir, but have failed hitherto. Is it too late for you to enjoy it? If not, appoint a day and the hour when you will be here and I will be on hand.

My present hour for driving is between 1 and 2 P.M.

The carriage drive duly took place on the second day after this letter was written, and it faced squarely the motherhood and church-"skyscraper" tendencies which would try to place a noose around Mrs. Stetson's neck. The following account is remarkable in that it is taken from her own notes and shows her ready ability to absorb the lessons Mrs. Eddy was providing.

After entering the carriage alone with Mrs. Eddy she explained that the New York newspapers had been making mistakes (about the plans of First Church, New York, to build a huge edifice--see CSS Vol.XI, No.14; CSJ

Vol.XXVI, No.11; and My.356:21-357:25). Mrs. Stetson's account continues:

S. We have made only one payment on the land to hold it. We have not begun to build yet.

E. Why are you going to build?

S. I said, why, because of the overflow. We cannot accommodate our people. We have been worshipping upstairs to avoid the congestion in the auditorium. We would have continued to worship upstairs but you made the by-law that two services could not be held in one building at the same time. From this I thought you wanted us to build another church.

E. Oh, darling, do you remember Mother's experience; she thought she could do or demonstrate for everybody and do everybody's work and started to build a church to help them build. I gave them money and how they turned upon me and rent me. Never give your students money, give them of your spiritual help and let them make their own demonstration. What did I do for you, Augusta? I put you out in New York City and let you make your demonstration or fail. What have you done? You have made the biggest demonstration and have done the most good and are still doing good. Just as sure as you give money to people--the overflow --you will have the same experience as Mother had. They must make their own demonstration.

S. But, I said, they will need the strong support of the old, advanced students. The overflow are all young students, they do not know much.

E. But, never mind that, let them go out and demonstrate.

S. They have not the means perhaps to build a church.

E. How did you get your money? I did not give you any. How did you build your church? Look at your demonstration; if they haven't the means to build they will find it by struggling and your people can loan them money but not give it to them. You are having the same experience that Mother had and she loved her people so she thought she could put them in a place. That was human love, and, oh, how I suffered for it. Now I know that divine Love trusts them to God and if they are good and if they hold on to God and my teaching, as you have done, God will do as much for them as He has done for you....

S. I said, there is no separation, all one body we.

E. Answered, we have no material body.

S. I said, no, we are the embodiment of Spirit.

E. Answered, the material body is not anything and we must not believe in it.

Although Mrs. Stetson dropped her plans for a huge temple in New York, the "one evil" did not drop its fear of rivalry among its many minds nor its claim to a material body. Those who did not understand what was meant by Mrs. Eddy's successor feared that Mrs. Stetson was more likely to get the position than they.

For her part, when Mrs. Stetson became aware that malpractice among her students was being laid at her door, she apparently felt she could brush it aside as no part of the divine reflection. Unfortunately the denial of a "lie" is not the same as the establishment of a truth. She told her students that if challenged they could claim that their real self never malpracticed.

This was no more a healing attitude than her accusers were adopting against her.

Virgil Strickler, First Reader in F.C.C.S., New York, made the following notes after conferring with Augusta Stetson on July 31, '09 on the growing crisis:

> I said, "Mrs. Stetson, if we tell this [that we were taught to work against an evil person], they will expel you instantly from The Mother Church." She said: "I know it; what shall we do?" After awhile she said: "We must deny that I ever said any of those things. I deny that I ever said them."
>
> I said: "But Mrs. Stetson, you did say them, and you have habitually taken up people by name and treated them." She replied that it was not she that took them up; that it was the human that said those things, and that the human was not her real self, and that she could say that she never had said them, and do it with a mental reservation that her real self had never said them....
>
> One of the practitioners [who had worked under Mrs. Stetson's guidance while they were using offices in the church building] then broke in to say that she had denied in this way in a certain lawsuit, and that it was perfectly proper to deny something you had said if you only did it with the mental reservation that while the human self may have done the thing, it was the real self that was denying having done it....
>
> Another practitioner said that she had been on the witness stand for two days in the lawsuit mentioned, and had testified throughout from the "absolute", and the opposing lawyer had never caught her once.

The lesson here is the lesson of duality. Jesus and Mrs. Eddy "beheld in Science the perfect man" and destroyed the lie about this perfect man. They did not have two men--one a real sinning mortal and the other a convenient substitute when the sinning one became unpopular. Mrs. Eddy agreed in Un.21:7 that "good and evil talk to one another" but immediately added: "Yet they are not two but one, for evil is naught, and good only is reality."

Although Mrs. Eddy kept calling on church officials to see the reality, many in Boston had already classified Mrs. Stetson as a "sinning mortal" when they decided to examine their own concepts of her fitness to be a member of "my church."

Visible "churches" are but individual examples of the One Church, and this lesson has to be learned in such easy stages as are necessary for stumbling footsteps. The one recommendation and demand Mrs. Eddy kept making to churches was, above all, unity (for example '00 1:17; '02 1:5; My.212:17; My.274:24; Man.70:19; CSS Vol.VIII, No.7; and her letters to Augusta Stetson of 11/30/99 and 4/11/03). The belief or conviction of a church-split may have to be lived with before negative unfoldments do lead clearly to the lesson of His Unity.

The circumstances of the examination of Mrs. Stetson by the Board of Directors in Boston, and their subsequent excommunication of her, are introduced in CSS Vol.XI, No.48 etc., and given in considerable detail in her book "Vital Issues in Christian Science." A simple rehearsal here of charge and counter-charge will add nothing in the right direction.

Suffice it to say that the mothering or control of "young students" by the "old, advanced" domineering mind had not been dispelled in one carriage drive, and the effect of this mothering on students caused Mrs. Eddy to send Mrs. Stetson the warning letter of July 23, '09 (My.359:27).

The purpose of this book is certainly not to provide "perfect man" or "sinning mortal" labels for individuals. But it hopes to record a few of the scientific and corrective attitudes recommended by the Revelator of Christian Science.

So far Mrs. Eddy had intervened in Boston in cases involving Josephine Woodbury, Joseph Eastaman, Abraham Sulcer, Stephen Chase, and others, but the opportunity thus given to understand God at work was not always grasped. As she told Mrs. Stetson during the carriage drive, at one time "she thought she could do or demonstrate for everybody", but soon discovered that students "must make their own demonstration."

If the Boston Board could not immediately demonstrate Church unity, she knew there would be times when "the Stranger shouts, 'Let them alone; they must learn from the things they suffer'" (Mis.328:1).

Nonetheless it is always permitted to "give them of your spiritual help"; and at Pleasant View and in Chestnut Hill there was positive guidance for correcting negative thoughts about Mrs. Stetson and others.

The negative thoughts about Mrs. Stetson had been very evident at the time of the dedication of The Mother Church. And during the years that followed many examples of outright condemnation could be cited--with very few examples of determination to invoke "the alterative effect produced by Truth upon error."

Perhaps as good illustrations as any can be found in Dr. A.E. Baker's "Notes on Metaphysical Work Done while Associated with Mary Baker Eddy". This work came at the turn of the century, a few years after the sniping at dedication time.

Dr. Baker was one of those given the task of keeping the truth about the Discoverer and Founder of Christian Science ever in consciousness. From this point of view he was required to be firm in his understanding of what was the basic truth about "Mother", particularly as this word was used to indicate qualities associated with Mrs. Eddy.

The "Work" included such reminders of basic Truth as:

> "Mother is governed by God. Mother is God. Mother has all consciousness. Mother is all consciousness.... Mother's energy is spiritual, not nervous. The lie that Mother is neurotic is powerless....
>
> "Mother's home is God, Love. Mother's household is the earth and the fullness thereof, Love. Mother's household will be chastened by Love.

They will not fear or hate our humble and lowly Mother in her beautiful and holy Christ-way....

Mother's students cannot label or talk about her as a person. No one can know, or see, or move Mother's mind but God....

Mother's mind is God. The pulpit and the press belong to God, Mother. They will be favorable to Christian Science and its Leader, Mary Baker Eddy.

([Dr. Baker's] Note: this treatment brought great growth to the Cause, attacks subsided, and favorable publicity appeared through the world.)

"The courts belong to Mother. God is the only justice. The courts will be favorable to Christian Science and its Leader, Mary Baker Eddy", etc.

References to Mrs. Stetson and her protagonists (the Directors) included:

1) "Clothed in the panoply of Love, Mother cannot be reached by human hate. Mother is clothed in the panoply of Love. Mrs. Stetson and no one else can clothe Mother. [Mrs. Stetson often used to shop for clothes for Mrs. Eddy.]

"Mother needs nothing. Mother is God-idea, complete. TRUTH IS." [This was the Tuesday "work" during a particular week.]

2) "Mrs. Eddy knew that A. Stetson was using audible treatment, 'You are dead' with success; making a law; the law to be made manifest. Mother refused to treat A.S. as error, which Dr. B [i.e. Dr. Baker himself] did not understand. Mrs. Eddy explained it as, 'A.S.'s work is not finished in New York.'

Mother's treatment for A.S. was 'You are a lamb of God. You must lie down in Truth'."

3) "Mother said, 'My students give me all the trouble I have. It is difficult for me to cope with their error.' Mother wrote the Manual because she said, 'If the success of the Church depended upon the Board of Directors, they would be taking up penny collections in the streets.' At one time Mother said, 'Half the Board of Directors are stuffed shirts, and the other half are trained monkeys!'"

As shown by the above, Mrs. Eddy was prepared to reveal the types of thought to be handled in "my church"; it is not an error "out there." As she counseled on many occasions: "Error comes to you for life, and you give it the only life it has." The belief of aggressive, pretentious directors on the one hand, or passive, dutiful directors on the other, is handled with the understanding of what the One Director IS.

When the major crisis with F.C.S.S., New York, was finally in the open, a member of Mrs. Eddy's household made some reference to the "dreadful Mrs. Stetson", and Mrs. Eddy spun around on her and warned:

> If you take sides in that dispute, you render yourself incapable of working on the subject metaphysically.

This corresponded with the declaration she had already made to Mrs. Stetson about taking sides in the latter's quarrel with Anne Dodge (letter of April 15, '09). And as for positive work, based on Principle, which Mrs. Eddy expected her household to do to heal their conceptions of Mrs. Stetson, this one which Dr. Baker recorded is typical of the truisms she gave them:

> She is a lamb of God; she must lie down in Truth.

In effect Mrs. Eddy is telling her students to know that the truth about Mrs. Stetson, the Board, Dittemore, McLellan, whomever, is what God knows of them. Moreover she proclaims in Un.19: "With God, knowledge, is necessarily foreknowledge; and foreknowledge and foreordination must be one, in an infinite Being. What Deity foreknows, Deity must foreordain; else He is not omnipotent, and, like ourselves, He foresees events which are contrary to His creative will."

This reflection of foreknowledge answers all questions as to whether Mrs. Eddy was ignorant of what was going on in New York and Boston, or was being kept in the dark by evil minds, or was too senile to know or care about it. The Revelator of Christian Science (Christlike Knowing) has knowledge of all that the Christ is bringing forth to the glory of God; hence reflects His knowledge, His foreknowledge, His foreordination.

And that is the lesson she brings to all mankind: Know that "ye have the mind of Christ", and know that this Mind sees and foresees all events that are in accord with His will.

~ ~ ~ ~ ~ ~ ~

The following statement by Mary Baker Eddy entitled "Church Work" makes a suitable summary of all that comes under the heading of PREACHING:

There is no such thing as a mortal despot, no personal control, in our church thought.

Do not declare there is no channel through which evil can operate. We do not destroy evil by removing channels, so-called. Evil will find channels so long as we think it is something. Work impersonally by declaring that the church is an association of active ideas, governed by divine Life, Truth, and Love.

Divine Life, Truth, and Love assemble the audience and "when I shall be lifted up, I shall draw all men unto me." Love is the only attraction, divine Life, Truth, and Love deliver the message. Love is the only impulsion and there is no mesmerism, resistance to Truth. There is no reversal of the Word through the so-called law of reaction which claims to equal the law of action, God's law.

Our Readers, our Board of Directors, our President, is divine Love. Our service is to seek, not our own, but another's good. There is no law of monopoly or exclusion, no personal control. There is eternal and perfect influence, it is the influence of divine Mind. There is no mental malpractice or mortal mind government.

All government is of God.

In unity there is strength. Unity of thought and action is the protection of the Christian Science Church. God's ideas are equal, each in his right place (at-one-ment). Differences between Christian Scientists are the devil's best workers.

Comparisons are wrong. Each man is complete and perfect and we must know no other man. God is the only cause, Spirit the only substance, Love the only Force, harmony the only law. Unselfed interest is the right attitude for church workers.

~ ~

IV - HEALING

~ ~

Healing the sick and reforming the sinner are one and the same thing in Christian Science. S&H 404:26.

The Revelator saw...the spiritual ideal as a woman clothed in light.... The Revelator was...beholding what the eye cannot see--that which is invisible to the uninspired thought. S&H 561:10, 573:2.

Members [of The Church of Christ, Scientist] can so protect their own thoughts that they are not unwittingly made to deprive their Leader of her rightful place as the revelator to this age of the immortal truths testified to by Jesus and the prophets. My.vii:5.

Healing as dealt with in this chapter is the revealing of the one Spirit or Soul, controlling all phenomena. It is the uniting of manifestation to Supply or Source--the seeing of the whole or healing Principle at work in any and every example of Principle's idea. Consequently it is not primarily a catalog of changes from one false material belief about God and man to a better material belief.

The prime example of Christian Science healing in the full sense (i.e. seeing the One Whole or the One Principle at work) concerns Mary Baker Eddy. The need to start correctly with Mary Baker Eddy is widely stressed in her own writings and statements in addition to the quotation above from *Miscellany*.

One of the most widespread examples comes from her letter to Judge Hanna (DCC p.109) where she observes: "The united plans of the evildoers is to cause the beginners either in lecturing or teaching or in our periodicals to keep Mrs. Eddy as she is (what God knows of her and revealed to Christ Jesus) out of sight; and to keep her as she is not (just another white-haired old lady) constantly before the public."

The observer who looks for Mrs. Eddy in person (and thus loses her entirely, as explained in Mis.308:4 and My.120:2) has lost also "the Science of Christianity [like] the man who could not see London for the houses" (My.149:22).

To try to "generalize from the particular" about a personal Mary Baker Eddy is as destructive as describing Christ, Truth, by starting with a physical Jesus and believing Truth must have a beard, two eyes, and a date of birth. Scientific "a priori reasoning shows material existence to be enigmatical" (S&H 467:25).

When Jesus said "I can of mine own self do nothing", he meant he was obeying Principle and could make no personal deviations therefrom. To understand Mary Baker Eddy we begin with the Principle she revealed and not with a material personalized presentation. On the other hand there is no reference of any kind to Mary Baker Eddy which cannot be used to gain a wonderful glimpse of Principle always at work.

It is the same as understanding that anything recognized as a "7", no matter how crudely drawn, carries the full force of SEVEN into its operation; or similarly, that an electric heater, no matter how wrongly or awkwardly placed, has no choice but to glow--if correctly connected to its source of current. Such discernment is precisely what Christian Science Healing is--the discernment of "the spiritual fact of whatever the material senses behold" or would like to invent. (See S&H 583:10.)

This chapter is not afraid of glimpses of "Mary Baker Eddy" which try to start with a "white-haired old lady". Previous chapters have not been afraid to illustrate Church, Nation, Man, even when a self-important mortal mind would want to confine itself to buildings, territories, mortal men and women.

The "Next Friends Suit" of 1907 hoping to belittle Mrs. Eddy is "a picture of error throughout", just like the "second biblical account" (S&H 526:24); but this biblical picture of error enjoys 36 pages of the C.S. textbook, without apology --showing that error can be rightly translated, not ballooned into something to be deplored or avoided. Christian Science takes the things of God and shows them unto the creature--takes everything that comes as consciousness and heals it (relates it to the one and only Principle). It should be easy to do this first with Mary Baker Eddy and the Revelation, but it extends to everything in consciousness, however mistaken the material or mortal thought of it is.

To appreciate the Revelation is to appreciate its ideal, its Revelator. But once a revelator is personalized (i.e. unhealed, localized) the fullness of the Revelator may be missed. In fact Revelator can never be confined to some particular person, however beautifully this one is pictured as struggling forward, sharing evil's rebuff and often winning out against evil's "persons."

Christian Science clearly shows that Christ cannot be confined to Jesus; or, to quote from the letters to Mrs. Stetson (p.290): "Jesus was not Christ, for Christ is the spiritual individual that the eye cannot see."

If Principle does appear as a person, place, or thing, the channel which illustrates the Principle does of course share in the honor. Moreover, to paraphrase a quotation from "Church Work" (p.301): Principle indeed "will find channels so long as we" realize there is one Principle ever operating; and as Mrs. Eddy worded it to Judge Hanna, any failure to see her as she is simply "misstates the idea of divine Principle that you are trying to demonstrate."

At this point it may be useful to recall the twentieth century message of the Revelator as foreshadowed in the article in The Seed quoted on p.151, and as found in the letters to Judge Hanna:

1) [in The Seed]: Jesus ever sought to detract from himself as person, and to point to the Father as the Principle of being.

He knew that the physical expression was but an emanation of mortal thought and itself nothing, as was proved by the Ascension when it disappeared.... He thus showed that there is no personal God--there is no personal Jesus--there is no personal Founder of Christian Science--there is no personal self; all is Mind.

2) [to Judge Hanna]: Keeping the truth of [Mrs. Eddy's] character before the public will...do more than all else for the Cause. Christianity in its purity was lost by defaming and killing its defenders. Do not let this period repeat this mis-

take. The truth in regard to your Leader heals the sick and saves the sinner.

3) [to Judge Hanna, Aug.26, '02]: Whosoever opens most the eyes of the children of men to see aright and to understand aright that <u>idea on earth</u> that has best and clearest reflected by word or deed the divine Principle of man and the universe, will accomplish most for himself and mankind in the direction of all that is good and true.

<u>Harmful Personalization</u>

Shortly after Mrs. Eddy had demonstrated "Six Days" of Creation to the world and was encouraging students to comprehend the whole example in the "Seventh Day", she sent the following:

-- <u>Letter</u> to James A. White [dated Sept. '95]:

> My dear Mr. White: How kind, true, how just like my idea of you is your last letter and its interesting enclosure.
>
> The cry in the Wilderness is by no means misunderstood by me, neither is it foreign to my earth life all the way.
>
> I have a house but live in it among strangers. I value and regard my help indoors of three females and one male, my bookkeeper, typewriter, driver. But they will always remain afar off from my life and its tenderness, its secrets, its sorrows, its joys. I am one in the house with them but not of them.
>
> I am more lone than the exile of Siberia. Yet never alone. There is a Divine Presence to whom I speak in terms dearest, whom I address in the most loving words that I know, and I am assured heart to heart. My dear friend, do not think that I mean a personal man or woman, but an incorporeal God, Good, Love. Hence the one side to my idealism is the Infinite and only, the four sides than which there are no other.

To uncover and reverse materialistic views of the everlasting Discoverer and Founder of Christian Science, Mrs. Eddy gave instructions or treatments such as the following to "Watchers" in her home:

1) Matter and personality are your gods. When will you turn from your idols! Unless you do, leave me out of your thoughts.

2) Take your thought off from me. You have no right to keep your thought on the person of anyone. Your thoughts should always be on God.

3) She [Mrs. Eddy] doesn't feel...any of her helpers' beliefs nor mine. She does not feel the readers of her books, nor any other mortal beliefs. The belief in fear, sin and disease is destroyed and cannot return again. My long continued treatment of her has not materialized her thought, nor made disease real, nor prevented her from being well. She can help herself. No mental condition can cause suffering any more than a material. Neither fear nor malice can produce suffering or bring back old beliefs.

There is no overaction, inaction, stoppage or clogging of the heart, for the heart is Love.

Mrs. Eddy's face is not deformed. Her eyes are large, natural; sight, hearing and memory are <u>never lost</u>. Her fingerjoints are natural.

<u>Further Corrective Statements</u>

The following written or verbal statements by Mary Baker Eddy pertaining to healing in the full sense, and to the <u>whole</u> evaluation of Discoverer and Founder, have also been preserved:

1) My [Mrs. Eddy's] thoughts form my face and its expression, hence their variation. No photograph has caught the expression of my highest thought, nor the thoughts of my highest expression. It cannot be done. My expression lies in my Works.

2) Always give God the glory. Say: "With God's help I will do so-and-so." Loyal Christian Scientists will have to make it clear that it was not "Mrs. Eddy" who did the healing, but Truth and Love (see S&H 495:1: "<u>God</u> will heal the sick through man"....) Their duty will be to overcome the belief in mortal mind of worshiping her personality.

3) [Message to "Beloved Students" not part of the household, dated Nov.28, '06 and signed "Lovingly in haste, M.B.

Eddy"]: I have so much on hand I cannot see you as often as I would like to. Please do not think of me unless I request it. Try to be happy and have faith.

4) If we are thinking of what flesh can do unto us, it is proof that matter is our God. "Ye shall be as gods." "All things work together for good to them who love God." We do love God, good, hence can claim this promise to us.

~ ~ ~ ~ ~ ~ ~

She was thus all the time driving home the lesson that the Revelator of Christian Science is not a person, is not in matter, has no life in matter, never lived or died in matter; but does appear as Mind to the awakening thought.

Some examples are given in Six Days (pp.113-4) of students' brief glimpses of the fact that Revelator is not a material body, even if appearing as a human body to the unillumined mind. Students have left these records, amongst many others, of the various outgrowings of personality which they faced and by which they were being urged to correct immature views of Revelator claiming to be their thought:

1) Mary Baker Eddy's hand disappeared to personal sight of Ella Peck Sweet when she laid her hand on the latter's arm--later became visible. She said: "Ella I am showing you things I could not tell you."

2) It was the third day after Mrs. Eddy's passing. In the room with the body, which lay on the bed, were Mrs. Elizabeth Norton and Miss Grace Collins. In the room next to them were Mr. Frye and two of the directors. There was a great noise--almost like an explosion. The directors went to investigate--they went through the house and to the cellar and could find no cause for or results of the detonation. Immediately following this noise Mrs. Eddy appeared to Mrs. Norton and Miss Collins. She walked across the room and disappeared through the wall. She appeared as youth, dark hair, and most radiant. Mrs Norton turned to Miss Collins and said: "Grace, did you see what I saw?" Grace said "Yes". Mrs. Norton told the directors what they had seen and the directors said it must not be told yet.

[Some students undoubtedly had marvelous glimpses of the fact that the one and only "Mrs. Eddy" is "idea in Mind." But is a body that walks across the room less or more spiritual than the body still lying on the deathbed?

[The question recalls the answer Mrs. Eddy {then Mrs. Glover} wrote out for Daniel Spofford when he posed a question about Jesus' resurrection. She told him: "To his disciples {Christ} died, so when they saw him they were afraid because they thought him a spirit...but they had not forgotten his identity Jesus or flesh and blood.... If the Christians of this day had been there, with their present beliefs, I have doubts whether they would have seen anything or heard a sound. I believe that Christ did appear and show himself as dense as their belief could be made."

[The only <u>substance</u> of an appearance is the Truth that was <u>never born</u> and never dies.]

3) [Frye Diary, Nov.28 '98]: Mother gave me a cutting rebuke this eve. for what I did about circulating article from [Concord] Monitor, about 2 hours afterward in talking pleasantly with me again, she said to me "This will go on for a little while and then I will be young and won't be with you any more (or I won't need you any more)." I'm not sure which of these two she said.

4) [Frye Diary, Jan.26 '98]: At about 10 o'clock [this morn, Mother] came in from her swing in belief completely overcome and seemed passing on but after I talked to her and worked for her she rallied but told me later that she had felt she wanted to go and be with the angels. She...opened S&H to 206 pars 3 & 4 [now 106:15-29].... In about an hour she laid on the couch for her usual morning nap and opened S&H to page 114 par 2 [now 218:9].

5) [Frye Diary, 1894]: she requested me yesterday that if she should seem to die, not to bury her body for 3-1/2 days, and to keep perfectly quiet about it during that time.

6) [to Adam Dickey, 1908]: I am now working on a plane that would mean instantaneous death to any of you. [Is this not saying that an understanding of the real and only Mrs. Eddy has abandoned any belief in, or claim to, a self-operated material life--once more confirming John xii:24?]

It would be hopelessly wrong however to try to shrug off some misunderstanding of Mrs. Eddy by laying the blame on a person or group of particular persons. When Gilbert Carpenter Sr. lived in Pleasant View he beheld many unsettling things about the personalized sense of Mrs. Eddy which m.a.m. wanted to present to him--until he realized that this belief in, and his surrender to, m.a.m. was all that was wrong, never what personalized channels were supposed to be saying about the Discoverer and Founder of C.S.

He records that Mrs. Frank Leonard, a trusted member of the household, warned him that Mrs. Eddy showed "mental weakness" at times, and he must excuse some of the things she might say or do on such occasions!

This was simply aggressive mental suggestion asking for his acceptance. And years later those who want to believe there are five misguided persons called directors who are responsible for what they think has gone wrong with C.S. can take heart from that wondrous lesson which God has in store for devoted men like Gilbert Carpenter about the truth and error of a situation.

THE MANUAL AND MRS. EDDY'S SIGNATURE

As the first decade of the twentieth century drew to its close, the legal mind of Judge Hanna and Judge Smith had understandable doubts about the correct procedure under the Manual should the signature of the Pastor Emeritus be no longer physically obtainable. The two judges sounded out a newcomer to the Eddy household in Chestnut Hill (William Rathvon) and together the three of them drew up a plan for an advisory council to act in Mrs. Eddy's place should she be unable to give the necessary signature.

They asked Adam Dickey, who had greater access to Mrs. Eddy, to get her reaction and consent. Probably aware that she never had any real doubts as to whither God was leading, Mr. Dickey refused even to present it.

His position in the household had been growing in stature, and he records that from the day of his arrival in February 1908 he had been made aware of some sort of pecking order even among the employees at Chestnut Hill! The temporary secretary whom he was replacing quietly advised him to "cultivate Frye" if "I were you" (Memoirs, p.28) as a valuable member to be "in" with.

Calvin Frye for his part records that about six months after this Mrs. Eddy told him: "Mr. Dickey yields to m.a.m. to such an extent he affords me very little help in anything. I have to correct him continually." Yet within a few days (on August 25) Mrs. Eddy was choosing Adam Dickey to "write a history of what has transpired" at Chestnut Hill, if she "should ever leave."

Gilbert Carpenter Sr., who saw at first hand the ups and downs of members of the household and of Boston officials, told friends that she could indeed find no human to provide a spiritual 100% for her; but he felt she got the 100% needed for her Cause by taking a few per cent from each of those available until they made up the 100% between them.

The human mind however remained much concerned about "Who shall be greatest?"--that is, about the pecking order when, rather than if, Mrs. Eddy "should ever leave." When she wrote the Directors on Aug.2 '09 advising dismissal of the charges against Augusta Stetson (thus demanding their own demonstration of the universality of Church) this mind took fright at the idea that Mrs. Stetson could remain to be the new leader of the C.S. movement in place of "me."

Advocates of the proposed "advisory council" openly stated that it was right and appropriate to "save" Mrs. Eddy from the Stetson influence--and from that of Adam Dickey!

Mrs. Eddy thereupon let things run their course in accordance with her statement in Mis.278:24: "I have felt for some time that perpetual instruction of my students might substitute my own for their growth, and so dwarf their experience. If they must learn by the things they suffer, the sooner this lesson is gained the better."

~ ~ ~ ~ ~ ~ ~

Below are many statements of "Mrs. Eddy as she is (what God knows of her and revealed to Christ Jesus)" and some of m.a.m.'s misunderstandings of Mrs. Eddy that become glorious as m.a.m. is reversed and handled. This is the work "that, in the words of our Master, 'ye know not of'" but are now called upon to do, even as Mrs. Eddy showed in her foresight found in My.147:26-30. She knew what m.a.m. was saying about darkest Africa and the wretched in "the utmost parts of the earth" and wrote: "I am helping them." Likewise whatever m.a.m. (any belief in more than one Mind) is saying about Mrs. Eddy is not true; and the "I" is helping when this truth about the "is not" of Mary Baker Eddy joyfully gives way to the truth that is.

-- Statement to Adelaide Still [Oct. '10]:

The surface of the sweetest nut is often a burr, and the thought that guides our life and expresses our being is unseen, except in the outward expressions and actions thereof. Hence the folly of declaring obstinately who is who and what is what, unless we have tested and proven the who and what. The wisdom of the wise is not as much expressed by their lips as by their lives.

One afternoon one of the workers at Pleasant View was in the room where she thought Mrs. Eddy was taking a nap. The following conversation ensued:

"Did you think I was asleep?"

"Yes."

"No I wasn't; this is the time every afternoon when I work for the world."

[Similarly]: Can you get tired? (No.) Can you be tired, fatigued from loss of sleep? (No.) I have worked hours day and night for you and the world and been rested and refreshed when I got up in the morning.

At another time she said:

I always handle claims of abnormal weather. They do not come from God. You can have rain without thunder or lightning.

[And again]: I sit quietly alone in my room conversing with the world, and the people thereof answer me intelligibly. The good in man comforts me, affords me pleasure and gives me no displeasure, and our communings are sincere and sacred. All this has its fulfillment, without a sign dishonest, insincere, ungrateful, unjust. But the positive of this experience claims as much feasibility and reality as the experience itself.

In the parable of the sower, the seeds sprang up and bore fruit, but the good fruit was productive and the evil fruit withered away and produced nothing, for good is real and evil is unreal. The wisdom of this hour and the proper labor of this hour is to know of a certainty the quality of the seed which takes root in our thought.

Who believes what I have written? He who has the most experience of good. Who disbelieves it? He who has the most fear of evil. What is the remedy for this belief? It is experience, for every moment, hour and day of mortal existence brings each one of us nearer the understanding of the nothingness of evil in proportion to our understanding of the allness of good.

Admonition by Mrs. Eddy

1) [to Adolf Stevenson, dated March 17, '08, after Mrs. Eddy's move to Chestnut Hill, causing the materialist to "look over the fence" to ogle at the new personality there]: I hereby tell you that no garden or flowers shall be cultivated on my place. Make no road for one to see such things on this place; the road to heaven is not one of flowers, but it is straight and narrow; it is bearing the cross and turning away from things that lure the material senses, denying them and finding them all in Spirit, in God, in good and doing good.

2) [to the Chestnut Hill household--at much the same time]: What I have to meet, you will all have to meet, now or again. Therefore know that the mesmerist cannot afflict either you or me with erroneous beliefs.

If you keep your watch I shall be a well woman. If you stay here until you learn to handle animal magnetism, I will make healers out of you. I had to do it, and did it for forty years, and you must do it.

You must rise to the point where you can destroy the belief in mesmerism, or you will have no Cause.... I cannot do it for you. You must do it for yourselves, and unless it is done, the Cause will perish and we will go along another 1900 years with the world sunk into the blackest night.... You have all the power of God with you to conquer this lie of mesmerism. [Dickey Memoirs of Mary Baker Eddy, pp.128-9.]

3) [to Edward A. Kimball, complementary to her insistence in 1902 that the "Babylonish woman" is a self-made quality of thought, not a particular person "over there"]: The "woman clothed with the sun" means no particular woman. It refers to conditions of thought, or the revelations of Truth. [See also CSJ Vol.XIX, No.4 "The Lawsuit Decided"].

4) [to Nemi Robertson, 1902]: One God, one Mind. All is Truth, Life and Love. This is the path strait and narrow, leading to the Father's secret reward. You must follow every step of the way. I alone know what this means.

[To Mrs. Robertson on another occasion]: Many minds are at work at this instant to stop our work for humanity and for the Cause. Yet their effort will fail. Why? Because God speaks to me as He has spoken from the earliest days when He guided me to the founding of this Cause. He speaks and I must follow. This is my cross. How I wish I could explain to you what this means!

5) [to Laura Sargent]: Do not teach that I am the Way. I am the wayshower. The Life, Truth, and Love that I teach are the way, and I am the wayshower. Teach them this thought through to the Principle.

6) [to Directors, 1905]: If the Publication Committees neglect their duties, so plainly stated in the By-laws of The Mother Church, they alone must be responsible for it or our Cause at the very hour of its triumph will go down. I say this prophetically. The Manual of our Church requires the Publication Committees to defend Christian Science, and its Leader. I have laid myself on the altar for you and all, almost forty years! I can no longer bear the strain. The officers who are salaried and responsible to God for performing their offices must do it. I can no longer do it for them.

7) [to Archibald McLellan, Oct.12 '07, seven months after he became one of her trustees]: I pity you dear student to be my best man and Trustee, but God will bless you and give you wisdom.

THE CREATION OF THE TRUST AND THE NEXT FRIENDS SUIT

Archibald McLellan, Henry Mark Baker, and Josiah Fernald were on March 6, '07, appointed by Mrs. Eddy to be trustees of her physical property for the remainder of her life-span--subject to safeguards written into the trust. McLellan was the only official Christian Scientist of the three.

The move followed a vicious attack on her person in the *New York World*, a Pulitzer newspaper; a distorted life-history run as a serial in *McClure's Magazine*, beginning Jan. '07; and the evident preparations for the Next Friends Suit which actually was filed March 1. The purpose of malicious mind at this stage was:

To eliminate S&H and other Eddy writings by gaining control of the copyrights;

To prevent her large accumulation of funds from promoting and extending the religion of Christian Science as stipulated in her will;

To have "so-called Christian Science [shown by judicial decree] to be the creation of a disordered mind" [as admitted by counsel for the "Next Friends"];

To have the Revelator of C.S. reduced to a person under the control of hostile persons.

The final result showed even the human mind that the wayshower who knows the Way <u>is</u> competent to be the guide, and that the idea of Mind that makes no pretence at having a clever and separate mind of its own is as holy as the Mind Itself.

Most of the story was published in the periodicals as it progressed, and extracts are given here of those portions which are not included in the separate chapters devoted to "Mary Baker Eddy's Published Writings."

The *New York World* Onslaught

The *New York World* sent two reporters to Concord near the end of 1906 to establish that Mrs. Eddy was dead, or completely enfeebled, and that a dummy or sometimes a substitute took the daily carriage ride which was preserved by the Christian Scientists to prolong an illusion.

They persuaded a janitor in the New York building where Mrs. Pamelia Leonard C.S.B. had her teaching offices to come to Concord to identify the substitute as Mrs. Leonard (who was now residing at Pleasant View as one of the helpers there). This lie was exposed by affidavits from Mrs. Leonard and others as follows:

Rodolph B. Frost, who worked at Pleasant View and had "done all the painting there for the last four years" testified Oct.29:

> I have known Mrs. Mary Baker G. Eddy for over seventeen years, and have known Mrs. Pamelia J. Leonard for four years.
>
> ...During the last two weeks I have seen Mrs. Eddy enter her carriage every day, except once, and on that day I met her at the gate.
>
> ...I have never known Mrs. Leonard to enter Mrs. Eddy's carriage, nor even known her to go to the door when Mrs. Eddy entered her carriage.

Mrs. Leonard (who was described in the current *Boston Herald* as a woman for whom "all resemblance to Mrs. Eddy absolutely ceases with the color of the hair") testified:

> The statement that I have impersonated Mrs. Eddy and ridden in her carriage in her place is entirely false, for I have never stepped inside of her carriage, and have never even looked inside of it....
>
> At the time Mr. Hennessy [the janitor] claimed to identify me...I was at home at Pleasant View.
>
> Had he taken the pains to have come out here to Pleasant View, I would have gladly seen him....
>
> I deny most emphatically that Mrs. Eddy has any such disease as cancer, or that she has any other disease. As I am and have been in daily contact with Mrs. Eddy, seeing her many times each day, I am in a position to know as to what I am stating.
>
> And she has not palsy of the hand.

Mr. Lewis Strang, associate secretary at Pleasant View, made the following statement Oct.15:

> I first encountered Messrs. Slaght and Lithchild [the two reporters from the *World*] on Saturday, Oct.13, 1906....
>
> At noon the next day, Sunday, Oct.14, [these] two men called at Pleasant View [and] asked for Mr. Frye. ...at Mr. Frye's request I was in the room during the interview....
>
> Mr. Slaght said...that the *World* had received many letters declaring that Mrs. Eddy was dead; that Mr. Frye was the real head of the Christian Science movement, and that money was being received--in short, that a fraud was being committed....
>
> He said it was not Mr. Pulitzer's purpose to use the material they had collected, provided they could satisfy themselves that Mrs. Eddy was alive....
>
> Mr. Frye asked them what they would consider satisfactory testimony, and they said that they would be satisfied if Professor Kent who lived across the way, would identify Mrs. Eddy in their presence....
>
> On Monday, Oct.15, [Mrs. Eddy] sent John Salchow, one of the men about the place, to see Professor Kent and arrange with him to identify her.... [Messrs. Slaght and Lithchild] reached Pleasant View about three o'clock...again emphasizing the point which they desired us to believe, that a positive identification of Mrs. Eddy was all that Mr. Pulitzer and the *World* were after.
>
> As soon as Professor Kent arrived, the three men and myself went at once upstairs to Mrs. Eddy's office. She arose and stepped to the middle of the floor to meet them.... She explained in a few words that her duties made it impossible for her to receive visitors....
>
> When we were going down the stairs...Mr. Slaght gave me to understand he was thoroughly satisfied as to the soundness of Mrs. Eddy's physical and mental condition. They furthermore led Mr. Mann, who drove them back to the hotel, to understand that they purposed leaving town that afternoon....

~ ~ ~ ~ ~ ~ ~

"Mortal mind sees what it believes as certainly as it believes what it sees" (S&H 86:29). The dupe of m.a.m. therefore assesses the Discoverer and Founder of Christian Science according to its own erroneous image, whether base or beautiful. Yet the remedy is always at hand: "to keep

Mrs. Eddy as she is (what God knows of her and revealed to Christ Jesus)" permanently in sight.

This alone takes care of whatever the Slaghts and Lithchilds may write about "their" Mrs. Eddy. In their story as it would appear in the *World*, inspite of what others thought they had seen and said, "Mrs. Eddy" was still going to be portrayed as a helpless invalid surrounded by people who were spreading illusions purely for their own benefit!

The editor of the Concord *Patriot* hoped he could correct mortal mind by correcting its channel, but as usual that was not sufficient. He wrote the proprietor of the *World* as follows:

-- Letter to Mr. Joseph Pulitzer [dated Oct.27, '06 and signed "Very truly yours, Michael Meehan"]:

My dear Mr. Pulitzer: I have met and talked with you once. I have met and talked with Mrs. Eddy more than once. I know her; she knows me.... If the intent of "*The World*'s" representatives to Concord be carried out in its columns, "*The World*" will say in substance that Mrs. Eddy is dead, and that a dummy or substitute, and not she, is in the carriage each day; ...or it will say Mrs. Eddy is enfeebled and decrepid, and that those brilliant faculties which in the past made her wonderful accomplishments possible have departed.

To every statement, or even insinuation, of this kind I, as one who knows, say it is not true, in whole or in part....

This letter to you is not occasioned by any special zeal on my part in the cause of CHRISTIAN SCIENCE, nor is it occasioned by any blind adherence to or worship of persons or advocacies, but solely in a spirit of justice, truth, square dealing....

[The letter was neither acknowledged nor acted upon.]

Charles Corning, mayor of Concord, came to the rescue as best he knew how with the following press statement Oct.28:

I have known Mrs. Eddy by sight for many years and have seen her in her carriage many times, and within the past season Mrs. Eddy has passed up Pleasant Street and down Green Street daily, and I

> know that the sole occupant of the carriage has been Mrs. Eddy.... Mrs. Eddy received me this afternoon in company with Gen. Frank S. Streeter, who is and has been an attorney of Mrs. Eddy for several years....
>
> I spoke to Mrs. Eddy, and I listened for nearly half an hour to her conversation. She is keen of intellect and strong in memory. She is a surprising illustration of longevity, with bright eyes and emphatic expression, and of an alertness rarely to be encountered in a person so venerable.

General Streeter made a statement confirming the interview--which he had requested for the mayor and himself and which was granted "almost immediately." He said:

> She arose and most cordially greeted the mayor and myself, exhibiting no appearance of weakness or decrepitude, but a physical activity not ordinarily to be found in persons many years younger.... She spoke briefly and without bitterness...and said that she was in the hands of an infinite God in whom she had perfect trust, and that He would care for her.
>
> Reference was made to business transactions of some time ago, about which her memory was exact and accurate....

Later the same day Mayor Corning introduced a C.S. lecture given by Hermann Hering, and in it he said <u>inter alia</u>:

Recently there have been in Concord representatives of one of the great metropolitan dailies, alleging that Mrs. Eddy was no more.... This afternoon, less than four hours ago, for the first time in my life, I stood face to face with Mrs. Eddy for a half hour. I listened to as bright, as vigorous, and as sprightly a conversation as I have ever listened to in my life.

The following day he made this statement to a reporter from the Boston *Herald*:

> ...I had gone expecting to find a tottering old woman, perhaps incoherent, almost senile. Instead, when she rose to greet me, her carriage was almost erect, her walk that of a woman of forty....
>
> "You have a cosy corner here, I see, Mrs. Eddy", said General Streeter.
>
> "Yes, and some people would like to see me in a closer corner", remarked Mrs. Eddy, quickly.
>
> I call that a good repartee....

After yet another day several members of the press from New York and New England descended on Pleasant View for an interview in which they saw what they had predetermined for themselves. Perhaps the most objective account came from Harlan C. Pearson for the Associated Press who wrote:

A representative of the Associated Press who interviewed Mrs. Eddy...ten years ago, went to Pleasant View...and was granted another interview by the same woman....

The interview, which was granted to half a score of newspaper representatives who had assembled in [Concord] after the publication of the sensational stories in connection with Mrs. Eddy's health, was arranged early in the day by H. Cornell Wilson, head of the Christian Science publishing committee, at the earnest request of the reporters. ...they were escorted to the double parlors on the east side of the house. A moment or two after they had been seated Mr. Frye announced Mrs. Eddy.

The Leader of the Christian Science faith walked to the doorway and stood, unassisted, before her interviewers. She did not approach farther than the threshold of the door, and when it was seen that she would not enter the room for a prolonged interview, a woman reporter [Sibyl Wilbur], who had previously interviewed her, was delegated to talk to her today.

That Mrs. Eddy was more anxious to demonstrate that she was in good physical condition than she was to answer questions was demonstrated by the abrupt manner in which she left the assembled newspaper representatives.... The brief interview consisted of the following questions and answers:-

"Are you in perfect physical health, Mrs. Eddy?" was the first question after Mrs. Eddy had made her appearance.

"I am", was the brief reply, given with distinct enunciation.

"Have you any other physician than God?"

"No, indeed", answered Mrs. Eddy, with emphasis, and then she added slowly and solemnly: "The everlasting arms are around and above me, which is enough."

"Do you take a daily drive?" was the next question asked, to which Mrs. Eddy replied as briefly and distinctly as she did to the first question. "I do", she said.

It was at this point...that Mrs. Eddy unexpectedly indicated that the interview was at an end, for she turned without another word and walked to the porte cochère at the front of the house, where her carriage was waiting to convey her on her usual drive about the city.... She was then driven away, while the newspaper representatives were escorted through her home, which they inspected with interest.

The Allegations of the "Next Friends"

The following is the:

Petition of Mary Baker Glover Eddy
who sues by her next friends George W. Glover [son],
Mary Baker Glover [granddaughter] and
George W. Baker [nephew] against

Calvin A. Frye, Alfred Farlow, Irving C. Tomlinson,
Ira O.Knapp, William B. Johnson, Stephen A. Chase,
Joseph Armstrong, Edward A. Kimball, Hermann S. Hering,
and Lewis C. Strang:

~ ~

1. [Locations of parties involved.]

2. [This section...covers allegations of Mrs. Eddy's inability to guard and manage her property, ending "The plaintiffs say"]:

3. That the said Mary Baker G. Eddy lives in her own house in said Concord under the charge and in the custody of said defendants Frye and Strang, who live in the house and keep her carefully surrounded and secluded by themselves and by household servants of their selection....

5. That the said George W. Baker...has on several occasions during the last twenty-five years written letters to Mrs. Eddy but has never yet received from her a direct reply and only occasionally a letter from some person near her; that on November 17, 1905, he made a special effort to communicate directly with her...but the respectful letter was withheld from her by her Assistant Secretary, Gilbert C. Carpenter, and her Secretary, the defendant Frye, as they said the rules of the house required, because not pertaining to the great work she had in hand,--and the last letter he wrote, dated April 6, 1906, was not even answered by said Frye....

6. That the property of the said Mary Baker G. Eddy for a long time has been and now is extensive and valuable...and that the business of managing said property has been and is important and difficult [and] has been done either in her name by others or by her while unfitted for the transaction thereof....

8. That in particular certain transactions require investigation and judicial consideration, being the following:

COPYRIGHTS

[Extensive details of copyrights, publications, sales, dates of issue, etc., of "all Mrs. Eddy's books, writings and periodicals" and in particular]:

Various transfers have been made by Mrs. Eddy of her copyrights and various retransfers made by her, and particularly the following:

On January 12, 1896, "Science and Health" and nearly all her other works were transferred by her to the defendant, Calvin A. Frye, and on October 6, 1899, he retransferred them to her. On October 9, 1899, she transferred them to the defendant, Edward A. Kimball, and on May 21, 1906, he retransferred them to her.

THE METAPHYSICAL COLLEGE

...During the first seven years of the college life over 4000 students were taught by Mrs. Eddy. The "Christian Science Journal" for December 1906, copyrighted 1906 by Mrs. Eddy, publishes a list of Christian Science practitioners now advertising in that monthly periodical for patients throughout the United States, from Alabama to Wyoming numbering 3133, and also in the Dominion of Canada, Mexico, Australia, Queensland, Victoria, China, Great Britain, Ireland, Scotland, France, Germany, Holland, Italy, and Switzerland numbering 200.

The healers must be Christian Scientists who use as their only textbooks the Bible and "Science and Health", and use and distribute the writings of Mrs. Eddy....

The receipts of this college from the 3333 practitioners now advertising their power of healing have been over one million dollars ...but the plaintiffs are unable to state the amount nor how much Mrs. Eddy has received, nor how much has been received and retained by the defendants.

THE MOTHER CHURCH

"The Mother Church"...with its extensive membership of 40,000, has a large income. Mrs. Eddy is Pastor Emeritus. Without her approval of the particular person selected no Church officer can be chosen. Nor can the by-law making this limitation be amended or annulled without her written consent.... No bequests from the Church can be made without her consent.

[Then: details of the official positions held in the Church by the defendants.]

REAL ESTATE

On February 12, 1898, and on other dates, she conveyed for her natural life her real estate in Concord and all the personal property thereon to the defendant Frye to hold according to the terms of a certain deed of trust.... On September 5, 1901, the defendant Frye retransfered to her all said property....

Her rightful income as owner of all the aforesaid copyrights, as the president of the Metaphysical College of Healing, as the head and Pastor Emeritus of the Mother Church, and as proprietor of all the real estate aforesaid has been of immense value, and has all been controlled or received by the defendants, some or all of them, and yet she has had no complete or sufficient accounting from them therefor.

9. That...there is abundant reason to believe the defendants and their associates have wrongfully converted to their own private use or otherwise misappropriated, or unlawfully diverted large sums of money and large amounts of property of the said Mary Baker G. Eddy; and the plaintiffs claim that the defendants should now be adjudged to have been trustees thereof and to make restitution therefor.

Wherefore the plaintiffs pray:

1. That defendants be required to disclose and give account of all the business transactions aforesaid....

2. That if they shall be found to have wrongfully received and held or disposed of any of the property...they be required to restore the same....

3. That they be enjoined during the pendency of the present suit in equity not to pay out any money or part with any property of the said

Mary Baker G. Eddy now held by them...and not to act whatever in her name....

4. That a receiver...be appointed to take possession of all the property of the said Mary Baker G. Eddy now in the hands of or under the control of the defendants....

[signed] George W. Glover
Mary B. Glover
George W. Baker

[The three new trustees {McLellan, Baker, and Fernald} petitioned the court to be substituted as "plaintiffs" as they were now legally in charge of Mrs. Eddy's property and should be the ones demanding restitution if any, but the request was denied.]

WHAT THE TRUST REQUIRED

[Under the terms of the new trust Mrs. Eddy did]: Grant, convey, assign, and transfer...all my interest...in and to any real estate; also to...any estate, personal or mixed, which I can own or possess, including stocks, bonds, interest in copyrights, contracts, actions, and causes of action at law or in equity against any person...nevertheless for the following purposes and upon the following conditions, viz:

First: To manage, care for, and control all the above granted real estate and interest therein during my earthly life and, at the termination thereof, to dispose of the same in accordance with the provisions of my last will and the codicils thereto; but I hereby reserve for myself the right of occupancy and use of my [homes in Concord and Boston and their furnishings].

Second: I give unto my trustees full power to manage, care for, control, invest, and reinvest all said trust property.... It is my wish that, in the making of investments, preference shall be given to the state, government, city, and muncipal bonds; but I leave this to [their] judgment....

Third: Said trustees shall pay to me, from time to time, out of the net income of said trust property, (1) such sums as I may need or desire for [the usual expenses of my] homestead "Pleasant View"; (2) such sums as I may desire for my own personal expenses and for charitable purposes; and (3) such sums as I may personally desire to use for the advancement of the cause and doctrines of Christian Science as taught by me....

Fifth: Said trustees are hereby appointed my attorneys in fact and, as such, are hereby invested with full power...to bring, appear in, prosecute, defend, and dispose of...any actions, causes of action, suits at law or in equity....

Ninth: The trustees shall receive a reasonable payment from the trust fund for their personal services as such, and shall also be reinbursed for all expenses incurred by them in the management of the trust estate.

Tenth: The trustees shall render to me personally, semi-annual accounts of the trust property and the income and expenses thereof.

IN WITNESS WHEREOF, I have hereunto set my hand and seal this sixth day of March, A.D. 1907

MARY BAKER G. EDDY

~ ~ ~ ~ ~ ~ ~

The defendants in the Next Friends Suit duly introduced their rejoinders and the court then set about determining what was the real challenge: the state of mind, past and present, of the C.S. leader. The prosecuting lawyer (Senator Chandler) maintained that Christian Science was itself an absurdity proving the insanity of its inventor; and his point of attack lay largely with its alleged beliefs about m.a.m.

Mrs. Eddy sought the testimony of the alienist Dr. Allan McLane Hamilton, even though he had gone on record as hostile to Christian Science in a New York case. His highly favorable findings are given in full in the second chapter of "Mary Baker Eddy's Published Writings."

Judge Chamberlin, the judge in the case, appointed Judge Aldrich as Master to examine Mrs. Eddy in her own home together with a Dr. Jelly and a Mr. Parker. As the account of this examination is not given in the "Published Writings", and as many of Mrs. Eddy's answers were wisely metaphysical, the main points are now given herewith:

The Masters at Pleasant View (Aug.14 '07)

Judge Aldrich [A]: ...the gentlemen present want to ask you some questions, and...if you feel fatigued, we want to have you speak of it and let us know.

Mrs. Eddy [E]: Thank you. I can work hours at my work, day and night, without the slightest fatigue when it is in the line of spiritual labor....

Mr. Parker [referring to the property] [P]: ...I see you have fruit trees.

E: ...there were no trees except pines when I came here. The rest of the trees I have planted, and when I suggested that a large tree be planted they laughed at me, but I said, "Try it and see if it will succeed." Every one of these trees around here was planted by myself,--that is, not by myself but by my direction....

When I came here they had no State Fair grounds and very little pavement. A one-horse car moved once an hour. There was very little being done in Concord then compared with what I anticipated when I came.

It seemed to be going out, and I admire the apparent vigor and flourishing conditon of this dear city now. I had a great desire to build up my native place.... They asked me in Boston to remain. Jordan & March, White, and other firms requested me not to leave the city, and they said to me, "Have we not helped you to accumulate money since you have been here?" And I replied, "Have I not helped you?" And they said, "Yes, you have, and that is why we want to have you stay." Then I said, "I want to go home and help my native state a little."...

A: Someone was telling me that you had given to the public streets....

E: I have, $10,000 at one time.

A: Where was that expended?

E: It has been expended on this street and on other streets, Main Street and State Street.

A: Was that done at the suggestion of anybody, or was it your own idea?

E: It was mine. They consulted me with regard to it. My students contributed towards it also and left the decision to me....

A: My life insurance is coming due pretty soon, and I want to make good use of it. What do you consider good investments?

E: I do not put it into life insurance. God insures my life.

A: I carry a little life insurance and it is coming due, so I am interested, you know. You wouldn't advise throwing it away, would you? For instance, my life insurance comes due next year.

E: Yes, I respect that. I respect the life insurance; I think it is very valuable to many, but I have not any need of it.

A: It was not really in that sense that I suggested it. I wanted to get your idea as to what would be a good investment....

E: Shall I tell you my ideas?

A: Yes.

E: Trust in God. God is Life. God is infinite. Therefore, if we are the image and likeness of Infinity, we have no beginning and no end, and are His image and likeness; that is my life insurance....

A: Now this is all interesting and useful, but still I have not made myself understood. For instance [if you had a hundred thousand dollars to invest today] what kind of investments would you consider sound?...

E: I prefer government bonds.... I have not entered into stocks.... I did not think it was safe for me. I did not want the trouble of it, that was all. Perhaps I was mistaken, but that is my business sense of it.

A: ...what would be your idea, whether there was greater security of investment in Eastern municipalities or Western?

E: The East I should say.

Dr. Jelly [J]: Mrs. Eddy, are you willing to tell us something about the development of your special religion? Are you willing to tell us about how the matter came about, and how it has existed and developed?...

E: I would love to do it. I was an invalid born in belief, I was always having doctors--

J: When you say "born in belief", I perhaps do not understand what you mean.

E: I mean born according to human nature, born not of God but of the flesh. That is what I mean. I was an invalid from my birth.... My father employed M.D.'s of the highest character, and they were estimable men, and they would say--Dr. Benton was one, and he said, and the others said: "Do not doctor your child, she has got too much brains for her body; keep her outdoors, keep her in exercise, and keep her away from school all you can, and do not give her much medicine." That was all allopathy, you know.

J: Can you tell us how long ago that was, please--about how long? I don't suppose you can tell exactly, but somewhere near.

E: No. I should say I was eighteen years old, perhaps, and it came to me through Dr. Morrill, he was a homoeopath, and I had never heard of that before; it was a new subject in New Hampshire, and father said: "I thought he was a fine fellow, but he must have gone mad to have taken up homoeopathy." That was the general idea of things then. When Dr. Morrill came to Concord he healed cases that the other M.D.'s did not, and my father employed him, and I got well under his treatment.

Then you asked me to tell my footsteps? I said, I will study homoeopathy. I did. I was delighted with it. I took a case that a doctress considered hopeless, and I cured the case. It was dropsy.

[Mrs. Eddy here gave the story found in S&H p.156 and continued]: That was my first discovery of the Science of Mind. That was a falling apple to me that mind governed the whole question of her recovery.

I was always praying to be kept from sin, and I waited and prayed for God to direct me. The next that I encountered were spiritualists who were claiming to be mediums. I went into their seances to find what they were doing. Shall I go on with this unnecessary detail?

J: I will not trouble you to go into that in any further particulars just now, but Mr. Parker would like to ask you a few questions....

P: How many hours in the day do you keep your mind upon your work?

E: Well I rise in the morning early and have few hours during the day that I am not at work, and I have the care of the house as much as I ever had it.

P: Now, your intellectual work, or your work in connection with your subject. Do you write? Are you writing? Do you write letters nowadays?

E: I write them or dictate them. Others seldom write letters for me, save through dictation; then I look them over and see if they are right.

P: You look them over yourself?

E: Yes, I do.

P: Is that invariable? Don't you ever let letters go away from here without that?

E: I do not when they pertain to business of my own.

[As the interview began to close, Mrs. Eddy expressed her satisfaction with the trusteeship she had created to look after her business, and referred to her trustees as follows:

Mr. Fernald: "superintendent of the Old Folks' Home; he is a good man to take care of me, is he not?"

Henry M. Baker: "my cousin."

Archibald McLellan: "a better man we do not need to have."

And she concluded: "Now, I am thinking why cannot we have this all in love and unity and good will to man?"

[Mr. Parker had mentioned music, and Mrs. Eddy rang for an attendant to ask Calvin Frye to let the group listen to her "artificial singer" before they left. When Mr. Frye arrived to lead them out he explained: "It is a graphophone, gentlemen."]

A: I want to say before going that my mother is still living and she is eighty-seven years of age.

E: Give my love to her.

A: I will.

E: God bless her. She is not a day older for her eighty-seven years if she is growing in grace.

A: Well, she feels pretty happy.

E: I have no doubt she is. I mean mere decaying when I say "older." She is rising higher. Decay belongs not to matter but to mortal mind. We do not lose our faculties through matter so much as through mind, do we? Now, my thought is, that if we keep our mind fixed on Truth, God, Life and Love, He will advance us in our years to a higher understanding, our words into works, and our ultimate into the fruition of entering into the Kingdom.

[After listening to the graphophone, the Board of Masters returned to Mrs. Eddy's room since they also had received a message saying she felt she had omitted something. When they arrived, she said]:

E: I feel that I did not answer you fully; that I dropped my subject before I concluded it with regard to the footsteps to Christian Science. Now, allow me to complete that thought. I got to where I told you I found it was mind instead of the drug that healed--

A: Let me make one remark. There were two reasons why we suggested we would not pursue that branch of the inquiry any further. One was, that we were a little afraid we might weary you, and the other was that in certain quarters it is suggested that this investigation is an attack on your doctrines, and we did not want to have it appear that we were requiring you to make any statements about it.

E: Not at all. I shall regard it as a great favor if you will condescend to hear me in this.... When I came to the point that it was mind that did the healing, then I wanted to know what mind it was. Was it the Mind which was in Christ Jesus, or was it the human mind and human will?

This led me to investigate spiritualism, mesmerism, and hypnotism, and I failed to find God there; therefore I turned to God in prayer and said, "Just guide me to that mind which is in Christ", and I took the Bible and opened to the words, "Now, go, write it in a book." I can show you where this Scripture is in the Bible.

I then commenced writing my consciousness of what I had seen, and I found that human will was the cause of disease instead of its cure; that neither hypnotism, mesmerism, nor human concepts did heal; they too were the origin of disease instead of its cure, and that the Divine Mind was the Healer; then I found through the Scripture that "He healed all our diseases." Also the command, "Go ye into the world, preach the Gospel, heal the sick", and I felt there was my line of labor, and that God did the healing, and that I could no more heal a person by mortal mind, the mind of mortals, or will-power, than by cutting off his head. I know not how to use will-power to hurt the sick....

A Christian Scientist can no more make a person sick than he can at the same time be a sinner and be a Christian Scientist. He does not knowingly make people suffer or injure them in any way--he has not the power to do it. All the power that Christian Scientists have comes from on High. We have no other power and no faith in any other power.

~ ~ ~ ~ ~ ~ ~

Before committing the above to the history of the Next Friends Suit, Mrs. Eddy checked the stenographer's version for accuracy, in accordance with court and parliamentary procedure, and wrote as follows:

-- <u>Letter</u> to Michael Meehan [dated Nov.15 '07 and signed "Affectionately and gratefully, Mary Baker G. Eddy"]:

Beloved Student: I am glad to have had opportunity to read and revise my interview with the Masters....

> I fancy I have not exceeded my privilege. I have added nothing, have not changed my thought, but have erased some unnecessary statements and repetitions in both the questions and answers,--also I have corrected some errors in rhetoric and grammar that must have resulted from inability on the part of the stenographer to distinctly hear what was said.

Notwithstanding the Masters' disavowal of attempts to call Mrs. Eddy's religious views into question, counsel for the Next Friends considered these views to be their trump card in the prosecution. They made careful distinction between ordinary religious "beliefs" held by believers the world over, and "delusions" they said that Mrs. Eddy held.

The day before they were ready to admit they had no case regarding Mrs. Eddy's mental and business acumen, they had one more go at her alleged beliefs and fear of "m.a.m." Apart from early letters and statements, which the court sometimes refused and sometimes allowed, they did what they could with published assertions like those in '01 p.20, where the "crimes" of the "mental malpractitioner" and "crimes committed under this new-old régime of necromancy and diabolism" are proclaimed for all to read.

The "unconditional surrender of 'Next Friends'" the following day is recorded in CSS Vol.IX, No.52.

To Mrs. Eddy "Next Friends" are not persons in any case, any more than the one malpractitioner she identified in early days is a person--any more than Revelator or Christ is a person. The same one evil, the same one belief of minds many, may reveal itself in a form that will most easily beguile, but it is not that form, any more than omnipresent Soul which illustrates Itself as person is not forever one particular localized person.

Indeed evil's channel has no more initiative than the Christ-example which "can of mine own self do nothing"; and Mrs. Eddy showed she had impersonalized the whole legal proceedings in 1907 by including in S&H that year the following statement about what she clearly called "a mental case...on trial." On p.430:23 she wrote:

False Belief is the attorney for Personal Sense. Mortal Minds constitute the jury. Materia Medica, Anatomy, Physiology, Hypnotism, Greed and Ingratitude, "next friends" of Man. [The quotes are as in the original.]

In 1908, after the case had been concluded, she removed the reference to next friends, and reworded the paragraph as now.

The suit ended with the divine blessing that surrounds "those who discern Christian Science [who] hold crime in check [and] maintain law and order" (S&H 97:1-3). George Glover was offered a generous financial settlement in return for his agreement never to contest his mother's will. That meant that there was no one who would use ownership of her copyrights to stop publication of S&H and her other writings. The C.S. Publishing Society would keep them in print until in God's good time they entered the public domain.

The funds that would promote and extend the religion of C.S. "as taught by me" remained intact; and there was worldwide recognition that the mind that discerns C.S. is a pure reflection of the <u>sanity</u> of the Mind that is God.

In particular, there remained no excuse for the grotesque assumption that the Revelator had lost control of the revelation or was unaware of any part of what the divine Revelation reveals.

PEACE AND POLITICS

The Next Friends Suit coincided with an upsurge in the world's yearning for peace, also with Mrs. Eddy's part in the wide circulation of the Peace Flag and her appointment as <u>Fondateur</u> of the Association for International Conciliation. The offer to put up the fee for the appointment was made by First Church of Christ, Scientist, New York and accepted with deep thanks (My.282-3).

In April 1907 the CSS carried an editorial asserting that "the objects of the National Arbitration and Peace Congress...should appeal to all Christian people" and maintaining "that they do appeal to Christian Scientists."

The following month however the editor used the CSJ to query the general interpretation of Mrs. Eddy's connection with the Association for International Conciliation. About this William L. Johnson writes:

> This editorial written by Archibald McLellan shows his attitude of jealousy toward this action of love for Mrs. Eddy taken by First Church of Christ, Scientist, New York City, against which he was always bitter.
>
> There was no necessity to write as he did, for...careful reading will show that he actually belittles Mrs. Eddy's membership because it was purchased for her through the efforts of First Church. What entirely escaped his vision is the point that the people of that church recognized the fact, by what Mrs. Eddy had accomplished, she should be made a Founder of the Association....
>
> First Church, New York City, showed its deep appreciation of the gift of spiritual peace which Mrs. Eddy had given through her teachings, by presenting her with membership in the Association, and that body accomplished this action at a most auspicious time when powerful enemies, through the suit of the "Next Friends" were trying to destroy Mrs. Eddy mentally and physically....
>
> Considering for a moment, Mr. McLellan's innuendo about the true value of Mrs. Eddy's membership as a Founder, one cannot help but wonder...that Mr. McLellan dared to write as he did when the fact is considered, as shown by Mrs. Eddy's letter of acceptance, that she was pleased and grateful at being made a Founder.

The following month the CSJ carried some references to the Peace Flag which Mrs. Eddy accepted in May, passing it on "with loving words" to the Board of Directors to exhibit in Boston.

The Directors had received the following from her assistant secretary:

-- Letter to Clerk, Board of Directors [dated May 2, '07 and signed "Yours sincerely, H. Cornell Wilson"]:

> The flag pole and angel figure which mounts the pole are yet to go to you. A box must be made for them so they will await the next messenger returning to Boston.
>
> When instructing me regarding this matter, our Leader said, "Send the flag--the Peace flag--to them with my love."

The flag was made by "four hundred working men and girls representing all nations." According to the "description and history" issued at the time:

> It was first exhibited in Mr. Carnegie's home on Fifth Avenue, New York City; it next went to Washington where it was exhibited at the foundation of the American Group of the Interparliamentary Union, held in Washington April 1904, at the Capitol in the Special Room. On this occasion President Seward, who was ambassador to China for seventeen years, presided....
>
> Dr. Robert S. Freeman, the owner of the flag, telegraphed to Mr. Alfred Love of Philadelphia (President of the Universal Peace Union) to meet him in Philadelphia ...and together they laid the flag on the chair of Betsy Ross, who made the first American flag. They then went to the grave of Benjamin Franklin, and laying it over the grave prayed for the mission of the flag to be accomplished. From there they went to Independence Hall where they wrapped the flag around the Liberty Bell, and covered the table upon which the Declaration of Independence was signed....
>
> [After being taken to Albany, N.Y. and other places, the flag went to England where] Dr. McDowell took it to Westminster Abbey, and from there it was taken to Runnymede [after being] put on the stone which is placed in the Coronation Chair whenever a king or queen of England is crowned.
>
> [The "history" then added that] this stone is said to be the Bethel stone upon which Jacob rested his head when he saw the vision of the ladder reaching up to heaven....
>
> It is reported that this flag was used at the first Hague Conference, and a duplicate of it is to be presented to the Hague Court as soon as it is permanently established....

By the time Mrs. Eddy received the flag, she was reported to be the first <u>individual</u> to have custody of it. A duplicate flag had been made and was awaiting presentation to Andrew Carnegie as an individual, but this came later.

GOD'S PEACE vs. GANG-WARFARE

Regarding the McLellan editorial there is no doubt that Mrs. Eddy saw it, probably even before publication; and she would have made sure corrections were issued, as was her wont, if they had been really necessary. With peace there is the same distinction between God's Peace and the mortal sense of "peace, peace, where there is no peace", as there is between God's Nation and localized and feuding imitations.

Only one year earlier Mrs. Eddy had been making the same kind of distinction between the legitimate celebration of God's omnipresent Church, and a "conspicuous" display of "anything that includes materialism" (pp.247-8). The uncomprehending mind could even have claimed that poor Mrs. Eddy just could not make up her mind whether to dedicate the Extension at the Annual Meeting in 1906, or whether to postpone dedication until the building was materially complete, no matter how inconvenient these vacillations were proving to be!

The determining factor however was the students' own emphasis. Were they clear that they were recognizing God's universal Church or were they wanting to boast of a "church, church, where there is no Church"?

Similarly when Mrs. Eddy voiced "strict" support of the Monroe Doctrine, she meant strict prayerful recognition of the Principle behind that divine and wonderful message, a message not reduced to some selfish, materialistic or ecclesiastical gang-warfare.

At first, as history relates, all that was planned in 1823 was an Anglo-American warning to catholic Spain to abandon her imperialistic designs in South and Central America; but when God is seen to be in the picture, the document becomes one of the world's great calls to go first to God and to "handle animal magnetism."

As has been noted, animal magnetism is the belief that one idea (be it expressed as animal, man, church, nation) can impose its will, its mesmerism, on another idea; whereas idea has no power of its own, and the only connection between "ideas" is through their One and Only Principle. This becomes a healing, not a destructive, message.

Mrs. Eddy's strict belief is therefore "in the Monroe doctrine...and in the laws of God." Without "the laws of God" the human mind bends a doctrine to its own purposes, i.e. practices animal magnetism. This habit of the human mind, defying the defined principle of the Monroe Doctrine and becoming determined to "interfere", rather than seeking first the Kingdom of God and His righteousness, would merit Mrs. Eddy's "reluctant" foresight of "great danger threatening our nation,--imperialism, monopoly, and a lax system of religion" (My.129:3).

In My.282:3, while ready to admire President Roosevelt's interpretation of God's law and doctrine, Mrs. Eddy felt it necessary to add: "my hope must still rest in God, and the Scriptural injunction,--'Look unto me and be ye saved, all the ends of the earth'."

Where the perspective is "nations" rather than the several illustrations of God's One Nation, Mrs. Eddy could surely be expected to warn the field that it must instead pray to be in line with the peace "which passeth understanding", the peace that God knows and plans. This is the "wiser want" of which she spoke (My.281:2).

When she wrote to the most involved member of First Church, New York, wishing for "the success of the Association for International Conciliation [which] is of paramount importance to every son and daughter of all nations" (My.282:21), she felt the need to add "May God guide...this good endeavor." [Emphasis added in the above paragraphs.]

In the same way, in the hour when it is still felt necessary to preserve peace among nations, she concludes that "the armament of navies is necessary" (My.286:10)--but this is "navies", not a navy for a particular territorial nation.

At that date Mrs. Eddy's work and leadership had brought some response to her God-inspired call: "Brave Britain, Blest America! Unite your battle-plan" (My.338:1), and by agreement Britain preserved bases for its navy in the Atlantic and America preserved bases for its navy in the Pacific, so that together they could keep the sea-lanes open for the peaceful pursuit of international trade. [Later there was the 5:5:3 agreement giving Japan a naval patrol three-fifths the size of the other two--an agreement shattered by war.]

The true battle-plan is not shattered by war. It is "the love for God and man"--one God, one man--making "victorious, all who live it" (My.338:3-4).

In Nov.CSJ '98 Mrs. Eddy prophesies to an Englishman in Canada that "your flag shall wave at the right hand, and at the right hour, beside the stars and stripes of the American flag." Does this prophecy declare that the individual flag will and must be but an example of the one flag of the One Nation--of the one boundless, unlocalized America, God's example of "all the nations of the world"?

Mrs. Eddy's Translation of Politics

A small selection of some of Mrs. Eddy's recorded statements follow:

1) The dragon's "seven heads" are: Politics (dictatorship) --capital and labor--militarism--materia medica--machinery--commercialism--ecclesiasticism.

2) We are self-governed only when guided by no other Mind than our Maker's. There are no conflicting, ignorant motives. There is no mortal mind to conflict with, or to interfere with, another. The false claims of the world must be met in ourselves and others.

3) [To Augusta Stetson--for full text see p. 293]: Avoid being identified pro or con in politics.... Give all your attention to the moral and spiritual status of the race. God alone is capable of government: you are not, I am not, but God has governed through his anointed and appointed one in the way of divine Science--not politics nor the making or breaking of national laws or institutions....

4) [To Caroline Frame, see p.158]: After the Babylonian woman fell the true sense of Socialism appeared--man's unity with God, therefore at one with fellow man.... Government is unity and cooperation in society.

5) [In Boston Herald, dated April 16 '98]: In order to close the multitudinous questions addressed to me...I will say...it had been better that our friendly nation in the first

instance had wiped her hands of Cuba altogether. [This was strictly in line with the God-given Doctrine which outlawed mortal mind's interference, and which issued a call to "handle animal magnetism" first. As the call went unheeded, Mrs. Eddy's hope (My.278:1) remained in God's government and in the everpresent opportunity He gives to cut short future decades of unmastered lessons, such as with Cuba.]

6) [To Mr. Willis, C.S.B. {CSS Vol.IX, No.48}]: It is my desire that...you obtain a large number of Christian Scientists to become members of the American Peace Society. [Mrs. Eddy withdrew this request {see p.178} when she saw that the belief of many minds <u>allied</u> for even a good human purpose could be animal <u>magnetism</u> unless the members understood that the only strength came from their independent individual linkage with the unchangeable Principle of Peace --the "wiser want" of My.281:2.]

~ ~ ~ ~ ~ ~ ~

The healing message of this chapter and its contents concludes with a selection of statements by Mrs. Eddy grouped in four main categories.

1. HEALING AND THE ONE CONSCIOUSNESS

[Message to students in Mrs. Eddy's home who had ears to hear]: It is not enough to heal the sick. You have to demonstrate God's allness in all that you see and do.

Our treatment must be universal as well as individual. Whatever we see objectively is simply the subjective state of our own consciounsss.

The test of the Christian Scientist is whether he can heal <u>sin</u> (which is the "illusion of mind in matter").

Healing the sick and sinful is the greatest part and all must join in this work who wish not to see this Cause go down.

Bear in memory that if by reason of ambition or cowardice, sin ploughs again into the ranks, and students dodge the question, the effects will fall on them, not me, the next time.

The difference between Science and faith-healing: one makes the healed <u>know God</u>; the other simply heals the physical. Faith-healing is not really healing, or else the patient would be one with God.

Do not think because you "heal", you are a Christian Scientist--as medicine heals as regards the senses, and so does error. A Christian Scientist heals the moral as well as the physical.

There is one Mind, and this Mind is yours and mine, and governs us. All our thoughts come to us from this Mind, and go back to their Source. There is no other Mind to tempt, to harm, or to control. Know this, and you are the master of the occasion, master of yourself and others.

Shadows of various types come in contact with one another and no harm ensues, so the impact of material objects in what is called an accident makes no impression on the true consciousness and in the realm of Spirit nothing has happened.

Without the Infinite there would be no infinitesimal, and this is as mighty a truth as its converse. We should consider the minor applications of Science as well as the major.

I walk the earth in the atmosphere of Love which holds me in spiritual gravitation. The Love that I reflect repels every error of mortal mind, for Love is the only law and Love is all activity. Love fills all channels and expels all error. Love purifies, inspires, protects and satisfies.

Love contains, Love maintains, Love sustains, Love does liberate, unbind, unseal and deliver; naught can hinder Love. Love does supply with perfect freedom, Love does furnish, provide, adorn with great liberty. Love does glow, warm, shine, light with its rays of glory.

Love does illumine, irradiate, beam with resplendent brilliancy.

Love is the only and all of spiritual attainment in spiritual growth. Without it healing is not done and cannot be, either morally or physically. Every advance step will show you this until victory is won and you possess no other consciousness but <u>Love</u> divine.

When I first came to Christian Science I was lifted right out of the belief of sickness into the belief of health. And since then I am working out of the belief of health into the Science of health.

Christian Science is a state of individual consciousness of knowing God.

Every pure thought falling silently and gently into human consciousness does its part in cleansing the whole world, just as every falling snowflake does its silent share in transforming the noisomeness of the grimy earth into a soft white blanket of purity. We must remember that the smallest truth is mightier than the greatest lie the world has ever known. One is as enduring as eternity; the other is as transient as a shadow.

Take from a lie its power to deceive and it becomes nothing, for its very being depends upon its ability to mislead. A lie must have two willing accessories--one who is willing to be deceived; one who is willing to deceive,--the victimized and the victim; if either is wanting, the lie can do nothing.

God blesses and rewards prayer for the Divine Principle cooperates with the mind that is divinely inspired; in other words, that thinks aright. "Seek and ye shall find" "Ask and it shall be given you."

~ ~ ~ ~ ~ ~ ~

[An article by Mrs. Eddy entitled "Demonstration"]: I have learned a great secret, I have learned how to demonstrate, I have learned how to make Science a thing of life and not of words. I am going to tell you what the secret is, and it is wonderful. It is this: Not to see or hear or repeat any kind of imperfection. It is seeing and hearing and repeating good only, at all times and all circumstances, and inspite of everything that appears to the contrary.

I make this resolve every morning when I first open my eyes, and I renew it every hour of the day. I see perfection in myself, in my friends, and in my so-called enemy, in my affairs, and in world affairs.

I take my radical stand for the perfection of God and for everything and everybody He has created. I look upon the world with God's eyes, and I see it just as He sees it, and I refuse to see it in any other way.

I stop a dozen times a day, and renew the resolve, and make sure that I am not repeating error or giving way to criticism. I watch my thoughts about people, the lame, the old, the unloved to sense that I pass in the street, stray animals, I except nothing. I have taken my radical stand for perfection and I will not, absolutely will not, relax this perfect standard.

The result has been simply marvelous. Try it and you will find that you forget your glasses; they will become unnecessary.

You will be seeing with God's eyes, His perfect sight, and you will behold a perfect universe, the outward condition of your inward thinking. To change the picture you must change the sight that produced the picture.

~ ~

2. PREACHING AND THE ONE CORRECTNESS

[Along with the sense of total consciousness goes the sense of totally perfect surroundings where correction means seeing as correct--not forcing to become correct. Here "Christian Science...speaks to the dumb the words of Truth, and they answer with rejoicing" (S&H 342:23). Students have preserved these further statements by Mrs. Eddy]:

When love can love stronger than hate can hate, the demonstration is instantaneous.

To look into the world and see sin, sickness and death, that is hate--to look out into the world and see everything in God's image and likeness, that is love.

The purest stirs the depths of dirtiness in the hells of mortal mind.

Love your way out of hell into heaven. Be patient. Stop making much ado about little things.

As we are moving from one standpoint to a higher, we cannot be unbalanced, for Mind is each moment unfolding the Truth in a sane and orderly manner, and there is no other mind which can prevent, or oppose, or hinder that unfoldment, since God is Mind, and God is All.

Where divine Love is known there is no sense of limitation, for Love satisfies. To the loving trusting heart all things are possible.

The wilful sin we suffer from; the sin of ignorance we are delivered from. There is no remission of sins.

If human belief handles M.A.M. there is a fight, but Divine Love knows there is nothing to fight. When error appears it only appears to disappear.

[Instruction to a student who joined an anti-Jewish crusade, believing she could thus fight the Jewish mentality, not of course as persons]: The rule in Science is that our only fight is with our belief that there is something apart from us that we need to fight.

The only fear is error's fear of its own destruction. The only death is the death of error. Animal magnetism is already dead, and cannot deceive this child of God into any sense of life, substance or intelligence or good or evil through, or contained in matter.

The spiritual concept is always the direct opposite to the material. But behind every mortal thought, apparently expressed, is the spiritual thought.

Mosquitoes are an attack of mortal mind using our consciousness to annoy us. A belief of pest does not exist. Correct it, prove it, and then it blesses us.

God's child can never make a mistake, can never lose an opportunity, never cause regret. His life is bright with abundant gardens, hope, promise. Love has a plan and purpose for each and every one to fulfill and none can escape it or fail to perform the will of God. Failure to hold onto Truth means fear of letting go of error. Unwillingness to give up sin implies fear of not gaining something satisfactory in the place of it.

We shall never be without a tree, but the present sense of tree is a very bad one. Its leaves fall, lightning strikes it, and it decays and dies. Scientific affirmation and denial will give a better sense of tree by changing what we have accepted as consciousness. This is transformation.

To say that all things about one are nothing, would be annihilation, and the work of Christian Science is not annihilation but transformation.

See everything beautiful. Beauty must be brought out in form, surrounding and dress. We must not lapse into ugliness and old age, but manifest beauty in all things. The earth is simply what we recognize with the material senses.

Never feed the appetite, merely feed your hunger.

Declare every morning: I feel fine, I cannot be discouraged, dismayed, confused, influenced, or in any way affected by mortal mind. No thought, conscious or unconscious, felt or unfelt, known or unknown, no power seen or unseen, can in any way touch me, unless it originates in divine Mind.

We must be spiritual detectives and arrest every wrong thought that tries to gain admission and cast it out when the idea tries to present itself.

There is a perfect presentation of every idea of Love. We must think of ourselves as spiritual and perfect. Our sight and hearing, and our senses and faculties are spiritual, perfect and eternal, for God created all.

There is no mortal, feminine, masculine or neuter gender. No he, she, or it, no development of human concepts. To know this through demonstration destroys false spiritualism. We must handle the claim of trickery, slander, meddlesomeness, of the human mind.

It is in the mirror of Spirit that we see the brotherhood of Life and in the brotherhood of Life is the substance of understanding; let us reach out to the Word for help, for the Word is an everpresent help.

Never let error escape you undetected; never see it as something, always see it as nothing. What is the next step? The next step is: Go and prove it nothing; evil will never seem nothing to me until this has been accomplished.

(See S&H 562:29 - 565:5): To know that this dragon is in truth but a mythical creation saves us from it. If we make something of it and attempt to destroy it, we will be vanquished every time; only Truth and Love can destroy the dragon.

"The works that I do shall ye do also, because I go unto my Father." "I and my Father are one." Materially that has been made doctrinal, but in its spiritual sense it means, one with divine Principle, God the only I; yes, the oneness with the Father, the true individuality. As you rise to spiritual understanding, you lose your sense as an "I" in matter and gain your selfhood in Spirit. This brings the desired health which is not dependent on the body, but is of the Father, forever the same.

Seeing God (Good) everywhere inspite of sense testimony will heal anything. Of course we know that we have to deal with so-called evil, but as its master, refusing to give it reality or place. Christian Science teaches the oneness, allness, of God, (man in His likeness) and universe, spiritual and perfect now.

Instead of being a material man in a material universe, you are a spiritual man in the unobstructed realm of Spirit where nothing but good can find you. These truths, held to, bring liberty.

God is one, therefore divine Mind is not concerned with a dualistic belief termed "decision." Neither is there any duality of possibility in spiritual being.

[Question on Sunday by Mrs. Eddy to new members of her household]: Would you like to go to church today?

[An approved answer]: This [place] is our church, and our divine service is in serving the Discoverer of Christian Science.

[Observation by a student]: Mrs. Eddy refused to allow records to be kept by the church since she did not wish recitals of error to be preserved as realities. [See letters of May 1900, p.226.]

~ ~

3. TEACHING AND THE ONE MAN

Man is his obedience to God.

God is and man is His isness. God is one and all; all men are one--a million is one.

The Son of Man is the spiritual idea or Christ and is you and me.

What a wicked thing to say [that someone was "not ready for Christian Science"]!

In human love you seek someone to love; in divine Love you seek to love. Human love is to expect something for yourself; in divine Love you expect something for all.

Man's true individuality is the living expression of the Mind that is God. Deity and His expression must forever be united. Man lives to express God. Could we have a grander destiny? What you and I and our brothers think goes to make up the consciousness of the world.

We are not individualized outside of our brother, but are one with him, as the Christ, hence the command to love our neighbor as ourselves. We have no Science apart from our brother.

Sometimes evil argues we are out of place. No creature can be misplaced, displaced or unplaced. The practice in Christian Science is the displacing in thought of the evil and erroneous cause of life. The constant prayer of every student in Christian Science should be for the ever-increasing supply of the realization of God--His Allness and man's relation and duty to Him.

Christ is the compound idea of God, and includes all the universe and man, for Christ is the reflection of God; and when we see this and reflect the healing power we look up to Him, God, and the work is done.

At this moment there is harmony throughout the universe for God's law is harmony. At this moment each idea is in its rightful place and is satisfied and contented. As each idea is the expression of God's being and each idea reflects

Life, Truth and Love, therefore each idea reflects and expresses health, harmony and activity here and now.

Never recognize a person in the argument but take up the error only. Be conscious of the Truth and error will disappear. Overcome the evil mind with Good, with Love. Feel that no other presence exists. This will deliver us. There is no personality. This is most important to know. [See also items on p.150.]

[Similarly, to Dr. Foster Eddy]: Don't fight the mesmerists. ...Treat them as temptations of error and link them to no personality, but put them down and out of your mind.

What is M.A.M.? M.A.M. includes not only the nature of mortal mind but the action. What are the phenomena of mortal mind? Material beliefs that call themselves matter--a lie, belief, false concept, constitute the material universe and mortal man. Handle this by knowing that there is no manipulation of the lie--matter.

Mortal mind has no matter, all that it is is a lie about that which is good, perfect, immortal, complete. Matter is a misconception of Spirit. Mortal man contains within himself all the elements of the material universe, hence man includes the universe. Christian Science leads you out of mortal mind beliefs to man and woman.

The fiery furnace which they heated seven times hotter than usual for fear they would not kill the Hebrew Children revealed the "form of the fourth" which was the form of the Son of Man. The form of the fourth, in the fiery furnace was their realization of their spirituality, and was the one Christ.

To be born into the belief of matter is the last enemy to be overcome. Mankind has already reached the last enemy and knows it not.

Nothing has lifted me more rapidly into understanding than constantly dwelling upon the thought "God created man" both "male-and-female", not masculine and feminine.

[Said to a young student]: You have got to get out of this young woman and I have to get out of this old woman, and the only way we shall do this is through the discords of material sense.

We each dwell in our own world of consciousness. We look out through the windows of this consciousness and behold the passing procession of mortal mind. Day after day we have been lured forth, have been pressed into the whirl, lost our individual peace and poise in divine Mind, and found ourselves dragged through the uncleanness, the pain of the procession. We seek to regain our own home of consciousness, wiser for the experience, thinking we will not again become part of error's pageant: but here let the newer understanding of Love guard well your door. Stay in your own home of demonstration. Keep your peace, for idle curiosity, criticism, or even false sympathy may lure you forth.

~ ~ ~ ~ ~ ~ ~

[An article by Mrs. Eddy with the title "MARRIAGE--Unity of Principle and Idea"]:

When man comes to have a Soul sense of wife, he will have a wife he cannot lose. When we have a Soul sense of Life we have a Life we cannot lose. Explain man as living, moving and having his being in God. Ideas of Mind are forever held in and sustained by Mind. Explain how thought passing from God to man is the Life, action, power, intelligence and dominion of man. The power of God is reflected in His idea. If the divine Mind is activity as consciousness then heaven is now.

Man is the aggregation of Soul thoughts; that which expresses as life in divine Life; as power in divine power. Every Soul thought reflects Life, Truth and Love.

The presence of Soul thought is the consciousness of individuality. To spiritualize man is to spiritualize idea. Just as soon as this fact, that Life is, asserts itself in our consciousness, the belief in death will cease to be.

How would the thought of Omnipotence help in the case of cancer? The omnipotence of God precludes the presence of evil. I have healed a person who was said to be dying from inaction of the heart by knowing that "Action is Eternal."

Man is not somebody or some thing; man is not person; man is a condition of consciousness. Man is a Soul thought. True thoughts constitute the individuality of man. What are those thoughts about? Are they about personality or are they about God?

To destroy any desire, destroy the belief that man can or ever did create. See the false nothingness of the false presentation of Mind. If you had an axe and could strike just one blow at error, where would you strike--so as to destroy the very root of the tree of error? Answer: Mortal mind. God is infinite Mind--evil or mortal mind are one and the same.

~ ~ ~ ~ ~ ~ ~

POSSESSION

[an article attributed to Mrs. Eddy]

Mind is that which recognizes or experiences within itself all power, all ability, all achievements, all results. We are learning that Mind is infinite, therefore there is none else. There is none outside of Him to whom He can give as evidence of Himself. He is the One-adorable-One. It has been revealed to us that this consciousness of Himself, or the idea of Himself [that] moves in accord with Him, that is inseparable from Him, is the sense of Spirit of man. We should be in evidence as a sense of harmony and immortality.

Let us rid ourselves of an outside world, and learn that we possess all things and were given dominion. A sense of possession is as much a law of your being as the distinct sense of activity.

Practise having a sense of possession of all things. Taking possession of what God gives us is the step leading to God's giving us what we desire. If you take possession of what is at hand for you, it becomes the loaves and fishes for you, the basis of multiplication.

Jesus' first question was, "How many loaves have you?" You must first have the consciousness of something to multiply. Keep practising "this is mine" until the spirit of possession is gained, and you feel "all things are mine." Read Matthew, 15th chapter, and you will notice that he gave thanks for the loaves and fishes before he multiplied them, though the disciples belittled it, saying it wasn't enough, wouldn't do, etc. Mind joyous in strength dwells in the realm of Mind (S&H 514).

Taking possession does not mean contending outwardly with the rights of others, but a settled consciousness of possession of your own things (which are concepts or thoughts)--your own privacy, your time, your work, etc. It is that which will make itself felt and hold its own against robbery. Call it injustice, robbery, what you will, that has pursued you, but the lack of a sense of possession in you (the lack of denial of the opposite) has made all these limitations possible.

Man was made to have dominion. How can you have dominion over what you do not (believe you) possess? You must have a clear enough sense of possession to make others feel it. "All things that are the Father's are mine" means just what it says. Things that have no possessor, anyone can claim.

Now this does not mean a human sense of greed, but a conscious sense of Mind--a sense of the Kingdom of Heaven within that gives power and control. Conviction is dominion.

How many times do you dress yourself so that you don't mentally see the things you have not--instead of seeing the things you have, and give thanks. As we argue this sense of possession we shall see that a sense of loss is not possible. It will be wonderful to you if you awake. You will find yourself forging ahead in every line. If you see that you possess all things, you feel much better physically, mentally, in every way.

Why shouldn't we take possession of healing, of health, of demonstration, of results? Let the results be what you decide and not what some other mortal thinks for you.

Take possession of your life. Don't let it stop because of disappointment. Take it right out of depression and darkness and put it in the light, and go on with Paul saying, "None of these things move me." Take possession of results; the sense of loss is a lie. It is for you to take possession before the promise can be fulfilled.

Our land of Canaan lies before us. Let us go in and possess the land. No one else can do it for us. We must feel it. How can we have dominion over the whole earth unless we feel that the whole earth is ours?

We hear a lot about surrender and sacrifice and loss, but a sense of possession is the truth of being that refuses to be surrendered. As the idea of God is reflection there is a sense of achievement, capacity, efficiency, ability, all accomplishment. The sense of these qualities is man--I am that man.

We have things to the extent we understand their true character. Anything which is true in heaven can be proved true on earth.

~ ~

4. PUBLISHING AND THE ONE GOVERNMENT

Just as the publishing of Miscellaneous Writings was the release of teaching, so the publishing of Miscellany was the expansion of church, and of Footprints Fadeless the outreach from personality.

The publishing details are found in the following:

-- Letter to Mrs. Eddy's publisher [dated March 25, '13 and signed by Calvin A. Frye]:

> Mrs. Eddy about seven years ago requested Mrs. Laura E. Sargent to collect all articles which Mrs. Eddy had written and had been published and paste them on sheets suitable to compile for publication in book form and about the same time Mrs. Eddy requested Mr. Lewis C. Strang to examine said articles and correct any errors in grammar and punctuation and compile them ready for publication in a book similar to Miscellaneous Writings.
>
> This task was performed by Mrs. Sargent and Mr. Strang, but Mrs. Eddy thinking it not best to publish the book then, the mss were laid aside to be pub'd at some further time.I also remember that several years (perhaps ten years ago) Mrs. Eddy wrote the manuscript intending to publish a small book entitled "Footprints Fadeless" giving additional matter relative to her struggles in the early days in establishing Christian Science and

employed Rev. I.C. Tomlinson to assist her in getting the matter ready for the press. After completing the mss her legal counsel advised her not to publish the book at that time. So the mss was carefully preserved by her for future publication.

In 1907 Mrs. Eddy commissioned Michael Meehan to compile a documented history of the Next Friends Suit--then bought up all the copies when ready for publication and permitted no general distribution. [Most of the material in the Meehan book was covered in the CSS during the months the suit was pending, and can be found there or as summarized in the preceding pages.]

Mrs. Eddy also permitted Sibyl Wilbur to gather material for a biography to counter the strange and unfriendly concoction by Georgine Milmine published after the Next Friends Suit had been withdrawn.

She later requested that Miss Wilbur's work go unpublished. But after Mr. McLellan had notified Adam Dickey that Miss Wilbur was threatening a lawsuit for breach of agreement, she permitted the personal account of her life to go forth--and with a qualified endorsement (My.297).

~ ~ ~ ~ ~ ~ ~

[Some ultimate thoughts by Mrs. Eddy on the one God-governed world, as preserved by students, emphasize One Teacher and One Man, One Nation and One Church, One Consciousness and One Universe. The selected extracts follow]:

Each one must discover Christian Science for himself in my book and have the revelation.

The Revelator Jesus did not leave the ages comfortless. He saw the final adjustment of all things, and, in this vision he saw symbolically the crown of power placed upon the head of womanhood. May not America's greatest gift to the world be the gift of God's Motherhood proclaimed and woman's equality demonstrated in the substance, essence and Science of true democracy, and broader fulfillment of the message graven for universal humanity upon the great Seal of the United States--"Novus Ordo Seclorum"--the "New Order of the Ages"

Foreign nations are all allied, but the United States stands alone in her glory. This little leaven of righteousness will finally leaven the whole lump of nations, till armies and navies are not required and the brotherhood of man is established on the Principle of one God and Father and loving our neighbor as yourself.

[This profound declaration amplifies the message sent to Mrs. McKinley after her husband's death {DCC 117} and removes the animal magnetism that would link the material sense of nations. There is One Nation united in deriving its glory direct from its One Principle. Any sense of nation which is foreign to this truth believes that it gets its strength through an alliance or magnetism with others. Dependence on others is answered by that independence which means dependence only on Principle.]

~ ~ ~ ~ ~ ~ ~

[The implication of omnipotent rule by the Word of God is awe-inspiring, as shown in the following statement by Mrs. Eddy which has been preserved by devoted students]:

Friends, I have little to say to you, since I have already written all there is to be said of genuine truth until the last trump is sounded.

The time cometh and is not far off when the Czar of Russia, the Emperor of China, the Queen of England, the Mikado of Japan, the Sultan of Turkey, the King of Italy, the Presidents of France and of the United States, and all potentates, together with every mortal man and woman within their domains, shall bow before the little book whose right foot is set upon the sea and his left foot on the earth, and whose hands compass the universe.

And wherefore? Because it is the Word of the one God, the one crowned Head of the universe, the Mind, Spirit and Soul of man. It hath the words of eternal life; it giveth health; it destroyeth death; it hath victory over the grave; it is the unction of Spirit; it hath the law of the spirit of Life which through Christ freeth men from the law of sin and death; yea, it interpreteth the divine Principle of all that is real and eternal, and giveth the divine rule of the application of this Spirit and its demonstration with signs following.

Let this book and the Bible be forever the Pastor of The First Church of Christ, Scientist, in Boston.

~ ~ ~ ~ ~ ~ ~

When I established the Christian Science Monitor I took the greatest step forward since I gave Science and Health to the world.

-- Letter to Frederick Dixon after he had returned to England from his training on the Monitor in Boston [dated Aug.19, '09, signed "Sincerely yours, Mary Baker Eddy"]:

My beloved Brother: Words can never express the gratitude I owe and feel to you for your God-guided work in England for Christ's cause here and on earth.

May the Divine presence be and abide with you, and that called evil and designed to harm you or to defeat your labor fall powerless and joy be thine.

[Dated July 24, '00 and signed "Mary Baker Eddy"]: The need of divine wisdom and Love--Christ's assurance of prayer answered--and the absolute Science of God's Allness, moves the Christian Scientist to pray for the peace, prosperity, and brotherhood of all nations and peoples. No will-power is used in the Scientist's prayer, since human will must be lost in the Divine, for prayer to be efficacious. In the words of Zechariah, "not by might, not by power, but by my Spirit, saith the Lord of hosts."

I would ask that all Christian Scientists unite in prayer for the cessation of sin,--the oppression of the weak,--the accession of power at the sacrifice of individual rights; and especially that divine Love shield the innocent from the wrath of the guilty, and cause it to praise Love.

~ ~ ~ ~ ~ ~ ~

The love that is going out to the world through Christian Science is the greatest power there is and the only thing that will change that thought.

I have often felt these hard unloving thoughts of others come about me like dark clouds and seem to surround me, but they never touched me and why? Because my thoughts were going out to them all the time in love and with a desire to help them.

[Extract from a letter]: I thank God for your faith in Him and your true sense of me. Why? Because in over one quarter of a century I have never in one single instance seen these fail to carry the student safely on in growth and prosperity. But in every single instance the loss of those mental conditions has wrecked the student. Once I was young (and now am young), but I have never seen the righteous forsaken--those who are <u>right</u>, misled.

There is one law and that is the law of God. There is but one court and that is the court of Heaven--it is the court of absolute justice, whose decision is final. Human concepts and opinions have been fortified in law and human courts administer these laws but God is the final arbitrator--the supreme Judge.

Heaven is the consciousness of law and government.

God is always with a good desire, giving it power, activity, energy, intelligent action and rich fruitage. He brings every right endeavor to its fulfillment, and gives more blessings than we have sought. So sure as is the law of gravitation, so sure is recompense.

[A student's recollection of instruction by Mrs. Eddy, who wrote {Mis.334:5} "Astrology is well in its place, but this place is secondary", that is, is effect not cause]: Astrology (if worshiped as cause) is a belief of mortal mind whereby it kills. It is entertained in the horoscope. This is something to handle. Every man, in belief, has a horoscope whether he knows it or not. Send a day and date of your birth to a hundred astrologers in various parts of the world, and ask for your horoscope, and every one will send you the same horoscope.

God alone governs man and no planetary, solar, lunar or stellar influence can touch you. Christ, Truth, destroys this belief.

~ ~ ~ ~ ~ ~ ~

[The following definition of Christian Science was prepared by Mrs. Eddy for secular publication]:

Christian Science was discovered in Boston, Massachusetts, A.D. 1866 by the Rev. Mary B.G. Eddy, author of Science and Health.

Christian Science is the explication of Truth, reducing to human apprehension and demonstration the infinite Principle, divine Love, God--manifested in annihilation of sin, sickness and death.

Christian Science is Christ-Science or Emmanual-knowledge, and involves the ultimate of all reason, revelation and inspiration.

In Christian Science God is demonstrated as Infinite Love, omnipotent, omniscient, and omnipresent Spirit; the only Life, substance, and intelligence of man as His idea or reflection. This at-one-ment of man with God Jesus demonstrated.

Christian Science unites Science to Christianity, basing its scientific character on demonstable Truth. In theology it worships God as eternal Love, the universal Father and Mother, thereby establishing the brotherhood of man. The Scientific Creation is the infinite expression of infinite Love, entirely spiritual. Its medicine is divine Mind.

The ultimate of Christian Science is the establishment and recognition of spiritual harmony; to this end it heals the sick and sinful as Jesus did.

In logic Christian Science is indisputable.

In demonstration of the power of Mind over matter, it is mathematical, irrefutable, and Biblical.

The fundamental truths of Christian Science are: the reality and allness of God, the unreality and nothingness of matter, the spirituality of man and the universe, the omnipotence of Good, the impotence of evil.

INDEX

The following index lists names and places mentioned in the text, besides adding references to some key subject words.

Names of recipients and senders of messages dealing with routine and general subjects are not included.

The format adopted is the same as that used in the Blue Book Concordance so that, for example:

Letters and words shown in parentheses indicate words or phrases found in some of the references that follow;
25ff means pp.25 and more than three following pages;
25-7 means pp.25 & 26 & 27, etc.

A

Abbott,Rev.Lyman 27,61
Abraham 105
Absalom 104
absolute (Truth,Science) 13,111, 116,126,147,195,296,352-3
acknowledge(d) 68,78,119,131, 149,166,211
acknowledging 24
Adam 16,197
Adams,Mary 95
advertise,advertising 42,62,63,80, 90-1,251
advertisement(s) 19,28-9
Advisor 87
Africa 89,311 (& see SOUTH AFRICA)
age,(old) 32,53,66,71,118,134-6, 147-8,342 (& see EDDY)
Alaska 92
Albany,N.Y. 333
Aldrich,Judge 324-6,328
Allen,Albert 285
Alpine 65
America(n) 87-9,154,333-6,350
  Peace Society 89
angel(s),angelic 46,56,67,86,183, 192,200,308,332
animal(s) 122,126,334,340
  poison(s) 154,156
animal magnetism 5-8,110,139ff, 157,165-6,210-1,230,351
  belief,evil 110,158
  channel,influence 115,121,163
  handling 62,100,102,107,120, 139,229,249,312,334,337,351
  (& see M.A.M.)
annihilate(d) 86,110,126-7,130, 159
annihilating,annihilation 175,342, 354
annual meeting 39,53,101,148, 243,247ff,334
Anthony,David 41
Apocalypse 66,72,122
  (& see WOMAN)
Apollos 123
appear(s) 3,56,60,124,126,134,

136,153,169
appearance(s) 26,33,63-4,66,70, 87,136,158,249
appeared 158
appearing,(second) 71,75,146,165
appoint(ed) 14,21-2,29,38,40,79, 96,224,293,336
appointing 122
appointment 10,19,21-5,38-40,42, 91,93
a,Apostles 71.88
Arena,The 215
argue,arguing 75,100,141,144,159
argument(s), 6,69,75,101,108,112, 132,140,143-4,146-7,154,156, 159,344 (& see MENTAL)
arm(s),arming,forearm 43,47,59, 114,117,119,130
Armstrong,Joseph 23-4,32,34,77-8,195,219-22,252,264,266,320
Armstrong,Mary 222
army 68
articles (good,kind) 43,45-6,52-6,61
 (special) 32,44,48,62,65,69,95, 99,128,158
 (various) 19,26-7,43,56-9,124 (& see EDDY WRITINGS)
ascend(ed),ascending 1-2,5,66,89
Ascension 151,304
assassin(ation) 74,94-5,102
Associated Press 52,274,319
association(s) 123,134,146,169, 181,198,208,275,301
 CSA 175-6,203-5
 for International Conciliation 331-2,335
 voluntary 170,204
astrology 142,230,353
attack(ed),attacks 50,94,141,167, 233,268,272,299,328
attacking 190,293
Atonement 16-7
Australia(Melbourne,Sydney) 92, 321
author 14-5,44,58,64,83,169,255
authority 27,33-4,58,96,134,157, 170,173,273
 no 9,12
 of Mind 185-6
authorities 50,83,189
authorization, authorized 9,61,81, 98,100,223,282
awake(ned),awakening 15,33,57, 65,75-6,113,137,139,155,198

B

Babel 52
Babylonish woman 158,216,313
Baker,Dr.Alfred E. 121,126,170, 298-300
Baker,(General, Mary Ann, Thomas) 236-7
Baker,George S. 50
Baker,George W. 320,328
Baker,Henry Mark 314,323,327
Bangs,Mr.,Mrs. 204
b,Banner 34,68-9
Bartlett,Lawyer 223
Bates,Mr.,(Mrs.) Edward 4,8,20, 187,193-6,211
battle 32,47,121
beautified 69,129
beautiful 66,69,89,117-8,142,160, 163,199,202,299
beautifully 34
beauty 33,67,128,134,272,343
b,Being 3,112,127,138,148,152-3, 156,158,163,168,237,343,347
 Principle,substance,Truth of 60, 136,143,147-8,150-1,164
 reality,truth of 131-2,135,153

belief(s) 1-3,6,72,84,86-7,95,103,
111ff,125ff,136ff,154ff,169,346
dangerous 211
false 2,116,145,151,331
human,material,mortal 118,134,
144,147,155,157,164,302,341,
345
(in,of)death,evil 53,86,129,145,
147,153,165,346
new,old 143,306
of birth,cause,time 111,134,136,
153
of body,cancer,leg,matter 100,
111,126,147,206
of nervousness,sickness 206,339
(& see EVIL,MORTAL)
Berlin 81
Bethel stone 333
Bible, Biblical 71-2,114,116,118,
215,264,329,354
(& S&H) 39,94-5,105,107,149,
171,179-80,189,234,248,250,
263,292,321,352
study 215
Bible Lessons
(Committee) 10,15-6,30,40-2
(International) 15-6,39
Bill,Annie 284
Bingham,Mr. 265
birth 67,134,136,156-7,353
(& see BORN)
bless(ed) 68,89,153,155-6,176,
283-5
blesses,blessing(s) 46,64,73,83,
141,150,155,163,232,254,290,
331,339,353
blind(ed) 67,75,118,125,143
Board
of Directors (see DIRECTORS)
of Education 3,29,32,77,94,
96,99-100,107,110,124,274
of Lectureship 21,219,264-5,269
of Trustees (see Trustees)
bodies 109,117,126-7,129
body 16,98,111,114-5,125ff,138,
146,148,150ff,158-60,167-8,308,
343 (& see BELIEF,GOD'S,
HUMAN,MATERIAL,ONE)
born 67,72,136,156,167,308,326,
345
Boston,Mass. 12,76ff,84-6,93,
182-3,220,250,270,275,289,300,
away from 190,261
Reading Room 37-9,265
(& see FIRST,MOTHER CHURCH,
OFFICIAL)
Boston Globe 92
Boston Herald 57,90,92,197,200,
202,224,234,315,336
Boston Post 46,59
Boston Transcript 92
Bostonian(s) 275,277
Bow,N.H. 136
branch church(es) 4,12,17,39,172,
175,177,220,250ff,280
b,Bride 67-8,158
bridegroom 68
Britain 321,335
Brookline 251
Brown,Miss 37
Bruno,Fraulein 81
Buckley,Dr. 268
Buddhism 142
Buffalo,N.Y 14.
Burnham,Mrs.(Frances) 62-3
business 4,9-10,23-4,93,105,146,
167,322
Business(Committee,Manager)
23,29,32
Buskirk,Clarence 98,271
Buswell,Mr.,Mrs. 216
Butler,Edward C. 92

b,By-law(s) 46,52,97,100,182-5,189, 192ff,218-9,224,236, 250ff,266-8
(for)church 13,31,63,100,178, 206,225,233,238,243,278,
(in)Manual 10,28,95,176,205, 228,255,270
(& see RULE)

C

Cameron,Mr. 265
Canaan 349
Canada 321
Carnegie,Andrew 333
Carpenter,Gilbert Sr. 101,112, 274,309-10,320
Case,Henry 260-1
Catholic(s),Catholicism 56,155, 229,246,334 (see also ROMAN)
cause (and effect) 5,16,30,111, 115-6,140,143,145,160,177,179, 229,337,344,353
cause(d)(vb) 6,44,147,155-6,158, 160,164
c,Cause(C.S.) 10,22,32,37,56,90, 104,117,142,183,218-9,310,352
dignify,serve 27,163
growth,prosperity 184,215,240, 273,299
harm,injure,insult,ruin 34,43,47, 95,104,159,
loss of 312-3,337
our 167,254,258,279,289
Chadwick,C.W. 56
Chamberlin,Judge 324
Chamberlin,Miss 37-8
Chandler,Senator 324
Chanfrau,Henrietta 220,272
change(s) 17-8,31,58,81,83,105-6, 135,150,220,229,251,293,302
colors,style 10,33,35-6
Manual,orders 32,39
Mrs.Eddy's Writings 60,85,133
changed 135,137,147,169,247,330
Charleston,S.C. 50,166
Chase,Stephen 187,222,243,278, 281,298,320
Chestnut Hill 179,294,298,310
Chicago,Ill. 41,99,251-2,282
Chicago Inter-Ocean 90,92
Chicago Tribune 43
c,Child 48,54,72-3,109,113-5,117, 119,143,156,158,263
childhood 75
c,Children 48,53,72,109,113,135, 158-9,187,192,345
(God's) 67,230,341
China 321,333
Emperor of 351
Christ 68-70,87,94,113,140, 151,157,289,344-5,352
(and)Jesus 304,308
comings of 64,70
follow 123,163
His(divine) 101,143,148
Jesus 56,70,72,109,329
person of 65,129,330
Truth 155,303
(& see ONE)
Christ & Christmas 2,234
Christ-example 330
Christ-Mind,Science 131-2,354
Christian(s) 72,194,214,
Christian(adj) 59,78,108,182,214, 216,228,254,331
Christian Science (as a universal subject) 1,2,12,44,73-4,87-8, 112,200,232,263,339,344-5
attitude to 43,314
basis,love,message 78,108,353
Discoverer,Founder of 101,205, 227

Discovery of,establishing 121, 158,177,349-50
in Germany 76,82
Christian Science (adjectivally)
club 178-91
Hall 107,244
healing,periodicals,work 60,169, 302-3
History 63,74-5,107,208,236, 236,245,251,263,310
seal 36-7
textbook(S&H)(see TEXTBOOK)
(& see ASSOCIATION,CAUSE, CHURCHES,DIRECTORS,HYMN-AL,INSTITUTES,JOURNAL, MONITOR,OUR PERIODICALS, PRACTITIONERS,QUARTERLY, SENTINEL,TRUSTEES)
"Christian Science & Legislation" 25
C.S.P.S.,CSPS (see PUBLISHING SOCIETY)
Christian Scientist 4,148,165,221
a,one 44,128,142,147,248,258, 267,273,329,338
no 274-5
the(true) 72,153,274,337,352
Christian Scientists 27,58,71-2, 108,111,141,145-7,248,271,331
behave as,disgracing 218,260
Boston,official 20,170
grand,real 95,284
independent 4
leading,well-known 59,92,217
number of 99,163,337
the,those 45,60,87,115,198,273, 315
(see also SCIENTIST)
Christianity 61,176,304,354
Christliness 182
Christmas 242
gift(s) 197,238
c,Church(es) 4,43,60,66,123,180, 219,226,273,275,343
bells,clock,corner stone 48,199-201
building,expansion 46,73,93, 228,239,243,248,266,287,349
business, property 208,225,227, 247,257
CS 10,15,80,174,181,185,209, 251,301
edifice 207,245,250
my,your(own) 198,210,229,291, 297,299
officers,president 11,13,29-30, 79,171,224-5
organization 12,22,208-9,211, 251,289
other 232,246
Parent 284
(& see BRANCH,BY-LAWS,EX-TENSION,FIRST,GOD'S,MANUAL, MOTHER,ONE,SERVICES, UNIVERSAL&TRIUMPHANT)
Church in the Wilderness 64-6
claim(s)(noun) 6,24,105,137,147, 149,151,157,164,206
Clark, Joseph 22-3,35
Clarkson,Judge 106,159,270,275
class 3,32,77,94,97-100,106, 120-1,205,240
of '98,"last class" 94,97,107-110,115,118-20
classes 3,96-7,99,126
(& see NORMAL,PRIMARY)
college (see MASSACHUSETTS METAPYSICAL COLLEGE)
Collins,Grace 307
Columbus News 285
command(s) 61,75,137,141,153, 238

Christ's 194
Commandment(s) 105,177,235
(& see DECALOGUE)
commerce 81
Committee
Building 279
Examining 189
Executive 188
Finance 243
on Help 121-2
on Publication (COP) 23,45,50, 92,217,219,226,228,259,265-8, 282-3,313,319
(& see LESON SERMON)
Commonwealth Avenue 197,202, 222,240-1
c,Communion 17,31,114,216,247, 249,263,266,292
Competence,incompetence 28,59
complete(d),completeness 1,4,59, 72,83-4,89,111,127,135,146-8, 153
concept(s) 3,12,71,88,111,117, 127,151,161
conception(s) 72,111,139,152,161
Concord, N.H. 8,26,38,48,84,122, 195,249,253,315,317-8,322-3, 325
Church (see FIRST)
Patriot 317
Cone,Mr. 265
conflict(ed),conflicting 32,97,102, 149,154-5,158
confronts,confronting 64,154
conscious 46,108-9,130,136,342
consciously 20,33,116,138
consciousness 57,75,93,108-9, 130,136,140-2,145ff,161,232, 337-9,346ff
c,Constitution 88,93
c,Constitutional 157,160,217
control(s) 8,61,69,130,150,155, 331,338
controlled 61,152,160
controversy 71,116,122-4,128
Conwell, Dr.Russell 180
copyright(s), copyrighted 9-10,15-6,18-9,26,41,60,78-9,83-6,93, 171,257,260,286
(& see LAW)
Corning,Mayor Charles 317-8
correct(adj) 7,76,81,125,128,148, 340
correct(vb) 3,14,43,46,48,56,128, 277
corrected 44,60,85,110
correctly 15,123-4
correction(s),correctives 27,42-3,51-5,96,124
course(s) 77,80,97,99,107,125
(see also BOARD OF EDUCATION,MASSACHUSETTS METAPHYSICAL COLLEGE)
create 16,137,157,166,347
created,creating 72,74,135,150, 156
creation(s) 72,130,134,143,148, 157,162,343,354
c,Creator 132,143,159,230
cross(es),crown 36-7,57,101,149, 282,312-3
C.S.B.,C.S.D. 77,80,110,274
Cuba 337
Cushman,Mr. 217

D

daily 42
deeds,events 87
(news)paper 59,89-93
study 107,120
Daily Capitol Journal 61
dark(est) 64,167,300,353

darkness 1-2,8,67,87,118,141,144, 150,183,280,348
darken(ed) 115,139,141,150,205 (& see THOUGHT)
daughter(s) 21,57,67,74,167
Daughter
 of the King 67
 of Zion 64-5,73-4
David 104
day(s) 1-4,7,38,46,106,148,153, 163 (& see SEVENTH)
dead 104,119,137-8,166-7,169, 177,237,299,315-7,341
 raise 5,36,108,113,119,137, 145
death 64,102,110ff,129,134ff,146, 148,169,181,308,341,352 (& see BELIEF,SIN)
debt,indebtedness 24,224-5,243
Decalogue 108,213
DeCamp,A.P. 243-4,278-9
decease 10,22,24
deceit,deceived 32,75
decide 23,25,28-9,38,125,187, 201,270,348
decided,deciding 191,243
decision 13-4,23,29,80,325,343, 353
decisions 188,208
Deed of Trust
 (Directors) 248,277
 (Publishing) 4,7ff,18,25,30, 93,100
defence,defense 49,223
 of C.S. 120.167
"Defence of Mrs. Eddy" 32
defend,defenders 32,104,223,304
demon(ology) 8,142,260,287
demonstrate(d),demonstrating 44, 47,49,84,114,138,154,162-3,298, 304,339
demonstration 15,47,59,115,118, 162,168,339,342,346,348,354
demonstrations 113,115,141
denial 98,110,129,145
denounce 98,110,129,145
Denver,Co. 230
descend(s),descending,descension 1,3,5,87
descent 61,87
destroy(s) 52,107-8,117,127,131, 136,140,144ff,156ff,163ff,347, 354
destroyed 6,94,100,110,140,151, 186,190,209
destroying 6,150,218
destruction,destructive 6-7,117, 137-8,144-5
Deutsches Monatsheft 76,78
d,Devil(s) 58,126,137, 140,231,273,301
diabolism 330
Dickey,Adam H. 133,138,184, 235,309-10,350
die(s) 110,114,118-9,136-8,153, 169,177,190,308
died 50 (& see DEATH)
direct(ed),directs 9,14-5,121,147, 160
directing 26,107
direction(s) 10-1,55,105
d,Director(s),(Board of) 10,18,37-8,47,121,123,183,186,196,200-1,223,241,299,307,332
 change,consult 8,220
 number of 11-2,276,280-1,285-7
discord 146,154,157
discordant 129,164
discover(ed),discovering,discovers 12,47,86,103
d,Discoverer (& Founder) 152, 205,304-6,309,343

discovery 1,75,88,158
d,Disease 1,5-6,58,94,115,130-3,
137ff,148,155,157,207,306
(& see SIN)
diseased,diseases 5,84,101,160
Dittemore,John 275,282,284,300
divine (other than before synonyms for God)
being,presence 131,352
character,nature 71,130
concept,idea 88,130,158
creation,fatherhood,origin 72,
102,130
command,decree,law,order 44,
74,88,100,127,141
control,direction,government 11,
59,101,158,181
duties,service 87,168
impulse,progress 7,106,146
language,understanding,word 87,
148
Science 5,45,109,139
scheme 74
(& see LAW,POWER)
Dixon,Frederick 92,352
Dodds,Alexander 90-2
Dodge,Annie 233,294,300
doubt 115,128,139,141-2,149,156
doubted 152
dream 64,66,113,115,131,139,
157,177,230,252?,277
dreams 113,116,131,138,277
Dresden 81
Dunmore,Lord,Lady 258
duties 11,13,15,25,37,92,250,268,
292,316
dutifully 285
duty 31,40,57,87,104,202,224,
232,236,259,283
(& see MENTAL)

E

earth 87-9,109-10,124,137,157,
342,349
earthly 88,101
Eastaman,Joseph 238,278-9,298
ecclesiasticism 86-7,120,143,210,
229,282,336
ecclesiastical 12,89,95,147-8,165,
179-82,186,190,273,334
control 172
self-righteousness 123
Eddy,Gilbert 252
Eddy,Mary Baker(G.),(Rev.)
addresses,articles,sermons 234,
245,249,346-7,353
advice 7,29,34,36-7,94,105,120-
1,184
age 32,53,119,242,253,300,307,
318,353
ancestry,family 71ff,88,102ff,
118,236-7,255,286
approval,consent 14,23-5,36-7,
39,42,64,69,93,172,181,234,
237,256,262,285,309,332
books,writings 2,18-9,53,58,120,
138,148,151,159,170,252,314,
327,329,331
burden,needs 26,49-51,58
chair,picture,portrait 234-6,241,
306
control,leadership,successor 10-
2,20-2,59,61-3,78,89,93,118,
220,232,243,250,256ff,273-4,
281,331
copyrights,estate,41,73,79,83,
85-6,121-2,286,314,321-3,331
directions,recommendations
173-5,181,192-3,220,229,251-2,
262ff,298
handwriting,signature 100,106,
256,289,309

home,household,property 178, 185,197,202,236,240-1,252,254, 259,298,305,309,314,318,320-3, 337,343
instructions 7-8,27,32,35,40,44, 48,85,108ff,127,182,195,208-9, 224,229,238,247,277-8,305,310
"Mary" 201,227
rebukes 27,30,33,43,48,105,112, 220,224-5,227,269,293
sayings,thoughts 1,5,73-4,88,94, 100ff
thanks(not routine acknowledg-ments in letters) 34,36,55,96, 168,196-9,238ff,272
(& see DISCOVERER,STUDENTS)
edition 77,79,84-5,94-5,100
edition of S&H
(Fiftieth) 95,99
(First) 98,126
(16th) 215
(226th) 280
editions 75,83,90,98
editor(s) 18,20,26,30ff,42ff,55-8, 63-4,76,83,91-3,193,202,224, 265
associate,assistant,second 26,30, 35,63,206,264,271,276
editorials 42ff,54-5,59,64-6,69-71,76,79,92,332-3
educated 12,139,150
evil 140,156
education(al) 44,123
(& see BOARD OF EDUCATION)
effect (see CAUSE)
Elder,Lawyer 207,286
elucidate(d),elucidation(s) 2,84, 100,108
enemy 8,44,47,64,100,128,136, 144,150,202,225,231,339
last 345
enemies 44,48,51,69,127,139,150, 283-4,332
England 65-6,88,92,199,352
English 76,78 (& see LANGUAGE)
envy 75,102,104,141,144,156
jealousy,110,139-40,142-3,147, 164,275,332
error 7,44-5,103,112,124,136,144, 149ff,160ff,274,338
belief and 6,125
destroy,destruction 94,282,341, 347
detect,dispose,handle 110,226, 274,299
nothing(but) 6,115-6,128,140, 342
picture of 303
recitals,rehearsals 58,343
Truth and/or 114-5,136,272, 277,289,298,344
erroneous 66,89,143,229,261,312, 344
errors 15,33,66,110,191,241,330
Essays 124-5
estoppel (clauses,references) 12, 173,181,256,281,285
European 81
Eustace, Herbert W. 3,8
evil 201,205,213,232,293,296, 304,330 343-4
as belief(unreal) 58,129,145,147, 152,165,312
as mind 105,142-4,154,344
as nothing 3,7,52,75,112,119, 342
as power 5,83-4,104,139,354
handling 7,32,58,61,110,116,149
(& see EDUCATED)
"Evil is not Power" 83
Ewing,Judge 270,275
Ewing,Ruth 265

Executive Members 198
exist(ence) 2,98,104,112-3,124-5,
 130,135,145,162,303,312
existed,exists 105,152,326,344
existing 71,151
excommunicate(d) 182,233
excommunication 191,214,216,
 226,233,297
expose(d) 6,61,123,165
"Exposure of Eddyism" 227
e,Extension 92,207,228,247-8
externalized 101-2,142,145
eye(s) 99,105,127-8,131,145,
 157,161
 God's 340

F

faction 81
faith 10,21-2,46,59,89,105,145,
 194,199,220,227,231,233,254
 healing 338
faithful(ly),faithfulness 78,96,111,
 239,290
false 59-60,67,127,134,155,158,
 193,346
 claim(s) 105,116,144,149,206
 theology 110,142,150
 (& see SENSE)
Farlow, Alfred 45,52,217-8,
 224-7,258,266,268,320
Father 74,93,102,109-10,114,117,
 144-5,151,168,208,343
Father-Mother 157-9,354
Fatherhood 72
fear 6,101,128-9,131,139ff,152,
 154,156-7,161ff,341
 of death 110,135,148
feel 103,108,119,146,166
feeling 128,157
female,feminine 67,72,157,237,
 342,345
 male and/or 72,74,110,157,159
Fernald,Josiah 314,323,327
Field-King,Julia 102-3
 fight 104,164
Fincastle,Viscount 258-9
First Church of Christ,Scientist,
 Baltimore 236
 Charleston 166
 Concord 137
 Edinburgh 253
 Germany (Hanover) 81
 London 253
 New York 287,294,300,331-2,
 335
 The,Boston 9-12,19-20,80,170,
 182,184,207,222,257-8,261-2,
 285-7,291,352
 Troy 248-9
first coming 64,71
First Members 9-11,22,173-4,
 188-90,203,208,210-3,222,233,
 238-9,250,255ff
 Membership 278-9
First Reader 24-5,38,172,193-4,
 240-1,266-5,277
Flynn, John J. 90,92
foe(s) 56,65,143,209
 (see also ENEMY)
food 27,138-9,150,161
Footprints Fadeless 349
foreign 24,76,80,144,305,351
Foss, Caroline 104
Foster-Eddy,Dr. 103,156,189-90,
 193-5,210-1,219-20,260
Founder,Founding 86
 (& see DISCOVERER)
"Fragments from the Study of a
 Pastor" 64
France 65,92,321
 President of 351
Franklin,Benjamin 333

Free Mason 84,167-8
Freshman,Mary 230
Frost,Rodolph 315
Frye, Calvin A. 6,18,52,136,228, 310,316,319-22,328
  Diary 146,159,183,210,308
fund(s) 25,64,74,196,202,229, 243,259,331
  building 278
  (see also MONEY)

G

Genesis 72
German(y) 12-3,24,65-6,76ff,92, 321
Gibbs,Charles 92
Glossary 88
Glover,Charlotte(Mrs.Shute) 167
Glover,Col.(Major) George W. (husband) 49-51,166-7
Glover,George W.(son) 320,323, 331
God,God's
  (and)man 101,109,198,263,302, 336,344
  being,body 129,133,344,346
  Church,Nation 334-5
  concept,face of 87,117,136,149, 193
  gets from,take 5,86,123,140,145, 164
  (go)to,let 5,7,14,20,33,110,145, 154
  idea(s) 98.125-6,128,130,132, 135,152,161,186,237,344,354
  image,likeness 2,109,118,155, 231,239,326,340,343
  (& see HEAVEN,LAW,ONE, POWER,WORD,WORK)
Godhead,Godhood 72,74
gold 62,69,196
g,Golden 141
  rule 176,182,191,233
  Shore 89
  text 16
Good 179,232,305,343,354
goodness 44,55,65,87,139,164, 274
govern 76,95,106,146,149,246
governed 4,135,147-9,161-2
governing,governs 170,178,338, 354
government(s) 43,88,101,147,158, 184,250,293,301,336-7
Gragg,Eldora 246
Greene,Eugene 41
Greenwood, Samuel 27
Gross, Willis 26
ground 70,73,177,202
grounded 140,177,183,195,274
growth 54,76,99,103,148
  intellectual 144
  spiritual 5-6,84,143,145
Gunther-Peterson, Frau 77-8,80

H

Hague Conference,Court 333
Haiti 167
Hall,Lydia 100
Hamilton,Allen McL. 324
Hanna, Judge Septimus 26,63,74, 107,118,218ff,227,302-5,309
  as editor 20-1,26,30-2,42,64,69-71,265,275
  as reader 172,193-4,240,246,265
  as teacher 97-8,123,126,282
Hanna,Mrs.246
harm(s) 7,63,104,126,150,155-6, 246,283,291,338,352
harmless 101,142,161
harmonious 80,129,131-2,134, 146,148,153,161,163

harmony 113,131,135,138,165,
185,192,301,344,347
hate(s) 68,104,116,132,139-40,
147,154,156,164,340
hated,hateful 116,135,149
hatred 110,142-4,155-7,164
Hatten, Thomas W. 21,279
heal 47,110,113,137,150,156,162,
165-6,168,233,338,343
sick 108,115,141,153,163,
198,273,290,305,329,337,354
healed 102,105,119-20,159,275,
328,346
healer(s) 23,29,100,112,121,312,
329
healing 5,22,28-9,47,89,102,119,
145-6,261,338,348
atmosphere,secret 108,190
business,work 152,288
Christian,CS 115,198
need 61,183
sick 75,100,290,337
(& see INSTANTANEOUS,
PRINCIPAL,THOUGHT)
heals 130,142
physical 338
health 113,132,135-6,144,150,
161,319,339,344,348,352
heaven(God),kingdom of 4,61,71,
197,199,229,254,294,312,328,
333,335,340,348-9,353
Herald,der Herold 35,76,81
Hergenroeder,Emilie 236
Hering,Hermann 172,241,265,318
Hering, Mrs. 38
Hill,Calvin 6
Holland 321
homoeopathy 326-7
human 57,89,101,106,120,151,
155,158
belief 118,155,157
bodies,body 117,126,151
concept,thought 49,108,111,342
consciousness 136,153,339
experience 140,152,169
form 72
law 226,285-6
love 143,295,344
mind 70,75-6,102,112,115,134,
216,310,334,342
nature 71
reason,will 154,161
sense 1,134,137,151-2
(& see BELIEF)
Huntington Library 289
h,Husband 49-50,68,73,146,158,
166-8
Huss 65
Hymnal(CS),hymns 9,18,200,
260-3
hypnotic,hypnotism 16-7,33,75,
142,147,157,230,329,331
hypodermic 185,271-2

I

I am,I AM 89,98,117,131,145,343
idea (see GOD's)
ignorance,ignorantly 2-3,144,147
ignorant 139,142-3,164,213,336
immortal 118,125,127,129,132,
135-7,150
imperialistic,imperialism 354-5
impersonal 151,164
healing 146
impersonality 164
impersonalization 151
i,Independence,independent(s) 4,
8,23,98,107,280,284-5,351
Hall 333
individual (adj) 4,26,71,87,97,
107,130,147,164,181,207,268,
336-7,346

man 146,177
rights 104,352
(& see THOUGHT)
individual(s)(noun) 4,43-4,71-2, 136,139,152,159,172,280,297, 304
individuality 71-2,147,152,346
individualized,individually 72,96, 277
influence(s) 43,68,115,132,141, 143-4,150,155,265,301,354
instant(aneous)ly,heal 64,112-3,115-6,136-7,145
i,Institute(s),C.S. 28-9,81,182, 226,286
instruct(ed) 6,49,97,114-5
instruction(s) 7-8,44,70,85,94,97, 124,127,134,169,212
(see also CLASS,EDDY)
insurance,investment 325-6
intellect(ual) 46,144,155
intelligence 98,125,130,136,139, 143-4,154,162
international 4,335
(& see ASSOCIATION, BIBLE LESSONS)
Ireland 321
Irving,Mr. 264
Isaiah,53rd,54th chapters 64,72
Israelites,lost Israel 156,236
(& see MOTHER-IN-ISRAEL)
Italy 66
King of 351

J

Jacob 333
Japan 335
Mikado of 351
jealousy (see ENVY)
Jelly,Dr. 324,326-7
Jenks,E.A. 62
Jesus 6,65,70-2,101-3,110,137, 151-3,156,176,290,303,347-8
(& see CHRIST, also MASTER)
Jewish,Jews 71,79,120,229,341
Johnson,Wm.B. 12,193-4,206, 222,227,281-2,284,320
Wm.L. 84-5,206,222,232,263, 282,332
Jones, Judge 27
Journal,C.S.(not quotes) 4,9-10, 32-3,35,51,79,99,103,234,257, 321
Judas 282
justification,justify 59,94,103, 142-3,150

K

Kains,M.G. 27
Kennedy, Richard 191,288
Studdert 8
Kent,Morgan 258
Kent,Prof. 122,316
Kent,Rose 94,110,258
Kimball,Mrs. 197
Kimball,Edward A. 27,32-3,96-9, 107,122ff,169,206,275,283,320-1
King Edward VII 43
kingdom of God (see HEAVEN)
Kinter, George H. 82
Knapp,Bliss 122
Knapp,Daphne 239
Knapp,Flavia 102,277
Knapp,Ira O. 12,42,102,222,281, 284,320
Knott,Annie 35,40,48,63,264
Kollmorgen, Miss 83

L

Ladd,Fred 255
l,Lamb 67-8,117,155,299-300
Lamb,Mr. 217

language 79,83,87,98,124,207
English 13
German 76,79,81-2
of Spirit 111,114
Lathrop,John 171,176,180,239
Lathrop,Laura,C.S.D. 180
law(s) 12,78-9,100-1,109,115-6, 129-32,140ff,160,198,331,336, 338
according to,at 187,220
copyright 79,85
divine,spiritual 44,127,135,176, 352
material 155
of God,Truth 88,134,144,146-8, 160-2,176-7,181,301,384-5,344
of reversal 164-5
(& see BY-LAW,HUMAN,SUIT, UNIVERSAL)
lawyer(s) 69,84,184,223-4,255
learn(s) 3,60,75,109,128,146,150, 160,168-9
learned,learner(s) 45,117,125,139
learning 5,105,114,119
schools of 94,100
lecture(ship) 22,47,63,98
(& see BOARD)
lecturer,lecturing 32,63,219,226, 229,269-72,302
legal 4,11-2,15,184,238,277,285-6,309,350
legalize 100
legally 12,85,110,186,286-7
"Legislation,Christian Science &" 25
legitimate 9,103
Leonard,Pamelia(Mrs.Frank) 309, 315
Lesson Sermon Committee 15-6, 26,29-30,39-42,211,224,264
Lewis,organist 222
liar 225
lie(s) 7,47,53,104-5,125,131-2, 159,165,224,226,232,267-8,291, 296-8,339,315,348
of animal magnetism,mesmerism 6,102,313
Lincoln,Elsie,soloist 222,260
Linscott,Ellen 270
Linscott,John 230,270
liver 126-7,129
localized,localizes 70,88,179,183, 226,287,304,330,334
London 92,200,253,302
Longfellow 35
Love,Alfred 333
Lynn,217,237-8

M

McClure's Magazine 314
McCrackan,Wm.D. 24-5,36,92, 226,283-4
McKee,David,C.S.B. 41
McKee,Dr. 50
McKenzie,Wm.P. 4,8-9,12-3,21, 31,63,241,270,275,278
McKinley,President & Mrs. 351
McLauthlin,Emma 38,235
McLellan,Archibald 31-2,35,42, 51,57-8,263,275-6,282ff,300, 314,323,327,332,350
Mrs. 18,54
MacNeill,Sir John 51
magazine(s) 27,49-50,61,63,74, 79,81,120,168,314
Malcon Company,Chicago 41
malice 75,102,110,140ff,147,154, 156-7,164-5,306
malicious{mind(s)} 33,226,314
m.a.m.(malicious animal magnetism) 48,70,100,120,128,135-9, 219-20,225-6,276,290,345

caused,lured,by 43,180,201,213
effect,influence,of 45,212,258
fear,victim,of 233,330
handle,master 6,100,311,341
misdirected 78
misunderstandings 311
obey,yields to 48,309-10
(see also ANIMAL MAGNETISM)
malpractice(M.M.P.) 75,139-40, 142,164,175,190-1,203,226,230, 287,291,301
handle 204,278
man 2-3,74,110,117-8,125ff,136-9,146-7,150-5,164-5,303,344ff
and/or woman 237,305,345,351
end of,good in 201,311
ideal 195
(& see GOD,INDIVIDUAL, MATERIAL,ONE,UNIVERSE)
m,Mankind 68,72,345
Mann,Joseph 29,182-3,316
Manual 3,10-3,18,95ff,176ff,195, 252,256ff,280,292,299
laws of limitation 171,181
(see also BY-LAW)
"Mary Baker Eddy's Published Writings" 7,178,183,314
Massachusetts(Bay State) 8,12,40, 268-7
Metaphysical College 77,80,96-7,99,106-7,126-8,322
Master,our 49,180,194,239
material(istic) 334
birth,origin 103,157
body,leg 114,129-30,206-7,282, 295-6,307
creation,history 103,157
gifts,things 87-8,162,198,235
man,woman 130,139,157,343
mechanism,organ 131-2
mind,thought 98,103-4,304
sense(s) 60,73,103,131,149,152, 303,312,342,346,351
universe,world 126-7,130,155, 180,343,345
work 178
(& see BELIEF,LAW,ORGANIZATION)
matter 306-7,345
as substance 115,139,341
belief(s) of 136-7
lie 268,345
no,nothingness of 345,354
spiritualization of 125-6
Meehan,Michael 317,329,350
meeting(s)
church 13,21-2,192-3,195,199, 238,350
committee 40-1
evening,experience(Friday, Wednesday) 74,111,189,203, 206-7,212,269
special,weekly 175,181
(& see ANNUAL,ASSOCIATION)
member(s) 42,60,84,122,216
church 52,174,178-9,182,194, 196,229,233,238,258,273
good 174,182,189,208,210,212, 257
local 247
of committees 29-30,40,42
of Directors 8,99,191,286
of Trustees 11-2,21-3,25
(& see FIRST,ONE)
Memorial Day, memorials 236-7
mental
action,case,work 110,218,226, 330
arguments 112,132,147,160,230
assassin,malpractitioner 74-5,94-5,101-2,107,137-42,145-7,155-7,162,212,330

attitude,illustration,picture 121,126,135
concept,condition,nature 6,98, 216,353
depression,drowsiness 143,155, 160,164,183
influence,liaison 129,211
poison 100,143,155-6,230
powers,quality 118,212
suggestion 60,139,259,309
(see also M.M.P.,SCIENCE)
mentally 190,205,211,214,217, 232,246,348
mesmerism 6,109,115,140-2,145-7,160-2,212,312-3,329,334
mesmerists 156,202,345
mesmerized 128
Messiah,Messianic 109
Metcalf,Albert 262
Mexico 92
metaphysical(ly) 2,7,75,94,124, 147,201,300,324
metaphysician,metaphysics 56,89, 107,117
Miller,Albert E. 93
Miller,Frederica L. 111
Milmine,Georgina 350
Mims, Mrs. Sue H. 27,53,118,272
mind(no{other}) 175,341
(& see EVIL,HUMAN,MALICIOUS, MORTAL,ONE)
Miscellaneous Writings,Miscellany (not quotes) 2,96,215,349
mission 94,103,156
missionaries,missionary 195-6, 210,269-72
money 9,20,43,48,62,73,117,162-3,186,252,295,322
Monitor,C.S. 4,86,90-1,93,352
Monroe Doctrine 334
Mont Blanc,Viso 65-6
Moore,Mr. 197
moral 110,143,145,159
morally 94,105,121,164,166
Morrill,Dr. 326
Morse,Lawyer 223
mortal 98,113,132,312
belief(s) 129,134,143,147, 155,164,306
man,men 112,118,130,157,296, 303,345
mind 24,28,70,105,125,129-31, 135ff,147-51,154-5,159,162, 165,169,342,345,347
sense 71,89,152
thought 121,143,151-2,157,304
mortals 87,154,169,230
Mosley, Prof.J.R. 56-7
Mother's Evening Prayer 260-3
(see also HYMN)
m,Mother 54,70,113-5,117-9
(& see FATHER)
Mother(God) 74,110,117,144,190, 298-9
Mother (Mrs.Eddy),Mother's 8, 16,26,78-80,101,112,118,202, 205,220,223,231,235,270,276
in Israel 175,189,289
Room 38,187-8,234,242,247,264
Mother Church,(t)The 22-5,39-9, 79,90,95,102,139,159,176,184, 186,206,215,285,322
(and)branches 17,251-3
building,expenses 73,222
channels,tenets 178,252,256
dismissal from 220,296
history,tones of 239,245
Motherhood,mothering 72,159, 190,280,292ff,350
Munroe,Mary 188.222
music 139,167,229,239,260-3,328
musician(s) 121,224-5

N

nation(s) 68,78,88-9,93,156,229, 303,334-7,351-2 (& see ONE)
national 4
 laws 293,336
navies 335,351
Neal,James A. 4,8-9,21-3,26,102, 239
Neal-McKenzie 14-5,20
New England 319
New London,Conn. 84-5
New Testament 4,128
New York,N.Y. 7,65,79,99,267-8, 275,282-3,286,294-5,299-300, 319,324,333
 (& see FIRST CHURCH)
New York Sun 47
New York World 156,314ff
news(service) 86,91-2
newspaper(men) 20,43-6,57,59, 89-90,93,219,224,232,257,320
newspapers 26,34,49,61,74,294
Next Friends(Suit) 229,252,286, 303,314,324,330-2,350
n,Night 1-2,6,65,87,131,151
Nixon administration 83
Norcross,Lanson 95,99,240
Normal (class,course) 77,97,99-100,126,211,281-2
Norwood,Edward E. 83-4,106, 167-8
Norton,Carol 109,219,239
Norton,Elizabeth 307
Nunn,Henry 219,227

O

Obstetrics 97,126
office 14-5,31,194,227
officer(s) 11,79,265,313,322
official(s) 20,65,76, 221,227,268,274,281-2,297,310
 Boston 20,310
 organ,periodical 76,81
 teachers,teaching 94,96,99-100, 281-2,295
Ogden,David B. 92
"On the Way There" 63
one
 body,hand 127-8,132,295
 Christ 70,131,345
 Church 86,177,209-10,253,297, 334,350
 God 70,135,338,343-4,347
 man 156,158,303,334,350
 m,Mind 105,109,112,126-7,137, 141-2,145-6,155,164,166,169, 186,208,227,229,338,273
 member 210
 n,Nation 253,273,334-6,350-1
 power 163,280
 Principle 115,178-9,303,334,351
 race 280
 world 350
Orgain,Alice L. 8,183
organ 125,127,130,132
 (& see OFFICIAL)
organization(s) 63,92,178-81, 242,273
 material 171,282,286-7
 (& see CHURCH)
organize(d) 12,120,253
organs 114,127-8,132,155,157
Osgood,Anna 191,196

P

Panama 92
parent(s) 106,113-4,158
Parker,Mr. 324-5,327-8
p,Pastor 65,171,179,185-6,226, 229,280,352
 Emeritus 11 ,172-3,181,184-5, 210,262,274,322

patience 75,113
patient(adj) 78,113,340
patient(noun) 100,111,114,119, 137-8,155-6,159-60,183,338
patients 113-4,136,143,148,156, 163-6,321
Paul,St. 58,62,123,152,180,184, 209,240,299,348
Peabody,Frederick 223ff,229,268
p,Peace(ful) 56-7,89,105,139,141, 169,229,331ff,346,352
  Flag 331-3
  (& see SOCIETIES)
people 38,47,64,78,103,150,156, 159
periodicals 4,14,33,42-3,76,79,89, 120,265,289,314
  our 2,19,24,32,37,47-9,53ff,268, 302
  (see also JOURNAL,SENTINEL)
Persia 197
person 2,65,113,129,131,139-41, 146,151-2,157,179,230
  in 302
personal 152,275,304
  accusations,rebukes 112
  praise,worship 56,235
  being,coming 71,73,197
  character,history 72,102
  control,interpretation,opinions 95,301
  envoys,intermediaries 123
  friendship 155
  property 9,288
  sense 136,138,150-2,172,176, 277,331
  teacher,teaching 3,125,280,282
personality 71-4,104,134-7,145, 150-2,163,191,197,307,345ff
pesonalization,personalized 70,72, 249,304,309
personally,personified 72,109, 115,122,227,232,246,293,312
persons 96,232,304,309,330,341
  four,five 11-2,(280)
  no 150
Philadelphia 180,193,196,210,333
Philbrick,Mary 104
Phillipine Islands 92
philosopher,philosophy 75,111, 121,126
physical 87-8,129,135,142,151, 338
  discomfort,disease,disorder 94, 160,164
  sense 74,131
  scientist 288
physically 94,101,145,338,348
physiology 48,141,331
Pittsburgh (Chronicle-Telegraph, Post & Sun) 90
Platform 97
Pleasant View (see EDDY HOME)
poisons 154-6,229
  (& see MENTAL)
political 4,61,92,292
politics 293,336
power 5-8,58,84,95,101,108,139-40,152-4,158,162ff,347
  divine,God's,Truth's 46,66,75, 114,119,135,153,156,161,346
  no 5-6,104,140-4,154-7
powerless 5,84,143,298
powers,special 235
practice,practise 22,38,107,121, 130
practitioner(s) 28,99,102,110-1, 148,321
pray(ed),praying 78,119,131,202, 258,265,283,327,352
prayer(s) 89,108,134,150,162, 168,170,232,276,339,352

preach(ed),preaching 4,88,107
Presbyterian Banner 34
 Church 65
Price,Forest 72
priest(s) 123,156,292
priestcraft,priesthood 56,65,110
p,Primary class,course 97,99,107, 281,287 (see also MASSACHUSETTS METAPHYSICAL COLLEGE)
principle(s) 10,88-9,110,125,156, 281,288
Principle 4,45,123,128,133,150-2, 157,161,281,304
 healing 302,334
 infinite 195
 (& see ONE,SCIENCE)
progress 7,91,115,139,148
Property Trust,Lynn 237-8 (see also MEMORIAL)
Protestant(ism) 66,155
psychic 75
publication 41,43,70,76,81,92, 103,286,349
publications 2-3,13,61
publish 9,26,46,52,63-5,83,94,104
published 18,27,50-1,56-7,62,81, 100
"Published Writings" (see MARY BAKER EDDY)
publisher 23-4,34
Publishing Society(CSPS) 4,8-9, 23,25,80,82,224,331
pulpit(s) 75,182,246,265,299

Q

quarrel(ing) 60,216,260-1,294, 300
Quarterly,Quarterlies 4,9-10,41, 186,234,263
queen,Queen Victoria 138
Quimby,Phineas 215
Quincy,Mass. 167

R

race 72,104,156,293,336
Rathvon,Wm. 309
reader(s) 41,44-5,48-9,55-7,106, 120,128,171,189,222,256,301 (& see FIRST READER)
reading room(s) 26,37-9,221,265, 267
Recapitulation 97
Reeder, John W. 38
reflect 86,88,112-3,132,147,158
reflected 119,121,130,157
reflection 89,117,135,145-6,165, 176,296,331,344-5,354
reflects 71,102,110,114,117
Reinke,Fraulein Bertha 82
religion 8,59,69,176,182,272,326, 331,335
religious 4,56,61,71,74,178,330
reorganization,reorganized 12, 171,204
r,Revelation 2,72,98,112,119,279, 303-4,350
Revelator 2,61,100,118,297,300, 304,307,314,330-1,350
reversal 2,116,136,154-5,164,195, 301 (& see LAW)
reverse 139-40,147,155,285
reversed,reversing 116,141,146, 150
Reynolds,Rev.C.D. 41
right 32,43,113,121-3,127
 ideas 130,163
 moment,place,time 7,90,152-4
righteous(ness) 86,102,116,284, 353
rights 49,55,104,159
Robertson,Nemi 313
Roman (church) 56,65,155

Rome,J.J. 39
Roosevelt,President(Theodore) 335
Roslindale 20
Ross,Betsy 333
Roxbury 38
rule(s) 8,13-4,43-5,48-9,106,140, 145,173ff,184,205,213,255,259, 276,320
 exception 75,77
 no 115,154
Runnymede 333
Russia,Czar of 351

S

Sabin,Col.Oliver 33,63-4,120,215
St.Paul (see PAUL)
St.Paul's Church,School 258
Salem 61
Sargent,Laura 69,102,187-8,238, 240,242,246,264,274,313,349
Sargent,Miss 37
Satan 20,101,134,220
Schoen,Marie 76ff
Schonfield,J 4
science 56,75,142
 mental 203
Science 49,113,122,145,338-9
 abstract 44
 in 45,87,114,124,138,149-50, 164,169,341
 no,not 12,344
 Principle of 177
 (& see ABSOLUTE,CHRISTIAN, DIVINE)
Science & Health 176,255 (& see BIBLE,EDITION,TEXTBOOK)
Science of Christianity 302
Science of Man 98,125,129
Science of Mind 75
scientific 4,58,61,88,130,132,297, 302
Scientific 5,108,354
scientifically 61,95,147,153,165, 232,277
Scientist(s) 7,61,63,95,109-10,114,120,123,207,217
 (& see CHRISTIAN)
Scotland 253-4,321
Scripture(s) 50,54,70,74,108,117, 231,248,329
Seal,Mrs.Frances T. 81-2
s,Second Church,Montreal 254
 Church,New York 171
 coming 64,70-4,88
self 59,113,143-5,152
 -abuse,pity,reproach 66,150,157
 -confidence,governed 68,336
 -conscious 46
 -destroying,perpetuating 4,165
 -love 142-3
 -righteous(ness) 87,123,142,150
selfhood,selfish(ness) 73-5,134, 143,150,229,276,334,343
sense(s) 57,62,70,86-9,103,105, 132ff,150,338,342
 object of 114
 of body,self 130,134,150
 of evil 149
 of life,power,wife 153,158,346
 true 3,158
 (& see HUMAN,MATERIAL, MORTAL,PERSONAL,PHYSICAL, SPIRITUAL)
Sentinel(Weekly)(not quotes) 4, 20,32-3
s,Sermon(s) 4,7,47
 on the Mount 108,111,177,194
 (& see LESSON)
services(church) 189,192,199, 207,215,234,246-8,252-3,287, 295,301,343

s,Seventh Day 1-4,50,61,86,100,
134,176-8,195,208,273,280,305
Shannon,Clara 95,101,211
sick 89,130-1,142
(& see HEAL)
sickness 7,113,115-6,129-30,150
sin 6,48,107,110-1,121,130,136,
142,150,156,161-4,198,213,220,
238,327,337,352
(disease,death) 24,53,113-6
no 128,149
sinner(s) 47,111,145,149,152,191,
226,279,305
sins 183,193
Six Days,Sixth Day 2,86
Slaght,Lithchild,reporters 316-7
Smith,Clifford 25,309
societies,(s)Society 158,179,336
Peace 178
Solomon 54
s,Son 74,85,109,157
adopted 103
of flesh 72
of man 67,344-5
South Africa 92
Spain 334
Speakman,Mary 30-1,48
s,Spirit(s) 44-5,98,238
and letter 120,124,128,171,259
language,thoughts of 111,114,
141
spiritual 72-3,103-4,108-11,117,
127,134-5,342,354
concept,meaning,sense 12,75,
114,125,130,139,153,156,342-3
growth,progress 5-7,84,143,145
idea,type 72,118,127,132,136
(& see LAW,THOUGHT)
spiritualism 230,327
spirituality 58,120,152
Spofford,Daniel 288,308
Spring,Rev.Gardiner 64-5
Stack,Mrs. 237
Stanger,Theodore 83
Stetson,Augusta E. 7,57,189-90,
261,263,275,283,287ff,310
Stevens,Henry 255
Stewart,Allison 19,23-4
Still,Adelaide 42,311
Stone,Albert C. 92
Strang,Lewis C. 42,92,122
Streeter,Gen.Frank 318
Strickler,Virgil 296
student(s) 12,33,45,54,62,73,76-8,
105ff,130,146,162
(dis)loyal 64,97,174,190,204-5,
211
German,Western 76-8,87-8
(Mrs.Eddy's) 38,47,53,89,102,
118,133
of Mrs. Eddy's books 104-6,120
subscribe(rs),subscriptions 46,61,
63,120
substance 132,139,147-50
matter 98,115,125-6,129,147
suit(lawsuit)(s) 197,216,218,223,
225,259,267,296,324,331,350
Sulcer,Dr.Abraham 271,278,298
Swazey,Miss 106
Sweet,Ella Peck 307
Switzerland 92,321
synonym(s),synonymous 44,109,
123,133

T

teach(es) 2-3,77,107,118,120,146,
149,169,343
t,Teacher 2-3,32,95,120,139,180,
258,350
local 172
t,Teachers 96ff,106-7,121ff,148,
269

teaching 2-3,29,44,74,77,94ff, 106,113,120ff,133-4
(& see OFFICIAL)
Tenets (see MOTHER CHURCH)
Testament (Old,New) 4,71,128, 198-9
testifying,testimonial(s) 47-8,53, 57-8,74,84,102,196,206,278
testimony 145,343
textbook(CS)(S&H) 13,44,79,95-6,105,199,236,305,313,338
theology 110-1,142-3,150,155, 354
theosophists 229
theosophy 75,142,202,211
Thinkright Bureau 19
Thomson,Mrs.M.S. 56
thought(s) 58,91,107,114,127, 139,147ff,239,305,313,338
current,public,universal 98,105, 157
darkened,hard,sad,tired 115,129, 139,150,162,353
enlightened,excellent,important 56-7,169,350
healing,helpful,loving,pure, tender 89,101,113,158,248
in 130-1,134
individual,own 145,155,157,160, 162,166,172,231,307,312,348
no 47,111,140,155,160
Soul,spiritual 86,117,119,141, 152-3,187,341,346-7
transference of 6,100,140,165
wrong 75,103-4,106,144,152, 164,231,342
(& see HUMAN,MATERIAL, MORTAL)
Tilton cemetery 236
Tomlinson,Irving C. 45,76-8,114, 118,236,257,266,271,320,350
tongue(s) 45,52,76-8,114,118,238
transform(ation) 62,110,127,151, 342
translate(s) 13,62,81-2,87,111, 114,118
translated,translating 13,61,76,79, 83,87,95,303
translation(s) 12-3,76-7,79,82-3
Treasurer 8-9,12,20,187,223,259, 277
Trustees (church) 179,248,256, 278,285 (see also DIRECTORS, BOARD OF)
(for Mrs.Eddy) 121,323-4,327
(publishing) 4,8ff,17ff,23ff,30, 38ff,59,63,76,82,93
Turkey,Sultan of 351

U

unification,unified 74,81
uniform(ity),uniformly 43,95,97, 126
Union,Peace 333
unite(s) 120,138,204,254,352,354
U(nited) S(tates) 321,351
President of 351
unity 78,109,127,157-8,167,175, 184,198,203-4,251,276,292,297-8,327,337
Unity of Good 60,87,124
universe 86,89,127,138,142,146, 230,273,345,350-1,354
and man 305
(& see MATERIAL)
universal(& triumphant) 71,74,88, 181,337,351,354
availability,message 4-5
church 86-7,210,273,287,310, 334,354
law 88,176
unlocalized 177,182,336

V

Vaudois 65
Vermont 211
voice(God's) 121,141,144,185,
 200-1,209
Vosburgh,Rev.Arthur R. 25,27,
 63,268

W,X,Y,Z

Wait,Horatio H. 99
Walker,Lawyer 222
war(fare) 123,145,154,333-4,336
Washington,D.C. 83-5,106,230,
 254,333
Washington News-Letter
 (see SABIN)
watch(ing) 4-5,106,126,166,201
Webster,Elizabeth 95
Weekly,C.S. (see SENTINEL)
Weller,Janette 264
Wertheimer,Rabbi 78
Westminster chimes 199-202
 Abbey 333
 catechism 201
Weston,Ames 92
White,Miss 262
White,Mr.James 305
Wiggin,J.H. 215,221,268
Wiggin,Mrs.H. 221
Wilbur,Sibyl 92,319,350
Wilcox,Martha 101-2,133
Williams,Mrs. 27
Willis,John B. 29-30,35,47,54-5,
 128,206,264
Wilson,Cornell 319
Wilmington,N.C. 167
Winans,Thomas C. 91,93
wisdom 103-6,108,133-4,141-2,
 154,161,233,312,314,352
wise 7,32,47,49,110-2,122
wisely 187,324
woman 35-6,63,103,157-9,166,
 198,255,290,313,345
Woman in Apocalypse 66,72-4,
 122,176
womanhood,women 229,350
Woodbury,Josephine 182,189-92,
 203-6,210ff,226-9,257,267,
 274-5,298
Woodbury,Mr. 216-7
word(s) 44-5,100,206,226,351
Word 1-3,5,61,70,74,142,342
 milk of 103,117
 of God,Lord 95-6,131,147,164-
 5,184-6,224,266,290,351
work 5-6,22-3,28,80-1,89ff,105,
 135,154,178,335
 against,at,out 101,137,161
 for,from,with 14,79,114,138,163
 go to 109
 God's 119,146,164-5,224,290
 own 20,143,348
workers 301
working 61,118
world 6,27,75,93,164,170,240,
 273,299,311,313,336,339-40,
 346-7,350
 go into 61,86-7,329,353
 your 229
 (& see MATERIAL)
worldly,worldwide 193,201,275,
 287,331
Wright,John L. 92
writer(s) 61,125,133
w,Writing(s) 61,125,133
 mistakes in 46
 my (Mrs.Eddy's) 19,55,75,149
 (& see EDDY WRITINGS)
Wycliff(e) 65
Yates,Katherine M. 63
Young,Bicknell 99
Zion 184 (& see DAUGHTER)

Made in the USA
Middletown, DE
20 January 2022

59192924R00219